Terrorism
and Organized
Hate Crime

Intelligence Gathering, Analysis, and Investigations

Second Edition

Michael R. Ronczkowski

CRC Press
Taylor & Francis Group
Boca Raton   London   New York

CRC Press is an imprint of the
Taylor & Francis Group, an informa business

CRC Press
Taylor & Francis Group
6000 Broken Sound Parkway NW, Suite 300
Boca Raton, FL 33487-2742

© 2007 by Taylor & Francis Group, LLC
CRC Press is an imprint of Taylor & Francis Group, an Informa business

No claim to original U.S. Government works
Printed in the United States of America on acid-free paper
10 9 8 7 6 5 4 3 2

International Standard Book Number-10: 0-8493-7829-X (Hardcover)
International Standard Book Number-13: 978-0-8493-7829-4 (Hardcover)

Library of Congress Cataloging-in-Publication Data

Ronczkowski, Michael.
    Terrorism and organized hate crime : intelligence gathering, analysis, and investigations / Michael Ronczkowski. -- 2nd ed.
        p. cm.
    Includes bibliographical references and index.
    ISBN-13: 978-0-8493-7850-8 (alk. paper)
    ISBN-10: 0-8493-7850-8 (alk. paper)
    1. Hate crime investigation--United States. 2. Hate crime investigation. 3. Terrorism--United States--Prevention. 4. Terrorism--Prevention. I. Title.

HV8079.H38R66 2006
363.325'165--dc22
                                                                           2006018580

Visit the Taylor & Francis Web site at
http://www.taylorandfrancis.com

and the CRC Press Web site at
http://www.crcpress.com

Dedication

For my family, and all the hardworking men and women in law enforcement, both sworn and nonsworn, and the armed forces who make sacrifices every day in honor of their country. Keep up the fight!

Foreword to First Edition

As I write this foreword, the entire world is focused on the Middle East and the continuing threat of more terrorist attacks against Americans, both here and abroad. And while the military continues its deployment of troops and equipment to address the possibility of war, law enforcement personnel in this country scurry to hire and train analytical specialists — individuals essential to our ability to address matters of homeland security.

The present-day practice with regard to the hiring and use of analytical specialists in law enforcement agencies is in stark contrast to the common practices in 1965 when I began my law enforcement career with the Miami-Dade Police Department (MDPD) in Miami, Florida. Throughout my 27 years in South Florida, I witnessed first-hand how detectives were forced to rely on personal contacts and individual practices to gather and analyze information. I still remember how, as a young General Investigations Unit lieutenant, I would sit at my desk every morning plotting burglary trends from the previous day's crime reports. I would gather the information, try to put it into some type of usable format, push pins into a district map in the uniform roll call room, and then provide the data to the uniform lieutenants for dissemination to their officers. It was the best that we could do at the district level in the mid-1970s.

What few analysts the department hired were devoted to organized crime analysis and plotting the relationships among the various organized crime figures plying their trade in the Miami area. It was, in fact, the combination of the successes enjoyed in the organized crime investigations arena and the attendant frustration the rest of us were experiencing in analyzing crime data that finally caused the agency to recognize the need to have personnel specialized in gathering and analyzing information assigned throughout the department. I was the deputy director when I left MDPD in 1992. By then, the use of analysts in the agency was much more widespread. Not only was the intelligence unit beginning to realize the value of having professionally trained analysts, so were many of the criminal investigative units both at headquarters and throughout the district.

As police chief in Tampa, Florida, I continued to recognize the need to have an effective medium in which to gather, analyze, and share information among agencies. The Tampa Police Department (TPD) had an effective analytical function. They did a great job of gathering and analyzing information and disseminating it to internal units. Unfortunately, and through no fault of the personnel, they did not do a good job of sharing information as it related to youth gangs. In spite of the plainly visible graffiti and gang tags on walls throughout the city, the city administration remained adamant in its position that there was no youth gang issue in Tampa. Through detailed briefings with the political structure, I was able to convince those in the administration of the importance of acknowledging the problem so that we could deal openly with other local authorities, law enforcement agencies, social service agencies, and the judiciary. The chief judge for the Circuit convened a summit on youth gangs, and we were well on our way to confronting this serious issue.

Not only do local agencies have to share among themselves, they must also share with state and federal agencies. Local law enforcement frequently possesses information that may be germane to state and federal investigations, but the conduit to share it is lacking. In fact, many agencies still rely on personal contacts and friendships among detectives as means for sharing information. As director of the U.S. Marshal's Service (USMS) from 1993 to 1999, I observed just how many federal agencies are dependent upon information from local, county, and state agencies to address matters of national security and interests. Terrorism and threats to homeland security have been major concerns in Washington, D.C. for many years.

As director at USMS, I witnessed first-hand the impact that terrorists, foreign or domestic, can have on our society and way of life. The 1993 World Trade Center bombing, the Oklahoma City bombing, and the 1998 embassy bombings in Kenya and Tanzania strained the resources of dedicated federal investigators. And, while I was not the director during the tragic and violent 1992 incident at Ruby Ridge involving alleged members of the Patriot movement, I was involved in the subsequent review of the actions of the deputy marshals. I certainly came to recognize the continuing need to monitor and comprehend organized hate groups such as the Patriot movement in the United States. There has been a constant need for national intelligence and analysis after these tragic events, but also a new emphasis on information that can identify possible future attacks. However, much of the training and materials available to law enforcement has focused on preparing and responding.

There has been a training and analytical void in law enforcement on the full context of the terrorism and organized hate crime issues faced by officers and analysts. That was, until now.

This book is extremely topical and current. Mike Ronczkowski has spent over 20 years in law enforcement — 8 years managing and teaching intelligence analysts. He serves as an adjunct professor at a local university, teaching a course on how to recognize and deal with terrorism. As he worked on his lesson plans, he came to recognize the need for a book like this. This book is relevant for law enforcement personnel around the world and, at the same time, appropriate for students seeking to learn more about one of criminal justice's hottest topics.

Material in this book undoubtedly provides personnel with an understanding and approach for gathering intelligence and conducting analysis on terrorism-related matters. The reader will also find that many of the concepts are applicable to other law enforcement investigations.

From a management perspective, I believe that hiring and training analysts is essential. I have seen many agencies promote clerical staff members into analytical roles and just assume that they would learn on the job. This is a fallacy. As this book points out, law enforcement managers and policy makers need accurate and quality intelligence. This will enable them to make informed decisions if they are to properly address issues. How can this be achieved without training and an understanding of the topic being analyzed?

I firmly believe that the author's approach, as detailed in this book, will greatly aid in addressing the analytical needs faced by agencies, filling in the gaps and voids that exist today.

In my current role as Commission Secretary for the Commission on Accreditation for Law Enforcement Agencies (CALEA), I have witnessed growth of an emphasis on agencies hiring, training, and even certifying analytical personnel to address such topics as homeland security, terrorism, and organized hate crime. The problem has been the lack of materials applicable to law enforcement — that is, until the author wrote this book. I congratulate him for addressing the needs of so many law enforcement agencies and for sharing his knowledge and experience with the rest of the law enforcement community. It has been an honor to review and write the foreword for this book, and I strongly recommend use of it by law enforcement practitioners, managers, and students.

Eduardo Gonzalez
Director, U.S. Marshal's Service (1993–1999)
Chief of Police, Tampa, Florida (1992–1993)
Deputy Director, Miami-Dade Police Department, Miami, Florida (1965–1992)

Foreword

Following the events of September 11, 2001, the International Association of Chiefs of Police (IACP) held a Criminal Intelligence Sharing Summit in Alexandria, Virginia, in which participants posited that failures of the intelligence process contributed in no small measure to the events of that tragic day. They further concluded that the ability of law enforcement agencies — at all levels — to collect, collate, analyze, disseminate, and share intelligence was key to fighting the war on terror. The IACP thus proposed the development of a federal initiative to enable accomplishment of this objective. In response to this proposal, the U.S. Department of Justice, Office of Justice Programs, Bureau of Justice Assistance in 2002 created the Global Intelligence Working Group (GIWG) and tasked it with the responsibility of developing what is now known as the National Criminal Intelligence Sharing Plan. This plan provides a framework to improve our nation's ability to develop and share criminal intelligence information and to bolster the safety and security of our communities.

> A recommendation that IACP Summit participants identified as core to achieving the goals of the National Criminal Intelligence Sharing Plan was to "promote intelligence-led policing through a common understanding of criminal intelligence and its usefulness." Intelligence-led policing is defined as the collection and analysis of information to produce an intelligence end product designed to inform law enforcement decision making at both the tactical and strategic levels. Intelligence-led policing is predicated on the production and application of intelligence information and products. For intelligence-led policing to be effective, the process must be an integral part of an agency's philosophy, policies, and strategies and must also be integral in the organization's mission and goals.*

Embodied within the term "intelligence-led policing" is the underlying concept that decisions regarding the delivery of police services should,

* U.S. Department of Justice, Office of Justice Programs, *The National Criminal Justice Sharing Plan*, October 2003, p. 3–4.

in fact, be led by intelligence. Yet for all of the acknowledgment given to the concept, few law enforcement agencies have embraced it to the extent that it truly influences, to any measurable degree, the decision-making process. As a result, many agencies, particularly those at the local level, continue to operate within the revolving door of the reactive "call-response" method of policing, forever letting the crises of the moment, instead of an intelligence-based plan, dictate the use of police resources.

Part of the reason for this phenomenon is that many agency administrators do not have a proper understanding of what intelligence is. As such, they will often use the terms "information" and "intelligence" interchangeably and make the mistake of assuming they are synonymous when they are not. When field officers and investigators take reports they are collecting information. That is, they are collecting raw data that may or may not be accurate, up-to-date, or complete, and that, by themselves, do little to indicate what the overall crime problems may be within a jurisdiction. Intelligence, however, is produced when information has been analyzed by a competent professional who can provide officers, investigators, and agency administrators with assessments of what, based upon their analyses, is likely to occur in the future. In other words, it is the task of the analyst to join together the individual pieces of a complex jigsaw puzzle (the information collected by officers) and transform them into intelligence products that provide the police administrator with one true picture of existing and emerging crime problems within the community.

Many agencies deliver police service based on perception rather than fact. Ask five officers their opinion of the greatest crime problem within the community and one is likely to receive five different answers based upon the officers' perceptions of what has occurred in their areas during their tours of duty. But no one officer works all areas of town, works 24 hours per day, or has access to information gathered by other officers or obtained from community members, parole and probation departments, other law enforcement agencies, and so on. As such, no one officer has all of the information relating to everything that has occurred, may be currently occurring, or is likely to occur within the jurisdiction.

In contrast, with access to — and through the analysis of — information that has been collected by officers, investigators, and the other entities mentioned above, the analyst is in a unique position to provide the agency administrator with a fact-based (as opposed to a perception-based) assessment of what existing and emerging community crime problems truly are, what the underlying causes of the problems may be, what current events may portend for community harm, and what might be done to ameliorate or eliminate them or to prevent their future occurrence. In possession of such an assessment, the police administrator can now make objective decisions as to what strategies should be employed and what resources, both now and in the future, will be needed to effectively direct the delivery of police services throughout the whole of the jurisdiction.

Unfortunately, however, as the Executive Director of the Alpha Group Center for Crime and Intelligence Analysis, an organization that conducts training programs for crime and intelligence analysts throughout the world, it is disheartening to me and to our other instructors, including Michael Ronczkowski, the author of this book, to see the lack of importance given to the role of analysis function within many law enforcement agencies and the resulting lack of benefits that police administrators could be receiving were they more fully cognizant of the contributions that can be made by the analysts they employ — assuming that they do, in fact, employ a crime or intelligence analyst or at least dedicate someone to the task at all.

The reasons why benefits go unrealized are many and varied. But primary among them is that many administrators are simply unaware of the tasks an analyst should perform, the types of products and services they should provide, or even what they, themselves, should be receiving from the analyst. In short, while they may hire an analyst, they do so without any specific knowledge of the job they are to do. When this occurs, analysts frequently become little more than historians within an agency and used, at best, to crunch numbers in an effort to explain what has happened in the past. Crime and intelligence analysts are not — and should not be — historians used simply to explain what has happened in the past but to present scenarios, based upon analyzed information, of what is likely to occur in the future. Armed with these scenarios the police administrator is in a significantly enhanced position to plan not only for the future and orderly growth of the organization, but for the heightened safety and security of the community as well.

The ability of the analyst to provide useful intelligence to administrators to accomplish this goal, however, is dependent upon several factors, not the least of which is the quality of the information upon which intelligence is based. Field officers and investigators have the potential to perform an incalculably valuable function as the information gatherers within a law enforcement agency. Unfortunately, few recognize the value of this function, with the result that crime reports, arrest reports, and field interrogation or field contact reports are often completed with little regard for detail. Ask any analyst, or, for that matter, any investigator, and they will frequently bemoan the fact that modus operandi (MO) factors of crimes and physical descriptions of people have been omitted, questions of victims, witnesses, or suspects went unasked, or that even such basic things as dates and times of occurrences were recorded in error. In such situations the old axiom of "GIGO" (garbage in, garbage out) prevents the analyst from creating the intelligence products necessary to accurately assess potential threats to the community. Worse yet is the tendency of officers to "kiss off" reports and to fail to gather information in the first place. For analysts, GIGO — garbage in, garbage out — is bad. NINO — nothing in, nothing out — is the kiss of death. Officers need to be reminded continually of their value as data gatherers, of the critical role they play in the subsequent analytical process, and of their need to collect accurate, up-to-date, and complete information to the greatest extent possible. Without information there can be no analysis. And without analysis there can be no intelligence. And without intelligence, there can be no basis to make objective decisions to guide the delivery of police services or to govern the effective use of law enforcement resources.

Another factor that will govern the quality and thus the value and usability of the intelligence product is the training the analyst has received to perform this type of work. Analysts are now being enlisted to help their agencies in the fight against not only crime but terrorism as well. Yet few have had any training to equip them with the skills needed to determine even the existence of terrorist threats, let alone the ability to provide any meaningful recommendations for how to respond to them. Sad to say, many police administrators have simply "knighted" people as analysts and given them the admonition to go forth and "analyze something." Without the requisite knowledge, skills, and abilities, however, the "analyst" fails to make a worthwhile contribution to the agency with the result that the analysis function is relegated to a relatively low level of importance within the organization. In light of the world situation today this is a luxury our law enforcement agencies can no longer afford.

In this age of global terrorism, today's analysts must be specifically trained to deal with new problems involving often previously unknown and shadowy figures whose objectives differ significantly from the traditional criminals we have come to know and understand. They must come to a knowledge of who the terrorists are, the groups and organizations they represent, and the motivations that drive them to commit their acts of mass violence. Moreover — and of vital importance — analysts must learn how to identify and interpret the often subtle yet critical clues that indicate the possibility of an impending terrorist action, and be taught the techniques to gather information and produce intelligence that truly enhances Homeland Security efforts.

The need for competent professionals to perform the analytical function is recognized by the National Criminal Intelligence Sharing Plan, the Commission on Accreditation for Law Enforcement Agencies, the International Association of Chiefs of Police, and a plethora of other major law enforcement organizations worldwide. In light thereof, funds must be budgeted for and analysts must receive the training necessary for them to fulfill not merely a secondary but rather a primary and dynamic role within the agencies they serve. So too must the people who supervise and manage the analytical function receive training so that they can fairly evaluate the performance of the analyst and guide the direction of the analysis program. Finally, the National Criminal Intelligence Sharing Plan recommends that even police administrators themselves receive the training and education necessary to acquaint them with the philosophy of intelligence-led policing, the nature of the intelligence process, and its role in enhancing public safety.

In that regard, *Terrorism and Organized Hate Crime: Intelligence Gathering, Analysis, and Investigations,* by Michael Ronczkowski, and his widely acclaimed Homeland Security and Terrorism Analysis course, are welcome additions to the educational arena because they provide a framework for exploring the many issues involved in the analysis of terrorism and organized hate crimes. Throughout this book Ronczkowski identifies the traits and structures of multiple forms of terrorism, demonstrates how to recognize the indicators of an impending act of terrorism or mass violence, how to deter and prevent an attack, how to gather information, and, of significant importance, how to transform information into intelligence products to meet community demands for safety and security. Moreover, in clear and concise language, this book illustrates how to establish and effectively operate a Homeland Security program and how to develop an analytical approach to terrorism that ALL law enforcement agencies, regardless of size, can use to address matters of homeland security, terrorism, and organized hate crimes within their jurisdiction, region, state, or province. As such, it is an excellent resource for not only analysts and intelligence officers, but for police administrators as well.

Steven Gottlieb
Executive Director
Alpha Group Center for Crime and Intelligence Analysis
www.alphagroupcenter.com

The Alpha Group Center is a premiere provider of Crime and Intelligence Analysis training to command- and line-level staff members of both civilian and military law enforcement organizations throughout the world. Offering onsite courses in Crime Analysis, Criminal Intelligence Analysis, Criminal Investigative Analysis, Homeland Security and Terrorism Analysis, Statement Analysis, Interview and Interrogation Techniques, and Law Enforcement Research Methods, the Alpha Group also serves as a training provider for the Certification Program for Crime and Intelligence Analysts, which is cosponsored by the State of California Department of Justice and the University of California and California State University Systems. This is currently the only certification program offered by — and with oversight from — a state governmental entity (as opposed to a private organization or association) that offers certification and confers the professional title of "Certified Crime and Intelligence Analyst" to program graduates. It is for this reason that this program is so well regarded throughout the law enforcement profession today. Furthermore, because the Alpha Group presents the curriculum to members of federal, state, local, military, and tribal law enforcement organizations throughout the world, this certification is available to people of any state or country who complete the program at any location in which it is offered.

Preface

Since September 11, 2001 the U.S. Federal Bureau of Investigation (FBI), as well as law enforcement agencies nationwide, have been thrust into the forefront of the "war" on terrorism. One may ask why law enforcement is fighting a "war" instead of "crime." For centuries, wars have been fought by the military. However, since the wave of "new terrorism" reaches beyond conventional boundaries by nonconventional methods, there is a need to attack from all fronts with all available resources. It has become apparent that a successful campaign against terrorism will require cooperation and coordination from military, law enforcement and private civilian agencies. The subsequent passage of the USA PATRIOT Act in October 2001 gave the role of traditional law enforcement a new direction. This enhanced the parameters in which agencies can communicate and gather good intelligence information. Since October 2001 the FBI staff alone sought to hire nearly 900 agents and 400 crime and intelligence analysts, also known as investigative research specialists, in the wake of perceived deficiencies in the gathering, analysis, investigation, and dissemination of intelligence data. This initiative may thwart future attempts to attack the United States and its interests. Only time will tell.

In an October 18, 2002 *Miami Herald* article, these deficiencies were made apparent. During testimony taken before a joint congressional hearing on October 17, 2002, FBI Director Robert Mueller stated that the FBI does well at collecting information, "… but will be the first to concede that we have not done a good job at analyzing it." This statement should not be viewed as an issue for only the FBI. Much of the information that the FBI gathers comes from the thousands of law enforcement agencies throughout the United States and other countries. Based on this, it can be argued that if the FBI has not done a good job of analyzing the information, then law enforcement has not done a good job of analyzing the same information. However, this is not the case. The public had not experienced any revelations that their domestic security was compromised or breached; the public only encountered criminals, organized hate groups, organized crime, gangs, and the occasional "whacko," all of which could be addressed by local law enforcement. Therefore, there was no precedent to look for or monitor "terrorists" or "terrorist-related" activity, and therefore no one to analyze this type of activity.

Terrorism, although not a new concept, is a relatively new variable for law enforcement agencies to consider on a regular basis. The need to effectively analyze terrorist-related and organized hate group information in a timely manner is critical. However, to analyze a topic, particularly terrorism and organized hate crimes, an analyst must have an understanding of the subject matter. This is perhaps the reason, as Director Mueller stated, that the FBI has not done a good job of analyzing this type of information.

This book is written to bridge that gap, to provide law enforcement agencies here — nearly 18,000 in the United States alone — as well as those in other countries, with an approach to analyzing homeland security needs and to aid the law enforcement community in understanding the vital role it plays in the war on terrorism. References to domestic terrorism cannot be construed as being specific to any one country. In this modern era of technology, communication, and transportation, placing boundaries on investigating and analyzing a topic such as terrorism is counterproductive. Based on history, terrorism is not going away any time soon. Therefore, law enforcement must develop methods and practices that address developing multifaceted links to local, regional, national, and international terrorism and hate crimes. Although many of the approaches detailed here focus on laws and practices in the United States, homegrown organized hate groups as well as domestic and international terrorism can strike in any country at any time.

Acknowledgments

This book would not have been possible without assistance from a multitude of people and entities. In no particular order, I would like to extend my gratitude to everyone who aided, directly and indirectly, this project over the past year: Sergeant Sean Holtz for his expertise in the area of cybercrimes and cyberterrorism matters as well as his technical wizardry; Dan Helms, Crime Analyst, National Law Enforcement and Corrections Technology Center, Rocky Mountain Region, and the Crime Mapping and Analysis Program (CMAP) for use of the GIS images; and Bair Software, Research and Consulting for the training project images. Thanks also to Julie Gonzalez for making the phone call and facilitating the foreword; Florida Atlantic University for giving me the opportunity to instruct in the Department of Criminology and Criminal Justice — in particular, the "Terrorism" course; the Miami-Dade Police Department in Florida; Steve Gottlieb and the Alpha Group Center for Crime and Intelligence Analysis Training, as well as the staff at the National Law Enforcement and Corrections Technology Center-Southeast in Charleston, South Carolina, for providing working environments that allowed me to gain experience and hone my skills and abilities. A special thanks to the staff, particularly Mark Potok and Russell Estes, of the Southern Poverty Law Center for their assistance, immediate responses, and work on the Center's Intelligence Report.

The Author

Michael Ronczkowski, M.P.A. began his law enforcement career in 1983 with the Miami-Dade Police Department in Miami, Florida, where he has risen through the ranks and continues to serve in an upper managerial capacity as a Major overseeing the department's Homeland Security Bureau. He is an adjunct professor teaching courses on terrorism and the criminal justice system at Florida Atlantic University in the Criminal Justice Department. Recognized internationally for his analytical skills, techniques and practices, and crime-mapping expertise, Ronczkowski has presented analytical material at numerous conferences, training classes, and workshops for various international associations, the Department of Justice, the Department of Homeland Security, and the National Institute of Justice. He managed a county-wide analytical intelligence unit for over eight years and has written analytical policy, procedures, and training protocols and has developed analytical databases and information resources. He also served as a certified Florida law enforcement instructor, field training officer, and supervisor. Ronczkowski has over 15 years of investigative experience and has supervised various criminal investigative units, including serving several years with the FBI and U.S. Marshal's fugitive task forces. He is an authorized Environmental Systems Research Institute (ESRI) Arcview instructor, and teaches crime and incident mapping and analysis for the National Law Enforcement and Corrections Technology Center (since January 2000). In addition, he instructs the Homeland Security and Terrorism Analysis course for the Alpha Group Center (since March 2004). In 2005 Ronczkowski became a board certification member for the United States Association of Professional Investigators (USAPI). Ronczkowski is the author of several writings on topics covering terrorism, analysis, and intelligence, including "The Robbery Clearinghouse: Successful Real-Time Intelligence Analysis" (*Police Chief Magazine*, September 1999), Tactical/Investigative Analysis of Targeted Crimes (*Advanced Crime Mapping*

Topics, NIJ — Crime Mapping and Analysis Program, April 2002), "Terrorism" (*Encyclopedia of Criminal Justice*, December 2004), "Analysis and Intelligence Driven Enforcement: The Future for Law Enforcement and Homeland Security" (*CALEA Journal* 85, June 2004), and "Using Police Information" (CDAP Project Partnership — Bureau of Justice Assistance and John Jay College, June 2005). He earned a bachelor of arts degree in criminal justice and a masters of public administration degree from Florida Atlantic University. Ronczkowski is also a graduate of the Federal Bureau of Investigation's National Academy, Session #217.

Introduction

"Terrorism" is perhaps the one word that creates more controversy and thought-provoking research than any other word, no matter where it is discussed. Debated, defined, and studied for decades by scholars and academics, terrorism remains at the forefront of many discussions, government debates, and media outlets. Now those in the field of law enforcement are debating, defining, and studying what terrorism is and what it means to the first responders of the world.

World events have shaped public perceptions for years, and these events have aided in the establishment of a framework that law enforcement managers use in guiding their agencies. With the advent of modern technology, law enforcement has sought to enhance its security, ability to work faster, process and analyze data, and develop avenues for sharing and consolidating information; working "smarter" and more efficiently.

Events surrounding recent terrorist activities now force law enforcement agencies to expedite and expand technological initiatives in order to aid in operational, tactical, investigative, intelligence, and deployment strategies. Facilitating methodologies with which to process these new demands within the law enforcement arena has led agencies across the country to hire specially trained criminal and intelligence analysts.

Since 1979 law enforcement agencies have sought to improve delivery of their services by standardizing practices and procedures through the development of the Commission on Accreditation for Law Enforcement Agencies (CALEA). The importance of crime analysis is noted in CALEA's documentation on accreditation. Based on this, many agencies have established crime analyst positions. The importance of these positions has not gone unnoticed. In 1996 Crime Analyst was listed as a "Hot Track" position in law enforcement, and the International Association of Crime Analysts was cited as saying "the demand for these technical whizzes has risen 10-fold in 15 years."

For individuals in the field of analysis, this was not a surprise. The International Association of Chiefs of Police (IACP) also recognized the importance of designing and implementing a standardized policy governing crime analysis, and has developed a blueprint for agencies to follow. In this document, which became effective on October 1, 1993, the IACP outlined a Model Policy for law enforcement agencies to use as a guide in its development of analytical protocols. IACP's Model Policy notes that crime analyst techniques began to emerge as early as 1972 in Dallas, Kansas City, and Sacramento. For nearly 20 years analysts have honed their skills, usually on the job and with little managerial direction. Many analysts anecdotally stated that their agencies were uncertain of how to utilize the talents of those in this largely nonsworn position. They also failed to see the importance of having a dedicated unit responsible for identifying patterns, series, and trends, usually without going on the street and generating statistics, such as arrests. However, this changed with the IACP's Model Policy. The crime analysis process was organized into five categories: data collection, data collation, analysis, report dissemination, and feedback/evaluation. This policy provided direction and helped define the role of the analyst within the agency.

Now that the concept of crime analysis has been with law enforcement for at least 30 years, and has been widely embraced in the past 10 years, why does it seem that agencies are still reactive rather than proactive? Perhaps it is because although the law enforcement community has implemented methods to standardize and categorize the analytical process, lack of understanding, education, and training of personnel throughout the ranks has impeded the process. How can one provide analysis for a topic for which one lacks knowledge, understanding, or formal training?

Traditional law enforcement methods have tended to be reactive rather than proactive, with an emphasis on identification and arrest of an offender in a specific jurisdiction. Analytical practices have enhanced this process; however, through experience, training, and technological advances, analytical personnel can aid the law enforcement community in looking at crime from a proactive posture across jurisdictional boundaries. Now that law enforcement agencies accept and rely upon analysts for the gathering, analyzing, and disseminating of "crime" information, a more exotic term has been added to the mix: "terrorism."

What is terrorism? How do we handle it? What information should we gather? How do we analyze it? For what are we looking? Why are crime analysts analyzing terrorism? These are just a few of the questions that an analyst outside a federal- or military-based agency might have. Analytical-based training for law enforcement analysts investigating crimes, although growing, has been limited over the past 30 years. Therefore, the importance of understanding "terrorism analysis" is exponential. The criminal relationships associated with crime, the knowledge and understanding of the topic, and the subject to be analyzed are of immediate importance if law enforcement agencies are to play a vital role in the war against terrorism. Waiting 30 days, or 30 years, runs the risk of missed information and perhaps many injuries or deaths. Provided in this book is a framework for answering and addressing these questions. Law enforcement now must target these much-debated issues and focus on understanding and defining its new and enhanced role in the war on terrorism.

Contents

chapter one

A need for understanding and analysis

Prior to September 11, 2001 the terms "terrorist," "terrorism," and "terrorist activity" were reserved for "other" countries and third-world locations struggling for an identity. This was especially true in the United States and the rest of the Western world or hemisphere. However, this perception could not have been further from the truth. Although only a country for over 225 years, the United States, just like many other countries, was born through the "revolutionary acts" of ordinary people. While viewed as revolutionary acts by citizens, according to modern definitions of terrorism those acts could be seen as terrorist activity today.

The United States, as well as other countries, has seen the need to gather and monitor terrorist-related activity and intelligence for many years. In the United States, the Central Intelligence Agency (CIA) was tasked with this mission for locations and groups outside the country. However, the need for internal monitoring was not seen as critical until September 11, 2001. With the demise of the Soviet Union and the end of the Cold War, the United States was viewed as the only remaining superpower — or in the eyes of some extremists, Satan. After the fall of the Soviet Union in 1991, many believed the need for spying and in-depth intelligence was diminished. The process, however, may have become more urgent and complex after the collapse. Being a superpower as well as a melting pot of cultures, surrounded by two oceans and neighbored by two cordial and passive countries, it is easy to become complacent and develop an "it can't happen here (or to me)" attitude. Now that this myth has been shattered forever, law enforcement is redefining its mission and purpose not only locally but also with respect to this international crisis.

What took so long for us to wake up? The United States was aware of terrorist activity and international reaches. It even convened a committee to investigate research on terrorism. The research was undertaken by a non-profit institution, RAND, which formally initiated terrorism research in 1972 in response to two significant terrorist events that horrified the world — the Japanese Red Army's attack at Lod Airport in Tel Aviv, Israel, and Black

September's attack at the Munich Olympic Games in Germany. This research was in response to then President Richard M. Nixon's creation of a Cabinet Committee to Combat Terrorism.[1]

Approximately 30 years later, we are still struggling with defining, dealing with, and addressing terrorism and the roles of officials and agencies in combating terrorism. Why is this? Is it because of politics and legal concerns? It is certainly not due to a lack of academic and scholarly research and writings. Countless publications have been written in the past 30 years covering virtually every aspect of the terrorism topic. However, outside of the field of terrorism research or military arenas there is a lack of awareness, especially by law enforcement personnel, as to how to best deal with and analyze terrorism and terrorist-related activity. Therefore, how are we to expect law enforcement personnel to identify something about which they do not have a conceptual understanding? Law enforcement academies have always focused on training and developing an individual so he understands every aspect of what he can do and what is expected of him in criminal-based situations locally, according to state guidelines. So how can law enforcement personnel be expected to effectively address the international reaches of terrorism without proper training and awareness of what they are attempting to identify and analyze? Much of the current law enforcement training focuses on the first responder handling hazardous materials and weapons of mass destruction instead of obtaining information and gathering intelligence. Providing training and a clear understanding of what needs to be gathered and analyzed are essential to effective management.

The mission

For years, many law enforcement agencies have employed civilian and sworn status personnel as crime and intelligence analysts. The role of these highly specialized individuals has gone largely unnoticed in the realm of law enforcement until now. Accredited law enforcement agencies currently follow the guidelines set forth in the CALEA Standards Manual, Chapter 15, "Crime Analysis," as well as the IACP (International Association of Chiefs of Police) Model Policy, as blueprints for its respective personnel assigned to performing crime and intelligence analysis. Chapter 15 of the CALEA Standards Manual alludes to the mission of an analyst as being that of a "support" position, stating that "The information obtained by analyzing the data is used to support management and operations."[2] Additionally, it is noted that the information obtained from analysis is to be used in strategic planning for topics such as crime prevention. However, is crime prevention the same as terrorism prevention? Much crime prevention is completed within the jurisdictional parameters of the respective agency. If this is the case, and local agencies are focused on a limited geographical area, the chances are that terrorism prevention is not a part of the mission.

The barometer often used as a measure of effectiveness and analyzed by an array of personnel is the FBI's Uniform Crime Report (UCR). Through the use of the UCR, law enforcement managers are capable of performing statistical management to gauge the effectiveness of their mission to reduce crime, to instill a sense of security in their citizens and the community they serve, and to follow a set of standardized procedures.

However, there is a flaw. There are just over 18,000 law enforcement agencies in the United States According to the U.S. Department of Justice, the FBI has attempted to collect basic crime and arrest data since 1930 from these agencies, but only over 17,000 of them have complied.[3] Although standardized, the voluntary nature of compliance and the various ways that states compile and submit information to the UCR leaves a gap in the basic collection of raw numbers. Given this gap in the collection of basic raw crime figures, the 18,000-plus independent law enforcement agencies are less able to define methods and practices designed to facilitate analysis of terrorism-related issues in a manner suitable to fit the immediate needs of concerned parties.

The missions and roles of analytical personnel and their duties need to be clearly defined in every agency's standard operating procedures for all employees to follow. Regardless of whether or not an agency employs analytical personnel, the need for information and analysis of data associated with terrorist-related activities or terrorists is vital to the interest of national security. Furthermore, it is imperative that this information be forwarded to concerned parties in an expeditious manner.

Actionable intelligence is essential for preventing acts of terrorism. Thorough analysis and expedient dissemination of information about domestic and international terrorists and their activities will improve the government's ability to disrupt and prevent terrorist acts and will provide useful warning to the private sector. Currently, the U.S. government does not have an institution (such as the CIA, which performs analysis regarding terrorist threats abroad) primarily dedicated to systematically analyzing all information and intelligence on potential terrorist threats within the United States. This will undoubtedly change with the establishment of the Department of Homeland Security, the instituting of a czar for intelligence, and the restructure of numerous government agencies. According to the documents establishing the Department of Homeland Security, working together with enhanced capabilities in other agencies such as the FBI would make America safer by compiling intelligence from a variety of sources.

Consolidation of resources is essential to any collective attack. In this mission, however, there are several underlying factors impeding the process that must be considered. The factors that stand in the way of effective homeland security and terrorism analysis are as follows:

- The Constitution
- Freedom of speech, press, and religion, and protection against unreasonable search and seizure
- The First Amendment
- The Fourth Amendment
- Traditional law enforcement approach to investigating crimes

- Reactive vs. proactive style of policing
- Lack of or insufficient number of crime and intelligence analysts
- Law enforcement that traditionally analyzes after the fact
- Proactive behavior or attitude when analyzing, which is usually met with skepticism
- Local law enforcement that is often consumed with local, civil, and community issues, e.g., racial profiling and community-oriented policing initiatives
- Proactive attitude requiring a change in philosophy, which law enforcement has not been traditionally quick to change or to accept

Currently, law enforcement analyzes and responds to the here and now. With homeland security, organized hate crime and terrorism analysts will need to be proactive and ready for the long term (at least 18 months) and look for nontraditional suspects.

An often forgotten component that may stand in the way is history. A quick snapshot of the last six decades may shed some insight to some of the skepticism surrounding intelligence as a whole.

- 1950s — McCarthy Hearings and the Communist boogey-man, FBI investigations of politicians and members of entertainment industry.
- 1960s — FBI investigates civil rights leaders and anti-war activists. Uniformed police deal with civil unrest and the 1968 Democratic Convention.
- 1970s — Vice President Agnew resigns, Watergate, Pentagon papers, more civil unrest. Freedom of Information Act extended to law enforcement. Information surfaces about CIA assassination plots.
- 1980s — Iran-Contra investigation.
- 1990s — Ruby Ridge and the assault at Waco.
- 2000s — 9/11 World Trade Center, Pentagon, and Pennsylvania hijackings.

This brief comparison can easily be played out for earlier years with everything from the prohibition era and the attacks on Pearl Harbor. One can oversimplify and sum it up to politics. Everything from shrinking budgets, the government's willingness to rely heavily on electronic and satellite-based intelligence over human intelligence, and the aforementioned high-profile eras have forged uncertainty in the public when it comes to intelligence.

Intelligence analysis units

Intelligence analysis units have existed in law enforcement for several decades. In *Applications in Criminal Analysis*, Marilyn B. Peterson provides historical background on intelligence and reports that it found its way into law enforcement in the 1920s and 1930s.[4] This was in response to the need to collect information on anarchists and mobsters operating during that time. Intelligence units operated sporadically in the United States until the advent of computers and adoption of analysis by many state and local agencies in the early 1980s. In the 1990s, perhaps the greatest growth and organization of intelligence units was seen. This was the decade in which the birth of many professional associations dedicated to intelligence and analysis, many of which still operate today, was seen. There were also several books written on the topic, and training programs began to emerge. Then came the new millennium. Just prior to the end of the century, everyone was consumed with the Y2K bug and computer meltdowns. Law enforcement was busy preparing for chaos and anarchy. Intelligence units, for those agencies who had them, were working around the clock in hopes of averting a catastrophic event. Today, these units are preparing for terrorism and threats to homeland security. However, "today" has been taking place for at least 10 years. Peterson dedicated a section of her book to terrorism, noting that it had blossomed in the previous 25 years as a threat, and she pointed out that groups such as the Skinheads and the Ku Klux Klan were then being considered domestic terrorist groups.[4]

While many agencies have intelligence units in place, many still do not. Or, if they have them, they fail to use their skills and abilities to the fullest. Another consideration is logistical. An informal cursory poll of analysts throughout North America over the preceding three years revealed that many analytical units are removed from the general investigative work area. They are usually relegated to a back room, or they work off-site in federal or state government intelligence centers. In order to be effective, analysts must be accessible to those personnel performing the line-level investigation.

Whether seeking to develop an analysis unit or to optimize an existing one, police administrators should strive to place these units in open areas that are readily accessible to their personnel. This is true whether the unit is composed of one person or several squads. Another practice to avoid is the use of cubicle jungles. Besides location and accessibility, the second most important factor for successful units is communication — which is greatly diminished by the use of any wall, including 6-ft cubicle walls. Interaction is essential to any intelligence unit.

With the logistics worked out, police administrators and managers — through the use of intelligence units — will be assisted in working smarter and in directing enforcement efforts of their organizations toward the right issues for the right reasons. Law enforcement is in the throes of an information age that is forcing the design or purchase of complex records management systems. Much of what law enforcement does is process information, but this does little to combat crime or to assist with terrorism matters without an effective intelligence analysis unit. To be effective, these units also require high-end computers, laser printers, plotters, and other peripheral devices, and complex software packages. All of these items are costly, and some managers fail to see the benefits of using scarce budgetary funds for a unit that does not produce traditional results — arrests. However, these items interpret the vast volumes of information collected annually. This interpretation pays dividends that indirectly drive a successful agency by providing direction that will lead to arrests and increased clearances. Properly outfitted units can also aid many facets of law enforcement, particularly special enforcement programs, including those dealing with terrorism, homeland security, and organized hate groups. This is done through analysis-driven enforcement (ADE) or analysis- and intelligence-driven enforcement (AIDE). Both rely on technology and the use of advanced crime analysis techniques, such as crime mapping, to identify critical need areas of policing. Managers then use this information to make informed decisions that will assist in dedicating resources to the endeavor at hand.

Intelligence analysis units will never lead an agency in statistical categories such as arrests, seizures, or citations. They will have few, if any, quantifiable measures. Intelligence units come with a high cost and require a professional, trained, and dedicated staff. Regardless of an agency's size, these units play an invaluable role with contributions that will be realized indirectly. All local agencies are at the forefront of the information gathering process. Every agency can and should either have the dedicated staff or be involved in a regional task force to address homeland security. The difficulty will be in a manager's ability to remove themselves from the need for instant gratification and results as well as seeing the need for overlooking jurisdictional limitations. This role will become evident as managers embrace ADE or AIDE and analysts train to look for criminal occurrences that may be linked to terrorist and organized hate crime activities.

Defining analytical positions and roles

With the mission defined, it is now necessary to standardize and establish working definitions for personnel assigned to perform the duties essential to developing effective and timely intelligence. This assignment would seem to be a relatively easy task. However, law enforcement agencies have spent the past two decades struggling with it. Job descriptions and requirements across the United States vary as much as the color and style of uniforms and badges.

Just as with uniforms, many agencies have written job descriptions and requirements to meet the needs of their particular agency. These have not impeded the level of service realized by any one jurisdiction, but if we as a country are to effectively tackle the issues surrounding homeland security and terrorism, it is essential that analytical requirements, practices, and procedures be standardized so that everyone is "speaking the same language." The importance of analysts has been realized locally by many agencies, and now this sentiment is echoed in the halls of the nation's capital. Analysts help protect the interests of the country through the development of useful high-quality analysis. The question that has lingered for years is, what is the difference between crime and intelligence analysis?

For many years, analytical and law enforcement practitioners have accepted the working definitions detailed in *Crime Analysis: From First Report* to *Final Arrest* by Gottlieb, Arenberg, and Singh, as best practices for their personnel. Written in 1994, these definitions were insightful. However, some of the details mentioned in the book may have been overlooked at the time. One such detail that was probably overlooked, or even questioned, was the mention of terrorism in the working definition of intelligence analysis. This occurred some seven years before most people realized that this would be something for law enforcement to consider, or even what the term "terrorism" meant. The definitions cited in the book are outlined below:[5]

> ***Crime analysis***: Allows the analyst to determine who is doing what to whom by its focus on crimes against persons and property (homicide, rape, robbery, burglary, theft, etc.)
>
> ***Intelligence analysis***: Aids in the determination of who is doing what with whom by its focus on the relationships between persons and organizations involved in illegal, and usually conspiratorial, activities (narcotics, trafficking, prostitution rings, organized crime, gangs, terrorism, etc.)

These definitions were incorporated into various job descriptions and policy protocols along with the premise that the world of analysis only encompasses administrative, strategic, and tactical practices. For law enforcement, this was true until September 11, 2001. We can now add another method of analysis, homeland security, which is actually a hybrid of the above types of analysis.

Intelligence disciplines

Throughout the years, differences in analytical definitions could be attributed to the fundamentally different missions experienced by various agencies employing analysts. The military, federal, state, and local law enforcement agencies employ analysts, but the job functions vary by agency. No matter how different the daily functions concerning administrative, tactical, and strategic analysis are for the various agencies, they now have one thing in common to strive for, and that is homeland security analysis. Regardless of the definitions used, an effective analyst will be part researcher, part psychologist, part historian, part investigator, and part linguist. In simple terms, any analyst is, or should be, a multitasker. As just noted, there are and will continue to be different missions. However, this can be overcome if we know how to apply them in our daily duties. Outlined below are five of the most common forms of intelligence disciplines that are not specific to any one mission or agency:

- IMINT — Imagery Intelligence — study and analysis of photos, videos, satellite images
- SIGINT — Signals Intelligence — study and analysis of signal communications (radios)

- MASINT — Measures and Signatures Intelligence — study and analysis of unique signatures produced by just about anything on the ground (radars, motors, generators, etc.)
- HUMINT — Human Intelligence — oldest form of intelligence — study and analysis based from human sources such as informants
- OSINET — Open Source Intelligence — study and analysis of open press, Internet, technical industry documents, group literature, etc.

Every one of the aforementioned disciplines can be found in everyday law enforcement. For example, MASINT is often referred to as modus operandi or M.O. and is used to find the unique characteristics of crime and attribute it to an individual. HUMINT is simply confidential informants or snitch. No matter which discipline or the mission at hand it is easy to point out that many personnel will focus strictly on one discipline. However, it is usually OSINET that is overlooked, misunderstood, and difficult to corroborate at most levels of crime and intelligence analysis. An issue to be realized with OSINET is the fact that terrorists and terrorist organizations, e.g., Al-Qaeda's training manual, note that approximately 80 percent of information needed to formulate an attack can be found through open source means. Even the U.S. military's Operation Able Danger noted that they developed many of their links and associations from terra-bytes of open source information. Part of the problem being faced is a clear understanding of the role and abilities of intelligence analysts.

In a 1997 document, 15 axioms for intelligence analysts were published by a member of the CIA Directorate of Intelligence and should be considered valuable insight into what principles can be used in everyday analytical conduct. Outlined below are the principles that should be used as guidelines for all analysts in their daily duties, regardless of agency size:[6]

Believe in your own professional judgments.
Be aggressive, and do not fear being wrong.
It is better to be mistaken than to be wrong.
Avoid mirror imaging at all costs.
Intelligence is of no value if it is not disseminated.
Coordination is necessary, but do not settle for the lowest common denominator.
When everyone agrees on an issue, something is probably wrong.
The consumer does not care how much you know, just tell him what is important.
Form is never more important than substance.
Aggressively pursue the collection of information you need.
Do not take the editing process too seriously.
Know your community counterparts, and talk to them frequently.
Never let your career take precedence over your job.
Being an intelligence analyst is not a popularity contest.
Do not take your job or yourself too seriously.

Not all 15 axioms will be employed by everyone or be applicable in every agency all the time, but they should be used as guidance in defining roles and missions of analytical personnel. There is, however, one more axiom that might be added to the list: Possess a fundamental grasp of the topic. Many of the cited axioms will be expanded upon in detail in subsequent sections. Use of the axioms is directed to the analysts, but they are only one piece of the whole. Agency leaders and command staff personnel also play vital roles in defining analytical positions and how they are used. In *Psychology of Intelligence Analysis*, former CIA employee Jack Davis stated in the Introduction (p. 7) that "to ensure sustained improvement in assessing complex issues, analysis must be treated as more than a substantive and organizational process."[7] Definitions mean little if the agency's leaders do not establish an organizational environment that utilizes an analyst in his intended role. It is incumbent upon these leaders to ensure that analysts are used to their fullest capabilities, are certified and trained properly, and are not relegated to mundane data entry duties.

What is homeland security and terrorism analysis?

Undertaking and employing analytical methods is a bold concept that can be construed as proactive and controversial. Both of these are contrary to traditional law enforcement practices of being reactive to crime and being wary of controversial situations. Now we are adding the exotic world of homeland security and terrorism that by necessity requires law enforcement personnel to be proactive. Waiting could have detrimental effects that would be felt beyond traditional jurisdictional boundaries of any one particular agency. It is usually after a tragic event that we observe many different people and agencies analyzing the occurrence and looking for what went wrong, what could have been done prior to the event, as well as what a law enforcement agency neglected to do. Performing analysis after a significant event, for law enforcement, is done to identify deficiencies and best practices and to improve future performance. However, with modern training, technology, and professional analysts, law enforcement has the ability to make an informed and educated statement to predict or anticipate future behavior.

One way of looking at analysis is that it is to law enforcement as market research is to business. Just like market research will investigate every aspect of a business from customer-based demographics to target market, analysts charged with homeland security and terrorism need to look at every available variable. Traditional analysis seeks to build probable cause in substantiating criminal charges, usually after developing some sort of investigative lead. With homeland security and terrorism analysis, law enforcement personnel cannot afford to wait for the lead to come in. They need to proactively seek not only terrorist activity but also potential terrorists, links, and targets.

Traditional law enforcement has been reluctant to share information due to jurisdictional reasons, confidentiality constraints, and case ownership. With a routine case, items such as case ownership are not seen as negatives and generally do not have detrimental effects on criminal cases. This is not the case with homeland security and terrorism. In homeland security and terrorism analysis and investigations, these limitations need to be overcome. Due to the nature of the assignment and the sensitivity of the materials to be analyzed, information must be handled carefully. Personnel need to understand that the intelligence they are dealing with is not limited to any one jurisdiction. Knowledge may be power, but in the world of homeland security, failure to share this knowledge, understand what needs to be analyzed, and think globally could have a devastating impact.

Understanding what needs to be analyzed

Since the advent of computer technology, law enforcement agencies have sought to enhance their capabilities to increase efficiency and effectiveness by implementing technological initiatives within their jurisdictions. However, due to bureaucratic and budgetary restrictions, many agencies strive to purchase the best systems possible from the lowest bidders. This has the potential of leaving an agency with outdated systems that meet the needs of their agency but lack compatibility with other agencies seeking to share information. Also, due to implementation phases and working out the bugs, many analysts may find themselves being trained only in the basics and learning the rest on the job. It is one thing to know which buttons to push but another to understand the topic you seek to analyze. In order to completely understand the topic, one must have a basic understanding of history, theories, practices, and needs prior to analyzing.

Not all terrorists or their organizations emanate from overseas. In *Countering the New Terrorism,* Ian O. Lesser stated that "In the United States, right-wing militia and survivalist movements are a prominent source of terrorist risk, and are increasingly networked with like-minded groups worldwide."[8] Law enforcement should therefore look in its own back yard before looking overseas for terrorists or terrorist-related activity. Terrorist groups, domestic and foreign, as well as organized hate groups constantly seek to enhance their membership and expand their reach of violence. What better way to reach the United States or any country than by locating, associating with, and collaborating with groups that have an antigovernment stand. This might be a shocking concept for some law enforcement agencies. After all, the media portrays a terrorist as someone coming from the Middle East who does not look or sound like the average American. Are we being publicly misled? Should we be looking in our own back yards or only overseas? The answer to these questions will probably vary from place to place, but one thing is certain. We are dealing with groups full of hatred that have a transnational reach or following. Therefore, law enforcement will not be able to deal with terrorism the same way it deals with crime. Also, an analyst is more apt to identify activity in an expeditious manner if armed with a fundamental understanding of terrorism and a skill for reviewing variables without prejudice or bias.

David C. Rapoport (1988) pointed out that he started preparing a terrorism report for the Canadian Broadcasting Company in 1969. Fifteen years later when he wrote and edited the book *Inside Terrorist Organizations*, he noted that the "academic enterprise" grew exponentially in such a short time.[9] More than 30 years later, with considerably more academic research and publications available on the topic, law enforcement is beginning to realize the magnitude of the field. Why reinvent the wheel? Many of the "who, what, where, when, why, and how" questions were answered for us. All we have to do is understand how to implement and use this vast knowledge and research to our advantage.

Keys to analyzing

Analysts employed by law enforcement agencies throughout the country utilize various approaches, methods, and techniques when analyzing crime. These methods will probably not have a negative impact in the world of crime fighting. The fundamental approach is relatively simple. If we cannot prevent the crime, then we must do what we can to identify, apprehend, and prosecute the subject. With this approach, analysts review an array of reported-crime reports and information usually submitted by their personnel. Whether this is done manually or through the latest technology is irrelevant, because unless a serial criminal is involved, time is often on the side of law enforcement when building a case. Many crimes go unreported, and law enforcement does not seek this type of information. Even worse is that some law enforcement agencies even encourage non-reporting of incidents as it helps lower the published crime rate. This is more of a "how can we analyze something we don't know" issue. The same cannot be said for homeland security and terrorism analysis.

The six keys to analyzing information for intelligence that will remedy the need to get beyond street crimes are as follows.

1. Seek reported and unreported information in an expeditious manner in order to thwart any potential activity that may penetrate homeland security or cause terrorist-related activity.
2. Validate the authenticity and the accuracy of information received and never discount anything without checking it against all variables or leads.
3. Know your data, resources, and capabilities.
4. Avoid becoming a one-dimensional analyst, and instead look at all global factors, including the organization at hand.
5. Do not to jump to extremes.
6. Immerse oneself in the process.

The first key is to seek reported and unreported information in an expeditious manner in order to thwart any potential activity that may penetrate homeland security or cause terrorist-related activity. We are still seeking to deter, prevent, and arrest, but the difference is that we are doing it without delay.

Martha Crenshaw said that "Intelligence failures may preclude warning of impending attack, or, paradoxically, an overload of warnings, especially if they are imprecise, may induce complacency or the 'cry wolf' syndrome."[10] Although these are valid concerns, it is up to the analytical and intelligence community to maintain a professional decorum, enhance training efforts, educate itself and its colleagues, streamline and standardize practices, and validate and document all information.

The second key is to validate the authenticity and the accuracy of information received and never discount anything without checking it against all variables or leads.

Specific tactical terrorist warnings of impending attacks are rarely received. According to Crenshaw's publication, "Governments often know that a terrorist attack is probable and what the likely targets are, but cannot predict the day or hour of the attack" (p. 15).[10]

Pursuant to this, the third key is to know your data, resources, and capabilities. An analyst who has an in-depth or intimate knowledge of the data is more likely to take a little bit of information and transform it into a viable piece of intelligence that may aid in operational and deployment strategies in order to curb terrorist or hate crime activity. Also, the analyst will be able to corroborate and challenge information as it is introduced, by analyzing it against a wide array of variables. Analysts who know what resources are available will be able to identify potential targets and their associations as well as recognize oddities.

The fourth key is to avoid becoming a one-dimensional analyst, and instead look at all global factors, including the organization at hand. Analysts who look at only one facet or variable will inevitably fail. With homeland security and terrorism analysis, analysts need to look beyond the potential of identifying a terrorist or a terrorist's target. Terrorist organizations cannot survive without support and membership. Crenshaw stated that "Organizational analysis explains not only why terrorism continues regardless of political results but why it starts" (p. 21).[10] We need to identify what would make it hard to recruit and keep loyal members, and we need to identify their weaknesses. Many law enforcement agencies did this for years by tracking gang members and their affiliations. It can be argued that many groups classified as terrorist or hate organizations today may have been viewed as elaborate gangs or extremist movements just 10 years ago.

The fifth key is not to jump to extremes. We cannot look only for those things that may lead to weapons of mass destruction (WMD). In the 1970s, the U.S. Army developed a spectrum of conflict. As demonstrated in Figure 1.1, terrorism is right after riots and disorders and before guerilla warfare on its Spectrum of Conflict. WMD are at the end of the spectrum, so why is the public focusing on the end? Is it because WMD are more sensational than terrorism? Whatever the views the public may have, law enforcement needs to remain focused, and approach the situation systematically, with care

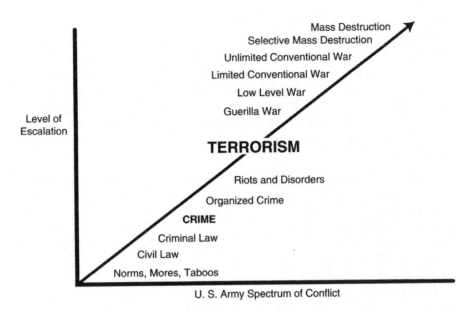

Figure 1.1 U.S. Army spectrum of conflict.

and caution. The media cannot be allowed to dictate the law enforcement analytical process when dealing with terrorism.

The sixth and final key is to immerse oneself in the process. No matter what technology is used, the human factor is essential and cannot be replaced. Analysts possess experience, preconceptions based on assumptions and expectations, and know the makeup and limitations of a jurisdiction.

Deterrence, prevention, arrest, and target hardening

"In meeting a threat, government has two basic alternatives: defense and deterrence."[10] This statement was published in 1988 by Martha Crenshaw (p. 16) when speaking of terrorism, and remains relevant for the government and law enforcement today. However, for law enforcement it is often construed as prevention and deterrence. Crenshaw noted that "The exercise of prevention is based on estimates of an enemy's intention and of its capabilities" (p. 16).[10] In this section, a modern, all-inclusive approach to prevention being used by analysts when aiding their agencies dealing with the criminal element will be expanded upon. This approach can be applied to terrorism-related matters as well as organized hate groups. Based on a review of earlier scholarly and academic publications, analysts will be able to be multidimensional by looking for variables that will enhance deterrence, prevention, arrest, and target hardening for homeland security, organized hate crime, or terrorist-related matters. These four components were also discussed in detail in a publication sponsored by the National Law Enforcement and Corrections Technology Center's (NLECTC) Crime Mapping and Analysis Program. They were discussed in the context of tactical and investigative crime but are applicable to matters of homeland security and organized crime. The publication *Advanced Crime Mapping Topics* was the result of a symposium held in 2001 consisting of a panel of experts from around the country. These experts came from all areas of the criminal justice world, including analytical practitioners, police managers, cartographers, academics, and policy makers. Outlined below are the four concepts presented at the symposium.[10]

Deterrence

"Analytically, deterrence of anything from street crime to biological terrorism may rely on fear of consequences such as prison or execution imposed by governments or on fear of social condemnation."[11] In the realm of law enforcement, when dealing with street crime the above statement is accurate and is often a goal set by agencies seeking to address a particular trend. Whether through the use of social programs, such as the drug abuse resistance education (DARE) program, or rehabilitation measures, law enforcement and governments continuously strive to find programs that will deter crime. The above statement regarding biological terrorism should not be discounted, even though this form of terrorism seldom occurs and will probably never be encountered by many of the thousands of law enforcement personnel. The best chance of deterrence when dealing with terrorism will come in sound analytical practices designed to place a stranglehold on terrorists' financial means and access targets, and limit their ability to recruit new members. Terrorists have little fear of social condemnation or execution. Their beliefs and their desire to be viewed as martyrs for their cause dramatically reduce the likelihood of any form of deterrence. If a person is willing to become a homicide bomber and die for his beliefs and his group, there is little that government can do in the form of sanctions to curb this activity. However, by proactively analyzing all terrorist-related information without undue delay, law enforcement personnel should be able to indirectly deter potential terrorists.

Prevention

Of the four areas of concern discussed in this section, prevention through proper and timely analysis of information is where law enforcement can have the greatest impact. Due to the structure and management of terrorist organizations, which will be discussed in depth later, the likelihood of law enforcement infiltrating a cell or column is highly improbable. This, coupled with the concept of a leaderless resistance or a lone wolf, would leave law enforcement personnel virtually handcuffed. However, through effective and accurate analysis, command staff and government personnel will be armed with intelligence that will greatly aid operational and deployment strategies designed to prevent a future attack.

There are three methods of prevention:[12]

1. Monitor groups suspected of planning terrorism in order to prevent their actions, or to arrest and incapacitate them.
2. Deny such groups what they need to access and to carry out acts of terrorism.
3. Monitor the acquisition of various supplies, information, or access that terrorists need, and then use that information to detect groups more likely to be contemplating acts of terrorism so that the group can be watched.

These three methods of prevention, although broad-based, can be readily adapted by virtually any law enforcement agency by expanding databases and documenting all potential information received. With these methods, the initial step in identifying potential leads for developing further intelligence and for enhancing investigative practices would be realized.

Just as law enforcement needs to successfully identify and prevent terrorist-related activity, a terrorist needs to successfully complete his mission. Prevention of terrorism requires depriving the terrorist of one or more of five specific conditions required to achieve his ends:[12]

1. Locate the target.
2. Get to the target.
3. Accomplish this with needed associates.
4. Have the necessary information, equipment, and facilities.
5. Expect enough safety to justify taking the risks.

Knowing that these conditions exist for a terrorist, it is important for analytical personnel to be aware of terrorists' needs when reviewing information for possible intelligence leads.

Arrest

In the world of law enforcement, locating and arresting a subject is the goal. In the realm of homeland security and terrorism, an arrest may come too late. We cannot afford to wait for an incident to be planned or to occur. Therefore every effort should be made to focus on prevention, deterrence, and target hardening.

Arrest with regard to organized hate group members can pose logistical and intelligence problems. Hate group members are often investigated and monitored in the same fashion as gang members. For law enforcement, opportunities for gleaning intelligence from the ranks of organized hate group membership are far greater than those for gleaning intelligence from a foreign-based terrorist organization. This is partly because hate groups publicly expose their beliefs and sometimes their actions. Once arrested, a larger issue of where and how to detain these individuals is created. Foreign-based groups are often incarcerated on a military installation or in a maximum-security federal penitentiary. Organized hate group members usually end up in county jails and state prisons. Hatred permeates so much from the ranks of these groups that several correctional facilities have implemented extensive databases and geographical mapping applications designed to capture hate group information while members are incarcerated.

Target hardening

The intent of target hardening is to reduce the possibility of attack by strengthening the perceived weakness of a given target. However, this is not a perfect science. As demonstrated through the course of history, terrorists do not shy away from secure or fortified targets, also known as hard targets. This is evident by the numerous attacks on military installations and equipment, such as the 1996 bombing of the Khobar Towers in Saudi Arabia or the attack on the USS *Cole* in October 2000, which killed 17 American sailors. Keeping this in mind, do not overlook or underevaluate any potential target. Another group of targets that requires consideration is what can be referred to as soft targets, such as hotels, restaurants, and public venues. These potential targets are often taken for granted and are seen as locations that have little notoriety to offer if attacked. However, in the world of terrorism nothing can be taken for granted.

By analyzing the array of information available to law enforcement, it is possible for government officials to identify likely targets of potential terrorists. Armed with this information and with the use of a wide range of intelligence tools, officials charged with preventing possible attacks can make better informed decisions and can assist identified targets in strengthening weaknesses that may cause them to be an attractive choice for a terrorist attack. When initiating a proactive target-hardening posture, all aspects should be reviewed. Physical as well as psychological targets need to be evaluated and addressed. Items such as access control, security, identifications, and ingress and egress are all part of target hardening. Terrorists are not just looking to inflict bodily harm, they also count on the psychological impact a tragic event will have on the public. Whether it is direct or indirect intent, terrorists know that through their course of actions they may injure or kill a small number of individuals in any one particular incident. They know that their actions will be repeatedly played in the media, creating a psychological impression on the public. All one has to do to see this is look at the impact felt by the airline industry after September 11, 2001, when the number of passengers dramatically decreased. The reason for the decrease in passengers was fear, and this is something that cannot be addressed with target hardening.

Chapter concepts

1. The mission of analytical personnel is that of support, and the information obtained is used for strategic planning. Also, the topic to be analyzed, and what is meant by homeland security analysis, need to be understood.
2. Currently, the U.S. government has no institution primarily dedicated to systematic analysis of intelligence on potential terrorist threats within the country.
3. Intelligence has been used by law enforcement since the 1920s. There is also a need to define analytical roles within an agency and to know the difference in the working definitions of crime and intelligence analysts.
4. Fifteen axioms for intelligence analysts are described. They provide valuable insight into what principles can be used in everyday analytical conduct.
5. Six keys to analyzing information for intelligence remedy the need to get beyond street crimes.

References

1. Jenkins, B.M., *Countering the New Terrorism*, Lesser, I.O. et al., Eds., RAND, Santa Monica, CA, 1999, p. iii.
2. The Commission on Accreditation for Law Enforcement Agencies (CALEA), *Crime Analysis*, The Commission on Accreditation for Law Enforcement Agencies, Washington, DC, January 1999, Chap. 15.
3. U.S. Department of Justice, Bureau of Justice Statistics, *Bridging Gaps in Police Crime Data*, Washington, DC, September 1999, p. 1.
4. Peterson, M.B., *Applications in Criminal Analysis*, Greenwood Press, Westport, CT, 1994, pp. 3, 115–117.
5. Gottlieb, S., Arenberg, S., and Singh, R., *Crime Analysis: From First Report to Final Arrest*, Alpha Publishing, Montclair, CA, 1994, p. 11.
6. Watanabe, F., How to succeed in the DI: fifteen axioms for intelligence analysts, *Studies in Intelligence*, 1, 1, 1997.
7. Heuer, R.J., Jr., *Psychology of Intelligence Analysis*, Center for the Study of Intelligence, Central Intelligence Agency, 1999; http://www.cia.gov/csi/books/19104/art1.html (February 17, 2003).
8. Lesser, I.O. et al., *Countering the New Terrorism, Implications for Strategy*, RAND, Santa Monica, CA, 1999, p. 104.
9. Rapoport, D.C., Ed., *Inside Terrorist Organizations*, Columbia University Press, New York, 1988, p. 1.
10. Crenshaw, M., Theories of terrorism: instrumental and organizational approaches, in Rapoport, D.C., Ed., *Inside Terrorist Organizations*, Columbia University Press, New York, 1988, pp. 14, 15, 16, 21.
11. Cooper, J., Nelson, E., and Ronczkowski, M., Tactical/investigative analysis of targeted crimes, in *Advanced Crime Mapping Topics*, National Law Enforcement and Corrections Technology Center, Denver, CO, April 2002, p. 28.
12. Heymann, P.B., *Terrorism and America: A Commonsense Strategy for a Democratic Society*, MIT Press, Cambridge, MA, 1998, pp. xi, xii, 84.

chapter two

Understanding and defining terrorism

In the late 1970s, Michael Stohl authored an introduction to the book *The Politics of Terrorism* entitled "Myths and Realities of Political Terrorism." He noted, referring to terrorism, that "The burgeoning journalistic and scholarly literature that has resulted from this increased awareness has unfortunately not been accompanied by a commensurate increase in the understanding of the phenomenon."[1] Here we are some 20-plus years later, and has anything changed? Does the law enforcement community understand any better? The short answer is "no." If academics and scholars continually struggle to understand terrorism and its repercussions, it is probable that law enforcement personnel are just beginning to understand and address the matter. This chapter is designed to aid the law enforcement community in understanding and defining terrorism, terrorist activity, and potential threat.

It has been explained that the terrorist and his adversary act in ways to change each other's behavior, and if a terrorist group fails it is because the government has virtually eliminated any possibility that its actions will be rewarded. If law enforcement personnel, particularly analytical and intelligence, have a sound foundation and understanding of terrorism, terrorist activity, and what a terrorist is, then government will be able to identify and change or eliminate the behavioral opportunities of those seeking to violate or encroach upon homeland security measures.

Terrorist organizational leaders may be reluctant to see their purpose accomplished and the organization's utility ended. Terrorists may look for incremental gains to sustain group morale but not to end members' dependence on the organization, which is similar to how many street gangs work. It is important that law enforcement personnel have a keen awareness of this because traditionally, with the arrest of a criminal, there will be closure to a crime series. Many crimes occur because there are opportunities for them to take place. However, with terrorism the activity or event is usually well planned, and once committed the organization will regroup and initiate a strategy for its next move. Just as the definition of terrorism changed over the decades, the causes of some groups have changed with time. This affords them the opportunity to garner support from different sectors and reinvent themselves in an effort to sustain life, enlist new members, and gain financial means. Defining terrorism is extremely difficult because it changes with time and historical context.

Defining terrorism

Defining terrorism has been greatly debated and written about for decades. Countless books have entire chapters dedicated to this topic. There are many working definitions of terrorism. In *Terrorism: An Introduction*, Jonathan R. White gives six "official" definitions of terrorism. Five of these are from various U.S. government agencies. Which is the most accurate? It depends on your position, mission, and the period in which you seek to define terrorism. Three of the more commonly cited definitions come from the FBI, the U.S. Department of State, and the U.S. Department of Defense, and they are outlined here:

> The FBI defines terrorism as "the unlawful use of force and violence against persons or property to intimidate or coerce a Government, the civilian population, or any segment thereof, in furtherance of political or social objectives."[2]
>
> The U.S. Department of State defines terrorism as "an activity, directed against persons involving violent acts or acts dangerous to human life which would be a criminal violation if committed within the jurisdiction of the U.S.; and is intended to intimidate or coerce a civilian population; to influence the policy of a government by intimidation or coercion; or to affect the conduct of a government by assassination or kidnapping."[3]
>
> The Department of Defense defines terrorism as "the calculated use of violence or threat of violence to inculcate fear; intended to coerce or to intimidate governments or societies in the pursuit of goals that are generally political, religious, or ideological."[3]

The similarities are evident, but which is correct, and why is it that one government cannot have just one definition? The answer is simple: their missions are fundamentally different. However, one should not get hung up on having an all-inclusive definition of terrorism, but rather focus on an understanding of what makes up terrorism. Phillip B. Heyman pointed out that there have "been many attempts to define 'terrorism' as clearly as we define murder, robbery, or rape. The effort has been less than successful."[4] In this section, the analytical practitioner and law enforcement investigators will be given a foundation from which to work in their daily duties concerning terrorism and terrorist activity, as well as a historical perspective of the topic.

Snow gives us the logical and simple explanation that "the root of the term terrorism itself is from the Latin word terrere, which means 'to frighten.'"[5] Looking at modern criminal statutes such as robbery, you will find terminology like "the taking of property by force or fear." Has law enforcement been dealing with terrorism for many decades without realizing it? Lesser et al. noted, "Terrorism is, among other things, a weapon used by the weak against the strong."[6] Again, using the robbery reference, many officers and detectives would argue that most robbers are intellectually and emotionally weak and use their social inabilities against those they see as financially strong in order to further their cause of financial gain.

Providing a definition of the root of terrorism can cause great debate and confusion. Deciding which definition should be adopted is another dilemma. Therefore, it is suggested that law enforcement agencies and analysts use a standardized and broad definition, if they must have one. The following definitions of terrorism, according to U.S. Code 22 USC Sec. 2656f(d), are straightforward and can be used by all parties when dealing with terrorism and terrorist activity:

> The term "terrorism" means premeditated, politically motivated violence perpetrated against noncombatant targets by subnational groups or clandestine agents, usually intended to influence an audience.
> The term "international terrorism" means terrorism involving citizens or the territory of more than one country.

Even though having a written definition of terrorism can be helpful, agencies should not dwell on the definition. Remember, this has been debated for decades, changed throughout the years, and is not going to be changed by any one law enforcement agency overnight. Besides, this is just one facet that needs defining. Terrorist activity and terrorists must also be defined.

Defining terrorist activity

Terrorist activity is designed to make a statement. This activity is a form of propaganda because the terrorist knows that the media will cover sensational and tragic events. Media coverage serves as a venue for expressing not only what physically can be done, but also what will likely psychologically affect those who view the activity. Terrorist activity takes many forms, including assassinations, bombings, arson, sabotage, hostage taking, property damage, and anarchy. According to White's citing of Gurr's empirical analyses, most terrorist activity lasts 18 months from the onset of violence.[7] Preparation to initiate the terrorist activity may go on for months, if not years, before the first incident. This is important for the law enforcement community to note, because law enforcement has traditionally been reactive to events. With terrorist-related activity, if you are not proactive, your community can be adversely affected. However, terrorist activity in the world of law enforcement has gone unnoticed, or has it? The fact is that many agencies have been gathering information on many activities classified under various other guises, such as labor movements, anarchy, social unrest, and anti-civil rights actions. The FBI does not measure criminal terrorism, but it has gathered information on numerous reported hate crime violations since the 1990s. Looking back, is it possible that some of these crimes could have been viewed as terrorist activity then, or even now? What is a working definition of terrorist activity? Let us look at how the U.S. Department of State defines terrorist activity from Section 212(a)(3)(B) of the Immigration and Nationality Act:[8]

> (ii) TERRORIST ACTIVITY DEFINED — As used in this Act, the term "terrorist activity" means any activity which is unlawful under the laws of the place where it is committed (or which, if committed in the United States, would be unlawful under the laws of the United States or any State) and which involves any of the following:
>
> (I)   The hijacking or sabotage of any conveyance (including an aircraft, vessel, or vehicle).
>
> (II) The seizing or detaining, and threatening to kill, injure, or continue to detain, another individual in order to compel a third person (including a governmental organization) to do or abstain from doing any act as an explicit or implicit condition for the release of the individual seized or detained.
>
> (III) A violent attack upon an internationally protected person (as defined in section 1116(b)(4) of title 18, United States code) or upon the liberty of such a person.
>
> (IV) An assassination.
>
> (V)   The use on any:
>
>   (a) biological agent, chemical agent, or nuclear weapon or device, or
>
>   (b) explosive or firearm (other than for mere personal monetary gain), with intent to endanger, directly or indirectly, the safety of one or more individuals or to cause substantial damage to property.
>
> (VI) A threat, attempt, or conspiracy to do any of the foregoing.

Although some activity noted above would appear to be an obvious fit for terrorist activity, those on the front line — law enforcement and analytical personnel — should not overlook anything as a potential for terrorist activity. It does not take the actions of an entire group to justify terrorist activity. It only takes one. Just like a 1000-piece puzzle, at the beginning it appears confusing, but as the pieces are put together the picture becomes more obvious. Lose one piece and the picture will never be complete. Analysts will be dealing with those pieces right out of the box, so it is important to maintain them and arrange them without delay. One piece of the puzzle that must be identified is the form of terrorism or terrorist activity being investigated.

Forms of terrorism

Terrorism comes in many diabolical forms that are as diverse as the definitions of terrorism. Whether to lessen the blow or to identify why a terrorist activity took place, being aware of the forms of terrorism assists the mainstream population in identifying and cataloging serious events. It is hoped that this knowledge will help deter and apprehend suspects.

Over the years, the term terrorism has been redefined and reinvented on many fronts. One word that will often be at the top of the list of definitions is "political." In Alex Schmid's review and analysis of 109 terrorism definitions, he reported that "political" was the second most common element used when defining terrorism, with a frequency rate of 65 percent. Only violence and fear had a higher frequency rate (83.5 percent).[9]

Political terrorism is not the only form of terrorism. Most definitions of terrorism have an underlying tone of politics associated with them. There is a need to expand upon political terrorism as a direct form of terrorism. Terrorism comes in many different forms, styles, types, and methods. However, for purposes of the law enforcement community, only six forms of terrorism will be discussed. These forms are the ones that most law enforcement officials are likely to encounter. Outlined below are working definitions of the six forms of terrorism enumerated in this section.

> *Political terrorism* — An act or series of acts directed toward bringing about political or policy change through the use of force, intimidation, or threatened use of force.
>
> *Ecological terrorism* — An act or series of acts designed to slow, impede, or halt the growth or harvesting of a nation's natural resources.
>
> *Agricultural terrorism* — The use of chemicals or toxins (biological means) against some component of the agricultural industry in an attempt to disrupt distribution or consumption of goods by the general public.
>
> *Narco terrorism* — Terrorist acts conducted in an attempt to divert attention from illegal drug and narcotic operations. This term is usually applied to groups that use the drug trade to fund terrorism.
>
> *Biological terrorism* — The threat of use of biological or chemical agents designed to injure, maim, or cause death.
>
> *Cyber terrorism* — The use of computer resources to intimidate and infiltrate public, private, and government computer-based infrastructures through the use of viruses or code breaking in an attempt to disrupt service, or destroy or compromise data.

Political terrorism

In Ted Robert Gurr's study of political terrorism, he noted several characteristics found in groups operating in the 1960s. Although this was roughly

40 years ago, many of the characteristics that he identified still ring true and are applicable to some modern-day groups.

Political terrorism has often been seen as a left-wing movement that virtually faded away in the United States after the 1970s. Individuals associated with these movements were considered political activists associated largely with underground movements. Although somewhat true for that era, political terrorism has existed for centuries. It is just now that we are coming to understand what makes up this form of terrorism and are identifying and developing methods of stymieing its activities.

Based on Gurr's characteristics of groups in the 1960s, activities associated with political terrorist or left-wing groups can be misclassified and labeled as other forms of terrorism. This is due to their methods of operation and their use of explosive and incendiary devices, the archetypical weapons of political terrorism.[10] In order to avoid this confusion, Gurr identified three objective elements associated with political terrorism and stated that all three elements must be present. The three objective definitional elements based on his definition of political terrorism are[10]

Destructive violence is used by stealth rather than in open combat.
Some of the principal targets are political.
Actions are carried out by groups operating clandestinely and sporadically.

Gurr went on to state that many of the targets of political terrorism are politicians, the military, and police, and that most terrorist campaigns were short-lived.[10]

Ecological terrorism

Incidents of ecological terrorism are sometimes reported publicly as random acts of destruction, and are seldom seen as having an underlying agenda or cause. Individuals operating in these groups are viewed as radical environmentalists (tree huggers and elves, as in the Earth Liberation Front [ELF]). These groups and individuals are not necessarily interested in garnering public support. They have little belief that any policy or legislative changes posed by the government will bring about sufficient social changes. They follow the premise that the ecosystems have an inherent worth that cannot be judged in relation to human needs, and that if action is not taken to effect changes there will be mass extinctions.

Two of the more prevalent target groups of ecological terrorists are the U.S. Forest Service and the logging industry. Many groups that carry out this form of terrorism dismiss the fact that they are violent and deny being terrorists. They consider actions such as setting large fires or inserting metal spikes into trees slated for harvesting as needed deterrents designed to keep logging companies from cutting down trees and destroying the environment. Their intentions are allegedly not designed to injure or kill individuals, but they cannot control the fires that are set or the lack of precautionary measures that could be employed to suppress the actions of outsiders.

Agricultural terrorism

Agricultural terrorism, or agroterrorism, is a relatively new form of terrorism that has many potential deadly scenarios. This form of terrorism has the potential to have a far greater impact on the multibillion dollar economic and international trade of a country due to contamination and disruption of the export of goods than the bombing of a single building. Opportunities to target designated sites are plentiful. There are approximately 1,912,000 farms and 87,000 food processing plants in the United States alone.[11] Most locations, e.g., farms, would be considered soft targets, and a terrorist act may go undetected for days or even weeks. Potential targets for agroterrorists include food handlers, processing facilities, grocery stores, restaurants, farms and ranches, livestock, crops, and food or agriculture transportation systems. This form of terrorism also includes the introduction of diseases to livestock.

Narco terrorism

Narco, or narcotic-related, terrorist activities are performed to further the aims of drug traffickers. These aims include financial gain, avoiding detection and apprehension, and establishing control over territories. This form of terrorism has been the focus of law enforcement and militaries from a wide array of countries for many years. Narco terrorist activities are often directed toward judges, prosecutors, politicians, and law enforcement officials in the form of assassinations, extortions, hijackings, bombings, and kidnappings.

Biological terrorism

Biological or chemical terrorism has received the majority of media attention in recent years largely due to its association with weapons of mass destruction. Just the thought of anthrax, smallpox, or some form of plague being spread can have crippling psychological implications. Biological agents gather a lot of media and Internet attention. Nearly 350,000 record results were returned in a recent Internet query with just one search engine. In reality, bioterrorism opportunities are perhaps the least likely scenarios to be encountered by law enforcement. However, due to the catastrophic potential of biological or chemical terrorism, law enforcement needs to become familiar with and prepared for the many different types of hazards that exist and the methods by which toxins can be ingested.

Cyberterrorism

Cyberterrorism, which will be detailed in a subsequent section, provides terrorists with the ability to operate in distant locations and to gain access to identities and financial records anywhere in the world. Terrorists operating in cyberspace are capable of accessing many secure data banks and stealing or altering information or destroying valuable data. Access to law enforcement, government, or military data files can aid a potential terrorist in avoiding detection. Cyber attacks may be geared toward disruption or denial of service, or financial gain. Financial gain is sometimes associated with identity theft or reallocation of funds from accounts, both of which are considered white-collar crimes and do not receive much attention from law enforcement agencies or the general public. Cyber terrorist acts, although void of mass physical casualties, have the potential to inflict mass hysteria and economic fallout that can be detrimental to global economy.

History and roots of modern terrorism

With a working definition of terrorism and terrorist activity in hand, it is important to know some of the historical content from which terrorism evolved. This will provide some insight into the growth of the term terrorism as well as how terrorism has become a modern-day obsession.

The Latin meaning of terrorism was explained above. However, the French are often credited with coining the term terrorism. The term terrorism grew out of the French Revolutionary period in the late 1700s known as the "Reign of Terror," and it has its roots in the Enlightenment Period of the eighteenth century. The Reign of Terror was the name for the bloody violence imposed upon the French citizens by their revolutionary leader, Maximilien Robespierre.

By the mid 1800s, the term changed to describe violent revolutionaries who revolted against governments. In the early 1900s in the United States, the term was used to describe labor organizations and anarchists. The anarchists garnered perhaps the most attention from law enforcement. Labor organizations were fighting for the working class and sought improvement in the work environment, employee rights, and financial equality. Although some labor organizations disrupted the flow of society, they generally did not create mass hysteria or death. Anarchists, on the other hand, did what they could to disrupt society by whatever means possible in order to achieve their end, regardless of who got in their way. Many of these anarchists eventually were rounded up and deported.

After World War II, the term changed again to be associated with nationalistic groups revolting against European domination. During the turbulent 1940s and 1950s, known as the postcolonial era, Europeans felt the repercussions of terrorism by nationalists seeking to end colonial rule. The two hardest hit countries were France and England — both had colonial settlements on various continents. Two of the major problem areas of the time were in Algeria and Kenya. The French suffered greatly from terrorist attacks in Africa against colonialism in Algeria by the National Liberation Front (FLN). English colonies in Kenya were targeted by the Mau Mau. Also during the 1940s, the State of Israel was being formed in the Middle East. When the British replaced the Ottomans as the governing colonial force over the Palestinians and Jews in Palestine in what became known as the Balfour Declaration of 1917, they promised the Jews a home in Palestine. Over time, this grew into a conflict that saw the Jews trying to remove the British. They turned to urban terrorism and established the Irgun Zvai Leumi, commonly referred to as the Irgun, as an underground terrorist organization to conduct actions against the British. These terrorist actions continued until about 1948, when Israel was recognized as a nation. Becoming a nation did not end the problem in the Middle East for Israel. Various groups, particularly the Palestinian Liberation Organization (PLO), continue to struggle against non-Arabs in the region.

As the Middle East conflict continued, much of the world saw a rise from the left. From the mid-1960s to the early 1980s, the term terrorism was associated with activities of left-wing groups worldwide, many of which were opposed to conflicts such as the Vietnam War. Much of the activity experienced in the United States during this period was viewed as the work of left-wing groups, also referred to as "radicals," "revolutionaries," or "extremists," such as the Symbionese Liberation Army. As left-wing groups diminished, the rise of religious extremists came into being with the Iranian Revolution in 1979 and the transformation of Iran into an Islamic republic. Shortly after the transformation, the Ayatollah Khomeini declared a holy war against Westerners. Iran is also said to have had an important role in the establishment of two current terrorist organizations, Hizbollah and Islamic Jihad. Today, terrorism is associated with large groups, such as Hizbollah, capable of working independently from a state, with members considered to be violent religious fanatics or extremists.

Terrorism was also characterized by changes in the ways intellectuals approached social problems and class-based revolutions or revolts, such as the Russian Revolution. One thing is certain: the meaning and style of terrorism has changed with society over time. Regardless of who defines terrorism, this fact is agreed upon consistently. Other driving forces that changed the meaning of terrorism over time are the media, communication capabilities, advancement in sophisticated weapons, and various socio-economic factors.

The evolution of domestic terrorism

Domestic terrorism is not a new phenomenon, and it did not suddenly appear on the shores of the United States on September 11, 2001. It has been around for over two centuries. The meaning of terrorism has changed with time. The differences in definitions of terrorism and in social viewpoints have led to many incidents of domestic terrorism being categorized as actions by extremists, anarchists, radicals, and revolutionaries, and even unions. Depending on the time and era, incidents we would now consider terrorism were seen as antigovernment or antisocial behaviors or were perceived as improving a way of life for a fledgling nation.

One of the first incidents of antifederal behavior in the United States occurred in 1791, when the federal government levied an excise tax on the production of whiskey. It has been said that this led to many revolutionary acts and might be construed as the first terrorist threat faced by the country. However, the actions taken against the King of England during this era were seen as revolutionary, not terroristic. Revolutionary, martyr, leader, and terrorist are all subjective labels.

Throughout the history of the United States there have been numerous incidents of antigovernment behavior that by today's standards would be considered terrorism. Prior to the Civil War in the early 1800s, an anarchist group known as the "Know Nothings" operated in the east. They were a secret society with an anti-immigrant agenda, committed to a white Protestant ruling class. No matter how many anarchist incidents they initiated, the membership would regularly claim that they were not involved, thus avoiding apprehension by law enforcement. Deborah Able reported that the "nativist" movement associated with the Know Nothings became the basis for a conservative political party known as the American Party.[12] This is the same party under whose auspices Millard Fillmore ran for president in 1856.

Violent ideological extremism also dominated many issues in the 1800s, up to and during the Civil War. Much of the war activity was geared toward southern states seeking to keep their rights. Most southerners were not fighting to preserve slavery, but rather to keep the power of local governments. Upon the conclusion of the Civil War, Revolutionary terrorism and Repressionist terrorism made appearances as labor movements and grew in the post-Civil War era. Primarily during the 1870s and 1880s, rural movements were complemented by labor violence, and anarchism from the left began to emerge. In the early 1900s, anarchists wrought havoc in the United States with one incident that led to the assassination of a president. The response at the time was to round up the anarchists and deport them, usually back to Europe. The assassination of President William McKinley in 1901 by anarchist Leon Czolgosz is just one example of the long history of political violence in the United States, but until recently it was not interpreted as terrorism.

In the era immediately preceding World War II, nationalistic movements were viewed as terrorist groups as they revolted from European authority. Throughout the decades, particularly in the 1960s, the character of American terrorism began to change. It became known as a radical phenomenon, even though the antigovernment behavior went beyond mere picketing and demonstrations. Left-wing terrorism began to sunset after the Vietnam War, and modern right-wing extremism began to emerge and came to fruition around 1984 with the violent activity of the Hate Movement. Upon arrival of the new millennium, terrorism became associated with large groups possessing strong beliefs based on religion and violent fanaticism based on a particular cause such as the environment.

Although this section only begins to scratch the surface of terrorism in the United States, domestic terrorism has been present for decades in many forms. Even though there were numerous changes over the years, the structure and makeup of domestic terrorist groups and classifications of domestic terrorists have remained relatively consistent for the past 25 years. Based on this consistency, the FBI ultimately developed a broad listing for

Table 2.1 Profiling Terrorists

Characteristic	Right Wing	Left Wing
Social change perspective	Reactionary	Revolutionary
Social class membership	Lower/middle	Lower/middle/upper
Leadership	Male dominated	Egalitarian
Marital status	Married	Single/divorced/separated
Age	16–76	25–45
Educational level	High school	College
Religious belief	Fundamental	Agnostic/atheist
Criminal planning	Impulsive	Meticulous

Source: T. O'Connor, North Carolina Wesleyan College (http://faculty.ncwc.edu/to-connor/392/spy/terrorism.htm, Nov. 2002). With permission.

the types of terrorist groups or terrorists found in the United States The three types of domestic terrorists according to the FBI are as follows:

Left-wing
Right-wing
Special interest (e.g., abortion clinic bombings)

Table 2.1 demonstrates the characteristic and demographical differences between left-wing and right-wing members.[13] Special interest terrorists are often seen as lone wolves or members of a leaderless resistance with views that are extreme and skewed and may be originally based on either the left or right wing. They randomly select their targets based on the presumption that they are associated with a segment of the population that opposes their point of view.

Domestic right-wing terrorist groups often adhere to the principles of racial supremacy and embrace antigovernment and antiregulatory beliefs. They generally engage in activity that is protected by constitutional guarantees of free speech and assembly. Many of these groups attempted to tame their rhetoric in order to appeal to a broader segment of the population. Left-wing groups, on the other hand, generally profess a revolutionary socialist doctrine and view themselves as protectors against capitalism. Special interest groups in the 1980s through the 1990s were often associated with abortion clinic attacks. Today, these groups are seen as anarchists and extremist socialist groups seeking to resolve specific issues rather than effect widespread political change. Groups and individuals often emerge from the extreme fringes of the animal rights, pro-life, and environmental movements. Although much of the terrorist activity seen in the United States could be categorized into the above categories, terrorist activity is too broad to be limited to just three types.

In 1987, the FBI expanded upon these three types of terrorism. In the *FBI Law Enforcement Bulletin*,[14] John Harris named five categories of domestic terrorist groups, which are summarized below. These groups, which were recognized by the FBI in 1987, are still applicable today:

Left-wing (white leftists)
Right-wing extremists
Puerto Rican leftists
Black militants
Jewish extremists

When reviewing the list of current domestic terrorist groups, one can readily associate the group to a category. But just as with the FBI's types of domestic terrorists, it can be suggested that a sixth group category could be that of "special interest."

In the United States, there are as many as 400 groups with anywhere from 10,000 to 100,000 members in right-wing groups that can be classified as domestic terrorist groups. In a speech before the Senate Select Committee on Intelligence on February 6, 2002, Dale L. Watson, executive assistant director of counterterrorism and counterintelligence for the FBI, reported that in the preceding decade right-wing extremism overtook left-wing terrorism as the most dangerous domestic terrorist threat to the United States. He went on to note that two special interest extremist groups, the Animal Liberation Front (ALF) and the ELF committed approximately 600 criminal acts in the United States since 1996 resulting in damages in excess of $42 million.[15] Interestingly, in this statement to the Senate these two extremists groups were viewed as domestic terrorist threats, but their actions were described as criminal. This can be attributed to the lack of coordinated and direct information available on domestic groups.

According to MILNET, the open-source military information database, no U.S. government agency maintains a formal list of domestic terrorist groups. However, there are two private nonprofit organizations that monitor groups in the United States under the designation of organized hate groups, the Anti-Defamation League (ADL) and the Southern Poverty Law Center (SPLC). The SPLC documented 676 active hate groups in the United States in its 2001 Intelligence Report.[16] In 2002 this number increased nearly 5 percent to 708 organized hate groups.[17] This is a dramatic rise from the 240 reported in 1996. The actual active membership numbers for hate groups are tough to ascertain because conservative estimates reflect 25,000 members, but there are possibly as many as 150,000 "armchair racists" who espouse the beliefs without necessarily taking any action.[18] The fact that there is no officially designated government agency that maintains a formal list is significant. Should some intelligence be developed regarding a domestic terrorist group, it may be hard to qualify and quantify the information within official government ranks.

In recent years, much has been written about international terrorist groups but little is available on known domestic terrorist groups. Domestic terrorist groups may be dismissed as a conglomeration of radicals, whiners, extremists, fanatics, and hate groups. No matter what the reference, they are dangerous. In a statement for the record before the U.S. Senate on May 10, 2001, then director of the FBI Louis J. Freeh remarked that domestic terrorist groups represent interests that span the full spectrum of political and economic viewpoints as well as social issues. He stated that FBI investigations into groups are based upon information regarding planned or actual criminal activity, not on information regarding beliefs.[24] This may be why little is officially documented concerning domestic terrorist and hate groups. Based on Freeh's remarks, it is probable that local and state law enforcement agencies are more cognizant of groups that would fall into the category of domestic terrorists, especially organized hate groups, because they may have operated in or near their jurisdictions.

A sampling of known domestic terrorist groups, many of which are also viewed as organized hate groups, is outlined below and explained in further detail in Appendix A.

Known domestic terrorist groups[19]

American Coalition of Life Activists
Animal Liberation Front
Army of God
Aryan Nation (aka Aryan Republican Army)
Branch Davidians
Christian Identity Movement
Colorado First Light Infantry
Colorado Militia
Citizens of the Republic of Idaho
Covenant (aka Sword and Arm of the Lord)
Earth Liberation Front (ELF)
Freeman
Ku Klux Klan
Michigan Militia
Militia of Montana
Mountaineer Militia
National Alliance
North American Militia of Southwestern Michigan
Patriot's Council
Phineas Priesthood
Posse Comitatus
Reclaim the Seeds
Republic of Texas
Southern California Minuteman
The Order (aka The New Order)
Unnamed California and Texas Militias
Viper Militia
World Church of the Creator (also known as the Creativity Movement)

The sheer number of potential groups or movements in the United States is alarming, and unconfirmed. A concern for law enforcement is that any one of the domestic-based groups can be seen as a potential place to recruit an extremist. An Internet search on general topics such as militias will garner over 200,000 results with the use of just one search engine. There are militia groups scattered throughout America, and their numbers are growing. Bruce Hoffman, citing works from the mid-1990s, stated that there are "an estimated 800 other similarly oriented militias — with a total membership claimed to be over 5 million, though more realistically put at no more than 50,000."[20] According to the SPLC's 2004 Intelligence Report, there were 152 identified active "patriot" groups (see Appendix B in this book) with cells in many states, compared to 171 in 2003. In 2004 SPLC showed that 45 were classified as "militias."[21] These numbers decreased in 2002, with "patriot" groups dropping to 143 and "militias" to 54.[17] Barbara Perry, in her book *In The Name of Hate: Understanding Hate Crimes*, cited the militia movement as being fueled by religious fanaticism and willingness to kill, and referred to it as a "full-scale terrorist underground."[18] Despite not having a definitive number to work with, law enforcement personnel need to exercise caution when monitoring information on these groups. It does not take a group to commit an act of terrorism; one person can also do a lot of damage. You only have to look at a homicide bomber to be convinced of this. Just as important, not every group or its members has terrorist ties or expounds violence, but they are at best unstable and pose fertile ground for the growth of domestic terrorism.

Domestic terrorism

With the ambiguity in defining terrorism, how can we possibly define domestic terrorism? In many parts of Europe there is no differentiation between domestic and foreign terrorism. There are factions of U.S.-based domestic groups that have overseas bases of support and operation. One of the few working definitions of domestic terrorism comes from the MILNET Web site, a research tool used by researchers, historians, and academics:

> Domestic Terrorism is the actions by persons seeking to persuade or dissuade the government or people of their home country using violent means that intend to frighten or coerce, ranging from threats to outright acts of violence such as kidnapping, beatings, or murder.[22]

This definition clearly fits many groups, from as early as the 1960s through today, and would surely fit everything from abortion clinic bombings to the Oklahoma City bombing.

However, much attention has been and continues to be focused on international terrorism and groups that are based overseas. Although the federal government has the means and authority to investigate and follow up on terrorist-related activity overseas, local law enforcement agencies do not, and they may fail to see the correlation between domestic or local events in the big picture of terrorism. The media focus on terrorist subjects from other countries as being the bad guys at the root of the entire epidemic known as terrorism. This may make a more attractive news angle to follow, and our citizens may find it easier to deal with than reading that one of their own could side with the enemy. After all, terrorists cannot look like mainstream law-abiding citizens, right? The truth is that domestic-related terrorism has taken place for many years and by those who would fit the mainstream citizen category. However, it is often classified as a routine crime somewhere in the criminal justice system.

It was not until the passage of the Uniting and Strengthening America by Providing Appropriate Tools Required to Intercept and Obstruct Terrorism (USA PATRIOT) Act in October 2001 that many American citizens came to understand a working definition of domestic terrorism. Although the text is laden with many enhancements designed to increase the effectiveness of law enforcement in the war on terrorism, domestic terrorism is not directly addressed until about three-quarters of the way into the document. For the purposes of this book, the following definition of domestic terrorism from the USA PATRIOT Act is suggested for use by law enforcement:

(A) Involves acts dangerous to human life that are a violation of the criminal laws of the United States or of any State
(B) appear to be intended
    (i) to intimidate or coerce a civilian population;
    (ii) to influence the policy of a government by intimidation or coercion; or
    (iii) to affect the conduct of a government by mass destruction, assassination, or kidnapping; and
(C) occur primarily within the territorial jurisdiction of the United States.[23]

This second definition is specific to the United States and its citizens, whereas the MILNET definition is more broadly based and can be adopted by almost any country.

A third definition to consider is that presented by Louis J. Freeh:[24]

> The unlawful use, or threatened use, of violence by a group or individual that is based and operating entirely within the United States or its territories without foreign direction and which is committed against persons or property with the intent of intimidating or coercing a government or its population in furtherance of political or social objectives.

Defining domestic terrorism and what constitutes domestic terrorism is increasingly becoming more complicated to achieve. Therefore, it is suggested that the definition overwhelmingly adopted in the USA PATRIOT Act be established as the standard used by law enforcement throughout the country.

The complex nature of terrorism and the transnational capabilities of virtually every person in the world are increasingly eroding traditional boundaries. Many so-called international terrorist organizations have sprouted roots in many countries, including the United States, and have tried to fall into the mainstream to avoid detection, reap financial gains, or exploit laws designed for law-abiding citizens. Elaine Landau pointed out that there are not many differences between domestic terrorists and the highly publicized terrorist bands operating in other parts of the world.[25] This also muddies the waters when trying to define domestic terrorism, but caution should be used, and the best way to monitor such groups is through categorizing and monitoring with link analysis in order to develop associations.

As noted earlier, domestic terrorism in the United States by American citizens has been prevalent for several years but has often been classified somewhere else in the criminal justice system. Walter Laqueur advised that statistics concerning terrorism focus on international terrorism. He said that terrorism statistics over the years are dependent on who is collecting the figures and what criteria are being used, but noted that "This is not to argue that statistics on terrorism are altogether useless."[26] Terrorism statistics are no different than many law enforcement statistics, which are at times subjective and completely dependent upon the reporting or collection criteria. What is important about statistics is that they are cited and compared with like variables. Outlined below are some statistics and examples of domestic terrorism, according to the Council on Foreign Relations, that show how prevalent it has been in the United States before September 11, 2001:[27]

> Between 1980 and 2000, Americans accounted for about three-quarters of the 335 terrorist acts committed in the United States.
> Weapons of mass destruction were used. In 1984, followers of the Bagwan Shree Rajneessh cult sprayed salad bars in Oregon with salmonella, causing 751 people to become ill in an attempt to change the outcome of a local election.
> In April 1995, the Oklahoma City bombing took place.
> In July 1996, the Atlanta Centennial Park bombing took place.
> In the summer of 1999, shooting sprees targeting minorities in Chicago and Los Angeles took place.

In December 2002, former FBI associate deputy director Buck Revell pointed out several factors that are changing and increasing the domestic terrorist threat. One point of particular interest is that "antigovernment reactionary extremists have proliferated and now pose a significant threat to the federal government and to law enforcement at all levels."[28] This point is well taken, but today's reactionary extremists were the turn-of-the-century's anarchists. People classified as anarchists were seen as opposing all forms of organized authority, including government, and they advocated the use of violence in order to improve a class of society, usually the working or lower class. Revell also noted that had it not been for modern-day nongovernment agencies such as the SPLC and the ADL, the federal government would have been totally clueless about right-wing extremists. It is these extremist or organized hate groups that can provide a conduit to international terrorist organizations seeking to expand their terror campaign into a country such as the United States.

Americans do not have immunity to the lure of violent ideologies or hatred. At the beginning of the new millennium, there were several U.S. citizens allegedly associated with known terrorist organizations such as al-Qaeda. Two of the more prevalent were the individuals who came to be known as "the American Taliban" and "the Dirty Bomber." The connection for each of these individuals was said to be religion. The Dirty Bomber reportedly converted or was exposed to an extreme version of Islam while incarcerated in a Florida prison. This does not mean that every disenchanted prisoner will join an international terrorist group, but prisoners' hatred often runs deep and represents a valuable recruitment source of potential candidates to join organized hate groups and antigovernment movements.

Organized hate groups and crimes

As alluded to in the evolution of domestic terrorism, organized groups such as gangs and crime families have a long-standing presence in the United States. The roots of modern hate have been around for centuries. From the early settlers of the United States to one of the first organized hate groups, the Ku Klux Klan, which has been around for over 135 years, hate has festered and been a contributing factor to many illegal actions. However, the presence of these groups has been seen as a crime threat, not a terrorist threat, but times have changed. In a speech before the U.S. Senate, Louis J. Freeh reported that on a national level, formal right-wing hate groups such as World Church of the Creator and the Aryan Nations represent a continuing terrorist threat. These two groups have formal followings throughout the country and probably have even more informal followers. Small splinter factions, such as the South Florida Aryan Alliance, spawned from the larger groups described above. These groups have continuously become more vocal and blatantly display their cache of weapons in photographs or public domains. Concern over hate crimes and actions of hate groups such as these prompted the FBI to initiate data collection on hate or bias with the Hate Crimes Statistics Act of 1990 through the Uniform Crime Reporting system.

In 2001, the FBI reported that there were nearly 10,000 reported incidents of hate within the United States. According to some private nonprofit associations that monitor hate crimes, this number may actually be as high as 50,000 per year. The discrepancy in numbers can largely be attributed to reporting practices and lack of training or awareness on the behalf of law enforcement. Measures are in place to remedy this discrepancy but only time will tell if the issue has been addressed. However, hate crime statistics for 2004 chronicle even fewer (7,649) criminal incidents that law enforcement agencies reported as motivated by a bias against a race, religion, disability, ethnicity, or sexual orientation and include information on 9,035 offenses, 9,528 victims, and 7,145 known offenders. Many reported hate crime incidents are focused on gender, race, and ethnicity, and they are reported as being committed by an individual rather than a group and are subjected to law enforcement being diligent in reporting. It should be noted that when we speak of gathering and analyzing information, analysts should remain cognizant of the detailed information found in hate crime reports and consider it for use in their analysis. The aforementioned is contrary to the way terrorism-related actions are reported. In these instances, you hear more about the group than the individual who committed the act.

During her tenure as attorney general of the United States, Janet Reno identified a need and requested that the FBI work in concert with state and local law enforcement agencies to develop a model hate crime training curriculum. This was in response to her deep concern about the problem of hate crime in the United States and perhaps to address the alleged differences in data. The result was four new training curricula for patrol officers, detectives, policy-level officers, and a mixed audience of all three levels. Interestingly, analytical personnel were not included. Regardless of this criticism, many personnel were trained on a variety of topics, including group characteristics that should be shared with analysts tasked with analyzing hate groups. Outlined below are some known characteristics of organized hate groups:

Group structure is loose on a local level and highly structured internationally.
A substantial number of members are white males under the age of 30.
Leaders tend to project a mainstream image.
Many are technologically savvy and use such venues as cable television and computers to promote their rhetoric.
Group members are often loosely affiliated and take inspiration and direction (e.g., Skinheads).
Groups focus on issues of concern to Middle America as a way of cloaking and marketing hate.
Members of these groups believe in an inevitable global war between races.

Another matter that needed to be addressed was a definition for hate crime. Much like defining terrorism, defining hate crime led to numerous working definitions. Some of the more prominent definitions come from the Hate Crimes Statistics Act of 1990, Bureau of Justice Administration in 1997, the ADL, and the National Education Association. For purposes of law enforcement, the FBI definition is widely used as a standard:[29]

A criminal offense committed against a person, property or society which is motivated, in whole or in part, by the offender's bias against a race, religion, disability, sexual orientation, or ethnicity/national origin.

Louis Freeh, in his statement before the Senate, also noted that anarchists and extreme socialist groups have an international presence and pose a potential threat to the United States. This is important to note, because foreign-based terrorist organizations that wish to attack on American soil must first gain access to the United States. As demonstrated with some disenfranchised American citizens such as those who joined the Taliban and al-Qaeda in Afghanistan, foreign-based groups recruited Americans and thereby reached American soil. Monitoring hate groups and their members, publicly and in prison, is vital. These groups represent potential recruitment grounds for well-financed foreign-based terrorist organizations that have hatred toward the United States and who can build upon this cause in an effort to solicit members of domestic-based groups to perform acts of terrorism. Law enforcement should also remain cognizant of members and leaders from groups conducting business behind bars either through visitors or communications. This has happened for years; just look at some of the larger-than-life organized crime figures. The hatred of domestic-based groups did not evolve overnight. It has been around for decades and without a doubt poses a great risk to homeland security and there are many potential recruiting grounds.

American organized hate groups are not only proprietary to the United States. Several groups have established chapters overseas and recruited members in many European countries, including England, Germany, and Austria. This is similar to the actions of terrorist organizations that are extending their reach to the United States. The roles these various groups play in the terrorism theater are expanding domestically and internationally.

Role of organized hate groups in domestic terrorism

Terrorism of any magnitude has an underlying tone of hate. All organized hate groups have beliefs or practices that attack or malign an entire class of people, and such is the case with terrorist groups like al-Qaeda, whose members overwhelmingly hate Americans and Jews.

Numbers concerning known militias and patriot groups are staggering. With potentially hundreds of home-grown organized groups active in the United States, law enforcement agencies should strive to categorize groups along the following suggested domestic ideological parameters, in addition to the FBI's domestic types, rather than treat them as individual organizations:

White supremacy
Hate groups
Neomilitia or Patriot movements
Sovereign Citizen movements
Militias
Tax protestors
Foreign or state-sponsored groups

Use of the suggested parameters will aid analytical and investigative personnel in narrowing criteria when tracking and monitoring activity as well as members. There are other categories available, but for analytical purposes most groups will fit into the above list. Categorizing domestic groups along these lines will also aid in identifying splinter groups, membership transfers, or groups that may associate with one another based on a common belief or hatred. Law enforcement is accustomed to using labels for such groups as career criminals. The difference is that most career criminal labels have structured guidelines and are usually progressive, so there is no need to change the category. When categorizing organized hate groups, law enforcement needs to be aware that members may change groups or associate with multiple groups. Therefore as new information concerning changes becomes known, it is important that a mechanism exist to facilitate the change in order to keep intelligence accurate.

Figure 2.1 depicts a hate map. Symbols are used to identify groups following the SPLC categories. The information demonstrates how virtually every area of the United States has been touched by organized hate groups. Categories used by the SPLC differ slightly from those just outlined. The SPLC's categories are valid but broad-based, and they may be too limiting for future analytical consideration. However, they should not be discounted. The SPLC uses the following organized hate group categories and definitions:[30]

1. *Ku Klux Klan* — The Ku Klux Klan, with its mystique and its long history of violence, is the oldest and most infamous of American hate groups. Although blacks have typically been the Klan's primary target, it also has attacked Jews, immigrants, homosexuals, and recently Catholics. Since December 1865 when it was formed, the Klan has typically seen itself as a Christian organization. However, in modern times Klan groups are motivated by a variety of theological and political ideologies.

    Started during the Reconstruction at the end of the Civil War, the Klan quickly mobilized as a vigilante group to intimidate Southern blacks (and any whites who would help them) and to prevent blacks from enjoying basic civil rights. Outlandish titles (like Imperial Wizard and Exalted Cyclops), hooded costumes, violent night rides, and the notion that the group comprised an invisible empire conferred a mystique that only added to the Klan's popularity. Lynching, tar-and-featherings, rape, and other violent attacks on those challenging white supremacy became hallmarks of the Klan.

    After a short but violent period, the "first era" Klan disbanded after Jim Crow laws secured the domination of Southern whites. However, the Klan enjoyed a huge revival in the 1920s when it opposed (mainly Catholic and Jewish) immigration. By 1925, when its followers staged a huge Washington, D.C., march, the Klan had as many as five million members and considerable political power in some states. A series of sex scandals, internal battles over power, and newspaper exposés quickly reduced its influence.

Figure 2.1 Hate map. (Courtesy of the Southern Poverty Law Center, Intelligence Report, 2003. With permission.)

The Klan arose a third time during the 1960s to oppose the civil rights movement and to preserve segregation in the face of unfavorable court rulings. The Klan's bombings, murders, and other attacks took a great many lives, including four young girls killed while preparing for services at the 16th Street Baptist Church in Birmingham, Alabama.

Since the 1970s, the Klan has been greatly weakened by internal conflicts, court cases, and a seemingly endless series of splits and government infiltration. While some factions preserved an openly racist and militant approach, others tried to enter the mainstream, cloaking their racism as "civil rights for whites." Today, the SPLC estimates that there are a total of 5,500 to 6,000 Klan members split among scores of different and often warring organizations that use the Klan name. The total number of groups counted in 2002 was 133 compared to 109 in 2001, a 22 percent increase.

2. *Neo-Nazi* — Neo-Nazi groups share a hatred for Jews and a love for Adolf Hitler and Nazi Germany. While they also hate other minorities, homosexuals, and sometimes Christians, they perceive "the Jew" as their cardinal enemy and trace social problems to a Jewish conspiracy that supposedly controls governments, financial institutions, and the media. While some neo-Nazi groups emphasize simple hatred, others are more focused on the revolutionary creation of a fascist political state. Nazism, of course, has roots in Europe, and links between American and European neo-Nazis are strong and growing stronger. American neo-Nazi groups, protected by the First Amendment, often publish material and host Internet sites that are aimed at European audiences. These materials would be illegal under European antiracism laws. For this reason, many European groups have their Internet sites on American servers to avoid prosecution under the laws of their native countries. The most important neo-Nazi group in the United States is the National Alliance, founded by William Pierce, the infamous author of the futuristic race-war novel *The Turner Diaries*, a book believed by some to have served as the blueprint for the 1995 Oklahoma City bombing. The total number of groups counted in 2002 was 220 compared to 209 in 2001.

3. *Racist Skinhead* — Racist Skinheads form a particularly violent element of the white supremacist movement and have often been referred to as the "shock troops" of the hoped-for revolution. The classic Skinhead look is a shaved head, black Doc Martens boots, jeans with suspenders, and an array of typically racist tattoos.

The Skinhead phenomenon began in the industrial cities of 1960s Britain as a working-class movement strongly marked by contempt for hippies and middle-class youth. Though drugs and violence were always part of the Skinhead scene, Skinheads originally embraced Afro-Caribbean music and were of different races. British fascists were able to precipitate a split in the movement between racist and antiracist elements — a split that has endured to the present day in Britain and in the United States, where "Skins" arrived in the early 1980s. Racist Skins are referred to by their enemies as "boneheads." Antiracist Skins are often referred to as SHARPS, a reference to a now essentially defunct group known as Skinheads Against Racial Prejudice.

Racist Skinheads in the United States, like those in other countries, often operate in small crews that move from city to city with some regularity. The largest and most dangerous Skinhead group today is Hammerskin Nation, with thousands of members and extremely violent track records in North America and Europe. The total number of groups counted in 2001 was 43, and in 2002 this number reduced to 18.

4. *Christian Identity* — The Christian Identity religion asserts that whites, not Jews, are the true Israelites favored by God in the Bible. In most of its forms, Identity theology depicts Jews as biologically descended from Satan, while non-whites are seen as soulless "mud people" created with the other biblical "beasts of the field." Christian Identity has its roots in a 19th-century English fad called British Israelism, which asserted that European whites were descended from the ten "lost tribes" of Israel and were thus related to Jews, who were descended from the other two Hebrew tribes mentioned in the Bible. However, British Israelism, which was initially friendly to Jews, was adopted and transformed in the 20th century into a rabidly anti-Semitic creed by a number of racist preachers in the United States.

For decades, Identity has been one of the most important ideologies for the white supremacist movement. In its hardest-line form, it asserts that Christ will not return to earth until the globe is swept clean of Jews and other Satanic influences. In recent years deep doctrinal disputes, the lack of a central church structure, and a shift among white supremacists toward agnosticism and racist variations of neo-Paganism weakened the Identity movement and reduced its number of adherents. The total number of groups counted in 2001 was 31 and in 2002 was 27.

5. *Neo-Confederate* — Many groups celebrate traditional Southern culture and the Civil War's dramatic conflict between the Union and the Confederacy, but some groups go further and embrace racist attitudes toward blacks and, in some cases, white separatism. Such groups are listed in this category.

The League of the South, founded in 1994 and counting some 9,000 members by 2001, is at the center of the racist neo-Confederate movement. Calling once again for Southern secession, the League's leaders say minorities are destroying the Anglo-Celtic (white) culture of the South. They oppose most non-white immigration and all interracial marriages. Founder Michael Hill, a former college professor, called blacks "a deadly and compliant underclass" and embraced well-known white supremacists such as North Carolina attorney Kirk Lyons. The total number of groups counted in 2001 was 124 and in 2002 was 91.

6. *Black Separatist* — Black separatists typically oppose integration and racial intermarriage, and they want separate institutions — or even a separate nation — for blacks. Most forms of black separatism are strongly anti-white and anti-Semitic, and a number of religious versions assert that blacks, not Jews, are the biblical "chosen people" of God.

     Although the SPLC recognizes that much black racism in America is at least in part a response to centuries of white racism, its members believe that racism must be exposed in all its forms. White groups espousing beliefs similar to Black Separatists would be considered clearly racist. The same criterion should be applied to all groups, regardless of their members' color. The total number of groups counted in 2001 was 51 and in 2002 the number reached 82, a 61 percent increase.

7. *Other* — Included in this category are hate groups with a hodgepodge of doctrines. Some, like the National Association for the Advancement of White People, are white supremacist groups masquerading as mainstream groups, with an interest in issues such as black crime, busing, and affirmative action. Others embrace racist forms of neo-Pagan religions such as Odinism, a pre-Christian theology that is largely focused on the virtues of the tribe or race.

     The Council of Conservative Citizens is a reincarnation of the White Citizens Councils that sprang up in the South in the 1950s and 1960s to oppose school desegregation. Like the League of the South, a neo-confederate group to which it has many links, the 15,000-member Council tried without success to mask its white supremacist ideology to further promote a right-wing political agenda. The total number of groups counted in 2001 was 109 and in 2002 this increased to 137.

Calculations and determinations that make up the SPLCs categories are based on group activities such as criminal acts, marches, rallies, speeches, meetings, and publications. Whether a group advocates or engages in violence or criminal activity is not applied. Therefore, use of the first seven domestic categories might be more applicable for matters of homeland security and terrorism analysis. However, for informational purposes and general relationship correlations, the SPLC categories would be of value pending further analysis.

As reflected in their maps, the SPLC also uses symbols to demonstrate the type of group being identified. Although these symbols are generic, few people have not seen these and know what they are intended to reflect. Although these symbols are used generically, they are hybrids of actual

Figure 2.2 South Florida Aryan Alliance banner.

symbols used by the various organized hate groups located within the United States (Appendix C). Symbols have played an important role in groups for decades and are used as badges of honor, often worn on clothing and uniforms, reflected on flags and banners (such as depicted in Figure 2.2), or painted on buildings. Some members go as far as tattooing the symbols on their bodies. Many symbols have been modified even further and adopted by street-level gang members and inmates incarcerated in correctional institutions. Symbols, however, are not proprietary to U.S.-based organized hate groups. They have also been used by numerous international-based terrorist groups, such as the Irish Republican Army (IRA), and they can be found prominently displayed on buildings in areas controlled by the related organizations.

The use of symbols and knowledge of their meanings will be discussed in Appendix C. Identification of symbols in large international groups, organized hate groups, or even street gangs, may provide information into associations, relationships, or terrorist activity signatures. It is also important for law enforcement personnel to remain cognizant of international or foreign-based terrorist organizations, such as those listed in Appendix D, that may have fostered relationships or support of domestic groups or are active in the United States. If a foreign-based terrorist organization is looking for a way to infiltrate the borders of a country, gaining access to an organized group of malcontents filled with extreme hatred opens new horizons for recruitment.

Now that we have an understanding of the types of terrorists and terrorist groups that exist, and where they exist, there is one last general challenge for law enforcement. What is a terrorist? After all, there is no stereotypical terrorist appearance, race, religion, or ethnicity.

What is a terrorist?

One person's terrorist is another person's freedom fighter. In some cases, a terrorist may be seen as a leader, martyr, or visionary. However, in the world of law enforcement this argument is not necessarily a concern. "Criminal" is not usually thought of as an option for how a terrorist is seen. According to Brent Smith, terrorists remain criminals but are motivated by ideology, religion, or political cause. If one were to look at just eight pictures — Osama bin Laden, Timothy McVeigh, Yasser Arafat, Mohammad Atta, Che Guevara, Menachem Begin, Yahweh Ben Yahweh, and William Pierce — there would be much debate as to who the terrorists are. The perception would depend greatly on the year and the definition of terrorist that is used. Two of the individuals, Timothy McVeigh and Yahweh Ben Yahweh, were not initially viewed as terrorists at the time of their alleged atrocities. These individuals were seen as radicals, extremists, and criminals. All one has to do is check their criminal records, and you will not find them labeled as terrorists, the way we label sexual predators or career criminals. They were charged with crimes and sentenced accordingly. On the other hand, bin Ladin, Arafat, Atta, Guevara, and Begin do not have criminal records, at least not in the United States. Menachem Begin, the former prime minister of Israel, is described in the media, published documents, and the Internet as being active in Jewish guerilla activity, fighting for Jewish independence, and a member of the Irgun. The Irgun was considered one of the more relentless groups of the 1940s. The Irgun can be classified as a terrorist group, yet Begin is not referred to as a terrorist. As for Arafat, Atta, and Guevara, their descriptors run the gamut. Arafat and Guevara are described as guerilla fighters, freedom fighters, revolutionaries, martyrs, and terrorists. William Pierce, also known as Andrew MacDonald, writer of the *Turner Diaries* (1978), the book that Timothy McVeigh was allegedly in possession of at the time of his arrest, was perhaps one of America's most notorious neo-Nazis. He was the leader of the West Virginia-based National Alliance. To some he was known only as a professor holding a Ph.D. in physics, which he once taught at Oregon State University — not your stereotypical vision of a terrorist. This listing of eight individuals is just a sample of the controversy that can be stirred on the topic of what a terrorist is.

When it comes to identifying a terrorist, one area that was alluded to is organized hate group leaders or members. This is not an indictment that all individuals associated with these groups are terrorists, but many of those in leadership ranks expound extremist beliefs in America similar to those of terrorist leaders in the Middle East. There are also some similarities between many hate group leaders and terrorists. Their educations, personas, and exposures to military tactics are similar to many known terrorists. A recent review of 20 individuals seen as leaders and associated with extremism in America, according to the ADL, showed that several were highly educated and had authored several publications and books. In addition, some sought to become mainstream by running for political office. The party ticket of choice was often the Populist Party. However, some ran under the traditional Republican and Democratic Parties. Two ran for the presidency. One was elected, and served as a state representative in the Louisiana legislature. One ran and won a primary in California, and one won a large percent of the first ballot when running for the Arkansas office of lieutenant governor. Several served in the armed forces. There is no definitive way to identify a terrorist, hate group member, or potential recruit. They come from all walks of life, social classes, and educational levels. Regardless of their diverse backgrounds or locales, there are approaches that can be employed by analysts or investigators that will aid in identifying who might be a terrorist.

In order to initiate any form of analytical or intelligence-based under-taking, law enforcement personnel need to have a starting point for gathering and cataloging individuals and their activities. One starting point would be beliefs. In 1988, essentially three types of terrorist beliefs were identified that apply to virtually any individual who can be construed as being a terrorist or belonging to a terrorist group:

> Nationalistic
> Ideological
> Theological

The U.S. military recognizes and describes nationalistic and theological in their general terrorism training courses, both of which are applicable for use in law enforcement. "Nationalist terrorists seek to form a separate state for their own national group, often by drawing attention to a fight for 'national liberation' that they think the world has ignored."[3] Many members of nationalist groups are not viewed as terrorists but rather are seen by the populous as freedom fighters. An example of a nationalist group would be the Irish Republican Army whose members began their struggle not as a Catholic vs. Protestant religious conflict but rather as a fight for independence and establishment of an Irish state. As for ideological terrorists, their actions are simply based on their beliefs. The differences between nationalist and ideological are usually found in their goals. Many ideological terrorists expressed frustration toward social structures and capitalism, and they seek a new order. The third type of belief group is theological or religious terrorists who believe they speak and work for their chosen deity. They "seek to use violence to further what they see as divinely commanded purposes, often targeting broad categories of foes in an attempt to bring about sweeping changes."[3]

Once a belief or point of view is established, analytical personnel need to avoid grouping these individuals in general terms based on membership in a left- or right-wing movement. Terrorists are multifaceted. They often approach their mission much like a business. They have beliefs, and businesses have mission statements. They have economic needs and seek funding, and a business is always looking at the financial bottom line. They develop geographic bases of support, and businesses often look for location, location, location. Terrorists develop tactics to take advantage of others, and businesses develop tactics to outdo the competition and convince the consumer to buy their product. Terrorists selectively choose their targets, and businesses look for the target audience. Another consideration is that they may even change affiliations or beliefs. With this said, how can analytical personnel in the field of law enforcement differentiate between a terrorist and a criminal?

Terrorist vs. street criminal

Jonathan White offers a comparison of terrorist vs. typical street criminal.[7] Although it may not be all-inclusive or fit every situation, the information provided will greatly aid analytical personnel when categorizing individuals.

This categorization is done much the same way as agencies decide what constitutes a gang member or career criminal. The difference is that we are now looking for the characteristics that might constitute a terrorist.

Differences between typical street criminals and terrorists[7]

Terrorist
Fighting for political objective
Motivated by ideology or religion
Group-focused
Consumed with purpose
Trained and motivated for the mission
On the attack

Typical street criminal
Crimes of opportunity
Uncommitted
Self-centered
No cause
Untrained
Escape-oriented

Members of the law enforcement community would probably readily agree about what constitutes a typical street criminal. It is the terrorist with whom those in the law enforcement community are unfamiliar and, except for a select few, have never encountered. Using the above list, law enforcement personnel will be able to inquire about these variables when determining whether to document someone as a terrorist. This information will also enhance opportunities of developing interrelationship links. Determining whether or not a suspect fits the category of terrorist requires investigators and analysts to ask the fundamentals — who, what, where, when, why, and how — when encountering individuals. Chances of developing a profile that will fit most terrorists are highly unlikely. Asking the proper questions is essential when encountering individuals in order to identify differences, but these differences will not always be apparent. Such was the case with the September 11, 2001, terrorists.

September 11, 2001 — subjects, criminals, or terrorists?

The 19 subjects from the September 11, 2001 attack on America were undoubtedly terrorists as opposed to criminals. However, in order to demonstrate the effectiveness of the above terrorist vs. criminal comparison, all one has to do is look at the activity that led up to the tragic events, and look at a profile of the September 11, 2001 terrorists. These terrorists did not commit any violations of state or federal statutes (other than traffic and immigration violations) that would have classified them as criminals in a traditional law enforcement sense. Following is a profile of the terrorists:

Ranged in age between their early 20s and mid 30s
Primarily originated from Middle Eastern countries, traveled and resided in several different countries
Were affiliated with an international group, al-Qaeda, known for its dislike of the American government
Were motivated by religious beliefs and extreme ideology
Usually had one spokesperson for the group
Mainly used bank branches located in highly populated Muslim areas
Usually came into banks as a group to open an account
Wanted to deal with one person at the bank
Nineteen hijackers opened over 20 domestic bank accounts at four different bank branches
Opened bank accounts with a few thousand dollars within 30 days of arriving in the United States, with three to four members present
Did not have Social Security Cards, and used nonpermanent addresses
Many lived within the same region, not all in one jurisdiction, and rented apartments
Primarily had wire transfers done from United Arab Emirates (UAE), Saudi Arabia, and Germany, and used identification from these countries
Made numerous balance inquiries
Made overall transactions that were below federal banking guideline reporting requirements
Purchased travelers checks overseas, brought them to the United States, and deposited a portion of them in accounts
Consumed with their mission and purpose, even willing to die for it
Trained at several aviation schools as well as known terrorist camps

Based on the limited information above, there would be little if any reason for law enforcement to be concerned, especially if they were only looking for evidence of a crime. They were not what traditional law enforcement personnel were trained to detect and monitor, which are street criminals. There were no red flags. Analytical and investigative personnel need to be cautious when reviewing and discounting any information. What appears to be legitimate activity by law-abiding individuals may turn out to be something more if looked at over time or with a certain perspective. Just as is noted in the profile of the 9/11 subjects, religion played a role. The perspective of religion is something new for law enforcement to consider. In many law enforcement circles there is little, if any, reference to religion when dealing with crime. There is also a reluctance to engage in any religious discussion. Understanding the religious perspective whether Islam or Judaism is just another aspect that law enforcement will need to consider.

Understanding the religious connection

Since September 11, 2001, many in the Western world have focused on one of the fastest growing religions with 1.3 billion adherents — Islam. However, it is important to note that the majority are peaceful people and do not condone the tragic events of 2001. Additionally, to follow this thought process will create a bias that will negatively impact any analysis. While it may be simple to blame the majority, law enforcement personnel must not forget that religion is used by many terrorists, both foreign and domestic. All you need to do is to refer to the number of domestic terrorist groups who adhere to the Christian Identity religion.

With much focus on Islam, this section will attempt to shed light on this religion and those who follow it, much like the 9/11 subjects. The Arab world is made up of approximately 22 countries and 300 million people of which about 3 million live in the United States, the vast majority, who are of Lebanese descent, living within the urban areas of Los Angeles, Chicago, Detroit, New York, and Washington, DC.

Islam is a monotheistic afterlife religion that follows Allah as the eternal all-powerful who sees all and knows all. God also has no physical description or gender connotation. There are several significant events in Islam, following an Islamic lunar calendar, many of which take place around the year 630. There are also many references to angels and at least 25 prophets noted by name in the Quran. Islam follows a system of rituals. They serve as a way to translate religious beliefs into reality. The main reference is to the Pillars of Islam or what is commonly referred to as the Five Pillars.

The Five Pillars, in order, are

1. Shahadah; the creed of Islam that declares allegiance to God
2. Salat or daily prayer; most important of all duties
3. Zakat or annual charity; addresses disparity (2.5 percent prescribed by Muhammad)
4. Saum or month-long fasting; ninth month of Islamic lunar calendar — Ramadhan
5. Hajj or pilgrimage; one journey to Mecca in their lifetime

Islamic extremism

The U.S. Army has studied Islamic religious extremism extensively and has declared it the most dangerous to U.S. interests. The focus of this section is on the word extremism. Islam is an Arabic word which means "submission" in the context of submitting to the word of God. It has its beginning in the early seventh century when it was founded by Mohammad ibn Abdulah. Mohammad was born in Mecca, Saudi Arabia in 570 A.D., and began his ministry in Mecca around 620 A.D. Mohammad spent much of his life in his ministry converting the then pagan population to Islam. As he converted the regional city-states, he left behind a religious institution and a religious form of civil government.

Religious extremist ideology in any religion can be dangerous. However, it is the Islamic religious extremist ideology that appears to be particularly dangerous to the West. Adherents to Shiism, for example the members of the Revolutionary Guard of Iran, have manifested themselves into the international terrorist organization known as Hezbollah. However, extremism is not limited to the Shiite component of Islam. Within the Sunni community, there are several organizations, e.g., Muslim Brotherhood and Hamas, which are a threat to western democracies. They seek to further the goal of a true Islamic state and promote the Islamic revolution and the formation of Islamic republics worldwide. At this level of extremism, there appears to be no or little strife between the Shiite and Sunni branches of Islam.

Hamas, the Palestinian branch of the Muslim Brotherhood, was born of the Intifada (uprising), which was a series of demonstrations, riots, and violence led by Palestinians against the rule of Israel. The Intifada began in 1987 in the Gaza strip and spread throughout the occupied territories. Hamas was founded on the principle of Islamic Nationalism and the elimination of the Israeli State. Hamas was loosely affiliated with the Palestinian Liberation Organization (PLO) and the Islamic Jihad, but became bitter enemies with the PLO when the PLO endorsed the concept of co-existence between the Palestinian state and Israel, with the eventual intent that there be a gradual phased creation of a Palestinian homeland. Hamas wanted an immediate and unrelenting frontal assault against Israel. In 1991 Hamas split from the PLO when the PLO refused their request for a Hamas presence at the Palestinian National Council.

Since the former leader of Iran and initiator of the Islamic Revolution, Ayatollah Khomeini, died in 1989 the political and religious leadership of Iran claims to have moderated its views on the West, worldwide Islamic revolution, and overt direct involvement in terrorist activities. This perception is skeptical and it remains to be seen. Regardless of the religious aspect that modern-day leaders such as Khomeini have played, it will continue to be the teachings and writings of Mohammed that will be interpreted by conservatives, moderates, and extremists.

Islamic sects

Upon Mohammed's death, there was controversy over the religious leadership, resulting in a division of Islam into the two commonly referenced sects, Sunni and Shiite. It should be noted that Muslims prefer simply to be referred to as Muslims. However, there are often two principal terms associated with Muslims: Sunni and Shiite. Additional references do exist such as Wahhabi but this will be explained further in Chapter 8. There do appear to be some differentiating traits or characteristics that can be derived. Outlined below are some of the behavior or belief traits.

Sunni

The term Sunni is used to denote those who practice Islam according to authentic traditional Islamic sources. There is unanimous agreement among them regarding its authenticity; the Quran is neither temporal nor newly created, but is eternal. Sunnis believe that believers will be blessed with the sight of Allah in the Hereafter, as is mentioned in the Quran. Since this religion has been completed, no one has the right to formulate new legislation or directives; however, one must refer to the qualified Muslim scholars who must work solely within the bounds established by Allah's Book and the sunnah of the Prophet.

Shiite

To some Shiites, the Quran's authenticity is doubtful and appears to contradict many of their sectarian beliefs or doctrines. The views and opinions of their Imams are the primary source of their jurisprudence. Shiites believe that to see Allah is not possible in this world or in the hereafter. The Shiites consider their Imams to be infallible, and to have the right to create new rulings and directives in contradiction to the revealed law.

Many terms need to be understood if one is to make an informed decision. Perhaps the most important thing to know is that extremists exist in every religion. Some of the terminology associated with Islam is highlighted in Appendix I.

Monetary restrictions are regulated in Islam. Muslims are forbidden from engaging in interest-based borrowing or lending. They are required to make written contracts for business dealings and to be honest in all financial exchanges.

It is apparent that financing placed an important role in the activities of the 9/11 terrorists. Much of the money they obtained came via other operatives, also known as supporters and sleeper cells, operating in various European countries. These individuals obtained the money through legitimate businesses and employment, such as masonry work and automobile sales and repair. Other terrorists with al-Qaeda affiliations stated that they received training on criminal activities such as bank robberies and fraud schemes to fund their activities. They were also instructed in street crimes, such as residential and vehicle burglaries, as well as the use of stolen telephones and credit cards in order to facilitate their communication needs.

What appears to be noncriminal and run-of-the-mill may just be the piece of the puzzle needed to avert a catastrophic event. Remember, you are not just looking for street criminals any more, and terrorists do not work alone. An infrastructure of support exists for every active terrorist. You must look at the big picture based on verified information, and you must avoid stereotypes. Terrorist groups are not just a ragtag bunch of individuals with fanatical or extreme beliefs. They are organized groups with structure and a management component.

Leadership

Organization

States

International Environment

Underlying Conditions

Figure 2.3 National strategy for combating terrorism structure.

Terrorism structure and management

Much like corporations, businesses, governments, and paramilitary or military organizations, terrorist groups have a structure and management component, as loose as it may appear to be.

In the 2003 government document *National Strategy for Combating Terrorism*, a basic structure of terror was presented, which is demonstrated in Figure 2.3. "At the base, underlying conditions such as poverty, corruption, religious conflict, and ethnic strife create opportunities for terrorists to exploit."[31] Terrorists use these conditions to justify their actions and expand support. An organization's structure, membership, resources, and security determine its capabilities and reach. Open borders, and to some extent technology, allow for access to international resources and new recruitment arenas. But no matter what, an organization must have a base of operation. Some organizations receive such bases of support, either physical or virtual, from states and countries all over the world. Groups such as al-Qaeda were able to establish and maintain bases and terrorist training camps in Afghanistan, and many others have done likewise in the Bekka Valley in Lebanon.

The leadership component becomes the catalyst for terrorist action. Regardless of size or structure, most organizations tend to utilize a chain-of-command style of management. Many terrorist groups, domestic and foreign based, and hate organizations also tend to follow a paramilitary or military organization

Figure 2.4 Command, active cadre, active supporters, and passive supporters.

when it comes to their training, structure, and tactics. The corporation or business world component is often displayed on the financial side of a terrorist organization. A tremendous financial need exists for an organization to keep a handful of operatives in the field, let alone to sustain the entire group. Therefore, many groups have turned to traditional criminal methods for gaining the capital they need to survive, committing crimes such as flimflams, credit card fraud, Internet scams, and robbery. However, these methods bring unwanted law enforcement attention to members of an organization. Therefore, many groups turned to business ventures, such as nonprofit organizations. Law enforcement personnel and scholars would probably argue that these so-called business ventures are an exploitation of a capitalistic and free society. Many international groups that have a pure hatred for the United States and everything that it stands for have exploited the use of nonprofit religious and aid groups within the United States in order to increase their financial coffers.

Similar to Maslow's Hierarchy of Human Needs, terrorists have needs, too. Jonathan White demonstrated the use of James Fraser's (former U.S. Army counterterrorist specialist) and Ian Fulton's analyses and writings from 1984. This was done in the form of a pyramid, similar to the National Strategy for Combating Terrorism and to Maslow's Hierarchy, to explain the structural needs of terrorist organizations. Fraser pointed out that terrorist organizations are divided into four distinctly separate levels dependent upon each other: Command, Active Cadre, Active Supporters, and Passive Supporters.[7]

Figure 2.4 shows the four levels of an organization as developed by Fraser and Fulton. The Command level is at the top and is the smallest. Just like many businesses, it does not exercise direct day-to-day operational control of activities and individuals. Command-level members would be well-educated planners, financial monitors, and target selectors. The second level is the Active Cadre. This is the hard-core component of the organization that consists of the field soldiers and, as some communities have come to experience, suicide/homicide bombers. It is at this level that the mission gets carried out. Active Cadre members are aware of the existence of other members and the organization's beliefs but will have limited knowledge of missions beyond their roles. The third tier in the hierarchal structure is made up of the Active Supporters. These are the individuals charged with logistics, field support, and intelligence gathering for the Active Cadre. In order to keep one terrorist in the field, it takes several individuals to actively support the mission. The largest group is the Passive Supporters. They are used to muster political or financial support. Many of these individuals do not even know they are supporting an active terrorist organization. Therefore, it is difficult to capture and identify verifiable intelligence on individuals who fall into this classification.

Organizational size varies. Terrorist organizations may have a handful of members or may have as many as 10,000 or more. Dealing with and managing such numbers of personnel is difficult enough in a legitimate business but in a covert terrorist organization of this size, opportunities for leaks exist. Leaders within these organizations realize the importance of being inconspicuous. Therefore, leaders keep communication, access to information, and mission details on a need-to-know basis, and often use small units, referred to as cells. The use of cells restricts the likelihood that law enforcement or spies can gain access to an organization. Cells are generally composed of four to six members, all with specialties to enhance the mission, and each member has limited knowledge of the overall mission. This ensures that if one is captured or intelligence is leaked, the entire mission is not jeopardized. It also makes infiltration of the group by law enforcement or a source of human intelligence nearly impossible. Similar to the military, where squads make up units and units make up divisions, a group of terrorist cells makes up columns. This form of command structure allows many individuals with various specialties to be under a single command. This is important for an analyst or investigator to know when developing leads and initiating a link analysis.

The makeup and structure of a terrorist organization make it ripe for dissent and problems. Management is difficult enough in the public sector, but couple it with a cloak of secrecy and you have a recipe for potential failure. Understanding the problems associated with terrorist management will give the law enforcement community the knowledge necessary to exploit the weaknesses of the enemy and to potentially turn these weakness into advantages.

Terrorist groups face several managerial problems. Outlined below are some of the more common problems of terrorist management:[7]

Communicating within an infrastructure of secrecy
Coordinating activities despite decentralization

Maintaining internal discipline
Avoiding fragmented ideologies
Maintaining logistics
Training
Financing

Terrorist leaders face many special operational problems. Communicating within an infrastructure of secrecy is perhaps an organization's primary weakness. Even with technological advances such as satellite telephones and the Internet, terrorists find it difficult to communicate because they are decentralized. With every communication they run the risk of being intercepted and compromised. Although secrecy is a tactical advantage, terrorists still need some form of communication to survive.

A second problem for terrorists involves coordinating activities, without centralization. This is something to which many law enforcement agencies can relate. Decentralization creates potential logistical nightmares and mishaps. Large-scale terrorist operations require a coordinated effort in order to be successful. Decentralization combined with the first problem, communication, increases the likelihood of errors and detection.

Third, maintaining internal discipline poses difficulties, because organizational leaders must continuously strive to keep members focused on the mission as well as on the group's ideology in order to prevent defection. This overlaps with the fourth problem, which is avoiding fragmented ideologies. For a terrorist group, it is important that all members share a common ideology. Regardless of their education, economic status, or nationality, the one factor that often bonds a group's membership is a common ideology or belief system.

The fifth problem faced by terrorist organizations is that of maintaining logistics. It takes 35 to 50 support personnel to keep one terrorist active in the field.[32] Support personnel are essential for providing food, transportation, funding, communications, and housing. Housing is perhaps the greatest challenge, because in order to avoid detection it may be necessary for a terrorist to relocate numerous times before completing a mission.

Training, the sixth problem faced in terrorist management, is as vital to a terrorist as it is to a law enforcement official. It is one thing to adopt a belief system, but it is another matter to be effectively trained in how to handle situations. Many law enforcement officials who have faced deadly scenarios and survived are cited as giving credit to their training. They noted that their training caused their instincts to take over. The same holds true for just about anyone with an extensive training background, including a terrorist. However, the problem of training for a terrorist is compounded by logistics and secrecy. Establishing a training facility especially for conducting a deadly terrorist act is no easy task and can bring unwelcome attention to the group.

Financing is the seventh and final problem faced in terrorist management, and it applies to all managers, legitimate and terrorist-related. Financing lies at the heart of any operation. Terrorist attacks do not materialize overnight;

they must be well planned and organized. They require considerable funding to sustain momentum. Financial means are needed for travel, lodging, food, supplies, training, and payoffs.

Using the above information, analysts and investigators must consider and evaluate these weaknesses. For every weakness in a terrorist organization, there is strength to be gained by law enforcement. It is up to the law enforcement community to become cognizant of terrorists' needs when gathering and analyzing information in order to effectively exploit a weakness and to seize the opportunity to thwart a tragic terrorist event.

Chapter concepts

1. For years, the definition of terrorism has been debated without concurrence on its meaning. This is because it has been defined within political and social contexts and has been influenced by history.
2. Terrorism has many different forms, including political, ecological, agricultural, narco, biological, and cyber.
3. Domestic terrorism is not a new phenomenon. It has evolved since 1791 and has gone through several different stages.
4. Different types of domestic terrorist groups are left-wing, right-wing, Puerto Rican leftists, black militants, Jewish extremists, and special interests.
5. Organized hate groups play a role in the context of domestic terrorism. These groups are categorized into white supremacy, hate groups, patriot movements, sovereign citizen movements, militias, tax protestors, and foreign sponsored.
6. There are three types of terrorist beliefs: nationalistic, ideological, and theological, and there are differences between a terrorist and a street criminal.

References

1. Stohl, M., Ed., *The Politics of Terrorism*, Marcel Dekker, New York, 1979, p. 1.
2. Justice Department, Federal Bureau of Investigation, http://www.fbi.gov/publish/terror/terrusa.html (February 21, 2003).
3. General Military Training, Terrorism, N.p., n.d., p1-3-10, pl-3-14, and pl-3-16.
4. Heymann, P.B., *Terrorism and America: A Commonsense Strategy for a Democratic Society*, MIT Press, Cambridge, MA, 1998, p. 3.
5. Snow, D.M., *September 11, 2001, The New Face of War?*, Longman, New York, 2002, p. 1.
6. Lesser, I.O. et al., *Countering the New Terrorism, Implications for Strategy*, RAND, Santa Monica, CA, 1999, p. 85.
7. White, J.R., *Terrorism: An Introduction*, 4th ed., Thomson Wadsworth, Belmont, CA, 2002, pp. 23, 33, 36, 39.
8. United States Department of State Immigration and Nationality Act, Section 212 (a)(3)(B).

9. Hoffman, B., *Inside Terrorism*, Columbia University Press, New York, 1998, pp. 40, 107.
10. Gurr, T.R., Some characteristics of political terrorism in the 1960s, in *The Politics of Terrorism*, Stohl, M., Ed., Marcel Dekker, New York, 1979, pp. 25–49.
11. President, Report, The National Strategy for the Physical Protection of Critical Infrastructures and Key Assets, White House, February 2003, p. 9.
12. Able, D., *Hate Groups*, Enslow Publishers, Berkeley Heights, NJ, 2000, p. 26.
13. O'Connor, T., Profiling Terrorists, http://faculty.ncwc.edu/toconnor/392/spy/terrorism.htm, Nov. 2002, North Carolina Wesleyan College.
14. Harris, J.W., Domestic terrorism in the 1980's, *FBI Law Enforcement Bulletin*, 56:5–13, 1987.
15. Senate Select Committee on Intelligence, The Terrorist Threat Confronting the United States, Statement for the Record of Dale L. Watson, February 6, 2002, p. 2.
16. Southern Poverty Law Center, 2001 Intelligence Report, http://www.tolerance.org/maps/hate/index.html (February 28, 2003), Hate Groups.
17. Potok, M., personal communication, March 10, 2003.
18. Perry, B., *In the Name of Hate: Understanding Hate Crimes*, Routledge, New York, 2001, pp. 138, 174.
19. MILNET, Known Domestic Terrorist Groups, http://www.milnet.com/milnet/tgp/tgpmain.htm (October 25, 2002), Profiles of Domestic Terror Groups.
20. Hoffman, B., *Inside Terrorism*, Columbia University Press, New York, 1998, p. 107.
21. Southern Poverty Law Center, 2001 Intelligence Report, http://www.splcenter.org/intelligenceproject/ip-index.html (February 2006, Known Active Patriot Groups).
22. MILNET, Domestic Terror: What it Holds for the Millenium, http://www.milnet.com/milnet/domestic/Dom-Terror.htm (October 25, 2002), Domestic Terrorism a Definition, p. 2.
23. Uniting and Strengthening America by Providing Appropriate Tools Required to Intercept and Obstruct Terrorism (USA PATRIOT Act) Act of 2001, 107th Congress, 1st session, HR3162 (October 24, 2001).
24. U.S. Senate Committees on Appropriations, Armed Services, and Select Committee on Intelligence, Threat of Terrorism to the United States, Statement for the Record, Louis J. Freeh, May 10, 2001.
25. Landau, E., *Terrorism: America's Growing Threat*, Lodestar Books (E.P. Dutton), New York, 1992, p. 45.
26. Laqueur, W., *The Age of Terrorism*, Little, Brown, Boston; New York, 1987, p. 335.
27. Council on Foreign Relations, Terrorism: Questions & Answers, http://www.cfrterrorism.org/groups/, American Militant Extremists United States, Radicals, (March 3, 2003).
28. Revell, B., A Long Path of Terror, http://www.adl.org, 1, 1, December 2002 (February 20, 2003), On the Beat.
29. U.S. Justice Department, Federal Bureau of Investigation, http://www.fbi.gov/ucr/Cius_98, (February 21, 2003).
30. Southern Poverty Law Center, Hate Groups, http://www.tolerance.org/maps/hate/index.html (March 6, 2003), Hate Group Definitions.
31. President, Report, *National Strategy for Combating Terrorism*, February 2003, p. 6.
32. Bodansky, Y., *Bin Laden: The Man Who Declared War on America*, Forum, Rocklin, CA, 1999.

chapter three

Homeland security and analysis

The Symbionese Liberation Army (SLA) operated in the 1970s and targeted banks, initiated kidnappings, and bombed and killed law enforcement personnel, but it was seen as a revolutionary or radical group that was disgruntled with the government. Even after the final arrests, convictions, and sentencing of the remaining members in 2002 and 2003, approximately 30 years after the crime spree and killing began, they were still viewed as a fad or leftist group. They were also described as a group whose time had passed, and its members were described as criminals who were convicted and sentenced for traditional crimes. What makes this group different from members of al-Qaeda, besides al-Qaeda's international ties and size? Perhaps it was the fact that members of the SLA were citizens of the United States and often looked and acted like the majority of other criminals or gangs.

For years, many groups such as these have operated within the country, dissatisfied with the government or the politics of the United States. Throughout the 1960s and into the 1970s, many individuals and groups demonstrated in various ways against the United States and its political points of view. The war in Vietnam was frequently used as a reason for these anti-government sentiments. Whether in the United States or in Europe, many factions sought to terrorize those associated with the war initiative. An example of this can be found in Germany, with the relatively small Bader-Meinhof Gang whose members had anti-Vietnam beliefs. However, much of the activity surrounding these rather small groups was seen more as a social or political nuisance rather than as terrorism. It was not until Ted Robert Gurr published the chapter "Some Characteristics of Political Terrorism" in *The Politics of Terrorism*[1] that what was taking place was shown to be more far-reaching than a mere nuisance: it was terrorism. Gurr noted that terrorist activity such as that demonstrated in the Vietnam era was conducted by very small groups and was ephemeral.

Regardless of the size of the group, terrorists and terrorism have a dramatic effect on the world, wherever the activity takes place. The victims or their family members are not concerned about the size of the group or if the group's activity was short-lived. However, they would have wanted some level of warning that an attack was imminent. Although the U.S. government cannot provide a warning system based on intelligence for the entire world, it has been able to design and impose a system in the United States known as the Homeland Security Advisory System. The Homeland Security Advisory System was designed to provide a comprehensive and effective means by which to disseminate information regarding the risk of impending terrorist attacks to federal, state, and local law enforcement authorities as well as to the American public. When instituted in March 2002, the federal government initiated numerous press releases and garnered a massive amount of media attention designed to inform the public about the new advisory system. However, today many individuals in the public sector as well as in the law enforcement community still have only a vague awareness of the system and what each level on the continuum means. The following subsections are presented to ensure a standardized approach and awareness of the advisory system.

Homeland security defined

Just like defining terrorism, terrorist activity, or a terrorist, homeland security has many meanings to different people. The U.S. federal government defines homeland security as follows:

> Homeland security is a concerted national effort to prevent ter-
> rorist attacks within the U.S., reduce America's vulnerability to
> terrorism, and minimize the damage and recover from attacks
> that do occur.[2]

The government elaborated on each phrase in the above definition. "Concerted national effort" is based on the principles of shared responsibility and partnership with Congress, state and local governments, the private sector, and the American people. "Terrorist attacks" covers kidnappings, hijackings, shootings, conventional bombings, attacks involving chemical, biological, radiological, or nuclear weapons, cyber attacks, and any number of other forms of malicious violence. "Reduce America's vulnerability" by constantly evolving the way the government works with the private sector to identify and protect our critical infrastructure and key assets, to detect terrorist threats, and to augment our defenses. "Minimize the damage" requires our efforts to focus on the brave and dedicated public servants who are our first responders. To "recover," we must be prepared to protect and restore institutions needed to sustain economic growth and confidence, rebuild destroyed property, assist victims and their families, heal psycholog-ical wounds, and demonstrate compassion, recognizing that we cannot return to a preattack norm.

Regardless of how homeland security is defined, a terrorist threat can come from anywhere. Based on the National Strategy for Combating Terrorism report, the terrorist threat is flexible, transnational, enabled by modern technology, and characterized by loose interconnectivity within and between groups.[2] These groups operate on three levels. The first level consists of those who operate within a single country and have a limited reach. The second level is comprised of the terrorist organizations that operate regionally. These operations transcend at least one international boundary. Organizations with global reaches constitute the third category. Their operations span multiple regions, and their reaches can be global. The United States is subject to attack from all three levels; therefore, it is imperative that intelligence be expedited and advisories posted as soon as applicable.

Homeland Security Advisory System

This advisory system was instituted in March 2002 by the U.S. Federal Government to provide a level of awareness of the likelihood of potential terrorist attacks to state and local governments and ordinary citizens, regardless of their locale. The determination of each level is decided upon by high-ranking government officials based on a wide range of information and intelligence received and corroborated by a multitude of sources worldwide. Once intelligence is developed, it is verified and corroborated against multiple variables and scenarios to determine if it is credible, if there is a specific threat, or if there is a grave threat. Only then is it presented for proper advisement and color designation, following the Homeland Security Presidential Directive.[4] The hierarchy used is called the Homeland Security Advisory System and is demonstrated in Figure 3.1. This system, which is used as a guide,[4] is an intelligence-driven system designed to aid law enforcement and the public in responding or preparing for a terrorist threat. One question that should be raised is where does the intelligence come from and whose information is used?

The advisory system was well publicized, but the public lacks finite understanding as to what each level represents. Outlined below is a summary of each level as posted on the Department of Homeland Security's Web site.[5]

Low condition (green)

This condition is declared when there is a low risk of terrorist attacks. Federal departments and agencies should consider the following general measures in addition to the agency-specific protective measures they develop and implement:

1. Refining and exercising, as appropriate, preplanned protective measures
2. Ensuring that personnel receive proper training on the Homeland Security Advisory System and on specific preplanned department or agency protective measures

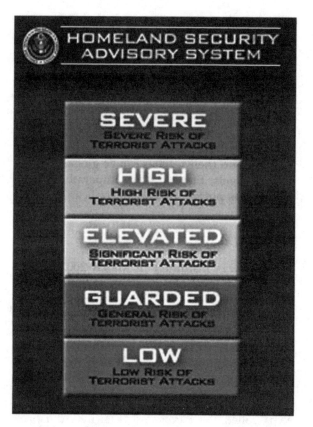

Figure 3.1 Homeland security advisory system.

3. Institutionalizing a process to ensure that all facilities and regulated sectors are regularly assessed for vulnerabilities to terrorist attacks, and all reasonable measures are taken to mitigate these vulnerabilities

Guarded condition (blue)

This condition is declared when there is a general risk of terrorist attacks. In addition to the protective measures taken in the previous threat condition, federal departments and agencies should consider the following general measures in addition to the agency-specific protective measures that they will develop and implement:

1. Checking communications with designated emergency response or command locations
2. Reviewing and updating emergency response procedures
3. Providing the public with any information that would strengthen its ability to act appropriately

Elevated condition (yellow)

An elevated condition is declared when there is a significant risk of terrorist attacks. In addition to the protective measures taken in the previous threat conditions, federal departments and agencies should consider the following general measures in addition to the protective measures that they will develop and implement:

1. Increasing surveillance of critical locations
2. Coordinating emergency plans, as appropriate, with nearby jurisdictions
3. Assessing whether the precise characteristics of the threat require further refinement of preplanned protective measures
4. Implementing, as appropriate, contingency and emergency response plans

High condition (orange)

A high condition is declared when there is a high risk of terrorist attacks. In addition to the protective measures taken in the previous threat conditions, federal departments and agencies should consider the following general measures in addition to the agency-specific protective measures that they will develop and implement:

1. Coordinating necessary security efforts with federal, state, and local law enforcement agencies or any National Guard or other appropriate armed forces organizations
2. Taking additional precautions at public events and possibly considering alternative venues or even cancellations
3. Preparing to execute contingency procedures, such as moving to an alternate site or dispersing their workforce
4. Restricting access to threatened facility to essential personnel only

Severe condition (red)

A severe condition reflects a severe risk of terrorist attacks. Under most circumstances, the protective measures for this condition are not intended to be sustained for substantial periods of time. In addition to the protective measures in the previous threat conditions, federal departments and agencies should also consider the following general measures in addition to the agency-specific protective measures that they will develop and implement:

1. Increasing or redirecting personnel to address critical emergency needs
2. Assigning emergency response personnel and prepositioning and mobilizing specially trained teams or resources

3. Monitoring, redirecting, or constraining transportation systems
4. Closing public and government facilities

Many terrorist acts are guided toward political change. The last line used under the severe condition (red) of the Homeland Security Advisory System might be construed as a way of submission. Terrorists would probably consider it a successful attack if the United States, or any other government, would close.

The Homeland Security Advisory System is managed by the U.S. Attorney General in concert with the Secretary of the Department of Homeland Security. They are responsible for developing, implementing, and managing the system for the federal government based on the latest verified intelligence. Again, whose intelligence? A potential concern, which is not publicly addressed, regarding the system is whether the information and intelligence being used to make informed decisions are inclusive of domestic terrorist activities or are just foreign-based. Also, it is not public knowledge whether the intelligence is a derivative of local and state law enforcement information or is just from federal and military sources. Despite this, it is imperative that law enforcement agencies submit all intelligence as soon as it is developed. In addition, state and local governments have been encouraged to implement the advisory system and modify it to meet the needs of their agencies.

Use of such a system is vital to standardizing practices, approaches, and contingency plans when dealing with homeland security or terrorism risks. However, one should not become consumed with the national advisory system or wait until a particular level is announced. This would be reactive, just like the system that is designed to help aid in preparing and responding. The system is full of suggestive reactionary practices that will aid any agency or its citizens in responding to threats, but law enforcement personnel are now looking to identify the threat and not just to respond. Waiting for the federal government or anyone else to initiate a threat level before doing anything would be neglect of duty. Every agency and its members are part of the solution, and analytical practices should be undertaken and be continuous, whether or not agency staff members feel they have anything to bring to the homeland security table. Furthermore, this system is based on "national" intelligence. Nothing prevents local jurisdictions or regions from implementing their own system. Regardless of the advisory level, information gathering and analysis should be continuous and should be routinely reconciled in order to paint the clearest picture. Analysis should be continuous and heightened as the advisory level is raised. Analysts must be well-rounded, look globally, and have an acute awareness of their roles and how their duties can benefit homeland security.

Homeland security and analysis

Several factors are used to assess a potential homeland security or terrorist threat. These factors include whether the threat is credible, whether it is corroborated, whether it is specific and imminent, and how grave it is. These four factors should be at the immediate crux of any form of real-time intelligence analysis being conducted. In the realm of law enforcement, the approach is often to follow a hunch or gut feeling, based on training and experience, when seeking out criminal activity or developing a trend or pattern. With homeland security, there is no such opportunity. When analyzing traditional crime many analysts will attempt to forecast, often based on probability, when and where the next incident in a serial crime will take place. Although this has its place in law enforcement, it is fair to say that the likelihood of predicting the next terrorist attack with any degree of certainty is not readily available. Rather than attempting to forecast there should be a concerted effort to identify weaknesses and understand how to anticipate behavior based on an array of known variables. When dealing with the traditional criminal element, there is rarely a situation that will negatively and tragically impact more people or countries than terrorism. Therefore, there is no room for anything less than credible, corroborated, timely, and well-defined information.

According to the Department of Homeland Security's White House Web site (2002), Information Analysis and Infrastructure Protection:

> The CIA will continue to gather and analyze overseas intelligence. Homeland Security will continue to require interagency coordination.[5]

Imposing vague terminology such as "require interagency coordination" reduces the chance that all law enforcement agencies will work together or in a real-time fashion. The fact that there is no mention of gathering and analyzing domestic intelligence, only overseas, is greatly disturbing and may cause law enforcement personnel to overlook potential threats to homeland security that may come about from factions in their own backyards. As alluded to in the White House's March 12, 2002, press release concerning the Homeland Security Advisory System, states and localities are encouraged to adopt and implement compatible systems. The question is, how many states and localities have adopted or implemented compatible systems? This question is not meant to be a criticism but is designed to demonstrate the need for self-initiated and documented processes and systems that will aid all parties involved in the war on terrorism. Since September 11, 2001, communication and intelligence processes have been thrust into the forefront of any successful antiterrorism campaign. However, these processes vary from agency to agency. Although international or foreign-based terrorist organizations can never be overlooked, there is a great deal of information from myriad resources on these groups, but there is little on domestic terrorist or organized hate groups. Based on the lack of domestic intelligence coordination and communication, it is incumbent upon law enforcement personnel, analysts included, to provide real-time intelligence analysis and to effectively disseminate it and provide accurate advisories without delay.

Dealing with homeland security and terrorism analysis has been addressed up to now largely by federal law enforcement and military analysts. Even though these well-trained analysts have a lot to offer, their traditional duties and practices do not always translate easily into effective local and state law enforcement procedures. The primary reason for this is that they have two distinctly different missions. Law enforcement analysts use federal and state guidelines, and they operate in defined jurisdictional areas. Military analysts use directives, treaties, resolutions, and international laws, and they operate in an international theater. Simply put, it is crime vs. war. Therefore, it is incumbent upon law enforcement personnel to develop the best of both worlds into methods that can be readily adapted and retrofitted in order to enhance the capabilities of analysts and investigators charged with handling homeland security issues.

One way to adapt is by developing a base from which to start. The National Strategy for Homeland Security report developed such a base. This strategy identified a strategic framework based on three national objectives that are also applicable to any agency. In order of priority, these are to prevent terrorist attacks within the United States, to reduce America's vulnerability to terrorism, and to minimize the damage and recover from attacks that occur.[6] The first two objectives are those that law enforcement, particularly analysts, can be successful at obtaining. However, the third objective seems to be the focus of many lectures and training courses given to law enforcement officials. As interagency and intergovernmental coordination is enhanced, the first two proactive objectives will overshadow the third, which is partially reactive. All these objectives were made slightly more attainable, in part due to legislative enhancements such as the USA PATRIOT Act.

The USA PATRIOT Act

The USA PATRIOT Act of 2001, formally known as the Uniting and Strengthening America by Providing Appropriate Tools Required to Intercept and Obstruct Terrorism Act of 2001 from the 107th Congress, HR 3162, was established to deter and punish terrorist acts in the United States and around the world, and to enhance law enforcement investigatory tools.[7]

The USA PATRIOT Act of 2001 was unprecedented. National and world events surrounding September 11, 2001, were the driving force behind the evolution and passage of what has become known simply as the Patriot Act. These events were the stimuli for the possibly record-breaking pace in which this act was passed and subsequently signed by President George W. Bush on October 26, 2001. This was just one month after being initiated and being passed in the Senate by a 98-to-1 vote. This massive sweeping legislation positively impacted law enforcement agencies and their roles in combating terrorism, and it covered a broad range of topics.

Some of the topics covered by the USA PATRIOT Act include the following:

Enhancing domestic security against terrorism
Enhancing surveillance procedures
International Money Laundering Abatement and Antiterrorist Financing
    Act of 2001
Protecting the border
Removing obstacles to investigating terrorism
Providing for victims of terrorism, public safety officers, and their families
Increasing information sharing for critical infrastructure protection
Strengthening criminal laws against terrorism
Improving intelligence
Protecting critical infrastructures

Interestingly, although the content of the act appears all-encompassing, domestic terrorism is not defined until about three-quarters of the way through the document. While this is not necessarily viewed as a negative trait, it is important that all law enforcement personnel remain cognizant of the numerous domestic-based organizations as well as the foreign-based international ones that have bases, outreaches, and supporters within the United States. The act was a product born out of international terrorist actions. However, it is also worth noting that this act is not meant just for investigating and analyzing exotic foreign-based terrorist groups. It applies to all groups, domestic and international, and all forms of terrorism.

Passage of this act greatly improved the tools available for law enforcement. Beyond the immediate benefit of the act, which is enhanced surveillance procedures, law enforcement at all levels will reap the greatest investigative rewards from the money-laundering and financial tracking capabilities as well as the increased information sharing among agencies. However, it is important to note that forfeiture aspects and associating them or identifying them to terrorists are going to lead to long, tedious, and arduous investigations that will require a great deal of expertise. This will pose great difficulty on the majority of law enforcement agencies that have fewer than 25 officers. The act is geared toward the one thing that no terrorist organization can do without, finances.

Importance of finances

Tracking, monitoring, and cutting off finances are tremendously important tools in the war on terrorism. As of October 2002, an aggressive international law enforcement effort resulted in the freezing of $113 million in terrorists' assets in 500 bank accounts around the world, with much activity in Western countries, including $35 million in the United States.[8]

The use of sleeper cells and activity associated with their efforts for financial gain has already been discussed. However, other forms of funding are used, such as nongovernment organizations (NGOs) and charitable organizations. Many of these are passed off as legitimate business ventures, but things are not always as they appear. International fundamentalist terrorists increased their use of NGOs and charitable organizations as a way to gain finances for use in their terrorist activities. NGOs are used much in the same manner as active supporters. They may offer logistical support in the forms of employment, documents, travel, and training. Uses of "fronts" by terrorist organizations (such as Hamas) in the United States uncovered charities, humanitarian foundations, and relief organizations that were used to raise funding in support of terrorist activities. Speaking in 1995 on the topic of protecting America, Oliver Revell stated that "Numerous front groups supporting Hamas have been established in the United States and several collect funds as tax exempt 501(C)(3) organizations."[9] Tremendous challenges exist for law enforcement personnel investigating terrorist fund-raising through the use of NGOs and alleged charitable humanitarian organizations. The line between legitimate and what may appear to be legitimate is often blurred.

Financing efforts by terrorist organizations have ranged from basic to sophisticated. There probably is not a financing method known that has not been tried at least once. Use of correspondent bank accounts, private bank accounts, offshore shell banks, Hawalas (see below), cash smuggling, identity theft, credit card fraud, drug trafficking, money laundering (which will be explained in further detail under enhanced analysis), and flimflams are prevalent. The terrorist's goal is to seek financial gain while remaining undetected. That is why the USA PATRIOT Act plays an important role with its emphasis on financial topics. Regardless of the form of terrorism being investigated, the Patriot Act opens new avenues for law enforcement. As law enforcement targets traditional financial methods, terrorists are more apt to use ancient and informal methods to move money, such as the Hawala system.

Hawala

The word "Hawala" means "transfer" in Arabic and in some circles Hawala is referred to as a Hundi. In some contexts, the word "Hawala" is used synonymously with "trust." Hawala is an ancient alternative or parallel remittance system that originated in South Asia and is processed with the assistance of a Hawaladar or agent. It is based largely on trust and extensive use of connections, such as family members and other known affiliations and is generally void of formal financial institutions such as banks. It was developed in India before the introduction of traditional banking practices and is often referred to as an underground banking system. There is little documentation and record keeping. There are many motivations for using the Hawala system, including its effectiveness, efficiency, reliability, lack of bureaucracy, lack of a paper trail, and ability to evade taxes. In some instances two terms are associated with transactions: Black Hawala and White Hawala. Simply put, Black Hawala refers to illegitimate transactions, particularly money laundering, and White Hawala refers to legitimate transactions. Many dealings associated with Hawala are done in the area of import and export businesses, travel services, jewelry, and currency exchanges. Transactions are usually completed in one to two days. There are many locales that rely or use the Hawala. Some of the most common ethnic locations are Pakistan, India, Somalia, and the Persian Gulf States. Three countries that tend to show on the radar screen are Great Britain, Switzerland, and Dubai.

There are several other common aspects to Hawala. First, in most cases, Hawala transactions go across international lines, such as with worker remittances to their home countries. Second, Hawala usually involves more than one currency, although this is not absolutely required. Third, a Hawala transaction usually entails principals and intermediaries. To accommodate requests of the principals, the intermediaries usually take financial positions. Later, much as in the case of conventional banking practices, these transactions will be cleared among the units to balance their books.

Tens of thousands of dollars are frequent. The only real limitations of a Hawala are the willingness and abilities of the parties involved. Invoice manipulations can be used to cover payments. For example, if an individual owes $10,000 to another, a purchase of goods is arranged at $7,000 and an invoice is sent for $17,000. This conceals the purchase of the goods as well as the money owed. Hawala quite often will not use any sort of negotiable instrument. Money transfers take place based on communications among members of the Hawala network.

This brief section is meant to provide an awareness of alternative forms of financial transactions that exist in the world. It is important to note that there are documented incidents of the use of Hawala in terrorist events and that the bulk of transactions are legitimate. Some scholars suspect that hundreds of billions of dollars are transacted in Hawala networks every year. The most obvious "legal" problem with Hawala in remitting countries is the lack of any registration or licensing, although the operations themselves are generally harmless. In receiving countries like India, there is in addition the more subtle potential clash between Hawala operations and exchange controls whereby Hawala transactions often result in increased black market transactions and expanded underground activity. Further details and references on Hawala systems can be attained by law enforcement personnel through the U.S. Department of Treasury Financial Crimes Enforcement Network (FinCEN) and Interpol. Knowledge of the various methods that a group may use to conduct financial affairs is another tool that will aid law enforcement in dealing with terrorism.

Dealing with terrorism

One of the great frustrations in dealing with terrorism is the wide variety of forms that terrorist acts can take.[10] Terrorism assumes many guises, such as those noted previously, e.g., political and cyber. These forms are compounded by the various types and styles of attacks beyond conventional bombings. If dealing with terrorist acts is frustrating, how are the investigative and analytical worlds to make sense of it? Traditionally, analysts and investigators have looked for common links and approaches that aided them in concluding their criminal investigations. An analyst assigned a case to monitor and gather intelligence leads and information will utilize various analytical techniques, often through the use of sophisticated software, in order to link common variables (also known as link analysis). Analysts have criminal and statutory guidelines to assist in the pursuit of developing probable cause and securing a criminal conviction. The numerous off-the-shelf intelligence programs are designed to expedite the intelligence process and graphically illustrate interrelationships that otherwise may be overlooked. These luxuries are not as available when dealing with homeland security and terrorism. There are thousands of law enforcement agencies in the United States, with 50 sets of varied state statutes, and much of what may be construed as a homeland security incident or terrorism becomes classified as a crime. An all-inclusive database or intelligence system that all agencies can agree upon does not exist. Whether it is a hijacking or a bombing, the first inclination of law enforcement personnel is to treat it as a violent crime that needs immediate response and attention, not a homeland security or terrorist action. This was true until September 11, 2001. How can we be sure that everyone is on the same page and is keeping an open mind as to the potential for terrorism to strike anywhere? The answer is simply through open communication, detailed information, proactive investigations, and the use of highly trained analytical and intelligence personnel.

Enforcing cooperation between the CIA and the FBI and the Immigration and Naturalization Service (INS) is essential in dealing with terrorism.[10] This is unarguably true; however, the same premise should be enforced between municipal, county, state, and federal law enforcement agencies. All levels of response, including investigation and information gathering, are crucial pieces to the puzzle when dealing with homeland security and terrorism. After all, it is not just international terrorist organizations overseas that need to be monitored. There are many domestic-based groups actively or passively operating in everyone's own back yard. Whether an investigation is local, state, or federal based, money is one nexus that, if exposed, can bring all agencies together. International- and domestic-based terrorist organizations generally have one feature in common: the need for financing. As documented in Steven Emerson's remarkable video documentary for the Public Broadcasting System (PBS) that aired in November 1994, titled "Jihad in America," terrorist organizations, regardless of how much they despise and loathe the United States, have no problem seeking support and financial backing in the United States. Based on this critical need, perhaps the best approach for dealing with terrorism is to track money and finances.

It can be detrimental to be one-dimensional and not to consider global approaches to homeland security and terrorist-related information. It has been demonstrated that terrorist activity can occur anywhere and at any time, but financial support is an ongoing process with many guises. This need exists and perhaps poses the greatest opportunity for law enforcement to expose and exploit in order to gain the upper hand in tracking and monitoring potential homeland security threats.

Homeland security and terrorism have received a great deal of public attention over the past couple of years. Most of the attention came from the federal government and the media. Law enforcement agencies, based on this attention, were forcefed a multitude of methods and practices for dealing with homeland security and terrorism matters. Some local and state agencies established homeland security units in an attempt to keep up with the growing concerns facing the ever-evolving world of terrorism. Traditional managers and administrators also reacted to this crisis, predictably, by having their agencies develop plans of action and contingency plans and by identifying potential targets that exist within their jurisdictions in case of an attack. However, this can be construed as nothing more than window dressing. Something near and dear to all managers is the budget, and this, perhaps, is the leading cause as to why only "window dressing" has been applied.

Agencies nationwide are continually being asked to do more with less. Homeland security and terrorism analysis is just another opportunity to do more with less. Overnight, agencies began assigning investigative and analytical personnel to address their agency's homeland security needs and to serve as points of contact. It has become the responsibility of these points of contact to expeditiously educate themselves in their new roles and to pass this knowledge and insight on to other personnel. Limitations were imposed on training and capital equipment purchases for numerous newly established units. Allocations were based on previously established budgets, and for many agencies the expansion of these monies is bleak. No matter what, law enforcement will have to deal with terrorism and continue to address concerns as they arise without excuses.

This has been only a cursory overview of some of the concerns facing government agencies in their attempts to deal with terrorism. The number of concerns needing to be addressed is yet to be determined, but there are some issues that can be overcome without draining the budget.

Law enforcement concerns

There are many concerns beyond budgetary to be faced by law enforcement personnel and agencies regarding homeland security and terrorism analysis. Throughout the decades, law enforcement personnel and academia have done a respectable job of educating and promoting awareness of criminal concerns across the board. There have been many models designed to standardize an array of law enforcement concerns ranging from community-oriented policing (COPs) to the New York Police Department's computerized statistics performance-based management approach (COMPSTAT). One model that is known to virtually every sworn law enforcement person is the SARA (scan, analyze, respond, and assess) model (Figure 3.2). These components were readily understood, but before the regular use of analytical

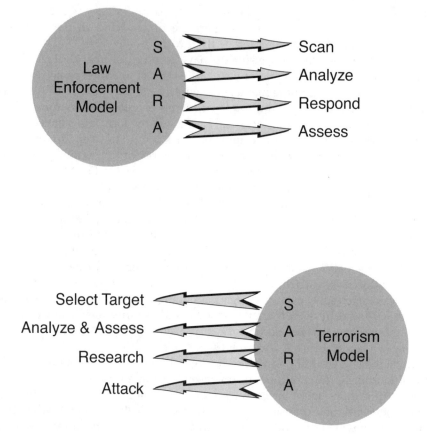

Figure 3.2 SARA and terrorism models.

personnel law enforcement circles often joked that the "A"s were overlooked or forgotten.

Just as law enforcement has organized practices into a model context, the same can be done with terrorism. Also demonstrated in Figure 3.2 is the use of the SARA model as a terrorist model. Terrorists have a planning stage (target selection, analyzing, and assessing the mission), a research (reconnaissance) and planning stage, and an execution stage (the attack). For a terrorist, use of all these stages is integrated and inseparable. Otherwise, the mission will fail. Terrorist activity is not designed to help anyone other than the terrorist, or the terrorist organization, in promoting their perceptions in the name of their cause. Terrorists do not randomly and spontaneously pick their targets. As history has demonstrated, terrorists are often selective in their targets, seeking to maximize the tragedy in physical and psychological terms in order to make a statement. This requires extensive analysis and assessment. It may take years, but when they are ready they will regroup and implement their plan of action. Dealing with individuals who have the patience and capability to undertake extensive campaigns poses a new concern for law enforcement personnel used to dealing with people who commit crimes of opportunity and greed.

American law enforcement is also worried about local issues and concerns, and most police managers do not think abstractly but pride themselves on a pragmatic approach.[11] Critical thought inevitably focuses on local issues. Often overlooked are issues of displacement and how actions may impact other jurisdictions. Terrorism is viewed as too exotic for most agencies to be concerned with. This is not necessarily the fault of chiefs of police or their staffs. The political and budgetary concerns of all government entities, not just law enforcement, drive the way these businesses are run. This has led many managers and leaders to stay focused on issues specific to their jurisdictions, and when necessary on the immediate region, but seldom beyond that. This attitude permeates from the unwillingness of the constituents being served to pay for services rendered outside their jurisdictional boundaries. It is important for the law enforcement community to educate not only its personnel but also the public and government officials on the vital need to work outside any one particular jurisdiction and to work in concert with regional, state, and federal agencies on matters of homeland security and terrorism.

Sharing information and intelligence by analysts, investigators, and counterterrorism agents is essential and probably poses the greatest concern for law enforcement at all levels. Jurisdictional haggling, credit claiming, and unnecessary secrecy permeate the counterterrorist and law enforcement communities. A sense of ownership and zeal to handle a case is commendable, but when dealing with homeland security and terrorism issues there is no time to play games among agencies — time is of the essence. Interagency cooperation also fragments on jurisdictional grounds or on the perceived level of threats being exhibited and the immediacy of response needed. Most agencies have specific guidelines outlined in their policies and procedures manuals covering traditional law enforcement response and investigation but they fail to cover intelligence gathering and matters of homeland security. Procedures and practices must be demonstrated in writing and not left to word of mouth or on-the-job training. The magnitude of homeland security investigations and the need to corroborate information are dependent upon details and documentation; therefore, proven and standardized practices must be used. Once standardized practices are put into place, agencies must arrive at some sort of consensus on a database structure before developing one. Using existing systems may not suffice due to limited data fields, too many narrative fields, or lack of compatibility with other agencies. Minimum database requirements need to be established. Not every agency will have the same database software, but by following predefined requirements, investigations can be enhanced and time can be saved.

Law enforcement agencies typically separate what would today be classified as a terrorist into criminal, political, or mentally unstable categories, and these classifications may be too simplistic. As demonstrated earlier, terrorist behavior differs from that of ordinary street criminals. Criminal investigation techniques must be modified to reflect these differences when examining terrorist cases. Another factor to consider is how agencies and the FBI have captured data on terrorist acts in the past. The FBI has labeled the majority of domestic terrorist activities under nonterrorist headings in the Uniform Crime Reporting (UCR) system. Many incidents were investigated, classified, and reported as hate crimes, or under the routine UCR reporting classifications of Part 1, Part 2, and noncriminal. The use of the FBI's classification, hate crimes, is expressly true when dealing with domestic-based terrorist groups. This can possibly be attributed to a group's lack of leadership, infrequency of action, members being "single-event wonders," or to the hatred by some groups toward a specific segment of the population. American law enforcement officers routinely deal with significant homeland security and terrorism issues and unintentionally dismiss any correlation, referring to the incidents as routine crimes. This can be largely attributed to a lack of coordination, training, and awareness.

Coordination, training, and awareness

Paramilitary organizations such as law enforcement have long prided themselves on their expertise, training, and adaptability. Training is the foundation upon which law enforcement practices are built. From day one, officers are trained in detail on everything from report writing to firearms. However, this training is generally geared only toward handling typical street crimes, and the closest they get to terrorism — on the U.S. Army Spectrum of Conflict — is riots and disorders through Field Force or Special Event Response Team training. On the other hand, many agencies have gone to the other extreme by providing training on law enforcement response to weapons of mass destruction, the last item on the U.S. Army's Spectrum. It is commendable that training is being provided concerning weapons of mass destruction, especially to first responders, but what about the rest of the spectrum, particularly terrorism? Although there are no hard numbers to go by, it is more likely that an officer will encounter a member of any one of the hundreds of organized hate and terrorist groups before he encounters weapons of mass destruction.

How do you train between 600,000 and 700,000 American law enforcement personnel, and where do you start? You start with the basics. Many basic law enforcement training initiatives relating to terrorism are focused on response. This is indicative of being reactive, and when dealing with homeland security and terrorism one needs to be proactive. Education on topics such as what to look for, questions to ask, identity concerns, and what homeland security and terrorism are should be emphasized. In addition to the training, many educational and reference materials available for law enforcement are geared toward response topics and some preventative scenarios. There is currently one federally funded program that since 1996 has addressed the material between these two topics and is designed to aid with intelligence and investigations relating to domestic terrorism. However, until September 11, 2001, many agencies were probably unaware of the existence of this program, or if they were, saw no need to attend. This deficiency caused many local and state agencies to turn to training from the military and federal agencies. Cooperation such as this is commendable, but agencies need to be mindful of the inherent differences in the style, mission, and type of law enforcement being practiced.

Coordination of law enforcement activities among various agencies is something that is done daily. Agencies often work under cooperative work agreements or memorandums of understanding (MOUs) and joint regional task forces. When operating under an MOU, agencies clearly spell out the guidelines to be followed and who will be in charge. The same cannot be said for homeland security, terrorism, and some routine investigations. It is these gray areas that often lead to confusion and, more importantly, lost information or intelligence. To demonstrate this point, several general incident categories are outlined below. Information and intelligence data are often routed to specific (different) locations or agencies whose members do not necessarily share all aspects of an investigation or all information:

Terrorist-related: Federal Bureau of Investigation (FBI)
Bomb-related: Alcohol, Tobacco, and Firearms (ATF)
Bomb hoaxes: Police general investigation units
Biohazardous materials: Fire departments
Arson: Fire departments, fire marshals, arson investigators, ATF
Explosive devices or chemicals: Bomb squads
Deaths involved: Homicide investigators
Fugitives: U.S. Marshal's Service, FBI, County Sheriff's Office
Miscellaneous: Gang units, robbery units, task forces, other jurisdictions, and county or state law enforcement agencies

Unless a terrorist-related event has a red flag associated with it, there is a great likelihood that the pieces of the puzzle can be scattered across multiple jurisdictions and databases.

The lack of awareness concerning homeland security, terrorism, and organized hate groups on many fronts is prevalent throughout law enforcement. Some of this is attributed to training matters and some is due to the lack of intelligence. The "I'll know it when I see it" approach will not work. In order to have effective information gathering and analysis, all members of an organization must be on the same page. Even if an agency had investigators dedicated to information gathering and analysis, these investigators cannot be everywhere and know everything. All members in an agency are part of the solution, and in order to be of value they need to have knowledge of the matter being faced and be educated to identify what pieces of information should be gathered. Once the logistics and educational issues are addressed, agencies can then focus on gathering information.

Chapter concepts

1. Despite the brevity of the homeland security definition, each phrase is replete with meaning and can be adopted by any governmental agency.
2. The Homeland Security Advisory System consists of five levels: green, blue, yellow, orange, and red, each representing varying degrees of alert, preparation, and response.
3. The USA PATRIOT Act has many roles in the war on terrorism, particularly with respect to finances.
4. Dealing with terrorism is novel for law enforcement, and there are many new concerns being faced by agencies and government managers.
5. Government and law enforcement agencies investigating crimes must be cognizant of the need to coordinate and train their personnel, as they encounter potential terrorist and organized hate crime activities.

References

1. Stohl, M., Ed., *The Politics of Terrorism*, Marcel Dekker, New York, 1979, p. 1.
2. President, Report, The National Strategy for Combating Terrorism, White House, February 2003, p. 8.
3. President, Report, The National Strategy for Homeland Security, Office of Homeland Security, July 16, 2002, p. 2.
4. Ridge, T., Gov. Ridge Announces Homeland Security Advisory System, Office of the Press Secretary, White House, March 12, 2002.
5. Department of Homeland Security, http://www.whitehouse.gov/ (February 21, 2003), Homeland Security Advisory System.
6. President, Report, The National Strategy for the Physical Protection of Critical Infrastructures and Key Assets, White House, February 2003, p. 1.
7. Uniting and Strengthening America by Providing Appropriate Tools Required to Intercept and Obstruct Terrorism (USA PATRIOT Act) Act of 2001, 107th Congress, 1st session, October 24, 2001.
8. Congressional Research Service, Report IB95112, Terrorism, the Future, and U.S. Foreign Policy, Lee, R. and Perl, R., Issue Brief for Congress, December 12, 2002, p. CRS-2.
9. Revell, O., Protecting America: law enforcement views radical Islam, March 1995, http://www.meforum.org/article/235 (March 11, 2003), *Middle East Quarterly*, p. 4.
10. Snow, D.M., *September 11, 2001, The New Face of War?*, Longman, New York, 2002, p. 11.
11. White, J.R., *Terrorism: An Introduction*, 4th ed., Thomson Wadsworth, Belmont, CA, 2002, p. 207.

chapter four

Working the puzzle
one piece at a time —
learning to anticipate behavior

No one profile exists for terrorists in terms of their backgrounds or personal characteristics. The differences in the origins of terrorists in terms of their society, culture, and environment preclude such a universal approach for foreign or domestic terrorists.[1] Much like understanding or interpreting languages, analysts and investigators need to have a familiarity, if not a total understanding, of the culture(s) of those they are investigating. Many open source information venues exist that can provide invaluable assistance in this matter. No matter how much someone attempts to assimilate into a society outside their own, there is a likelihood that they will revert back to something from their culture. It will be law enforcement's job to identify these behavioral differences.

In Chapter 2 there was an analogy reference to building the investigative or intelligence puzzle one piece at a time. The reference had to do with an analyst or investigator putting a picture together one piece at a time, using various tools of the trade. But this is not true for all cases, and a bit more clarification is needed. Cases having a nexus to homeland security are inherently going to be different in that personnel will be working with a piece that is not a corner or straight edge. Figure 4.1 demonstrates a piece in the middle of the puzzle, and traditional crime analysis as puzzle pieces with corners and straight edges. Even this may not always be true; it is more likely that homeland security cases are going to fall in the "gray" areas of standard investigative techniques. These gray areas will not have straight edges or corners with which to initiate the building of puzzles. The complexity, sensitive nature, and political nature of homeland security or terrorism cases present challenges not regularly seen in law enforcement since the days of organized crime and large-scale narcotics rings. Modern law enforcement may have lost some of its strategic investigative prowess over the last several decades and transcended into an environment of instant gratification

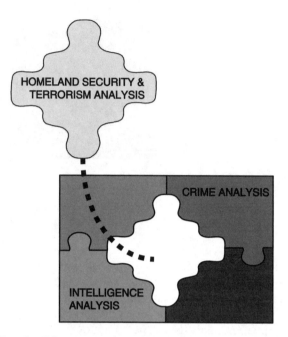

Figure 4.1 In Homeland Security and terrorism analysis, law enforcement will likely not have the luxury of corners or straight lines.

through arrests and case clearances, thanks in part to the use of computers. This is evident in the impact that the "Compstat" process has had on agencies, many of which worked on solely analyzing Uniform Crime Report Part I crimes — statistical management, if you will.

Today, there is a need to prevent the next attack. One of the leading intelligence agencies in the world, the Central Intelligence Agency, encourages the use of alternative analytical approaches in understanding complex transnational issues such as terrorism. In traditional crime analysis, analysts have struggled with "forecasting" crime patterns, often based on the use of historical events. With homeland security, forecasting is not necessarily going to be successful. Use of alternative analytical approaches reaches beyond use of technology. New approaches such as use of calendars, tracing e-mails and Internet protocols, and restructuring data sets will shed new light on topics. Analysts must also be mindful of potential failures when conducting analysis and testing hypotheses. Whether thinking "out of the box," or pursuing the use of new technology or tools, analysts are likely to be working with a deficit data. The reason for this is the lack of specific variables with which to work, missing data, as well as a worldwide theater. Techniques such as timelines, association matrices, link analysis, and data sorting, are and will continue to be staples in the analytical toolbox. These initiatives and forecasting events will continue to be frequently used techniques. However, instead of just forecasting the next attack or performing automated processes, an analyst or investigator should strive to look for behavioral patterns.

Anticipating behavior patterns can be done at the individual and group level. People are predictable and creatures of habit; if you are patient and skilled enough to locate the cues. There are a multitude of possible places to look for the puzzle pieces, usually in a data set.

Since the days of organized crime and narcotics, arguably the biggest change in law enforcement investigative techniques and tools has been the advent of the personal computer and office networks. With this change, agencies have had the opportunity to mine and further data capturing and extraction initiatives. However, the instant gratification component and the decades that have passed may have weakened the law enforcement strategic skill set, including inductive and deductive reasoning skills.

Data set challenges

Perhaps the greatest challenge in the information, analysis, and intelligence process is that of clean data. Imagine working with somewhere between 30 and 80 percent of the information from your jurisdiction, and probably even less if you obtain data from another agency that you are hoping to merge with yours. That's what many law enforcement agencies are dealing with. The reason, data systems, e.g., computer-aided dispatch (CAD) and data tables, are geographically specific to a jurisdiction. With traditional Part I crimes this is a challenge, but with homeland security it can be detrimental.

Names and addresses

Data in many analytical systems stems from CAD imports. The data is raw and limited to the accuracy when reported and that of the data entry specialist. Some agencies validate their data against geographical layers and addresses that do not match and are, at times, removed from their data set. Addresses from outside the jurisdiction, such as those visitors from out of the country, are sometimes entered into the "comments" section. This translates into the data dump that is requested now lacking these addresses because the extraction will come from the primary data table, not the comments. Figure 4.2 shows a fairly detailed data entry format and query screens that would be used by an analyst. In this figure, which is comparatively typical in many law enforcement agencies, there are some inherent problems. First, where and how would you enter a hyphenated name, a name with a suffix such as Jr. or III, and a multipart Hispanic or Arabic name? Second, where would you enter an address from outside the home country, or for that matter, an address from Washington, D.C. that was like 2950 Constitution Avenue, NW, Suite 303? Third, there is no designated field for a country code or formatting for a postal code, which is the sister to the United States zip code. Fourth, in this world of political correctness there are no identifying fields for religion or schooling. Fifth, where would you enter multiple known addresses, and which one gets designated as the primary? Lastly, what about post office boxes or military addresses?

Figure 4.2 Traditional law enforcement databases are often agency/jurisdiction specific.

The first item noted above deals with the mainstay of many law enforcement endeavors: names. Many names throughout the world stem from long-standing cultural origins. Some denote the region or city they are based in, while others may provide a descriptor to the family's line of work. It is likely to be the cultural aspect of naming conventions that will pose the greatest obstacle for law enforcement. While we like to categorize names as belonging to a country, it is the culture that may disclose the information needed to successfully understand the links. One group of names that has received little attention is Arabic names. Outlined below are some of the issues that should be understood when dealing with Arabic names.[2]

- Arabic = given name, father's name, grandfather's name, last name
  - Women are the same but have a female first name
  - After marriage = female first name, husband's name, husband's last name
- Bin or ibn in name = "son of"

- Hyphens are used in Arabic names to draw associations
- Names with KH, DH, GH in them denote that the name is composed of Arabic characters without a Roman alphabet or phonic equivalent
- Many note city of origin, e.g., Tikrit in Iraq = Al-Tikrit

These are just some of the daunting challenges with regard to names that law enforcement must come to understand and deal with. In Figure 4.3 you should note the use of a "Soundex" feature. This is used to aid with the numerous spelling mishaps as well as the multiple ways a name can be spelled, especially Arabic names. Just look at the variations that can be found for Sayyed Qutb. Which one is correct?

Syed Qutb
Sayed Qutb
Sayyad Qutb
Sayad Qutb
Sayyid Qutb

Addressing and locations are perhaps the next challenge. Not everyone follows a world atlas and observes geographical boundaries on a map. Many cultures in the world are, and have been for centuries, nomadic, clannish, and tribal in nature, often following religious values and traits. Just ask yourself, where are Czechoslovakia and the U.S.S.R. on a map today?

Data tools

Data will come from many sources. Besides CAD, the most common data are derived from documentation prepared by the first responder. One of the most comprehensive documents prepared by law enforcement officials, and underanalyzed, is the traffic accident report. Figure 4.3 is an example of the information collected in many traffic accidents. These forms are scrutinized largely due to the financial (insurance) implications and may not be entered in detail into a database, outside of raw CAD data. From a law enforcement perspective, these forms are cumbersome and require a fair amount of time to complete. The forms are rarely analyzed for much more than identifying problem intersections or as a base for studies such as racial profiling. However, from an analytical point of view, especially when seeking out individuals trying to avoid law enforcement encounters, these forms provide a tremendous amount of detail on both parties as well as all the individuals involved directly or indirectly, including witnesses. Names, addresses, identification, insurance carriers, relatives, associates, photographs, and vehicles are just some of the details that can be accessed.

Computers and numerous software packages (e.g., PenLink, I2, and Watson) are all powerful and excellent analytical tools that aid in everyday analysis as well as strategic intelligence. They can even assist in overcoming some of the aforementioned obstacles. However, for some agencies these

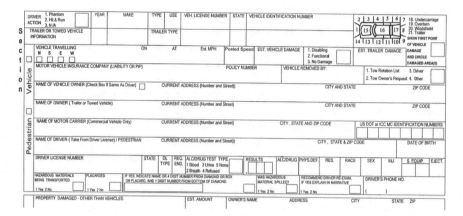

Figure 4.3 Typical representation of details collected in most traffic crash/accident reports.

software packages and suites are cost-prohibitive due to licensing, support, training, and hardware issues. Other tools such as Microsoft Office Suite, primarily Access and Excel, are readily available but like most software packages are not utilized to their fullest potential. The aforementioned is generally due to the operator's comfort level with the product and overall knowledge of the tool's capabilities, as well as lack of training. Regardless of which software or hardware tools are used, reliance on any of them to perform analysis should be carefully monitored. Any analytical/intelligence tool is good, but one should not let them or one's limited knowledge of them drive the analytical process. Remember, someone programmed them to perform a task or identify relational data. The primary problem that exists is the lack of knowledge concerning the data table. Users get too comfortable with the data entry interface and fail to see the true power of the query capabilities. The most powerful query tool and computer is already built into all analysts: the brain and common sense. Computers are great but they only do what someone directs or programs into them. Prior to the age of computers, strategic cases were successfully made, and when you started learning math, calculators were not allowed. You first learned to do things the "hard way." Many analytical/ intelligence training courses and scenarios are heavily focused on computers and software packages; thus we are forgetting to employ our own computer as another tool. With homeland security and terrorism analysis, it is important to use Soundex features and Boolean string and wild card queries. These are invaluable tools, but few understand how to use these tools, largely due to dependence on letting the software perform the link analysis.

Identifying what is needed

In the Heuer's analysis of competing hypothesis (ACH), which will be explained further in Chapter 6, reference is made to making a list of significant

KNOWN	NEEDED	EXPECTED

DIAGRAM WORKING AREA

Figure 4.4 KNED demonstrated.

evidence. The only caution here is that personnel should do everything possible to shy away from "checklists." The reason for this is that they are seen as milestones and can give a false sense of security, because as they are checked off it is easy to assume that the issue has been addressed and put to rest. Just as in ACH and the Macro–Micro–Macro continuum, all aspects should be reconsidered or reevaluated. One way to bring all aspects of the two approaches, common sense and the desire for a checklist, together is through an approach I refer to as KNED (Known, Needed, and Expected Direction) diagram (Figure 4.4). KNED is used to provide an approach for one to extract information that is often overlooked when visualized. This approach will train your visual senses into seeing the entire picture.

Computer programs are limited in their logic capabilities. As simplistic as the KNED process appears on the surface, I have noted over the past two years of teaching this approach, through use of real cases, that many analysts and investigators struggle. The primary assumption for this can be the heavy reliance on computer-based programs. Through the use of this approach I have witnessed that personnel who grasp the concept actually match and outdo computer software in the classroom. Another struggling point is the desire of personnel with arrest authority to develop probable cause and establish the elements of a crime. There is nothing wrong with this desire, but one should be cautioned that there is an underlying desire to focus on that crime and when the elements are not clear the information will be dismissed, forgotten, or other variables will not be pursued. Law enforcement personnel are faced with information overload. Therefore, one must be able to process and make sense of information as it becomes available. One caution, though, is not to put the most recently received piece of information on the top of the pile. Information should be processed in its entirety as it is received. When you jump ahead, the validation of data will suffer and something will eventually be forgotten or overlooked.

To demonstrate the use of Figure 4.4, the following small sample statement will be used.

> April 2006 — An off-duty sheriff deputy working as a security guard at a cigarette wholesaler reports that four men have come into the business and purchased 299 cases of cigarettes. The entire transaction cost was just under $30,000.

This example is from a real case, and while teaching this approach I have found that many law enforcement personnel immediately focus in on the significance of the 299 cases and the $30,000, while others want details on the four men. They immediately surmise that we are dealing with cigarette smuggling or a financial crime. When queried about what information they want regarding the four men, the response often "a complete workup." Can someone please define "complete workup" or even advise what systems or resources they would check? This varies based on the person's skill set, knowledge of data resources, and available technology. In this scenario there is no mention of a crime anywhere. And why focus on the four men? Is there enough to work with, and is there any relevance? Are you striving for an arrest to close the case? There are many other opportunities to glean information, if you know where to start. Traditional law enforcement training has focused on the "subject," and this variable is often described as a male between the ages of 16 and 24. Additional training has exploited the use of technology and use of computers. However, personnel have leaped into the computer age and often forget to use the most powerful computer available to them, their brain. Reliance on computers and software can be detrimental if not seen as what they are, an analytical tool. There is a need to understand the process just like when you first learn mathematics. You don't start learning with the use of a calculator.

Let's break down the above scenario. One, we know that a deputy reported something he thought was unusual or suspicious. We need to speak with this deputy. We expect to understand the circumstances through the deputy's eyes — subjectivity is always involved. Two, we know the deputy is working off-duty. We need to know how long he has been working there. We expect to understand what is considered normal and the time frames involved. Three, we know that we have a cigarette wholesaler. We need to obtain the corporate and business records, and who hired the off-duty deputy. We expect to identify principal parties and understand the volume of business being conducted. Four, we know that four males entered and made a purchase. We need a description of the males, who of the four made the purchase, how it was made, and method of transportation used to get to the business. Five, we know that 299 cases were purchased. We need the significance of 299. Is there a different reporting requirement for 300? We also need to know the weight and how much is contained in the case. We expect to identify a possible violation threshold as well as the possibility of a method of transportation, if we are dealing with significant weight. Six, we know that the entire transaction cost just under $30,000. We need to know the significance of the dollar amount and how the transaction was completed: cash, check, or credit. We expect to identify whether there is a reporting threshold and to identify account ownership information. Seven, we know that we are dealing with a business that deals in large monetary transactions. We need to know if there was a surveillance or camera system and what types of recorded documents are kept. We are expecting possible identifications.

As you can see, there is a tremendous amount of information that can be extracted from just a brief description. Is this overkill? Not if you are working homeland security. The experience and training of the law enforcement professional and available time when working this process will come into play, and overkill will likely be avoided. Had we just worked the typical reaction of looking for a crime, this information may have languished somewhere until further "obvious" developments had taken place. Once the "Needed" column is compiled, you will have that a working list of leads that fellow investigative team members can now work. Once worked, the information gleaned from the needs would then be brought back to the team and reevaluated using the Macro–Micro–Macro continuum. The process would then again be initiated based on the reconciled and validated information. You will also have a method by which to confirm whether a lead has been worked or not. Documented details are essential. Had this information gone directly to a data entry clerk and entered into a database, it may never be directly reviewed. Should the information have come in through a tip there, is another chance that it would be assigned for follow-up and eventually taken at face value, usually within 30 to 120 days.

It has been suggested by some law enforcement officials that a fourth column titled "Outcome" could be added to KNED. The problem with that is someone could easily see that an outcome is noted and dismiss the entire line item as being completed. Also, you should always have an "Expected Direction" for every line item. The reason for that is without it you are just fishing. You need direction for whoever may be assigned the particular "Needed" item. Each line item should be done completely from left to right. I have witnessed individuals tackle this initiative one column at a time. By doing this you are driving with one eye open and will eventually struggle when it comes to completing the last column. You can spend an inordinate amount of time applying this approach to all data. That's where your experience and training will kick in and you will know where to the draw the line.

Forms of analysis that can be used to identify the missing piece

There are many different ways in which to view and contrast data variables. There is no one right way that will work for every occasion. Analysts are encouraged to use multiple forms, usually three, in an attempt to validate their hypothesis. Not all forms utilize or draw from the same data set, and various software packages that perform the same base function can result in different outcomes. Outlined below are some of the more common forms of analysis.

1. Spatial: Geographic information systems (GISs) use techniques to examine and explore data from a geographic perspective to develop and test models and to present data in ways that lead to greater insight and understanding, largely from a visual perspective. This is done through layering geographically matched data over a base map.
2. Temporal: An attempt to understand items that are related by or limited in time, as well as time patterns within data.
3. Tempo: Looking for a characteristic or rate of activity, or pace, in a data set. This can be done by time, day, date, or other event such as lunar and solar.
4. Victim: Attempt to understand behavior or characteristics that can be attributed to the target of the incident. Applies to individuals or a group of individuals.
5. Subject: Attempt to identify behavioral characteristics or traits of a person responsible for a particular action. This may include ideological beliefs, statements, direct actions, and associations.
6. Target: Attempt to understand weaknesses or vulnerabilities attributed to a location or symbolic venue. Applies primarily to physical structures; however, can be applied to individuals who have a strong correlation with, or can be construed as being the same as, the venue either through name or address.
7. Tactic: Means to achieve a goal, or a course of action followed in order to achieve an immediate or short-term goal. This would include type or methodology used to pursue or obtain a goal.

Homeland security and terrorism analysis have placed emphasis on items that have significance. Terrorists perform their own analysis and intelligence. They learn from their predecessors; therefore, analysts need to identify past events. We will focus on two of the above analytical forms employed when reviewing prior events, temporal and tempo — the most common being temporal. The approach to these efforts often centers on use of a calendar. However, there is more to consider when it comes to dates, and they are or may not be what they appear.

Use of calendars and significant dates in your analysis

Calendars and dates have been used in crime analysis fairly consistently in order to represent crime patterns or trends. Identifying which day has historically had occurrences has been utilized in the development of operational and deployment strategies. Use of calendars and dates has been parlayed into many aspects of homeland security and terrorism analysis. One problem, there are differences between the analyses.

Calendars and dates, although used routinely in analysis and intelligence, are ripe for potential misuse and misinformation. The reason for this can be found in the 40-plus calendars currently in use as well as the lack of understanding by many on this matter. Also contributive is the inherent nature of a person to use what is known and subliminally adopt as a standard that everyone uses. Many other differences can be found when using calendars such as years, dates, eras, and religions. When working with calendars there are essentially three rules to remember:

1.   Calendars based on rules: These calendars are specified completely in terms of rules that are independent of astronomical events. Examples are the Gregorian, Julian, and Mayan calendars.
2.   Calendars based on astronomical observation: These calendars require either observation of celestial phenomena (for example, the first appearance of the crescent moon after a dark moon, the astronomical conjunction of Sun and Moon). The Islamic calendar is of this type.
3.   Calendars based on astronomical calculation: These have been based on astronomical observation, but with the development of astronomical theory, calculation of the times of astronomical events has replaced observation. Examples are the Jewish and Chinese calendars.

The Islamic calendar has drawn a considerable amount of attention. It is lunar in nature and follows astronomical observations. Figure 4.5 demonstrates the difference between an Islamic and Gregorian calendar for the calendar year 2006 (there are about 33 Islamic years to every 32 Gregorian). Having brought this to light, is there any significance as to why September 11, 2001 was chosen for one of the most catastrophic terrorist events?

When is 9/11 not 9/11? — depends on the calendar used

The title of this section can cause one to believe that there are only a handful of possibilities. In fact, there are over 40 calendars in use throughout the world. Outlined below is just a sampling of some of the dates associated with the question posed in the section title — when is 9/11 not 9/11?

- Gregorian
    9/11/01
- Julian
    8/29/01
- Mayan
    12.19.8.10.1
- Persian
    1310 Shahrivar 20

SAMPLE COMPARISON OF ISLAMIC CALENDAR VS. GREGORIAN
ISLAMIC DATES BEGIN AT SUNSET THE PRECEDING EVENING

| NY=
NewYear | Aa=
Aashurah | MN=
Miladun-Nabi | IM=
Isra/Me'raj | NS=
NisfuSha'ban | RM=
Ramadan | LQ=
Lailatul-Qadr | BF=
Eidul-Fitr | YA=
Yaum-Arafah | EA=
Eidul-Adha |

Solar Eclipses
T=Total A=Annular H=Hybrid(Tot./Ann.) P=Partial

Lunar Eclipses
t=Total(Umbral) p=Partial(Umbral) n=Penumbral

January
ZHJ 1426/MHM 1427

S	M	T	W	T	F	S
1	2	3	4	5	6	7
ZH	2	3	4	5	6	7
8	9	10	11	12	13	14
8			11	12	13	14
15	16	17	18	19	20	21
15	16	17	18	19	20	21
22	23	24	25	26	27	28
22	23	24	25	26	27	28
29	30	31				
29	30	NY				

February
Muharram 1427

S	M	T	W	T	F	S
			1	2	3	4
			2	3	4	5
5	6	7	8	9	10	11
6	7	8	9	Aa	11	12
12	13	14	15	16	17	18
13	14	15	16	17	18	19
19	20	21	22	23	24	25
20	21	22	23	24	25	26
26	27	28				
27	28	29				

March
Safar/Rabi-I

S	M	T	W	T	F	S
			1	2	3	4
			SF	2	3	4
5	6	7	8	9	10	11
5	6	7	8	9	10	11
12	13	14	15	16	17	18
12	13	n	15	16	17	18
19	20	21	22	23	24	25
19	20	21	22	23	24	25
26	27	28	29	30	31	
26	27	28	T	??	RA	

April
Rabi-I/Rabi-II

S	M	T	W	T	F	S
						1
						2
2	3	4	5	6	7	8
3	4	5	6	7	8	9
9	10	11	12	13	14	15
10	11	MN	13	14	15	16
16	17	18	19	20	21	22
17	18	19	20	21	22	23
23	24	25	26	27	28	29
24	25	26	27	28	29	RT
30						
2						

September
Sha'ban/Ramadan

S	M	T	W	T	F	S
					1	2
					8	9
3	4	5	6	7	8	9
10	11	12	13	p	NS	16
10	11	12	13	14	15	16
17	18	19	20	21	22	23
17	18	19	20	21	22	23
24	25	26	27	28	A	30
24	25	26	27	28	29	30
RM	2	3	4	5	6	7

October
Ramadan/Shawaal

S	M	T	W	T	F	S
1	2	3	4	5	6	7
8	9	10	11	12	13	14
8	9	10	11	12	13	14
15	16	17	18	19	20	21
15	16	17	18	19	20	21
22	23	24	25	26	27	28
22	23	24	25	LQ	27	28
29	30	31				
29	30	EF	2	3	4	5
29	30	31				
6	7	8				

November
Shawwal/Zul-Qa'dah

S	M	T	W	T	F	S
			1	2	3	4
			9	10	11	12
5	6	7	8	9	10	11
13	14	15	16	17	18	19
12	13	14	15	16	17	18
20	21	22	23	24	25	26
19	20	21	22	23	24	25
27	28	29	30	ZQ	2	3
26	27	28	29	30		
4	5	6	7	8		

December
Zul-Qa'dah/Zul-Hijjah

S	M	T	W	T	F	S
					1	2
					9	10
3	4	5	6	7	8	9
11	12	13	14	15	16	17
10	11	12	13	14	15	16
18	19	20	21	22	23	24
17	18	19	20	21	22	23
25	26	27	28	29	ZH	2
24	25	26	27	28	29	30
3	4	5	6	7	8	YA
31						

Figure 4.5 Islamic vs. Gregorian (traditional western) calendar — 1427 vs. 2006.

- Indian
  1923 Bahadra 20
- Hebrew
  5761 Elul 23
- Bahá'í
  Izzat Azamat Vav
- Islamic
  1422 Jumada t'Tania 22
- French Republican
  209 Frucitdor III
- Unix time() value
  1000166400
- ISO-8601 Week and Day, and Day of Year
  Day 2 of Week 37 of 2001
- Excel Serial Day Numbers
  1900 Date System (PC) Excel serial day: 37145
  1904 Date System (Macintosh) Excel serial day: 35683

As demonstrated above, there are clear inconsistencies. The United States Armed Forces follows a Julian calendar, so depending on who or what calendar format is used in any analysis, it is possible that one can draw more than one conclusion. Analysts and law enforcement personnel may spend too much time analyzing dates for significance. After all, what is significant? This will vary based on person, culture, and definition. Following the tragic train bombing events in Madrid, Spain, some analysts and academics looked for significance. It was noted that both events occurred on the 11th ... if you use a Gregorian calendar. Both took place on months that through their numeric equivalent are divisible by three. One last piece that was observed was the continuation of the number three, in the number of years between the two. Is any of this significant? What about the fact that 2004 was a leap year? What is the significance of that, if any?

Dates of terrorism significance

There are many significant dates in the world of terrorism beyond September 11, 2001. Outlined below is an example of many dates that may have potential significance in terrorism based on a traditional western Gregorian calendar. Any date of significance is based on several variables, including personal perception, personal ideology, group ideology, calendar used, religion followed, and culture. Items such as celebrations, major events, or even the weather should be noted when monitoring dates.

This listing is not all-inclusive and is largely based on events that have occurred since 1968. It is also void of many events that have occurred in North America such as abortion clinic bombings, ecological events, and many incidents attributed to domestic-based, Puerto Rican, Jewish Defense League, and anti-Castro groups.

January
  1 — 1964 Palestinian Liberation Organization is formed
  1 — 2001 Hamas suicide car bomb wounds 54 in Netanya
  5 — 1996 Hamas bomb maker, Yehiya Ayyash (The Engineer) is killed
  5 — 2003 Al-Aqsa Martyrs' Brigade detonates simultaneous suicide bombs in Tel Aviv
  6 — 1963 Columbian National Liberation Army (ELN) is founded
  8 — 1998 Ramzi Yousef is given life plus 240-year sentence for 1993 World Trade Center bombing
  12 — 2000 Turkey execution of PKK leader Abdullah Ocalan stayed
  17 — 1991 Operation Desert Storm air offensive begins
  18 — 1982 American University president is assassinated by Islamic Jihad
  20 — 1981 U.S. Embassy, Iran, hostages taken in November 1979 are released
  22 — 1999 France: GIA ringleaders get 8 years for terrorist acts, and 84 others are sentenced in a mass trial

23 — 2003 Daniel Pearl is murdered in Pakistan

25 — 1993 Mir Aimal Kasi kills two and wounds three outside CIA headquarters

31 — 2001 Scottish court finds Libyan al-Megrahi guilty in Pan Am 103 bombing

February

2 — 2000 In France, ETA leader Iglesias Chauvas and member Chonchita Alvarez are arrested for a 1995 plot to assassinate the King of Spain

3 — 2000 Syria and Sudan sign agreement on fighting terrorism in compliance with Arab Antiterrorism Convention

6 — 2000 In the UK, Ariana Afghan flight is hijacked with 20 hostages, eventually released, and the hijackers surrender on February 11, 2000

7 — 1991 In the UK, the Provisional Irish Republican Army is responsible for three-round mortar attack on No. 10 Downing Street, Prime Minister's home

13 — 2000 In Columbia, FARC and ELN stage series of attacks, killing 12 and kidnapping 16

15 — 1984 U.S. diplomat Leamon Hunt is murdered by Red Brigade in Italy

15 — 1999 PKK leader Ocalan is arrested and returned to Turkey, which sets off Kurdish protests throughout Europe

16 — 1992 Hezbollah General Secretary is killed in helicopter ambush

17 — 1988 Marine Lieutenant Colonel William R. Higgins is kidnapped and hanged in Lebanon

17 — 1998 Four al-Gama militants are hung for attacks in 1994 and 1995 in Egypt

20 — 1998 Japanese Red Army member, Tustomu Shiosaki, is sentenced to 30 years for attack on U.S. Embassy in Indonesia

21 — 1970 Swissair jet bombed by PFLP-GC in Israel; 47 killed

22 — 1969 Democratic Front for the Liberation of Palestine founded

24 — 1998 Bin Ladin issues Fatwa that allows attacks on Americans worldwide

25 — 1991 Ground Offensive launched in Operation Desert Storm

25 — 1994 In Israel 39 worshippers at Tomb of the Patriarchs are massacred

25 — 1996 Hamas bombs buses in Jerusalem killing 28

26 — 1993 First World Trade Center bombing kills 6 and wounds 1,000

27 — 1980 M-19 seizes Dominican Embassy in Columbia; ends April 21, 1980

March

1 — 2001 In the UK 21 groups are banned under new terrorism law; LTTE office is the first closed

1 — 2003 Khalid Shaykh Mohammed (KSM) is arrested in Pakistan

3 — 2005 In the Philippines MILF explodes a bomb in a crowded terminal, killing 21

4 — 1999 PKK suicide bomber injures four in Turkey

5 — 1998 In Sri Lanka LTTE is blamed for a bus bomb that kills 37

5 — 2003 Hamas suicide bomber explodes a bomb on a bus, killing 15

7 — 1999 In Bangladesh a bomb kills ten; Harkatul Jihad backed by Bin Ladin blamed

9 — 2002 Suicide bomb in Jerusalem kills 11; Hamas claims responsibility

10 — 2000 LTTE conducts a suicide motorcade attack in Sri Lanka, killing 29

11 — 1999 FARC founders Miguel Pascua and Commandant Oscar are killed in raid

11 — 2004 In Madrid, Spain al-Qaeda detonates 10 of 13 backpack bombs on the train, killing nearly 200

12 — 1993 Bomb attacks in India kill 250

15 — 2001 In Turkey a Russian plane is hijacked

16 — 1984 William Buckley, a U.S. citizen, is kidnapped and killed by Hezbollah

16 — 1985 U.S. journalist Terry Anderson is kidnapped in Lebanon

20 — 1995 Aum Shinrikyo commits a Sarin gas attack that kills 12 on Tokyo subway

20 — 2002 Islamic Jihad detonates a bomb on an Israeli bus, killing 7

21 — 2002 Suicide bomber detonates a bomb in crowd of shoppers in Jerusalem

22 — 1945 Arab League is founded

23 — 1998 In Algeria seven GIA militants sentenced to death for assassinating archbishop

26 — 1978 Egypt and Israel ratify Camp David Peace Accords

27 — 2001 In Algeria Abdelmajid Dahoumane is arrested for New Year's bomb plot

27 — 2002 In Israel Hamas claims responsibility for killing 29 via a suicide bomb

April

2 — 1986 Hawari group is blamed for a bomb that explodes on TWA flight 840 killing 4

2 — 2003 JI explodes a bomb on a crowded passenger wharf, killing 16 in the Philippines

4 — 1986 In Germany the La Belle disco is bombed, killing three

5 — 1988 Hezbollah hijacks Kuwait Airways and kills two

6 — 2001 Algerian Ahmed Ressam (the Millenium bomber) is convicted for New Year's bomb plot

10 — 2002 Hamas kills eight in Israel by detonating a suicide bomb on a bus

11 — 1968 Popular Front for the Liberation of Palestine — General Command (PFLP-GC) is formed

12 — 2002 al-Aqsa Martyrs' Brigade kills six in Jerusalem

18 — 1983 Car bomb explodes in front of the U.S. Embassy in Lebanon, killing 63; Hezbollah is responsible

19 — 1993 Mount Carmel at Branch Davidians compound in Waco, Texas shootout with ATF that kills 79

19 — 1995 Timothy McVeigh detonates a truck bomb at the Alfred P. Murrah Federal Building in Oklahoma City, killing 168

23 — 2000 Abu Sayyaf kidnaps 21 in the Philippines

26 — 2001 The Columbian government withdraws troops and allows ELN to claim territory

May

1 — 1993 Suicide bomber kills Sri Lankan President Premadasa during a May Day celebration

7 — 2002 Hamas kills 15 in a Tel Aviv suicide bomb at a club

8 — 1985 Firebombing of U.S. Citibank and Xerox in Spain

10 — 2002 Chechen separatists are suspected in a remote-control mine attack that kills 41

12 — 2001 ETA is suspected of a car bomb attack in Central Spain that wounds 14

13 — 1991 In Italy Mehmet Ali Agca attempts assassination of Pope John Paul II

13 — 2003 al-Qaeda bombs three housing compounds in Saudi Arabia, killing 20

15 — 1948 Founding of the State of Israel

16 — 1978 Italian Aldo Moro is murdered by Red Brigade

16 — 2003 Simultaneous attacks at 5 locations in Casablanca that kill 42

17 — 1989 Hijacker of TWA Flight 847; Mohammed Ali Hamadei, in 1985 is convicted in Germany

21 — 1991 Prime Minister of India, Rajiv Gandhi, killed by female LTTE suicide bomber

21 — 2002 Shining Path is suspected of detonating a car bomb outside U.S. Embassy, killing nine

22 — 1962 Continental Airlines flight from Chicago to Kansas City becomes the first suicide bombing of an American aircraft — 44 killed

22 — 2001 Abu Sayyaf raids beach resort and kills two

24 — 2000 Israeli troops pull out of Lebanon

25 — 2001 Hamas and PIJ use two suicide bombs at bus station for anniversary of Israeli pullout of Lebanon

26 — 1998 Japanese doctor convicted in Aum Shinrikyo Sarin gas attack in 1995

27 — 2001 Abu Sayyaf kidnaps 20 in raid on a resort

28 — 1964 FARC is founded

28 — 1997 Ship owner is slain in ambush by November 17

29 — 1997 Mohammed Abouhalima is found guilty of first World Trade Center bombing

June

1 — 2001 Hamas claims responsibility for Tel Aviv disco suicide bomb that kills 20

3 — 1989 Ayatollah Khomeini dies after 10-year rule in Iran

5 — 2002 Islamic Jihad uses car bomb to ram a bus and kills 17

6 — 2001 In Canada a bomb maker is charged in 1985 Air India bombing and jailed in Japan

6 — 2003 A taxi rigged with explosives rams a bus carrying Germans in Kabul, killing five

7 — 2000 LTTE suicide bomber kills 22 in Sri Lanka

9 — 1997 Suspected leader of al-Gama is killed in Cairo; 40 members arrested

11 — 1985 Jordanian flight hijacked in Lebanon and the plane is eventually destroyed

12 — 2001 Abu Sayyaf claims beheading of U.S. hostage

12 — 2001 Abu Nidal and three others are tried in absentia in Jordan for a 1984 murder

13 — 1999 Shining Path kills eight in village raid

14 — 1985 Hezbollah hijacks TWA flight 847 and murders U.S. Navy diver

15 — 1972 Cathway Pacific Airways flight from Thailand to Hong Kong explodes from a suitcase bomb that kills 81

18 — 2001 Islamic Jihad suicide bomber kills 19 on bus

19 — 2002 al-Aqsa Martyrs' Brigade kills seven in Israel suicide attack at a bus stop

21 — 1994 Sarin gas attacks kill seven by Aum Shinrikyo

21 — 2001 U.S. indicts 14 members of Hezbollah for Khobar Towers bombing attack that killed 19 U.S. airmen

23 — 1985 Air India flight off the coast of Ireland explodes due to plastic explosives, killing 329

24 — 2000 FARC leader Rey Palacios is captured in Columbia

25 — 1995 Khobar Towers in Dahahran Saudi Arabia is bombed by Hezbollah

27 — 1976 Air France flight is hijacked by PFLP

29 — 1999 PKK leader is sentenced to be hung in Turkey

July

4 — 1976 Israeli raid at Entebbe to rescue 246 hijacked hostages

4 — 1995 In India al-Faran guerillas kidnap U.S. and UK citizens

7 — 1998 GIA leader in Algiers is among 11 rebels killed by Algerian government

7 — 2005 Four bombs explode and kill 56 on subway trains and a bus in London

8 — 1965 Canadian Pacific Airlines explosion kills 52

10 — 2001 ETA car bomb attack in Madrid

11 — 1998 Abu Nidal responsible for attack on Greek island ferry, killing 9

12 — 2000 ETA car bomb wounds ten in Madrid's Callao Plaza

13 — 1999 Muslim militants storm Kashmir camp in India, killing 4

16 — 2000 In Japan Aum Shinrikyo members are sentenced to death for sarin gas attacks

17 — 2002 Greek police arrest leader and founder of November 17

18 — 1994 Hezbollah responsible for Buenos Aires Jewish Community Center bomb that kills nearly 100

21 — 2005 In London, attempted bomb attacks at three Underground stations and on one bus; only the detonators exploded, causing one minor injury

22 — 2002 Hamas leader and 14 others killed in Israeli airstrike

22 — 2003 Uday and Qusay Hussein killed in U.S. raid in Mosul

23 — 2001 Bicycle bomb kills seven in Kashmir

24 — 2001 LTTE attack on international airport and Air Force base in Sri Lanka, killing 18

25 — 1995 GIA suspected in Paris Metro station bombing that killed seven

27 — 1996 Army of God follower, Eric Rudolph, detonates a bomb a Centennial Park in Atlanta during events for the Summer Olympic Games, killing one and injuring 100

30 — 1997 Hamas responsible for double suicide attack that kills 16 in Israel

30 — 2001 Former ETA leaders sentenced to 1,000 years each

31 — 2002 Hamas responsible for bombing at Hebrew University that kills seven

August

2 — 1990 Iraq invades Kuwait

2 — 2000 Hindu pilgrims are killed in India on way to shrine and 102 are killed in Kashmir

3 — 1998 FARC and ELN coordinate attacks, killing 106 soldiers

3 — 2001 London railway station targeted with car bomb and the RIRA is blamed

4 — 2002 Hamas uses suicide bomber to kill nine on Israeli bus

5 — 2003 Car bomb explodes in front of Indonesian Marriott Hotel; Jemmah Islamiya is responsible

6 — 1991 Former Iranian Prime Minister is assassinated in Paris

6 — 2002 Militants attack Hindu pilgrims in New Delhi, killing eight

7 — 1998 Two blasts at U.S. embassies in Kenya and Tanzania kill 224

8 — 2000 Chechen rebels suspected in Moscow Pushkin Square bomb that kills 12

9 — 2002 Grenade blast kills four at Christian missionary hospital in Islamabad

10 — 1987 November 17 detonates bomb near a bus of U.S. airmen

11 — 1982 Member of Palestinian terror group, 15th of May, responsible for bomb on Pan Am flight from Tokyo to Hawaii; 1 killed and 15 wounded

12 — 2001 Suicide bomb in Haifa restaurant kills 21 and PIJ is suspected

14 — 1994 Carlos the Jackal is arrested in the Sudan and extradited to France

15 — 2001 Lashkar-e-Tayyiba responsible for Handwara bombing that kills 18

17 — 1995 Bomb explodes near Arc de Triomphe in Paris

18 — 2001 ETA responsible for car bomb near tourist area near Barcelona

19 — 2003 Hamas suicide bomber detonates bomb on a bus, killing 20

21 — 1995 Hamas suicide bomber on a bus kills five

23 — 2001 ELN is blamed for car comb outside police station that kills one

28 — 1999 Car bomb in Yemen kills six

29 — 2001 Mahmoud Haballah arrested in Canada for involvement with al-Qaeda bombings of U.S. embassies

30 — 2001 LTTE bomb outside building in Kalunai that kills three

September

4 — 1999 Bombing of apartment block in Russia kills 64

5 — 1972 Israeli athletes held hostage in Munich Olympics by Black September and 11 are killed on September 6, 1972

6 — 1970 PFLP begins the simultaneous diversion of a Swissair DC-8 and a TWA Boeing 707 to Jordan, followed 6 days later by the hijacking of a BOAC VC-10. The aircraft are forced to land at Dawson Field, 30 miles from Amman, which was quickly renamed Revolutionary Airport. The planes are blown up on September 12.

6 — 1986 Abu Nidal attacks synagogue in Istanbul, killing 21

7 — 1995 GIA is suspected in car bomb that explodes outside Jewish school in Lyon, France

8 — 1999 Bombing of apartment block in Russia kills 94

11 — 1978 Camp David Accords

11 — 2001 al-Qaeda responsible for four hijackings; two crash into the World Trade Center Towers, one crashes into the Pentagon, and one crashes into Pennsylvania field; nearly 3,000 casualties

13 — 1993 Israel and PLO sign peace agreement

14 — 1986 Bomb at Kimpo airport kills five

14 — 2003 ELN kidnaps eight in Columbia

15 — 2003 Truck bomb detonates outside security building in Moscow

18 — 1997 Bomb on Cairo tourist bus kills nine

19 — 1989 UTA Flight 772 to Paris explodes over Niger, killing 170

20 — 1984 Islamic Jihad responsible for truck bomb at U.S. Embassy in Beirut, killing 23

23 — 1983 Omari Gulf Aircraft bombed in United Arab Emirates, killing 111

24 — 2004 Lashkar-e-Tayyiba suspected of Hindu temple attack in India that kills 31

27 — 1987 November 17 responsible for U.S. Commissary bombing in Greece

29 — 1998 LTTE blamed for shooting down Lionair flight in Sri Lanka killing 55

29 — 2003 FARC blamed for motorcycle bombing that kills ten

Between September and October in 1984 the town of Dalles, Oregon about 80 miles from Portland, experiences a bioterrorist attack when followers of the Indian guru Bhagwan Shree Rajneesh spike salad bars at 10 restaurants in town with salmonella and sicken about 750 people with the goal of changing a political election.

October

1 — 1995 Shaykh Omar Abdel Rahman is convicted in New York bomb plot

1 — 2001 Jaish-e-Mohammed is responsible for suicide bomb in Srinagar that kills 38

2 — 2000 LTTE suicide bombing kills 23 in Sri Lanka

3 — 1996 November 17 blamed for Greek NATO bomb attack

4 — 2000 Shining Path leader captured in Peru

5 — 2000 LTTE suicide bomber kills ten in Sri Lanka

6 — 1973 Yom Kippur War begins

6 — 1981 Egyptian President Anwar Sadat is assassinated by Egyptian Islamic Jihad

7 — 1985 The Achille Lauro cruise ship is hijacked

12 — 2000 Boat bombing on the USS *Cole* that kills 17 in Yemen; al-Qaeda responsible

12 — 2002 Multiple car bombs explode outside nightclubs in Bali, killing 202; Jamaah Islamiyya responsible

15 — 2003 Palestinian terrorists bomb a U.S. Embassy motorcade, killing three

16 — 1997 LTTE truck bomb at hotel next to Trade Center in Colombo kills 18

17 — 1995 GIA suspected in Paris subway bombing

19 — 2000 LTTE suicide bomb wounds 23 in Sri Lanka

20 — 1981 Antwerp synagogue bombed, killing two

21 — 2002 Car bomb explodes next to bus in Karkur, killing 19; PIJ suspected

23 — 1983 Islamic Jihad bombs U.S. Marine barracks in Beirut, killing 299

23 — 2002 Chechens seize theater in Moscow, taking over 800 hostages

29 — 1975 Three Black September members hijack Lufthansa flight

November

1 — 1955 Dynamite bomb kills 44 on a United Airlines flight from Denver to Portland, Oregon

4 — 1979 U.S. Embassy in Tehran seized and 66 taken hostage

4 — 2001 PIJ responsible for shooting attack on Jerusalem bus

6 — 2001 ETA suspected in Madrid rush-hour car bomb that wounds 100

7 — 1985 M-19 captures Supreme Court building in Columbia, more than 100 killed

8 — 1987 PIRA bombs Remembrance Day celebration in UK, killing 13

9 — 2003 al-Qaeda suspected in Riyadh residential compound attack that kills 18

10 — 2003 Luxury residential compound in Saudi Arabia bombed, killing 17

13 — 1995 Car bomb at U.S. military facility in Riyadh kills seven

14 — 2002 Mir Amai Kasi executed for 1993 attack outside CIA building

17 — 1973 Group November 17 takes its name for student uprising on this date in Greece that kills 34

19 — 1995 Egyptian Islamic Jihad bombs Egyptian Embassy in Islamabad

20 — 2000 Hamas responsible for roadside bomb that targeted Israeli school bus

20 — 2003 al-Qaeda responsible for vehicle bomb in front of British Consulate General, killing 30

23 — 1985 Egyptian plane hijacked by Abu Nidal in route to Malta; 60 killed

23 — 1996 Hijacked Ethiopian plane crashes in Comoros Islands, killing 127

25 — 1984 The 25 April Movement responsible for U.S. Embassy mortar round attack

28 — 2002 Three suicide bombers drive vehicles into the front of the Paradise Hotel in Kenya, killing 15

29 — 1987 Korean Airlines Flight 858 is blown up, killing 115

December

1 — 2001 Hamas responsible for two suicide bombing attacks in mall that kill ten

3 — 1984 Hezbollah Islamic Jihad hijacks plane bound for Tehran

6 — 2000 LTTE suspected for landmine attack that kills four bus passengers in Sri Lanka

12 — 1983 Hezbollah responsible for U.S. and French embassy attacks in Kuwait

14 — 1987 Founding of Hamas

16 — 1983 PIRA bombs Harrod's Department Store in London, killing nine

17 — 1996 MRTA rebels take 700 hostages at Japanese Ambassador's residence in Lima, Peru

18 — 1999 LTTE blamed for two bombings in Sri Lanka, killing 34

21 — 1975 Carlos the Jackal kidnaps 11 OPEC ministers in Vienna

21 — 1988 Libya responsible for Pan Am Flight 103 bombing over Scotland, killing 259

23 — 2001 Richard Reid attempts to ignite an explosive device concealed in his shoes on an American Airlines flight from Paris to Miami

25 — 2000 Bomb blasts in India and Pakistan by Jamiat-μl-Mujahedin kill 11

27 — 1985 Abu Nidal attacks Rome and Vienna airports, killing 18

27 — 2002 Chechens blamed for two suicide bombers with truck bombs, killing 72

28 — 1972 Black September seizes Israeli Embassy in Thailand

30 — 2000 Abu Sayyaf blamed for series of bombs in Metro Manila that kills 16

Learning from past behavior

Regardless of the group, terrorists have historically learned from their predecessors. Whether a significant date or a failed attack, a terrorist can garner information about prior incidents quite easily, especially in the United States. Entrepreneurs and the corporate world have exploited the use of the Freedom of Information Act or Sunshine Records Laws to gather case records and files. They then consolidate, link, and repackage the information that some agencies already had and sell it back to law enforcement and others. Figure 4.6 demonstrates an example of repackaging. This reference is not meant to be negative. Law enforcement agencies do not always have the skill set or time to prepare such information.

One reason a terrorist or terrorist group would find such information attractive is the detail. A cursory review of law enforcement personnel with security clearances working homeland security over the past 2 years has revealed an interesting fact having to do with how many people refused to discuss case information, but once an arrest was made they failed to pursue having the court record sealed. I have walked into classes with an affidavit and information from agency cases that provided what may be considered too much detail. Some even provided the Who, What, Where, and When. There are Web sites that exploit these documents and sell them for as little as $2.00.

Figure 4.6 Public records laws afford opportunities for individuals and businesses to gather data. These data are then "repackaged," computerized, and sold publicly in easy-to-use formats such as the example here.

Skill
Knowledge
Resource
Access (ability)
Motive

Figure 4.7 Five key components analysts should look for when identifying terrorist activity.

A terrorist group would seek out these documents to learn details such as what brought their actions to the attention of law enforcement, techniques used by investigators to gather information, and locations and individuals used. They are essentially looking for the same thing investigators are: skills, knowledge, and resources. In an open society information is often too readily available, and there is a hesitancy to seal documents.

Looking for SKRAM

Analysts and investigators need to be cognizant of what goes into developing a terrorist activity or event. Many variables and individuals will ultimately come into play. The issue of variables has been discussed. When looking into individuals, or subjects, there are five components that should be explored in depth. It is important to be aware of not only the individual but also the group. The five components are outlined in Figure 4.7, SKRAM (Skill, Knowledge, Resource, Access[ibility], Motive).

Behavior patterns of individuals and groups are to some degree dependent upon SKRAM. Many organizations and their affiliated groups (such as the Irish Republican Army and Palestinian Liberation Organization) have remained fairly consistent with tactics they have employed for years. When putting the pieces together you will be continually looking for items that will comprise SKRAM. Say that a terrorist organization is going to deploy a "dirty bomb" somewhere in a particular country. Without the Skill and Knowledge within their membership to build a dirty bomb, there is little chance this can occur. If this scenario were in question, you should determine whether they have the Resources necessary to build one or have access to one. Access to a location and/or ability to carry out the attack is also essential. The last piece, Motive, is probably the easiest to develop. All aspects of

SKRAM can be attainable if you know where to gather the requisite information needed for successful analysis. SKRAM components can often be found in recruiting attempts, techniques, and locations.

Recruiting opportunities

Perhaps one of the greatest opportunities for law enforcement to regularly thwart terrorist activities is at the recruitment level. If terrorists cannot successfully recruit, their activities will be stymied or altogether eliminated. This tactic by the law enforcement community has been successful on many fronts. From street gangs to organized crime, membership is the key. One place to find many malcontents (potential recruits) in a single location is a jail or prison. Typical street gang members to organized crime figures, including the drug cartel type, can be found in an institution designed to rehabilitate. Although these groups might appear to have little in common, they tend to find common ground on ideology and religion. Many already have hatred toward the government or another segment of the population.

Prisons — recruitment and communication

According to *The Sociology and Psychology of Terrorism: Who Becomes a Terrorist and Why?* individuals who become terrorists are often unemployed, socially alienated individuals who have dropped out of society.[3] This describes most people incarcerated in prisons. Beyond ideology and social adjustment, religion is rapidly growing behind bars. One of the fastest growing religions is Islam. Couple this with the years that idle minds have to formulate thoughts or be molded, there is little doubt why the prison population would be fertile ground for recruitment. However, from a law enforcement perspective, prisons are overlooked largely due to the perception that the arrest is complete. The amount of information available at the prison level is phenomenal. Accuracy and details prevail, in most instances. There is little expectation of privacy outside of legal or religious interactions. Essentially, the law enforcement community has a venue in which individuals must find covert ways to communicate internally and externally. Organized crime figures have for years continued to run their criminal enterprises from within the prison system. The same is true of terrorists. An example is an Egyptian man named El-Sayeed Nosair who is serving a life sentence in New York for the 1990 murder of Rabbi Maier Kahane in Manhattan. Nosair was also indicted for his involvement in the plotting of the 1993 bombing of the World Trade Center while in prison.

Ability to communicate from within

Nosair was not the first and will certainly not be the last to communicate from behind prison walls. Another example of terrorism continuing to operate behind bars is the case of Sheikh Omar Abdel-Rahman, also known as

RESTRICTIONS ON SHEIKH ABDEL RAHMAN'S
COMMUNICATIONS FROM PRISON

16.   Beginning in 1997, and continuing to the present
day, the Bureau of Prisons (at the direction of the Attorney
General) pursuant to 28 C.F.R. § 501.3, imposed Special
Administrative Measures ("SAM") upon SHEIKH ABDEL RAHMAN.   I have
reviewed the SAM and related documents.   A summary of certain
provisions of the SAM is set forth below.

17.   Among other things, the SAM limited certain of his
privileges, including his access to the mail, the media, the
telephone, and visitors, for the express purpose of protecting
"persons against the risk of death or serious bodily injury" that

Figure 4.8 Court record limiting Abdel Rahman's access to the world outside of prison.

the Blind Sheikh. In October 1995 Sheikh Abdel-Rahman was convicted of engaging in a seditious conspiracy to wage urban terrorism in the United States, which included the 1993 World Trade Center bombing and plots to blow up landmarks (an FBI building, and the Lincoln and Holland Tunnels). In January 1996, he was sentenced to life plus 65 years in prison. Beginning in 1997, the United States Bureau of Prisons imposed special administrative measures (SAMs) upon the Sheikh, who was serving his sentence at the United States Penitentiary Federal Medical Center in Rochester, Minnesota. These measures limited specific privileges such as access to mail, media, telephone, and visitors, for the purpose of protecting others (Figure 4.8). Despite this, he still found a pipeline by which to communicate with members outside prison.

Federal prosecutors charged four associates of Abdel-Rahman with helping the Islamic militant to continue to direct terrorist activities from his U.S. prison cell, as noted in the indictment (Figure 4.9). Abdel-Rahman's lawyer, Lynne Stewart, an Arabic translator, and two others were charged with providing "material support of a terrorism organization" by helping Abdel-Rahman pass and receive messages while incarcerated in a federal prison cell.

Communication from within prison walls is neither new nor limited to terrorists. Over the past several decades organized crime figures and street gangs have sought out methods by which to continue their criminal enterprises. Everything from tattoos to sign language has been used. Analysts must not rely solely on modern technology to intercept communications. Old methods of communication such as International Morse Code or use of Mayan images, are now used by inmates and others. Individuals using these methods are acutely aware of the technology employed by the law enforcement community, and they may even know the community's weakness,

UNITED STATES DISTRICT COURT
SOUTHERN DISTRICT OF NEW YORK
- - - - - - - - - - - - - - - - -X

UNITED STATES OF AMERICA   :

         -v.-   :   INDICTMENT

AHMED ABDEL SATTAR,   :   02 Cr.
     a/k/a "Abu Omar,"
     a/k/a "Dr. Ahmed,"   :
YASSIR AL-SIRRI,
     a/k/a "Abu Ammar,"   :
LYNNE STEWART, and
MOHAMMED YOUSRY,   02CRIM. 395

                                            :

         Defendants.

                                            :
- - - - - - - - - - - - - - - - -X

                    INTRODUCTION

      The Grand Jury charges:

           Background: The Islamic Group

      1.   At all relevant times described herein, the

Islamic Group, a/k/a "Gama'a al-Islamiyya," a/k/a "IG," a/k/a

"al-Gama'at," a/k/a "Islamic Gama'at," a/k/a "Egyptian al-Gama'at

al-Islamiyya," (hereinafter, "IG") existed as an international

terrorist group dedicated to opposing nations, governments,

institutions, and individuals that did not share IG's radical

interpretation of Islamic law. IG considered such nations,

governments, institutions and individuals as "infidels," and

interpreted the concept of "jihad" (struggle) as waging

opposition against infidels by whatever means necessary,

including force and violence.

Figure 4.9 Federal indictment for associates/acquaintances of Abdel Rahman.

which is "old" methods of communicating. To find this in practice today one just needs to visit a prison or review tattoos used by street gangs.

Prisons and other correctional facilities and their potential for recruitment were highlighted as a concern in an April 2004 U.S. Department of Justice report. In this report, which reviewed the Federal Bureau of Investigation's counterterrorism program post 9/11, it was noted that correctional intelligence was essential to Joint Terrorism Task Forces (JTTF). In Operation TRIPWIRE, an initiative designed to identify sleeper cells, JTTF members are identifying existing or former sources who are incarcerated and are involved in radical elements. The report noted that between September 2001 and April 2004 the efforts of Operation TRIPWIRE in gathering correctional intelligence led to the identification of approximately 370 connections between inmates and various terrorism investigations, as well as potential terrorism-related activity within the prisons.[4]

Gangs — today's street terrorists

According to the National Drug Threat Assessment 2004 Executive Policy Summary, there are an estimated 850,000 active gang members in the United States alone.[5] Every one can be seen as a potential recruit for a terrorist organization. Many gangs have received notoriety over the past 20 years, e.g., Latin Kings, Bloods, and Crips. Some groups have been alleged to have ties to terrorist organizations. One such group was the El Rukns. In 1986, members of the El Rukn street gang in Chicago plotted with Libyan leader Muammar Abu Minyar al-Qaddafi to obtain rocket launchers and to perpetrate terrorist acts against the United States in exchange for money. On the European and German front, the gang that set the stage for interacting and training with terrorist organizations such as the PLO and IRA was the Baader-Meinhof Gang, which eventually became known as the Red Army Faction (RAF). The RAF referred to its members as "urban guerrillas." It operated from the 1970s to 1998, causing great civil unrest, especially in the autumn of 1977. The RAF killed dozens of high-profile Germans in its more than 20 years of existence.

However, in the era of trained and violent organizations one stands above all: the MS 13.

MS 13 and SUR 13

Mara Salvatrucha (MS), also known as MS 13, an El Salvadoran street gang that grew out of the El Salvadoran civil war, emerged in Los Angeles during the 1980s in an area heavily populated with Mexican gangs. The group adopted the number "13" in its name (M is the thirteenth letter of the alphabet). Since its beginning, the gang has successfully migrated from southern California to the east coast, with a significant presence in over 30 states including Virginia, Maryland, North Carolina, Pennsylvania, Texas, Washington, DC, and New York City. They are also spreading to Nicaragua, Panama, Guatemala, Mexico, and Honduras.

During the 1980s, California gangs were divided into sureños (southerners) and norteños (northerners). These were umbrella terms used mainly in the prison setting for Hispanic gangs in California. Sur 13, also known as Sureño 13, originated in southern California; however, its formation is different from that of MS 13. As gang members began to appear in the southwest and on the east coast, they referred to themselves as both Sur 13 and sureños. However, as California gang members representing various southern gangs migrated from the state, many began to unite under the name sureño.

Some of the differences between MS 13 and Sur 13 are that MS 13 migrated to the east coast, maintaining ties with California-based members and members of La Mara in El Salvador. Sur 13 gangs on the east coast are emulators, rarely connected to the west coast sureño gangs. MS 13 tattoos and graffiti include both "eme" and "ese" (Spanish for the letters M and S), while Sur 13 does not include "ese." Although both are Hispanic, MS 13 membership tends to be El Salvadoran, while Sur 13 consists mostly of Mexican nationals. Regardless of this, these differences may not always remain constant, and change or adaptation is always possible.

In March 2005 federal agents together with local law enforcement effected the arrests of over 100 members of MS 13 in seven cities throughout the United States. The reaches and membership are largely unknown. Cliques of the MS 13 are prevalent in the United States, Canada, and Central America. The actual membership numbers are not known, but it has been suggested by federal law enforcement authorities that the numbers in the United States alone may be in the neighborhood of 50,000. Law enforcement officials have expressed concern about the emergence of MS 13 and its potential to partake in terrorist activity either independently or as part of a larger organization such as al-Qaeda.

MS 13 criminal activity has included homicide, robbery, drug trafficking, money laundering, illegal exports, and auto theft. In encounters with members of this formidable gang, law enforcement personnel have noted numerous identifying features of members, e.g., large gothic-style tattoos, the area code where the clique originated in the tattoos, theatrical happy or sad faces, three dots on the hands or face signifying "Mi Vida Loca" (my crazy life), as well as the number 13. The reference to the number 13 may be in a mathematical component such as the numbers 6 and 7, which add up to 13. The wearing of bandanas and the colors blue and black are also prevalent.

Street gangs are not the only means to recruit potential terrorists. Many organizations claim to be student organizations or associations, often found near or on the campuses of higher education. Much like gangs, they seek to exploit their ideology and find individuals who may be weak minded or who seek a sense of belonging.

Besides traditional methods such as lectures and writings, modern day anarchists, extremists, and radicals have found a new medium, music.

Music — another means to recruit

Rap, hip hop, religious, and rock music are some music genres that can be used to spread ideology, hate, and extremist points of view. Growing up, some people have felt that the biggest difference between themselves and the prior generation was the music. This is still true. During the explosion of rap artists many young people thought it was chic to be or follow "Gangsta." Now some are following a jihad, terrorist, or extremist point of view and associating with some questionable parties.

In February 2004 a British-based group calling themselves Sheikh Terra and the Soul Salah Crew produced a rap video called "Dirty Kuffar," an Arabic term that refers to a non-believer. Distributed by British Muslim extremist Mohammed al-Massari, many aspects of this propaganda video are geared toward a jihad and recruiting point of view. Some striking images splash across the screen, and wording such as "peace to Hamas and Hezbollah." Images such as KKK and Nazi members seem out of place in a jihad rap song — unless you are seeking to recruit.

Dirty Kuffar is not the only song with a questionable existence. Many other music groups, particularly in the hip hop genre, may be considered extremist. A Puerto Rican group from Brooklyn, New York, The Mujahdeen Team or The M-Team, has appeared at Islamic Circle of North America (ICNA) and Muslim American Society events. Like Sheikh Terra and the Soul Salah Crew, Mujahdeen Team refers triumphantly to the September 11 attacks. This group exploits the world of electronic media and even has a site on myspace.com, a favorite among thousands of youths. Electronic forums by these fringe elements should be monitored. Besides chat rooms, Web sites, and instant messaging, groups can exploit the use of hidden code within music disks to launch Web site videos. Regardless of the means or purpose, there is much to be learned in this formidable venue. Use of music is not without controversy, though.

There is some debate with regard to music in the Islamic religion and Muslim culture. Perhaps the largest debate surrounding music in Islam is the issue of whether it is allowed or forbidden. Some people believe that music is pure and a beautiful creation of God Almighty, who set the tone for everything in the universe. Therefore, if it is a creation of God it should be enjoyed. According to the same segment of the population who believe the Quran is complete and perfect, there is no prohibition of music or singing. Prohibition of music is allegedly attributed to some scholars and clerics who interpret the Quran and follow man-made laws and books of Hadith and Sunna.

One thing that cannot be debated is the use of music to sway society's youth, regardless of the country. Music is a powerful and inspiring tool. Every group, from white supremacists to jihad extremists, uses music and song to express its beliefs. The Palestinian government used music on a grand scale, complete with an orchestra, to celebrate the life of their first female suicide bomber, Wafa Idris. This event was broadcast on television on July 24, 2003. Idris had detonated a 22-pound suicide bomb in Jerusalem in late January 2002 that killed her and an 81-year-old Israeli man, and injured more than 100 others.

Chapter concepts

1. The complexity, sensitive nature, and political nature of homeland security cases present new challenges necessitating new ways to look at data.
2. Data and data sets pose challenges in the way information is collected, database field structure, data relationships, and data cleanliness.
3. Arabic names present unique issues in databases due to naming conventions and spelling inconsistencies.
4. A process for reviewing and analyzing information is KNED: Known, Needed, and Expected Direction.
5. The seven common forms of analysis are: spatial, temporal, tempo, victim, subject, target, and tactic.

6. In homeland security and analysis, dates are considerations to understand, such as the need to understand 40-plus calendars and what constitutes significance.
7. Importance of knowing past initiatives in the effort to understand current and future behavior.
8. Looking for SKRAM in homeland security analysis and investigations as well as recruiting efforts; also looking for additional recruiting and SKRAM variables in gangs, prisons, and music.

References

1. Deputy Chief of Staff for Intelligence, *Military Guide to Understanding Terrorism in the Twenty-First Century*, U.S. Army Training and Doctrine Command, August 15, 2005, p. 2–1.
2. Anonymous, *A Law Enforcement Guide to Understanding Islamist Terrorism*, First Capital Technologies, LLC, Baton Rouge, LA, March 2003, pp. 82–87.
3. Hudson, R.A., *The Sociology and Psychology of Terrorism: Who Becomes a Terrorist and Why?*, Federal Research Division, September 1999, p. 20.
4. U.S. Department of Justice Federal Bureau of Investigations, The FBI's Counterterrorism Program Since September 2001, Report to the National Commission on Terrorist Attacks Upon the United States (14 April 2004), p. 15.
5. National Drug Intelligence Center, http://www.usdoj.gov/ndic/pubs10/10330/#Gangs, National Drug Threat Assessment 2004 Executive Policy Summary (25 February 2006).

chapter five

Gathering information, the key to the process

Several definitions of what constitutes the duties of an intelligence or crime analyst have been debated throughout the law enforcement profession since at least 1972. This was noted in a review of numerous job descriptions from around the United States in March 2000. Although at all levels and professions these analysts perform a wide range of tasks and skill sets, researchers consistently noted that gathering, analyzing, and disseminating crime information are among the daily duties of those they examined.

When gathering crime information for a law enforcement agency concerned with predefined jurisdictional limitations, most information is derived from one source, the offense and incident report. The inherent restriction here is that the information is limited by the fact that it must be reported. Therefore, it is reactive; and it must be written from the perspective of the responding officer, thus it is subjective. Other forms of information used by law enforcement come from a variety of sources. Outlined below are some additional informational sources along with their restrictions or potential concerns.

- Confidential Informants
  - Concerns — what is the source, is the source documented, has the source been "black balled," what is the source's motivation?
- Covert Operations
  - Concerns — what is the format of the operation, what are the jurisdictions' legal requirements, what are the time constraints or periods?
- Interview and Interrogation
  - Concerns — what is the legal basis for the interview, is the case criminal or informational, what are the limitations or arrangements?
- Open Sources
  - Concerns — what is the source, has the source been validated and corroborated, is it being used as a basis for furtherance of a case, how is it accessed?

- Equipment
  - Concerns — what type of equipment is used, what is the training of the operator of the equipment, what are the legal requirements of its use, is it automated or manual?
- Professional Interchange
  - Concerns — what is the relationship, are there any biases, is the information factual and based on documentation or just hearsay?

In dealing with terrorism, these restrictions must be exploited and exposed. Being proactive is a must, and in order to spawn intelligence you need as much information as possible, for without information you will have no intelligence. There is no such thing as a bad source, only bad information. Information equals intelligence, not the other way around. Gathering or obtaining good, clean, timely, and accurate information is key.

Intelligence gathering

The primary objective of intelligence gathering "is to deal with future danger, not to punish past crimes."[1] This rings especially true in the world of terrorism. Although you are not seeking to punish past crimes, you cannot discount their usefulness when attempting to understand the future. In the world of law enforcement, intelligence has often been used in a reactive manner to formulate and establish policy.

Information is endless in terms of quantity. There are no limitations to the resources that can create useful and viable information. Perhaps the best source of information is that which comes from human sources. However, in law enforcement the use of undercover officers and informants is limited. The costs and risks associated with such operations are exponential. Also, many of the terrorist groups and organized hate groups are closed societies and are difficult to infiltrate. Therefore, much of the information gathered comes from traditional sources such as reports, search warrants, anonymous tips, public domain, and records management systems. This information is used to populate various investigative databases.

When investigating a crime or developing answers to ongoing patterns, series, or trends, law enforcement personnel often rely upon numerous databases and records management systems. These systems, the majority of which are based on offense reports, are used to gain information and insight to prior incidents with similar signatures or modus operandi. Police reports, field interview cards, property pawn transactions, public records, and traffic citations are some additional common sources of information on known criminals. Ordinary street criminals often have lengthy arrest histories and numerous encounters with law enforcement officers documented on their criminal records. Criminals do not seek to have run-ins with the law, but they do not shy away from them. Terrorists, on the other hand, go to great extremes to avoid detection. As noted in the profiles of the September 11, 2001 hijackers, other than a traffic infraction they had little if any contact with the law enforcement community. Therefore, gathering information on these individuals requires analysts to think outside the box and to identify nontraditional sources of information. One example of these sources would be purchases that perhaps an ordinary person would not make, especially if in bulk. Other sources would be the Internet, published material, court records, handouts, radio (including citizen band and ham radios), and self-published books such as *The Turner Diaries* and *Hunter* by Andrew MacDonald.

There are inherent difficulties in categorizing terrorism that are compounded by the shaping of policy for a type of behavior that fits poorly into more familiar categories. "Terrorist acts are both crimes and forms of warfare, and in both respects are unlike what we are used to."[2] Understanding the larger possibilities, such as warfare, law enforcement will be able to make informed decisions on matters concerning data collection. When gathering information, it is important to document and standardize every step of the process. This will alleviate any complications when categorizing behaviors or activities and will ensure that all participants in the process are on the same playing field.

Terrorism is different from street-level crime on many fronts. "Most crimes are the product of greed, anger, jealousy, or the desire for domination, respect, or position in a group, and not of any desire to 'improve' the state of the world or of a particular nation."[2] When gathering information or intelligence for homeland security, one must be cognizant of the differences between most crimes and terrorism. It is important to think globally and not just make decisions about collection based on jurisdictional parameters. When dealing with terrorism, most law enforcement databases are not structured to capture information from a wide array of sources. Intelligence databases, if designed for a single-use agency, should be designed with the understanding that the information may be exported for use outside the jurisdiction; otherwise, information may need to be integrated from other sources. In addition to the jurisdictional parameters placed upon an analyst and those self-imposed, other restrictions may include politics, interpretation of regulations, exotic military operations, and fear of impending actions.

The gathering of information can be complex or rudimentary. Regardless of the degree to which an agency is willing to develop a database, there are nine basic considerations that should be captured in detail.

Individuals
Associates
Relatives
Employers
Telephone subscribers
Organizations, groups, or gangs
Businesses
Corporations
Educational records/background (missing in most law enforcement data sets)

Use of these nine basic considerations for gathering detailed information on matters of homeland security, terrorism, or hate crimes will greatly aid the investigative and analytical processes, especially if the information is shared with multiple jurisdictions. Remember to include owned or leased properties, e.g., vehicles and office space, with respect to individuals and the like. By doing this you will identify other potential variables to use in link analysis. These nine considerations will allow for immediate link analysis and will readily demonstrate interrelationships and associations. In order to do this in an expeditious manner, analysts often turn to their records management systems. There are some inherent problems with relying on only one system. If an agency is using an off-the-shelf records management system, it will generally be insufficient for use as a criminal intelligence database. These systems do not usually automatically collect all of the nine basic considerations. Many systems capture dispatch and self-initiated activities but more in-depth information is needed, and this will probably come from documents prepared by the first responder. Other problems center on the method or style of the tabular data fields. Bad addresses, incorrect zip codes, and the inability to capture information from outside a particular jurisdiction are prevalent in most databases.

Role of the first responder

The gathering of information must start somewhere. In the field of law enforcement, information gathering is initiated when a responding officer, or first responder, is dispatched or comes upon an incident or scene. The first responder is the eyes and ears of intelligence analysis. Traditionally, the starting point for the formal process of data gathering for most law enforcement agencies is the moment that documentation begins and an offense incident report is generated. For years, officers would respond to an incident, record relevant facts, and document the incident in a manner designed to encompass all elements of the crime being investigated. The importance of detailed data gathering in a post-9/11 world cannot be limited (as a once-famous fictional television character would say, "just the facts"). Although critically important, facts are routinely centered on criminal statutes and utilized to fulfill the requirements of probable cause in order to successfully prosecute an offender. While this is extremely important and should not be overlooked, first responders need to expand their reporting repertoire to include details that may seem mundane or inconsequential to the incident being addressed. Link analysis and corroboration of information are dependent upon details, e.g., telephone numbers for cellular phones and pagers, addresses, apartment numbers, or property. If analysts and investigators cannot link similarities, only have generalities with which to work, or have to follow up on an investigation to gain details, valuable time is wasted. As the saying goes, time is money, but in homeland security and terrorism, time can save lives.

Officers must be trained in what to look for and on how to accurately portray or explain details within a police report in order for it to translate properly into databases. Traffic stops provide perhaps the best opportunity to harvest information. Outlined below are some traffic stop indicators that may provide assistance and warrant further investigation.

- Driver entering through a minor border checkpoint (Washington State — Millennium bomber)
- Driver mainly drives rental cars (Japanese Red Army and 9/11 skyjackers)
- Driver adheres to major interstates
- Driver use of valid drivers license and state identification card (need to integrate with society)
- Invalid or expired visas or possession of passports
- Vehicle contains weapons, propaganda, or residue
- Vehicle plates or registration differ from drivers license
- Peculiar license plates, homemade plates, or no plate
- Bumper stickers (e.g., "Abolish the IRS" or "Remember Waco")
- Decorations or militia identification numbers
- Vocal resistance to documentation (citing constitution or bible)
- Anti-government literature

Human intelligence is usually the most desirable form of gathering information, but this can be extremely difficult in the world of terrorism. Officers are essentially forms of human intelligence that, if trained properly and if shortcuts are avoided, can yield leads and details that may prove beneficial in the future. This should be evident when one reviews some of the more notable leads and arrests that have been made possible by traffic stops initiated by road officers. Outlined below are a few samples of some high-profile traffic stops:

- 2002 — al-Aqsa Martyrs' Brigade Suicide Bombers (Israeli National Police) stopped en route to a mission
- 2001 — Mohammed Atta (Tamarac, Florida) ticketed for invalid drivers license and ultimately had a bench warrant for his arrest issued
- 2001 — Zaid Jarah (Maryland State Police), al-Qaeda 9/11 skyjacker, stopped for speeding on 9/9/2001; car was found at airport following the attacks
- 2001 — Hani Hanjour (Arlington, VA), al-Qaeda 9/11 skyjacker, stopped in vehicle with New Jersey tag and had a Florida drivers license, stopped for speeding
- 1999 — Ahmed Ressam (Port Angeles, WA) stopped by U.S. Customs, possessed two Canadian drivers licenses, airline ticket New York to London, hotel reservation in Seattle, used a route that did not require him to go through Victoria, British Columbia — Millennium Bomber

- 1994 — Timothy McVeigh (Oklahoma State Trooper), no license plates, *Turner Diaries*, carrying a weapon, wearing a shirt that read "The tree of liberty must be refreshed from time to time with the blood of patriots and tyrants"
- 1988 — Yu Kikumura (New Jersey State Police), Japanese Red Army bomber, vehicle stopped for routine violation; led to discovery of bomb materials

Address data, which often come from traffic stops or details, are crucial in just about any law enforcement database. Quite often, address data will not be verified or questioned. Knowing one's jurisdiction is something most officers have ingrained in their minds from day one. By knowing the community, officers should have an advantage over subjects and possess the insight to question addresses and information provided by them. Use of a post office box, cluster box, packing company group box, shelter, or "refused" or "unknown" as a residential address is not sufficient and will only delay investigations. Another problem is the number of reports that show addresses of occurrence as being the police department, jail, impounded lot, hospital, or as vague as "Smith's Department Store on Main Street." All of these scenarios will not only delay investigations but will also negatively impact the use of analytical databases, link analysis software, and geographical information systems.

Details are the most important factor in developing quality intelligence that can be readily validated. When dealing with the typical street criminal or investigating a street crime, many investigative leads are developed through generalities such as a subject being described as a white male with a specific tattoo or mark. This is because many street criminals have encountered law enforcement officials at some point, by arrest, field interviews, pawned property transactions, or traffic stops, and law enforcement systems are laden with known subject descriptors obtained from the various encounters. Thus, criminal justice information systems are lined with a wide array of relational attributes on these suspects that, once queried, will provide numerous workable leads for investigators. The same cannot be said of potential homeland security and terrorist suspects. These suspects go through great pains to avoid law enforcement encounters and attempt to fit into the mainstream as everyday law-abiding citizens. Perhaps the greatest chance for a first responder to encounter potential suspects is through traffic crashes, traffic stops, or random calls for service, when potential suspects may only be seen as witnesses or neighbors at the time. Timothy McVeigh, the Oklahoma bomber, was initially apprehended for a traffic stop. Based on this, it is vitally important that first responders document in detail all encounters with individuals, including place of work, educational facility currently attended, phone numbers (beeper and cellular), alien card, passport, drivers license, and license plate numbers. It is equally important to document details about associates who may accompany a suspect. Just as important for investigators to remember is the fact that many road officers keep "informal" notes for traffic stops and encounters either on their copy of the citation that they issue or notebooks. Items such as mannerisms and conversations may be noted in detail.

First responders or road officers routinely conduct traffic stops, subject checks, and field interviews. These are golden opportunities to gather information that will dramatically enhance any homeland security database. In order for this to be effective, questions must be asked in detail. One thing an officer asks for is identification. For many officers, presentation of any form of a drivers license or state-issued identification card suffices as authentic and legitimate and causes little concern or need for further questioning. However, this is a new era in law enforcement. Officers should question all forms of identification and should look for multiple sets of documents, use of different addresses, and evidence of tampering. If other individuals are accompanying the subject, questions should be asked for the purpose of comparing intentions and knowledge of one another. Also, information obtained by examination of vehicles or residences, in accordance with applicable laws, for signs of foreign travel (i.e., photographs, maps, video cameras and tapes, airline and hotel receipts, training manuals, and radical or questionable writings), is extremely important and should be recorded in reports, as further questions may be warranted. These items are just the beginning. Many crimes can yield further links or, through the use of search warrants, can corroborate previously received information.

Crimes and incidents that may yield information or links

Just about any encounter with law enforcement may yield a link to the missing piece of the homeland security and terrorism analytical puzzle. The key is to have the opportunity to attain that piece, no matter how mundane or insignificant it may appear at the onset. Many crimes or incidents that first responders encounter provide the greatest opportunity for gathering valuable details for inclusion in their reports. The information received by first responders is fresh, and any reported scene is likely uncontaminated. In this section, several types of crimes and incidents that warrant careful review and consideration in the analytical process will be explored.

Stolen identities

One type of reported crime that can be directly associated with those in the terrorism trade is that of stolen identities (use of someone else's personal information) and issuance of fake or stolen identification papers, e.g., social security cards, drivers licenses, passports, resident alien cards, military identification, and credit cards. Modern technology has made counterfeiting identification about as easy as desktop publishing. Identity crimes provide access to financial venues and a way to fit into the mainstream of society. Identity theft is often considered a nuisance and a crime that is a challenge to investigate. This type of crime is not one that attracts the attention of the media or that of high-ranking members of law enforcement. It is viewed as a white-collar crime that lacks the violence of homicides and home invasion robberies. However, if you analyze the potential direct and indirect relationships that are possible through this type of crime, it is not difficult to fathom the potential gains that may be realized by a terrorist. One attractive feature of identity theft is that the chances of detection and arrest are minimal. If apprehended, the time sentenced might be minor, and the crime can be carried out by street criminals or organized enterprises through technology from just about anywhere in the world. This makes it more complex for local law enforcement personnel to pursue.

False identification

Other problems related to the manufacture or sale of false or altered identification are possession of false identification and lack of supporting documentation. Incidents such as these are often encountered by first responders on traffic stops or in field interviews. Officers seldom question the identification's authenticity unless there is some obvious indicator. Although response times and minimizing the time calls are being held for dispatch are areas of concern for road patrol officers, failure to question a document's authenticity may make the critical difference. Documentation of the identification in question and responses to questions should be noted in an incident report. In the case of an arrest, impoundment of the document and making of copies, as well as notification of concerned government entities are crucial to follow-up investigators. In the case of foreign residents, visitors, and registered aliens, identification items such as passports, alien cards, visas, airline tickets, and hotel bills are all forms of supporting documentation that should be readily accessible.

Counterfeiting of goods

Today it is difficult to tell what's real or fake because of the sophistication of today's counterfeiters. Counterfeiting to many is seen as a business, an illegal one, which has a high profit margin and low probability of apprehension. Everything from clothing, leather goods, alcohol, toys, electronic media, and pharmaceuticals are routinely counterfeited and sold worldwide. The problem is so widespread that Fortune 500 companies spend millions of dollars each year to fight counterfeiters. Some of the more popular countries that are the originating point of counterfeiting are Hong Kong, Peoples' Republic of China, Mexico, and Korea. In Asia the problem is so bad that a museum of counterfeit goods was built in 1989. Estimates demonstrate that the counterfeiting problem is over $500 billion in sales each year. Bogusly branded items are found on the WorldWide Web, flea markets, businesses, and street corners. Outside of customs inspectors and trained investigators, few officers know the signs of a counterfeit item from a real one.

Illegal trafficking of cigarettes

One type of crime associated with aiding terrorist groups is illegal trafficking of cigarettes and smuggling of cheap cigarettes across state lines. This is done to avoid paying higher taxes and to resell them at greater profits. In the early 1990s, law enforcement personnel in the Miami, Florida area conducted several operations, known as Operation Gaza Strip, targeting illegal cigarette sales and government-subsidized food stamps. The targets of the operations were mom-and-pop convenience stores, most of which were owned and operated by individuals of Middle Eastern descent, and were in lower-income and high-crime areas. Allegations were raised that the profits gained from the illegal acts of the subjects were being routed to individuals in the Middle East, possibly to support fundamentalist causes. State and federal charges were eventually brought against a multitude of individuals, but charges of supporting terrorism were never brought, because this was not even considered then. Now, the climate has changed. Fast-forward 10-plus years to Charlotte, North Carolina, where nearly 20 individuals were charged with numerous crimes, some of which included smuggling cheap cigarettes to Michigan. The individuals were characterized as from a Charlotte-based cell that aided terror. At least one individual of Middle Eastern descent was found guilty of sending $3,500 to the militant (terrorist) Lebanese group Hezbollah. He was also convicted on 16 separate counts and was sentenced to a series of consecutive prison terms that add up to 155 years.[3]

Cigarette traffickers can easily make somewhere between $50 and $70 per carton of cigarettes sold illicitly. Because of the great potential to make money, and low penalties if apprehended, cigarette trafficking to support terrorism can be popular. More important is the fact that various terrorist organizations have been involved. Groups such as Hezbollah, Real Irish Republican Army (RIRA), Islamic Jihad, and the Kurdish Workers Party (PKK) have directly or indirectly benefited and made millions of dollars from the cigarette trafficking trade. It is important to note that research indicates that Internet sales of cigarettes are somewhat prevalent in places such as Gibraltar and the Colon Free Trade Zone.

Misappropriation

Thefts of any magnitude should be reviewed in order to identify potential internal leakages or outright misappropriation of items that can be used for illegal activities, such as construction of explosive devices. Large-scale theft, in particular, is another type of crime that poses a potential problem. Many of these crimes take the forms of truck hijackings, cargo thefts, construction thefts, industrial thefts or losses, in-transit (airlines, shipping, and railway) thefts, and military-related crimes. The attractiveness of these crimes is twofold. The criminals are often in or go through remote areas, and there is little or no security. Whether the theft is to further a campaign of terror or to sell for financial profit, large-scale thefts provide opportunity to gain access to mass quantities of chemicals, fertilizers, explosives, fuel, technical equipment, and logistical support items and items used in the making of explosives. Items classified as explosives should pose the greatest concern. However, most law enforcement personnel are unaware of the numerous items that can be used as explosives or in developing explosives, and there should be concern that any theft of these items may be classified as theft of chemicals or merely be lost in the shuffle. In addition to thefts, mere possession of any of the explosive compound materials warrants immediate attention, but again, for what should law enforcement be looking? This question is addressed in the provisions of Section 841(d) of Title 18, United States Code (USC), and 27 CFR 55.23. The director of the ATF must publish and revise at least annually in the Federal Register a list of explosives determined to be within the coverage of 18 USC Chapter 40, Importation, Manufacture, Distribution, and Storage of Explosive Materials (Appendix E). Chapter 40 covers not only explosives but also blasting agents and detonators, all of which are defined as explosive materials in Section 841(C) of Title 18, USC. While the list is comprehensive, it is not all-inclusive. The fact that an explosive material may not be on the list does not mean that it is not within the coverage of the law if it otherwise meets the statutory definitions in Section 841 of Title 18, USC. Also, some chemicals may be inert, and if stolen in one jurisdiction may not receive further immediate attention. However, the counterpart to the inert chemical may be stolen in another location by other members of a group and if combined can create an explosive. That is why it is imperative that any possession or theft of any material listed on the ATF list be identified and investigated immediately.

Cargo crimes

Cargo crimes, a largely unregulated area due to lack of statutory coverage, are often documented as thefts, burglaries, or robberies. There is no precise data collection process in place within the United States. According to the South Florida Cargo Theft Task Force, there is as much as $25 billion in cargo direct merchandise losses each year. A single tractor-trailer can have between $1 and $2 million in merchandise that can be easily sold or used by the person who steals it, and if captured, the risk of being jailed for an extended period of time is likely to be less than for a bank robbery. Also, robbing a bank has a high risk factor associated with it, and for the most part a low return, usually about a couple of thousand dollars. Analysts should be cautious when dealing with cargo crimes. Most cargo crimes are a result of tractor-trailer thefts. This seems simple, but on many occasions the tractor may be recovered in one jurisdiction and the trailer in another without the cargo. The problem is that when this takes place, the reporting agency may consider the case closed once one component is recovered and further review or investigation is discounted.

Another consideration regarding cargo crime is what is referred to as leakage. This is the removal of property or insertion of articles, including explosives, without tampering with or removing the container's seal. There are many methods of doing this, but the two most common are by removing bolts and panels or drilling out rivets. Once access is gained, the subjects conduct the illegal act and reinstall the hardware without the knowledge of the driver, who may be picking up the trailer or container from a port. This process can also be reversed, and individuals may place items into a container outside the country without tampering with the seal.

Cargo crimes come in several different forms and involve a wide variety of merchandise. Some items that are routinely targeted due to their high ticket value are computers and peripheral devices, cellular telephones, cigarettes, alcohol, perfume, and designer clothing. In a 1998 publication,[4] a cargo security expert noted that access to automated computer files is of serious concern because these files contain sensitive shipping information that allows criminal insiders to case entire shiploads of containers for the most lucrative cargoes. Shipments can even be electronically passed to other destinations via computers and may go undetected for weeks, especially if the shipment is transnational. This same article noted several emerging trends in cargo crimes. The first trend involves an insider who is part of the criminal conspiracy or is paid off. The second is international infiltration of cargo transportation systems. The third is fraud. Fourth is the widening intelligence information gap on cargo theft. Fifth is the stealing-to-order phenomenon, where specific items are taken in order to fill a specific request. Besides the lucrative financial advantages, cargo crimes provide an international nexus for foreign-based terrorist organizations to exploit. One area of concern cargo theft detectives focus on is seaports. This is because seaports are critical gateways for the movement of international commerce. More than 95 percent of our non-North American foreign trade arrives by ship. According to JayEtta Z. Hecker's testimony concerning container security in 2001, approximately 5,400 ships carrying multinational crews and cargoes from around the globe made more than 60,000 U.S. port calls. More than 6 million containers (suitable for truck-trailers) enter the country annually.[5]

An additional form of cargo is that of humans. Human trafficking or smuggling has recently been making a blip on the federal radar. Law enforcement personnel should not dismiss or overlook the amount of funding associated with human trafficking and understand the laws associated with this form of modern slavery.

Suspicious vehicles

Incidents involving suspicious vehicles (especially rental vans and trucks) and suspicious persons should be immediately reviewed for consideration. Instead, these incidents are often filed away as information for future reference or "not reported" by the responding officer, due to no police action being taken. Also, civil matters such as landlord and tenant disputes or defaulting on a lease should be given consideration, particularly if they occur at strange hours or involve instances where no apparent justification is given. Reports for incidents such as those just cited should be written in great detail and include complete suspect and associate information, identification used by the suspect, actions taken by the suspect, time periods covered, vehicle information, method or form of payments made, and the existence of security monitoring videotapes, if any.

Found or abandoned property

The last type of incident that may yield leads is found or abandoned property, particularly if symbols or foreign writings are on the property. Such items often go straight to "property and evidence" rooms pending claim by the rightful owner, or they undergo some form of legal destruction. These items should not be overlooked. Property items deserving further review are computers, packages and letters, baggage, photographs and drawings, contraband, weapons, and anything labeled with foreign markings or symbols. Certain guidelines, limitations, and restrictions must be followed concerning entry of these items into a criminal intelligence database.

Gathering limitations and restrictions

Gathering intelligence information and entering it into a criminal intelligence database, whether for the purposes of homeland security, terrorism, monitoring of hate groups, or criminal enterprises, is governed by state and federal legislation. The predominant regulation in the United States is set forth in the 28 Code of Federal Regulation (CFR) Part 23, and is interpreted in guidelines updated and maintained by the U.S. Bureau of Justice Assistance. 28 CFR Part 23 is a guideline for law enforcement agencies operating federally funded multijurisdictional criminal intelligence systems under the Omnibus Crime Control and Safe Streets Act of 1968. It provides information for submission and entry of criminal intelligence information, security, inquiry, dissemination, and review and purging. It does not provide specific information on how standards should be implemented by individual agencies.

The CFR makes it clear that entry of information into a criminal intelligence database must be supported by reasonable suspicion. This applies to databases that will be shared with other law enforcement agencies that may be classified as criminal intelligence, intelligence case information, or similar designations. On an evidentiary scale, as shown in Figure 5.1, reasonable suspicion is just above mere suspicion (a hunch) and just below probable cause, the standard for initiating an arrest.

Figure 5.1 Evidentiary scale.

The federal regulation 28 CFR Part 23, 23.20 (C) defines reasonable suspicion as follows:

> Reasonable suspicion or Criminal Predicate is established when information exists which establishes sufficient facts to give a trained law enforcement or criminal investigative agency officer, investigator, or employee a basis to believe that there is a reasonable possibility that an individual or organization is involved in a definable criminal activity or enterprise.

Case law suggests that reasonable suspicion as applied in the context of whether information should be entered into a criminal intelligence database will not necessarily be the same as when applied to situations supporting the stop and frisk of a suspect. In court cases, reasonableness should be judged objectively from the perspective of a cautious and prudent law enforcement officer based on the officer's experience and training. Additional guidance and information relating to reasonable suspicion can be found in the following court cases:

Ornelas v. United States, 517 U.S. 690, 696, 1966
Illinois v. Wardlow, 528 U.S. 119, 124, 2000
U.S. v. Jimenez-Medina, 173 F.3d 752, 756, 9th CA, 1999
U.S. v. Garzon, 119 F.3d 1146, 1451, 10th CA, 1997
Jackson v. Sauls, 206 F.3d 1156, 1165, 11th CA, 2000

Federal regulation 28 CFR 23.20(a) goes on to state that a system will only collect information on an individual if there is reasonable suspicion that the individual is involved in criminal conduct or activity and if the information is relevant to that criminal conduct or activity. A 1998 policy clarification removed any ambiguity regarding information not supported by reasonable suspicion, declaring that the entry of individuals, entities, organizations, and locations that do not fall under reasonable suspicion can be included providing this is done solely for the purposes of criminal identification or is germane to the criminal suspect's activity. However, three requirements must be met prior to placing such information into a criminal intelligence database:

Appropriate disclaimers must accompany the information, noting that it
is strictly identifying information and carries no criminal connotations.
Identifying information may not be used as an independent basis to
meet the requirement of reasonable suspicion.

The individual who is the criminal suspect identified by this information
must meet all requirements of 28 CFR Part 23.

There is no limitation on nonintelligence information being stored on the
same computer system as criminal intelligence information, provided that
sufficient precautions are in place to separate the two types of information
and that access is limited to appropriate personnel. Law enforcement agency
personnel should be cognizant of various state public record (Sunshine) laws
before storing information on the same computer system. The above
standards are only applicable to agencies that enter information into a multijurisdictional intelligence database, such as with task forces investigating
homeland security, terrorism, and hate groups. Single-agency databases
where no information is supplied outside the agency may maintain information in their agency. They would be subject to internal policies and procedures
as well as state public record laws. In either scenario, personnel should be
cognizant of record-purging requirements. Some locations require that
information and intelligence not currently active or without activity during
a specified time period, often between 2 and 5 years, be purged.

Tips

Gathering information from tips is another gray area that should be reviewed
cautiously. Limitations and restrictions concerning tips vary from state to state,
but if they are entered into a multijurisdictional criminal intelligence database
as enumerated above, they are subject to many of the same guidelines.

Tips are vital sources of information. They can come from a variety of
sources, internal and external, such as informants, anonymous letters, tip
lines such as Crime Stoppers, and online e-mails and forms, such as the one
established by the FBI that allows anyone to submit information via their
Web site. However, it is important to remember that tips are stand-alone
pieces of information that need to be evaluated, verified, and corroborated
prior to being acted upon and entered into a criminal intelligence database.
Tips should be kept separate or be denoted as pending verification. Every
detail of the tip, including the date and time received, caller (if known),
nature of the information, and investigator assigned to followup, should be
entered into a data form in order to avoid miscommunication.

Once a tip is received, it must be assigned for a timely investigative
followup so that a determination of status can be made promptly. If it is
determined that the information does not have lasting value, it should be
removed from the database. Tip information should be reviewed every 90 to
120 days after entry to determine whether reasonable suspicion has yet been

developed, thus justifying its move to the criminal intelligence database. Review processes can be continuous if warranted. However, if no real developmental activity is demonstrated on a tip, it should be purged from the system after 2 years. This will ensure that a data set remains relevant to the mission at hand and is not a conglomeration of information that can possibly result in erroneous leads or links.

Regardless of whether a law enforcement agency has only an internal database, a database in which information is shared with multiple jurisdictions, or a database just for the purpose of tracking tips, there should be a written protocol to follow, as well as formal training. In addition, agencies should back up their data daily and have security measures in place to limit access and avoid being compromised.

Intelligence gathering and information interpretation

Interpretation of the information gathered is dependent upon analytical and investigative techniques used to transform it into intelligence. In a publication from the CIA, it was reported that "Major intelligence failures are usually caused by failures of analysis, not failures of collection. Relevant information is discounted, misinterpreted, ignored, rejected, or overlooked because it fails to fit a prevailing mental model or mindset."[6] Analysts and investigators need to keep open minds, be creative in approaches, and avoid assumptions that are not based on fact and corroboration.

Information that has been gathered according to the guidelines above — properly standardized, formatted, and entered into a secure criminal intelligence database — is the starting point for the intelligence interpretation phase. However, no matter what the quality of the data or the magnitude of the database, it is analytical processes that extricate the intelligence. One workflow process that is followed is referred to as the intelligence cycle.

In the cycle, noted in Figure 5.2, there are five steps that constitute the cycle: planning and direction, collection, processing, all source analysis and Production, and Dissemination. These five steps are used to develop raw information into a finished intelligence product for use by policymakers. Many law enforcement and investigative entities follow this process, including the Central Intelligence Agency (CIA). Regardless of who employs the intelligence cycle, the approach is the same. However, the differences are likely to be in the volume of information available, manpower, law enforcement mission, technology, and legal limitation. There are several pieces that are constant but will vary based on the depth of analysis. These items would include jurisdictional concerns, problems, or personalities in various contexts — political, geographic, economic, military, scientific, or biographic. Current events, capabilities, and future trends should also be examined.

In order to attain success in the intelligence cycle there are several basic data collection techniques along with goals that law enforcement personnel can pursue. The goals of basic intelligence analysis are:

Figure 5.2 Intelligence cycle.

- Identify and define existing conditions
- Identify, rapidly, changes in existing conditions
- Accurately anticipate trends from existing conditions

In addition to the goals, analysts will generally categorize or pursue leads based on three identifiable pre-incident indicators. Three of the more common breakdowns that are used for the purpose of link analysis or intelligence gathering are:

- Group Related
    - Ongoing campaigns
    - Protests against the treatment of member
    - Names, dates, commemorative actions
    - Visible group preparations for activity
- Target Related
    - Specific collection or threats against a target
    - Actions by the target that place it in focus
    - Prior activity directed against the target
- Incident Related
    - Previous threats and announcements of intent
    - Tips from other sources
    - Equipment stolen, logistic movements, rehearsals, prior attacks

Regardless of the goals or incident indicators used, it is essential to have an approach and to know the data. Random querying based on a mere hunch or memory is like driving with one's eyes closed. Analysts must have a hypothesis or a structured analytical problem as their roadmap, and then they can start breaking down the information into manageable or working parts. Listed below are four general "intelligence gathering and interpretation" factors.[7] These factors and/or the above variables should be used as a starting point when initiating analysis concerning homeland security, terrorism, or organized hate groups:

1. Group information — Name(s), ideology (political or social philosophy), history of the group, and dates significant to the group (including dates on which former leaders were killed or imprisoned); publications (some groups also have a bible or manifesto that outlines activities — current, future, or hypothetical); gatherings, meetings, and rallies (often posted in periodicals or on the Internet).

2. Financial information — Sources of funds, proceeds from criminal activities, bank account information (domestic and foreign); the group's legal and financial supporters (generally, anyone who would write an official letter of protest or gather names on a petition for a terrorist is a legal-financial supporter, and sometimes an analysis of support will reveal links or mergers with other terrorist groups).

3. Personnel data — List of past and current leaders; list of active members and former members; any personnel connections between its members and other groups of similar ideology; group structure, particularly if the organization's pattern is based on columns and cells; and the skills of all group members, e.g., weapons and electronics expertise, and explosive training. (Knowing the skills of the group is an important part of threat assessment. If the philosophy revolves around one leader, it is important to know what will occur if something happens to that leader. Often, the analysis of family background is useful to determine how radically a leader or member was raised or to identify military tenure or training.)

4. Locational data — Location of group's headquarters; safe houses; training facilities owned or attended; and stash houses, where weapons and supplies may be stored. (It is important to specify the underground to which terrorists can flee. This is more difficult than determining safe havens. Terrorists also usually prefer to live in communal homes rather than alone.)

One way of conceptualizing the information is through the use of a table. Placing the above information into a table provides an at-a-glance reference for investigators and analysts to use to view the data, and provides an easy reference for future reports. This is demonstrated, based on four well-known international terrorist organizations, in Table 5.1.

Besides giving a starting point to the intelligence process, use of the four working parts will allow for sharing of the workload among agencies or personnel. Once the intelligence gathering process is initiated and completed in detail, the basic interpretation process can be undertaken. One analytical method that can be used is referred to as the "loop effect."[8] This method

Table 5.1 Sample Intelligence Table

	Tupamaros (Uruguay)	IRA (Ireland)	ETA (Basque)	Red Brigade (Italy)
Type and History	Revolutionary; urban student radicalism	Nationalist; second-class treatment	Nationalist; unique language	Revolutionary; economic change
Aim	Socialist economy	United Ireland	Own nation	Societal betterment
Organization	Students organized sugar workers into cells	First tried military battalions, then cells	Shadow government, central committee	Pyramidal paired cells called brigades
Strength	Two per cell, 3000 members	Five per cell, 2000 members	700 members	800 actives, 8000 underground
Attacks	Sabotage, demonstrations	Protests, clashes, executions	Demonstrations, assassinations	Kidnapping, robbery, extortion
Social	Students and sympathizers	Average age 21, married with children	Average age 25, middle class	Average age 27, radicalized students, criminals
Support	Ideological neo-Marxist support	Relatives and friends abroad	One-third mass support, some ideological Marxist support	Many sympathizers; ideological Maoist support
External Aid	Cuba	Russia, United States, PLO, others	France, Cuba, Russia, Libya, links to IRA, PLO	Czechoslovakia, links to Sicilian Mafia

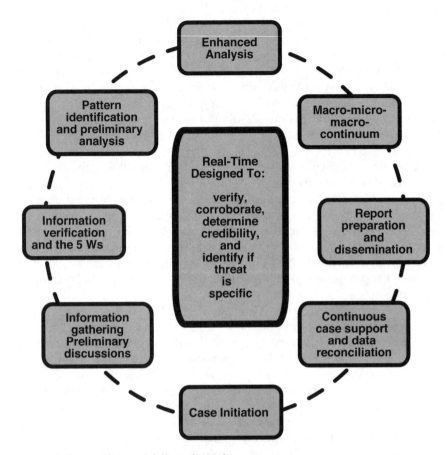

Figure 5.3 Loop effect and follow through.

was initially employed as a tactical and investigative tool, but with some minor adjustments it is easily adaptable to investigations concerning terrorism and organized hate groups, as shown in Figure 5.3. The loop effect is a step process for analysts to ensure continuous follow-through, thus the "loop" reference.

Every piece of information, case, or report has a starting point, referred to as case initiation. The first two steps in the loop effect are the gathering of raw information manually and electronically. Analysts receive and categorize the information as it arrives, seeking to prioritize it according to protocols and attempting to identify items needing immediate attention. Steps one and two are the triage of analytical work.

The third step of the loop effect is also an information-gathering component, but the information gathered here comes from an investigator or an analyst asking questions and looking for initial associations and verifications. Questions asked center on the five Ws: who, what, where, when, and why, and usually how. Once the questions are satisfactorily answered, the analyst begins the preliminary analysis, looking for pattern identification.

The fourth component of the loop effect is identification and documentation, and would also be characterized as basic analytical techniques.

These first four components, coupled with basic analytical techniques and followed by the four intelligence-gathering and interpretation parts, are only the beginning. Up to this point in the process, an analyst has undertaken massive amounts of information, striving to validate and identify patterns early on. Tentative conclusions should not be drawn until further investigation can be done to substantiate any findings and enhanced analytical steps can be initiated.

Step five consists of enhanced analysis. During this step, an analyst transforms the information and preliminary intelligence into a viable intelligence product. Relationships and associations will be elaborated upon and inferences drawn. Many variables will be examined using a wide range of analytical techniques including spatial and temporal analysis, victim, offender, and target analysis, threat and vulnerability assessments, and financial and toll record analysis. The list of techniques and tools is virtually unlimited and depends greatly on the skills, abilities, and data awareness of each analyst.

Once all available resources are examined, step six will come into play: the Macro–Micro–Macro continuum, which is explained in depth in Chapter 6. Analysts and investigators have traditionally gathered information, reviewed it, investigated it, drawn conclusions, and reacted. The Macro–Micro–Macro continuum phase does not discount the work already performed, but as a precautionary measure it provides for a second look at the data to ensure that conclusions are consistent with the available variables and that the intelligence was corroborated.

Step seven is the end product. Analysts prepare reports, maps, and bulletins designed to aid management in making informed decisions. The final step is a given for most intelligence units: continuous case support and data reconciliation. The latter two steps will be explained in further detail in Chapter 6.

The entire loop effect is designed to work in real-time environments in order to ensure verification and corroboration, determine credibility, and identify specific threats and their severities. Once the basic requirements are fulfilled, analytical personnel are ready to begin the enhanced stage, transforming information into intelligence.

Evaluating the information used

Information that is retained either in an intelligence file or intelligence database should be continually evaluated and determined to be reliable and the content valid prior to entering and using it in the analytical process. Source reliability can often be noted as one of four categories: reliable, usually reliable, unreliable, and unknown. Content should also be checked for validity and confirmed where known. With the aforementioned considered, it is the classification of criminal intelligence information that will be the greatest challenge when dealing with data. Classifications will continually evolve and be subject to change and the agency determining the category in which to place the data. Items classified as restricted should be based on credible facts not just because it is under the guise of homeland security. Classification systems and dissemination criteria should be defined and consistently implemented. The Law Enforcement Intelligence Unit (LEIU) recommends the following classifications:

Sensitive — significant case currently under investigation, informant iden-
    tification data, or reports that require strict dissemination requirements
Confidential — information that is received through official law enforce-
    ment channels and is for law enforcement personnel only
Restricted — reports that were previously classified as confidential or
    sensitive and no longer require those classifications
Unclassified — the general public can obtain direct access or open
    source information

It is the last classification, unclassified, that is often overlooked. On many occasions agencies fail to check the reliability of their source and will start in a higher classification listing and work downward. The flow should go upward and be based on credible, reliable, and valid information regardless of the nature of the case.

Chapter concepts

1. The gathering of information can be complex or rudimentary. Therefore, developing an understanding about the topic by everyone
   involved and using a standardized approach are essential.
2. There are nine basic considerations when gathering information:
   individuals, associates, relatives, employers, telephone subscribers,
   organizations, businesses, corporations, and educational records/
   background.
3. Thorough gathering of information is the role of the first responder.
   Detailed questions including the five Ws need to be asked.
4. Analysts and investigators need to look beyond routine street crimes
   in order to identify incidents that may yield information or links to
   terrorist activities.
5. State and federal laws and guidelines govern intelligence-gathering
   limitations. When entering information into a criminal intelligence
   system or database, reasonable suspicion is required.
6. There are four types of information classifications — sensitive, confidential, restricted, and unclassified — when working with criminal
   intelligence information.

References

1. Heymann, P.B., *Terrorism and America: A Commonsense Strategy for a Democratic Society*, MIT Press, Cambridge, MA, 1998, p. 129.
2. Heymann, P.B., *Terrorism and America*, p. 7.
3. Associated Press, N. Carolina man gets 155 years in scheme that aided terror group, *The Miami Herald*, final edition, p. 22A.
4. Badolato, E., Current and future trends in cargo security, *Security Technol. & Design*, August 1998, pp. 15–16.
5. Hecker, J.Z., *Container Security Current Efforts to Detect Nuclear Materials, New Initiatives, and Challenges*, U.S. General Accounting Office, p. 2.
6. Heuer, R.J., Jr., *Psychology of Intelligence Analysis*, Center for the Study of Intelligence, Central Intelligence Agency, 1999, Chap. 6, p. 1.
7. O'Connor, T., Counterterrorism Analysis, http://faculty.ncwc.edu/toconnor/392/spy/terrorism.htm, Intelligence Gathering and Information, November 20, 2002.
8. Cooper, J., Nelson, E., and Ronczkowski, M., Tactical/investigative analysis of targeted crimes, in *Advanced Crime Mapping Topics*, National Law Enforcement and Corrections Technology Center, Denver, CO, April 2002, p. 31.

chapter six

Enhanced analysis: transforming information into intelligence

Enhanced analysis is where "the rubber meets the road." Up to this point in the analytical process, personnel have primarily been cleaning data and analyzing information using broad approaches. Transforming the information into quality intelligence requires time and skill. Whether some forms of analysis are art or science is debatable. In the case of homeland security and terrorism analysis, it is both. Methods employed by an analyst can be replicated for use on many different fronts. In addition, there are numerous scientific models and tools available for analysts that can be utilized by anyone to prove or verify information. The data should yield the same results for whoever undertakes the process.

Use of a checklist is encouraged but not relied upon, due to the magnitude of events that can be faced by an analyst undertaking terrorism or organized hate group investigations. Too many steps are involved in the intelligence process, and information often arrives at intermittent times, making organization of the information difficult. Matrixes, link charts, time lines, and maps also play important roles in transforming information into enhanced intelligence. Whatever techniques are used to analyze the information, it is crucial to know one's criminal data and what information is available. In warfare, one needs to know the enemy, and in the analytical world one needs to know the enemy (subject or target) as well as the data. If you do not know what you have, how can you transform it into intelligence? What you see in data is determined to a large degree by the sum total of your knowledge, experience, and training.

Analyzing: transforming information into intelligence

Philip B. Heymann pointed out in his book about international terrorism that "A primary objective of intelligence acquisition abroad is to anticipate the action of terrorist groups."[1] This is also true for domestic-based groups. Applying this premise to the realm of law enforcement requires some adjustment. For years, analysts and investigators have spent the majority of their time focusing on linking, locating, and reacting to a suspect's action in hopes of facilitating an arrest. Forecasting and predicting a particular course of action for a suspect and responding to it is not the norm for many law enforcement managers, who usually focus on certainty, control, and the bottom line. Managers must alter their styles of operation when addressing homeland security and terrorism analysis. If law enforcement does not take the next step and anticipate the actions of terrorist groups, the results may be catastrophic.

The following is information used to develop a group's modus operandi:

Capabilities
History
Statements
Support
Intentions/causes/motivation
Current and future capabilities
Vulnerabilities of the organization
Location of operation
Dates of meaning or significance
Membership
Leadership (noting there may be a leaderless resistance)
Threatening calls or any other messages
Attacks
Financing or aid

New terrorist generations learn from their predecessors. They analyze the mistakes made by former comrades who were killed or apprehended. "Press accounts, judicial indictments, courtroom testimony, and trial transcripts are meticulously culled for information on security force tactics and methods and then absorbed by surviving group members."[2] In other words, they analyze records for intelligence much like law enforcement should. Information gleaned from scrutinizing court proceedings is often overlooked or taken for granted by law enforcement personnel, partly because law enforcement has traditionally considered a case closed once a defendant has stood trial and all court matters are over. Detailed information, including indictments and affidavits, is widely available for the taking, thanks in part to freedom of information or Sunshine records requests. Without the sealing of records, what good is a secret clearance if one only needs to wait for a case to be closed in order to understand how a law enforcement body pursues a case and identifies the tools used to secure the warrant or arrest. These measures can no longer be ignored if we are to completely understand and analyze terrorism. When transforming information into intelligence, one is continually trying to corroborate, advance, and reconcile data. Analysts and investigators must keep open minds when transforming information and should not discount learning from the enemy. Use of the above list, especially court-related documents and press information, will not always yield leads but these items should be monitored and routinely compared with other variables. However, do not limit yourself to media accounts and court cases in your immediate region. Terrorist organizations and organized hate groups are transnational, as represented with the list of known active patriot groups, and are located in many cities and states. Therefore a global approach is essential, where applicable. This is one aspect where law enforcement can learn from the enemy. In a terrorism training document seized in Manchester, England, from a disciple of Jihad, "Military Studies in the Jihad against the Tyrants" (based on translation), also known as the al-Qaeda training manual, information sources both public and secret were detailed. It was stated that by using public sources openly and without resorting to illegal means, it was possible for an operative to gather at least 80 percent of the information needed about the enemy. Methods cited were newspapers, magazines, radio, and television. If terrorists believe they can get 80 percent of the information needed from legal sources, then law enforcement should have an advantage on the remaining 20 percent through quality use of criminal intelligence databases and from considering all available factors.[3]

Other factors to consider are links to common crimes, such as theft, that may have hidden variables associated with them. One such factor is the collection of necessary components used to make homemade bombs, such as fertilizer, icing sugar, and diesel fuel. "Stolen" would not normally set off bells and whistles. These are common items that anyone can purchase and possess legally, in contrast to the theft of military ordnance, such as plastic explosives or dynamite, which would immediately alarm law enforcement and initiate notifications. Whether these items are stolen separately or collectively, there is a potential for disaster. Which items might a potential terrorist seek to obtain without being detected? Although the answers to this question could be endless, analysts need to document detailed and finite descriptions of items that are located, stolen, or purchased and are in the possession of suspects. These items can then be weighed against other variables in order to develop potential links or leads.

Analytical and investigative variables

Once the form, type, classification, and modus operandi are established, there are a multitude of analytical and investigative variables to consider. These variables are used in link analysis or in charting an individual, group, or activity. Outlined below are some of the variables that should be used when corroborating information for groups and offenders. The components of a group or an organization profile listed below should also be included in terrorism and organized hate crime intelligence databases. However, these variables can be expanded upon, and an analyst should freely search narratives or miscellaneous fields. The components of an offender profile are described in *Crime Analysis: From First Report to Final Arrest*,[4] and these components are now commonplace in many analytical databases.

Components of a group or organization profile

Culture
Cause
Sponsor
Religion
Ideology and beliefs
Symbology, if any
Membership
Make-up
Numbers
Recruitment
Origin
Prior arrests or detainments of members
Financial
Income generation
Supporters
Hierarchy
Chain of command
Political position
Target selection
Method of attacks
Weapons used
Current and future capabilities
Modus operandi
Base of operation, e.g., local, regional, national, international, or transnational
Court records
Media records
Historical references, e.g., records, reports, and news
Training
    Where
    By whom
Components of an offender profile[4]
    Age, sex, race
    Marital status
    Level of intelligence
    Sexual adjustment
    Social adjustment
    Appearance

Employment history
Emotional adjustment
Work habits
Location or residence in relation to crime scene
Personality/characteristics
Analysis of criminal act
Motive
Lifestyle
Prior criminal history
Sequence of events during the offense
Mood of the offender before, during, and after the offense

When considering the use of variables, personnel are cautioned on the importance of verifying the sources and differentiating between information obtained as tips vs. actual cases. It is also imperative that the information is obtained and entered in compliance with federal, state, and local laws. Use of any of the above variables for weighting, comparing, or linking is best done with intelligence-based software, providing that the data entry methods were standardized in the database. Attempting to analyze organized groups and their supporters through manual methods and matrix charts may be possible but will only delay intelligence and investigations. No matter what methods are undertaken to analyze and use the variables, it is vitally important that personnel document their actions. Methods and variables must be documented as well as dates, times, and software used. This will allow other personnel to replicate results, if necessary, and to know if additional information was received that needs to be analyzed.

Analysts and investigators usually give the most attention to linking individuals, telephone numbers, and addresses. With terrorism and organized hate groups these variables are not always easily available or accurate, but there is one variable that drives all groups — financial. Financial considerations should weigh heavily when gathering information. Without financial backing, terrorist organizations or individuals will have difficulty in succeeding. Terrorist and organized hate groups are committed for the long haul, and as noted earlier, they often have elaborate support systems that require funding. It has been demonstrated in criminal and some terrorist cases that trailing the money will lead to the source, but this can be laborious. Money laundering plays a role in terrorism support as much as it does in ordinary criminal activity. The three stages for money laundering and several methods for completing the stages are as follows:[5]

Stages
Placement — Entry of bulk money into a business-based financial system
Layering — Conduction of a series of transactions designed to conceal an audit trail
Integration — Legitimization of illegal proceeds

Methods
> Structuring (also known as "smurfing") — Possibly the most common method, many individuals deposit cash or buy bank drafts in amounts under $10,000
>
> Bank complicity — A criminally co-opted bank employee may facilitate the money laundering
>
> Currency exchanges — Allows customers to buy foreign currency that can be transported out of the country
>
> Securities brokers — A stockbroker may take in large amounts of cash and issue securities in exchange
>
> Asset purchases with bulk cash — Big ticket items are purchased, such as automobiles and real estate, and are often registered in a friend's name
>
> Postal money orders
>
> Telegraphic or wire transfers of funds
>
> Gambling in casinos
>
> Credit cards — Credit card bills are overpaid and a high credit balance that can be turned over to cash at any time is kept
>
> Travel agencies — Cash is exchanged for travel tickets, which is a common method of moving money from one country to another

When tracking the money, it is important to be aware of the above stages and methods. However, not all currency flows through money laundering arenas, traditional banking, or financial market systems. One such system being used legally and illegally is the Hawala remittance system that was mentioned in Chapter 3.

Web sites and other resources

Analysts and investigators must be creative and constantly look for new media from which to harvest information. Advances in cable and satellite television have provided international terrorist organizations, such as the Palestinian Liberation Organization (PLO), opportunities to exploit the media to their advantage and to promote their positions in the Middle East. What may be perceived as just another news broadcast or interview can yield insight to locations, individuals, and direct or indirect messages. However, this method places investigators at the whim of terrorist organizations and at the subjectivity of the news. More proactive and real-time measures are needed. The Internet is a good source of information. Organizations and membership Web sites, especially hate groups, often post their beliefs, causes, and calendars for upcoming events, propaganda, flyers, and even their manuals of operation. One can learn a great deal by viewing the world through their eyes. Figure 6.1 and Figure 6.2 are examples of flyers that groups create and distribute. The two groups with flyers depicted are the World Church of the Creator and the National Alliance. They readily demonstrate how concerns and topics can be conveyed to an international audience. Flyers such

ARE YOU PREPARED
TO FIGHT THE ARAB HOLY WAR ON AMERICAN SOIL?

End Muslim Immigration Now!

World Church of the Creator
www.creator.org   Post Office Box 2002, East Peoria, IL 61611   309-699-0135

Figure 6.1 WCOTC End Muslim Immigration Now flyer.

as these are meant to stir controversy and enlist new members. Rallies also arouse many emotions and create contention. Rallies or gatherings are held for the purposes of recruiting, promoting beliefs, and gathering attention. They may be held publicly or privately, as depicted in Figure 6.3. These venues provide valuable sources of information with uniforms and symbols (Figure 6.4) displayed. Speeches given at rallies provide additional information. Many groups utilize signs (Figure 6.5) to communicate their beliefs.

COMING SOON
TO A NEIGHBORHOOD NEAR YOU

- Black savages are flooding in from Africa.
- They will spread the HIV virus to every corner of America.
- They will reproduce like cockroaches; despite being poor, uneducated, and jobless.
- They will bring murder, rape, and robbery to every community in which they are placed.

TOP LEFT: BLACK AFRICANS LINE UP TO BE TAKEN TO AMERICA. TOP RIGHT: CHILDREN LAUGH AND PLAY AMONG THE CORPSES LEFT TO ROT IN THE STREET; A COMMON SIGHT IN AFRICA.

A campaign has been launched to bring more non-Whites to America. Recruiting teams are being sent to Africa to persuade Blacks to move here as government-approved immigrants.

The Jews want as many non-Whites as possible mixed in with the White population as quickly as possible. They believe that once they have done that it will be too difficult a task for us to unmix what they have mixed. They'll be surprised at what we are willing to do to repair the damage they have done.

WHITE REVOLUTION: IT'S COMING TOO!

NATIONAL ALLIANCE

P.O. Box 90 • Hillsboro, WV 24946 • USA • 304-653-4600
www.natvan.com • www.natall.com

Figure 6.2 National Alliance Coming Soon flyer.

Figure 6.3 Florida Ku Klux Klan followers gathering at a public park.

Figure 6.4 Alleged member of a branch of the Ku Klux Klan. The military-style uniform and symbols of hate are proudly displayed and worn.

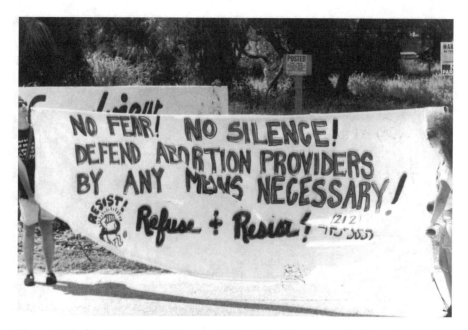

Figure 6.5 Left-wing group "Refuse and Resist," with suspected relations to a Klan faction, at a rally in Florida allegedly advocating disobedience.

There are many Web sites associated with organized hate groups. These are promulgated by individuals and educational institutions and have a wide range of information and insight on activities and events that may prove helpful to law enforcement. These sites should be viewed with some level of skepticism, however, because their content is often skewed and subjective. Other than a group's "official" Web site or those operated by their leadership and members, there are two sites that are dedicated to the collection of detailed and reliable hate crime and hate group information: Southern Poverty Law Center (SPLC) Intelligence Report (http://www.splc.org) has resources on symbols, hate groups, attacks, legislation, and government resources and the Anti-Defamation League (ADL) (http://www.adl.org) has resources directed toward law enforcement personnel and training, postings of upcoming extremist events, a terrorist attack database, and listings of extremism by state. Both of these are nonprofit organizations that also aid law enforcement. Raymond A. Franklin's "The Hate Dictionary" is also available on the Internet (http://www.bcpl.net/~rfrankli/hatedir.htm). It provides links to a tremendous number of Internet sites as well as servers, chat rooms, groups, and several other locations.[6]

There are thousands of Internet sites that can provide insight into a group or individual, as well as information geared toward law enforcement. Listed below are some of the many resources available concerning intelligence for terrorist groups or threats:

http://www.dhs.gov — U.S. Department of Homeland Security

http://www.fbi.gov/terrorinfo/counterrorism/waronterrorhome.htm — FBI Terrorism Information

http://www.terrorism.com — Terrorism Research Center, calendars

http://www.mipt.org — Significant dates, calendars

http://www.tkb.org – Terrorism Knowledge Base

http://www.whitehouse.gov/homeland — Homeland Security contact listing

http://www.state.gov/s/ct — U.S. Department of State

http://www.nipc.gov — National Infrastructure Protection Center

http://www.justice.gov — U.S. Department of Justice

http://www.naco.org — National Association of Counties

http://www.defendamerica.mil — U.S. Department of Defense News

http://www.counterterrorism.com — Examines counterterrorism tools available to law enforcement and first responder personnel

http://www.nlectc.org — National Law Enforcement and Corrections Technology Centers, daily terrorism update newsletter

http://www.intelligence.org.il/eng/ — Intelligence and Terrorism Information Center from Israel

Although it is impossible to provide an all-inclusive listing, the above sites will provide a good starting point and direction to many other online resources. If past behavior is an indication of future behavior, law enforcement personnel should routinely review the many online calendars of significant terrorist events and meaningful dates for the numerous groups all over the world. Dates of significance, anniversaries, and holidays may assist in forecasting or validating the possibility of future threats. Also, many groups or their members have published online memoirs, diaries, and books that may cite specific dates. These publications are available through various rogue Web sites and through some popular online bookstores.

Critically needed is an awareness of the various media venues available to the general public. Venues such as the Internet, shortwave radio, print media (magazines, papers, and books), and independent nonmainstream publishing companies offer an array of how-to guides that virtually anyone can purchase for $30 or less. Although some of these media may have a legitimate target audience, it is the quick and easy access to these items by potentially dangerous individuals that should be important to any analyst. One such example is a publishing company in Colorado that is referred to as the publisher of the "action library." This publisher is operating legally under state and federal laws. However, law enforcement should be aware of many of this publisher's publications for insight into the information they provide. There are hundreds or more of such publications of which law enforcement personnel should be aware. One such book invited the reader to tap into a unique storehouse of forbidden knowledge, with information on building weapons and explosives, opposing big government, changing one's identity, and sniping. This is just one book. Many other books are available that give instructions on forging identity documents. Numerous writings on building bombs and silencers, sniping, explosives, and ammunition are also prevalent.

These books are not necessarily written with malicious intent. Some have been written by individuals who do not have relationships with terrorist or organized hate group organizations. Some books are "how-to" manuals, recently authored, and some books are decades old, written by individuals with direct ties to terrorist and organized hate groups. One such book, a fictional publication that recently claimed revisited notoriety, was *The Turner Diaries*. After the Oklahoma City bombing and the subsequent apprehension of Timothy McVeigh, the FBI reported that McVeigh was in possession of *The Turner Diaries*. This easily obtained publication was allegedly used as a blueprint for his illicit activities. There are many eerie similarities to the bombing and the book's content, including the type of bomb used. If one person can use this writing as a blueprint for destruction, how many others are using the multitude of other books available for illegal and illicit activities? How many law enforcement personnel, including analysts, have read or are even aware of these publications?

Law enforcement personnel strive to prevent crime and identify weaknesses in their jurisdictions through analysis that may be exploited by the criminal element. This information is then used to develop operational and deployment strategies. The criminal element does not have access to this information, thus giving law enforcement the analytical advantage. However, it has access to many publications that it may use to self-train, so why should law enforcement ignore the obvious? Analytical personnel should be aware of these publications in order to gain insight into the thinking of potential terrorist-related individuals and their activities in areas such as the following:

Robberies (financial gain)
Gathering and making weapons and ammunition
"Leaderless" resistance
Cause and ideology
How to hide out and avoid authorities
Use of disguises
Hideout needs (supplies)
Making and using explosives
Column and cell organization as well as supporters
Symbols

Another source of published documents that may provide valuable insight for terrorists or terrorist groups is information that can be extracted from official court and criminal case documents, as described earlier. Many investigators and analysts overlook the amount of information available at the conclusion of their cases or during subsequent prosecution. Virtually every aspect of a case, including plaintiffs' and defendants' testimonies, is available for the taking. Those engaged in terrorist-related activities can easily obtain unsealed documents and use them to gain information that can have detrimental effects on future law enforcement endeavors. Analytical personnel should be aware of the availability of this information and should include a review of these documents in their post-case analysis. An example of one such document is a how-to terrorism manual that was admitted as evidence by prosecutors during the federal trial of four men for their alleged involvement in the 1998 bombing of the U.S. embassies in Kenya and Tanzania. This document included 18 chapters on how to operate as a terrorist. Topics that were covered in detail included counterfeiting currency and documents, communication, use of apartments, transportation, training, kidnapping and assassinations, espionage, explosives, use of poisons, and interrogations. Although this material was written for potential terrorists, law enforcement personnel can also use this information against them. In addition, law enforcement personnel should consider these publications important to future intelligence-gathering initiatives and, where applicable by law, should strive to have the information sealed from public review.

Another concern for law enforcement, particularly with organized hate groups and their members, is information available from jail, prison, probation, and parole databases. Information in these systems is often overlooked, probably because many law enforcement personnel view this part of the criminal justice process as out of their hands. Stockpiles of information are waiting to be harvested in these untapped databases. Institutions capture a great deal of detailed information about inmates' activities and associations. This resource is an excellent source of information, and many correctional agencies are more than willing to share insight they may possess about these groups.

Macro–Micro–Macro continuum

Armed with an arsenal of databases, resources, checklists, and variables, an analyst must begin to validate inferences, probabilities, and hypotheses. In order to avoid tunnel vision on any one piece of data, analysts should employ the Macro–Micro–Macro continuum.[7] This technique will aid analysts in reevaluating and double-checking initial results.

The first macro includes the numerous pieces of information, intelligence, and variables present in a case. It gives the big picture. Shown in Figure 6.6 are six potential sources of information that flow into the analytical resources. This includes raw computer-aided dispatch (CAD) or records management system (RMS) data that are available to local law enforcement and form the first macro step. The problem often encountered is that many data sources, with the exception of the above two, stand alone and can create delays. Therefore, use of data warehouses is encouraged where feasible.

Providing there are no database connectivity issues or data sharing restrictions, the data are then extracted, transported, transformed, and loaded into the appropriate criminal intelligence data tools. Once the data

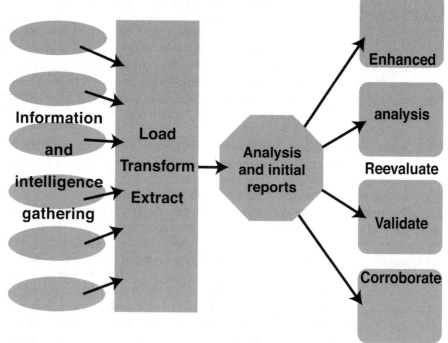

Figure 6.6 Macro–Micro–Macro continuum.

are consolidated, any number of analytical techniques can be initiated. This starts the micro step of the continuum. During this step, analysts seek to identify potential targets, relationships, associates, and supporters. The micro step requires definitive answers and results. Every piece of information is scrutinized from every angle, and nothing is left out. However, this is not the end of the process. Using the results obtained after the micro step may lead to incorrect assumptions. These results must be extracted and reevaluated against the big picture in order to validate them. Caution must be exercised at the micro level, especially with terrorism groups, because of their use of sleeper cells and their widespread networks of supporters. This is why the third step, macro, is used as validation. The results from the micro stage are reevaluated and analyzed using analysis methods such as spatial, temporal, target, victim, and subject, in order to look for outcomes that may contradict the first step.

Throughout the process, analysts should continually search for one-to-many and many-to-one relationships. Too often, analysts will focus on one-to-one relationships, thus creating a potential void that leaves associations undetected. Once all three steps are performed, then the final analytical reports are completed and submitted for consideration. However, this is not the end of the analysis. The process is continuous and is never complete unless there is definitive proof to the contrary. By using the Macro–Micro–Macro continuum, analysts will follow many of the same methods that have been used for years, but now they will be taking a step back after their initial findings and will be comparing again, with a fresh look. However, this continuum is only a technique with which to avoid errors and omissions. Analysts still must have some type of approach or method.

Analysts cannot rely upon only one method. For the purposes of verification, a minimum of two methods should be utilized. Four of the more prevalent methods used by analysts to verify leads and substantiate information are link analysis, matrix tables, timelines, and flowcharts. Three of these methods are described below.

Link analysis charts

Link analysis charts provide visual or graphical overviews of interrelationships. They are great analytical resources for long-term and complex investigations. Although there are many software packages available that provide link charts, this can be manually done with the use of virtually any computer software package that allows for the drawing of graphics. Some basic rules for developing link charts, such as the one shown in Figure 6.7, are as follows:

> When connecting relationships by using lines, it is important that only confirmed relationships be connected with solid lines and arrows to demonstrate the direction of the relationship, where applicable. When a relationship cannot be confirmed, use of a dashed line is appropriate.
> Groups or businesses are reflected through the use of a box, and in some cases individuals are drawn as individual circles within a larger circle.
> Individuals will be reflected as circles, with the appropriate annotations reflected in same.

Link charts can be drawn using link analysis pictograms, such as that shown in Figure 6.8, to reflect individuals, telecommunications, currency, and computers. Use of link charts becomes cumbersome when there are many relationships and a large organization. When this occurs, there is the likelihood that relationship lines will overlap. This is not necessarily a concern, but when there are too many the charts can be difficult to read. This can sometimes be remedied by using a curved line where the lines intersect, as if it were jumping the other line.

Association and directional matrixes

The second analytical method is the use of association and directional matrixes. An association matrix, as shown in Figure 6.9, is often used in

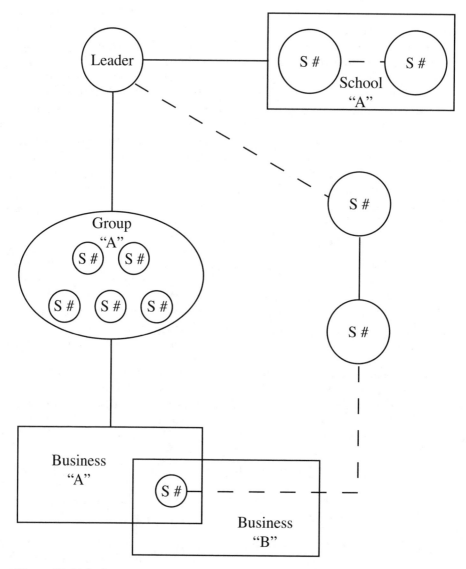

Figure 6.7 Link chart.

support of a link analysis chart. The names of individuals are entered alphabetically, with the group name on the bottom line. As associations are uncovered, criteria symbols are entered into the appropriate boxes, with a legend identifying the symbols provided. The most commonly used symbols are circles, shaded and unfilled, plus signs, equal signs, and checkmarks. A directional matrix is commonly used to track the flow of goods, money, and weapons. If there is a substantial intelligence case being worked, it may be necessary to compile a separate chart for each commodity being monitored. The directional matrix looks similar to an accountant's ledger and is done

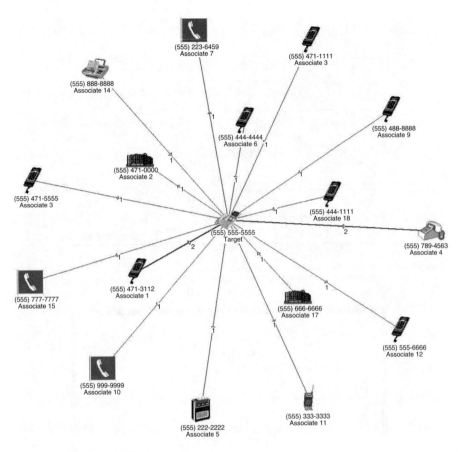

Figure 6.8 Link analysis chart using pictograms.

with the same purpose as a link chart, but shows commodity and money flow between relationships. The left axis represents whence the commodity originates, and the top indicates where it went. The right axis has a column reflecting the "total from" and the bottom a "total to."

Event flowcharts

Event flowcharts are another tool to help visualize relationships among events. They are similar to time lines. Several charting methods are available, but two of the more prevalent are the Birch Method (Figure 6.10), and Mercer Method (Figure 6.11).[5]

The Birch Method uses some of the same rules as a link chart. If an event is confirmed, then the box is drawn with a solid line. If it is unconfirmed, a dashed line is used. There are no limits to the number of event boxes, but it is important that directional arrow lines be used between events, and solid and dashed lines be used accordingly in order to establish the flow of events.

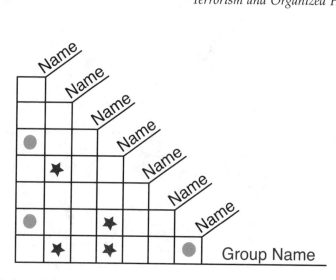

Figure 6.9 Association matrix.

DATE

**Background
Information or
Brief Description
of Event**

Figure 6.10 Birch Method event chart.

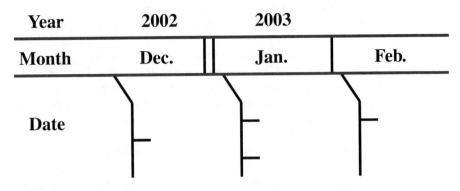

Year	2002	2003	
Month	**Dec.**	**Jan.**	**Feb.**

Date

Figure 6.11 Mercer Method event chart.

The Mercer Method places the year on the top line, the applicable months on the second line, and the years separated on the month line, using two vertical lines. A diagonal line is then drawn from the month down and is connected to a vertical line, with the dates on the left and a brief description on the right. As with the other charts, an unconfirmed connection is marked with a dashed line and a confirmed connection with a solid line. If an event date is unknown, the month span can be specified (such as March to July) and the unknown date marked with a question mark.

Use of either of the above two methods will greatly enhance the understanding of any intelligence case. Personal preference will usually dictate the method used. Once the final diagram is generated, it should be reviewed by someone who was not directly involved in its production. This is important because an analyst can become too close to a case, and relationships may be taken for granted or overlooked.

Heuer's analysis of competing hypotheses (ACH)

Another assessment method is Heuer's 1999 analysis of competing hypotheses (ACH). ACH is an eight-step procedural tool used to enhance judgment on important issues and to minimize common analytical pitfalls, as listed below:[8]

1. Identify the possible hypotheses to be considered. Use a group of analysts with different perspectives to brainstorm the possibilities.
2. Make a list of significant evidence and arguments for and against each hypothesis.
3. Prepare a matrix with hypotheses across the top and evidence down the side. Analyze the "diagnosticity" of the evidence and arguments — that is, identify the items that are most helpful in judging the relative likelihood of the hypotheses.
4. Refine the matrix. Reconsider the hypotheses, and delete evidence and arguments that have no diagnostic value.

5. Draw tentative conclusions about the relative likelihood of each hypothesis. Proceed by trying to disprove the hypotheses rather than prove them.
6. Analyze how sensitive your conclusion is to a few critical items of evidence. Consider the consequences for your analysis if that evidence were wrong, misleading, or subject to different interpretation.
7. Report conclusions. Discuss the relative likelihood of all the hypotheses, not just the most likely one.
8. Identify milestones for future observation that may indicate that events are taking a different course than expected.

Heuer's list is comprehensive. It also complements two methods already discussed, the Macro–Micro–Macro continuum and the loop effect, by demonstrating a consistent approach to tackling complex issues.

Use of any one of these methods alone or together will greatly enhance the quality of a report as well as aid in threat and vulnerability assessments.

Assessing the threat

Terrorists are strategic actors. They choose their targets based on the weaknesses they see in the victim's defenses and preparedness. This is where threat assessments come into play. Government agencies have used threat assessment models and reports to identify sources and potential threats for many years. Assessments also assist with identifying the likelihood of the threat's occurrence. Assessments should emphasize well-documented events in terms of dangers or opportunities that exist due to a terrorist or organized hate group against an agency's interests. Agencies have a tremendous need to detect and intercept security threats that may impact their jurisdiction. However, gathering information and analyzing it solely based on individuals or groups creates a void. The void is the target that may be threatened. These threats should be measured against venues within a jurisdiction by law enforcement agencies using a set of predefined standards to ensure that all communities are evaluated in like terms.

In a post-September 11, 2001, International Association of Chiefs of Police (IACP) Project Response report, a team of law enforcement experts identified a four-level standardized system for locating and measuring community risk. The four tiers of the risk system are:[9]

1. First Priority Level — Fatal (functions that upon failure could result in death, severe financial loss, or legal liability)
2. Second Priority Level — Critical (functions that would be difficult to do without for any length of time)
3. Third Priority Level — Important (functions that are not critical to an agency)
4. Fourth Priority Level — Routine (functions that are not strategically important and that, if they fail, would only be an inconvenience)

The IACP four-tier system is more of a criticality assessment rather than a threat assessment but should be included as part of a threat assessment. According to a U.S. General Accounting Office publication:[10]

> A criticality assessment is a process designed to systematically identify and evaluate important assets and infrastructure in terms of various factors, such as the mission and significance of a target. For example, nuclear power plants, key bridges, and major computer networks might be identified as "critical" in terms of their importance to national security, economic activity, and public safety.

Criticality assessments or the IACP's four-tier system should be used to bolster a threat assessment because they provide a basis for identifying which assets and structures are the most likely to be at risk.

The purpose of a threat assessment is to evaluate the likelihood of terrorist activity against a given asset or location. It is a support tool for making decisions concerning how to establish and prioritize security program requirements, planning, and resource allocations. Raymond J. Decker, Director of Defense Capabilities and Management, stated, "A threat assessment identifies and evaluates each threat on the basis of various factors, including capability, intention, and lethality of an attack."[11] For several years, the Department of Defense has been utilizing threat assessments in its antiterrorism program for its military installations.

Threat assessment approaches involve many factors, but three of the most common are a terrorist group's intentions, past activities, and capabilities. These factors are detected throughout the analytical and investigative processes and should be applied when developing threat assessments.

Threat assessment models are designed to be generic in nature unless specific details dictate otherwise. They are not based on worst-case scenarios, as are vulnerability assessments. It is impossible to develop a model for every feasible threat scenario or group, but threat assessments provide a foundation from which to build. Developing a threat assessment model requires knowledge and survey of the jurisdiction or region in order to identify potential threats or areas of concern. Much focus of threat assessments is tailored toward buildings. Personnel should not forget the significance of key individuals. Heads of Fortune 500 companies can make attractive targets, as has been done in the past, for terrorist groups seeking to weaken an economy. In order to emphasize this point, just imagine the repercussions of the stock market should one of these individuals be targeted.

Threat assessment reports usually begin with an introduction, a description of the geographical area being considered, and a list of reporting or participating agencies. This is followed by the report body, and the report usually concludes with related activities, a synopsis, and a forecast. The following layout is suggested for regular assessments in matters of homeland security. It should be followed by the completed site survey in the body's text:

List identified targeted groups, members (suspects), and incidents.

Report results from checking Web sites and publications; report target
and suspect analyses.

Initiate link analysis.

Provide link charts and matrixes; sort based on numerous variables.

Provide results of reviewing against other link charts and older data.

Report data search results on victims, suspects, groups, and targets
(based on findings).

Identify specific details: groups, members, targets, and geographical
limitations.

Verify leads and information (should be done at all steps).

Report results of site file reviews and visits.

Determine posture of the sites' physical security status.

Report results of briefings conducted (should be done at all steps, as
needed).

Identify all splinter groups.

Identify all supporter groups (active and passive).

Identify financial links.

Continually update all links and information without delay.

Perform final analysis review of all available data.

Threats or terrorist activities do not occur overnight. They are often
elaborate and well financed and are planned months or years in advance.
This is to the advantage of law enforcement. The chances of gaining information or insight to a group are enhanced by time and by attending the
following types of gatherings and investigating the following propaganda
for potential threat indicators:

Public demonstrations
Meetings, rallies
Unrest at colleges and public speeches advocating violence
Training
Antigovernment posters and leaflets
Publications and CDs
Phone threats

Evaluation and assessments should be continuous. Because threat assessments are invaluable decision-making tools, they need to be updated at least
annually. Threats can change and new threats emerge; failure to reconcile
assessment data can produce invalid information. While assessments are key
decision-making support tools, it is important to understand that they might
not properly capture emerging terrorist threats.

Vulnerability assessment

Vulnerability assessments help provide in-depth analyses into the inner
workings of a facility or designated site in order to identify components that

may be at risk for attack. The following is the U.S. General Accounting Office's working definition of a vulnerability assessment:[12]

> A vulnerability assessment is a process that identifies weaknesses in physical structures, personnel protection systems, processes, or other areas that may be exploited by terrorists and may suggest options to eliminate or mitigate those weaknesses.
> Vulnerability assessments are related to a current period of time and should be performed at least annually. All possible "what if" and worst-case scenarios should be researched. The "what if" scenarios involve security, design, engineering, mitigation, response, and damage buffers. Once an assessment is initiated and the site to be protected is identified, the perimeter of the identified target should be expanded to ensure that all possible ingresses and egresses are secured.

Typically, vulnerability assessments are conducted by teams of skilled experts. Areas such as engineering, security, finance, and information systems are generally beyond the scope of law enforcement personnel. Therefore, the experts and those with an intimate working knowledge of the site will conduct the assessment. The level of protection needed should be determined, and the site in question should be evaluated against different threat levels. Some factors to consider when determining threat levels are national security, critical infrastructures, on- and off-site hazards, proximity to population centers, and adequacy of the site's existing preparedness plans. These factors will help law enforcement personnel make key management and deployment decisions should the need arise.

Government facilities are not the only facilities that should have vulnerability assessments performed annually. Many private-sector facilities could be attractive targets for terrorists and organized hate groups. Therefore, law enforcement officials should try to get copies of private industry assessments, especially for high-risk-style businesses such as power plants, natural gas facilities, and schools. Conducting an assessment is only one part of the process. Any identified exposures should be addressed and rectified before conclusion of the assessment or within a specific time frame.

With the information from threat and vulnerability assessments, law enforcement managers and government officials will be armed with sufficient information to make judgments concerning risks of terrorist attacks. Threat and vulnerability assessments can be expedited and made readily available through the use of spatial analysis geographic information systems (GIS). Examples of how GIS can aid law enforcement are shown in Figure 6.12, Figure 6.13, and Figure 6.14. These figures can be used to demonstrate the vulnerability of a dirty bomb in an urban setting. Figure 6.12 is a bird's-eye view of a metropolis before the scenario begins. A 1000-lb conventional high-explosive device contained in a sport utility vehicle and laced with powdered and liquid radioactive waste is detonated in an intersection. Figure 6.13 shows the fallout pattern of the device one hour after detonation,

Figure 6.12 Bird's-eye view. (Courtesy of Dan Helms, Bair Software Research and Consulting, 2003. With permission.)

demonstrating the vulnerability of numerous buildings within close proximity to the blast site, which will help law enforcement to evacuate and quarantine the area. Figure 6.14 reveals the extent radiation levels can reach within the blast area. Using the results of GIS modeling algorithms such as these, it is possible to conduct detailed vulnerability assessments that go beyond the mere recognition of a building or specific target. Analysts are thus able to immediately assist homeland security plans with command center and staging area logistics, establishment of perimeters, and model contamination of soil and groundwater.

Spatial referencing and its use in homeland security analysis

Geography and space are substantial variables to consider in analysis, threat assessment, response, recovery, and investigation. GIS can provide decision makers with the data needed to confront a wide variety of threats including disasters, sabotage, and terrorist attacks. It will also provide decision makers with a better understanding of the data. Mapping, or spatial referencing, of terrorist threats and capabilities, current and future, is done with specific facilities and vulnerable targets. This allows authorities to determine the organizations that pose the greatest threats and the facilities and sectors that

Figure 6.13 Fallout pattern. (Courtesy of Dan Helms, Bair Software Research and Consulting, 2003. With permission.)

are at greatest risk. It also allows planners, managers, and policy makers to develop thresholds for preemptive or protective action through the use of attribute data via what are referred to as layers. Layers of data in geographical software allow the user to paint a picture in a wide variety of patterns by activating one layer against another in order to visualize and identify important factors that may otherwise go undetected.

Spatial analysis, although growing in popularity with the analytical community in the form of crime mapping, is often bypassed by agencies due to the perceived complexity of operation and associated costs. This may be why law enforcement and military personnel rely so heavily on tabular data and matrixes. Although the military uses satellite imagery as well as other forms of spatial referencing, the law enforcement community lags behind. In recent years this has started to change, partly due to numerous federal

Figure 6.14 Radiation levels. (Courtesy of Dan Helms, Bair Software Research and Consulting, 2003. With permission.)

agencies such as the National Law Enforcement and Correction Technology Centers, and several private corporations that have offered funding and training for GIS. The law enforcement community has also begun to reap the benefits of spatial analysis through the recent use of affordable and user-friendly desktop GIS. However, personnel need to understand GIS.

According to the Federal Interagency Coordinating Committee on Digital Cartography, GIS is "A system of computer hardware, software, and procedures designed to support the capture, management, manipulation, analysis and display of spatially referenced data for solving complex planning and management problems."[13] The latter part of the definition, solving complex planning and management problems, is appropriate when dealing with homeland security and terrorism, because terrorism is complex and poses a variety of management problems for law enforcement managers.

Through the use of GIS, law enforcement and government agencies can share information on several different platforms. This is particularly important when analyzing data from locales outside traditional jurisdictional boundaries. With GIS, law enforcement personnel are capable of mapping incidents or potential targets at various levels, from statewide (small scale) to street level (large scale). Virtually the only restriction placed on this capability would be the projection, or real-world reference, at which the base map data are displayed, but this is easily transformed via most desktop GIS applications. Issues such as not having a neighboring jurisdiction's base map can be easily rectified through the use of free resources such as the U.S. Census Bureau's Topologically Integrated Geographic Encoding and Referencing (TIGER) files. These files provide a wide variety of geographical layers available on the Internet that when downloaded (and projected if needed) can enhance analysts' abilities to visualize areas with which they are unfamiliar. In addition, there are many Internet sites and resources, some free and some fee-based, that show new ways to view intelligence and the world. This is just the beginning. GIS has an extensive range of applications, some of which have been used for decades and are just now being discovered by the law enforcement community. However, it is important to note that the majority of the data used to formulate spatial analysis in law enforcement comes from their own data. Herein lies the problem. The geocoding (address matching) process used in GIS often demonstrates that many law enforcement agencies only attain an 80 percent accuracy rate, which translates into potential decisions being made knowing that possibly 20 percent of the data is missing.

Range of GIS uses

The range of uses and benefits of GIS are exponential. Beyond the previous obvious use of enhanced information sharing, GIS offers an integrated analysis for law enforcement personnel. The ability to map a city's infrastructure against a wide range of potential homeland or security targets will enable personnel to make informed decisions based on the whole picture.

GIS can assist in homeland security analysis through many facets. First are detection, deterrence, and identification. It is essential that all potential at-risk locations be identified and properly referenced on a map. This allows an analyst or first responder to visually detect other potential indirect targets, thus enhancing the likelihood of deterring future attacks. Additionally, first responders would be able to instantly identify a potential field of fire if a gunman or sniper were to open fire from any given location. This capability would also be helpful during the evidence collection process, because it would limit the search area.

The second facet is preparing and planning. Law enforcement personnel, regardless of assignment, are trained in planning and preparing for the worst-case scenario. This is particularly important in homeland security. Proper preparation and planning are crucial at all levels. Through the use of GIS, all personnel involved in a plan of action can gain a multidimensional view of various layers of data. By developing layers that account for the "what if" scenarios, analysts will be able to readily call upon and visualize a variety of data without interfering with any one aspect of an operation.

The remaining three facets are resource deployment, response and evacuation, and recovery. All are critical to any emergency preparedness plan, but they can easily go unnoticed by an analyst not looking at the global picture. Deployment and evacuation are two facets that pose perhaps the greatest concern for local and state law enforcement agencies. Deployment scenarios, depending on the seriousness of the operation or incident, are something for which most agencies have contingency plans. These usually occur during civil disorders or demonstrations, but they are adjustable to fit most plans. In addition to basic deployment planning and monitoring, GIS software will enable managers to estimate response times of field units.

Evacuations add a new dimension, because most agencies do not have control over civilians and outside parties. Evacuation plans are often established when a particular segment of the population is affected, as with natural disasters or nuclear accidents. These plans are frequently used by emergency operation command centers that have a specific criterion for evacuation and predefined locations to which to send evacuees. In a terrorist situation, law enforcement does not have the luxury of dictating all of the evacuation or deployment criteria. The use of real-time spatial data can greatly enhance an ad hoc plan of action.

The Federal Geographic Data Committee (FGDC), a 19-member interagency committee composed of representatives from the executive office of the President and cabinet-level and independent agencies, posted a document entitled "Homeland Security and Geographic Information Systems" on their Web site, detailing how GIS and mapping technology can save lives and protect property in a post-September 11, 2001 America. They cited several uses for GIS within homeland security, some of which have been described above, and expanded upon the topic.

According to the FGDC, the following characteristics that make up geographic information technologies, combined with appropriate sets of geospatial information, constitute an invaluable tool for handling, displaying, and analyzing information involved in every aspect of homeland security. Outlined below are the characteristics, as cited by the FGDC:[14]

Detection: Geospatial information provides the spatial and temporal backdrop upon which effective and efficient threat analysis is accomplished. By linking and analyzing temporally and spatially associated information in real time, patterns may be detected that lead to timely identification of likely modalities and targets.

Preparedness: Emergency planners and responders must often depend on geospatial information to accomplish their mission. Current, accurate information that is readily available is crucial to ensuring the readiness of teams to respond. Geospatial information access and interoperability standards are essential elements, as they support the means for the nation's response units to react to terrorist attacks, natural disasters, and other emergencies.

Prevention: Geospatial information provides a means to detect and analyze patterns regarding terrorist threats and possible attacks. This information, coupled with information about borders, waters, and airspace, in turn, may lead to disruption of terrorists' plans or prevention or interdiction of their attacks.

Protection: Geospatial information is an important component in the analysis of critical infrastructure vulnerabilities and in the use of decision support technologies such as visualization and simulation to anticipate and protect against cascading effects of an attack on one system as it relates to other interdependent systems.

Response and recovery: Geospatial information is used by many organizations in response to and recovery from natural disasters. Similarly, this information is invaluable for emergency response services of all kinds, as well as for carrying out long-term recovery operations. The Federal Response Plan, developed by 26 federal agencies and the Red Cross, identifies overall responsibilities and the concept of operations for presidential declared disasters. A number of emergency support functions are identified, with the Federal Emergency Management Agency (FEMA) in the lead for coordinating response to natural disasters and the federal wildland agencies responsible for coordinating response to wildland fires.

These are examples of the potential that can be achieved with the use of GIS. GIS is a relatively new tool for many law enforcement agencies that are just beginning to discover and harness the power of these systems. Powerful GISs are now available that quickly render one to several layers of digital geospatial data into map-like products. These systems can facilitate near-real-time performance of a wide range of relevant geospatial analyses. They can also be used to access and process digital geospatial data virtually anywhere because digital data, unlike analog data, can be instantly transmitted. This ability will be of great benefit during preparation and planning stages.

Preparation and planning

Use of GIS in homeland security is dependent upon good, clean, accurate, and timely data. The two fundamental components to using GIS are incident data and base map data. Clean incident data, particularly addresses, are extremely important and are one of the leading reasons that information does not get geocoded or mapped. That is why it is essential that all participants have a complete understanding of the importance of standardized data. The second component of GIS is the quality of the base map used by the analyst. Analysts often have to work with layers of data that are maintained and updated by independent contractors or other departments. These can contribute to the learning curve associated with mastering the use of GIS-based programs. No matter who is charged with maintaining or updating the numerous GIS layers, updates must be done consistently and with a sense of urgency. Changes need to be shared with all end users, either through word of mouth, or preferably through formal means such as metadata (data about the data). The National Spatial Data Infrastructure (NSDI) is a working example of compiling metadata to facilitate integration of data and support decision making. The NSDI is a network of federal, state, and local geospatial information databases that provide metadata for all information holdings to make information easier to find and to use.

Effective planning and analysis require that officials anticipate the future while remaining cognizant of the past. When assessing and evaluating potential hazards and risks spatially, the integration of historical incidents against current issues may provide a vision for the future. Terrorists often seek to learn from those they consider to have achieved some level of success with their tactics. Their continuous review of historical material, such as writings and court material, is designed to assist them in developing future plans of attack. Law enforcement must not overlook the same tactic of learning from the past, locally and nationally.

GIS linking

In the field of GIS, three words are commonly mentioned: points, lines, and polygons. Points are often referred to as dots or pins. They are known to law enforcement as the locations of crimes, but they can also be residential locations and potential targets. Lines usually represent street center lines, roadways, and property lines. Polygons are often used to depict building footprints, land use and zoning, and jurisdictional boundaries. Perhaps one of the greatest benefits of GIS is the capability to link images, documents, data tables, building floor plans, operational plans, points of contact, and guidelines through a process known as hot linking. Hot linking provides a valuable tool for all law enforcement officials. It allows for the use of the full power of technology by incorporating a mechanism designed to reduce or eliminate manual efforts and multiple sources of data within one single project or file. Once information is plotted within GIS and saved as a project, law enforcement officials have a venue in which they can link a wide array of documents and images. The end user can simply point and click on a map location in order to gain access to all of the linked items.

Additional benefits of GIS

Additional benefits to be gained from GIS include the ability to anticipate and visualize fields of view that may be available to field commanders as well as the ability to see other possible points of interest and dispersion patterns for chemical and toxic plumes. The latter are critical aspects of the planning stage, when anticipating and developing evacuation models, as well as when developing deployment strategies that ensure the safety of all first responders. Figure 6.15 shows a hypothetical scenario of a chemical plant along a waterway and possibly within five miles of residential areas. In this scenario, responding officers and managers would be able to readily identify areas affected by toxic plumes through use of the one- and three-mile buffers. This would include the water and railways that may otherwise go

Figure 6.15 Radius buffers.

undetected, because they might be perceived as barriers but toxic plumes do not recognize such barriers. The ability to identify potential exposure areas is one facet. Another is the ability to identify potential targets that terrorists and organized hate groups may seek out.

Figure 6.16 Three-dimensional modeling of a target. (Courtesy of Dan Helms, National Law Enforcement and Corrections Technology Center — Rocky Mountain Region, Crime Mapping and Analysis Program. With permission.)

Identifying potential targets

GIS is a powerful tool that allows for more than a one-dimensional view. It can depict orthophotography images, satellite images, three-dimensional (3D) modeling (as demonstrated in Figure 6.16), and elevations. However, before enhanced models or projects are built, law enforcement personnel should consider all potential targets and vulnerable areas. Although no list can be all-inclusive, the following list of potential targets and vulnerable areas may be used for review, analysis, and geographical consideration when developing and conducting spatial analysis for the purposes of homeland security and terrorism initiatives. Figures in parentheses are approximate for the entire United States as reported in The National Strategy for the Physical Protection of Critical Infrastructures and Key Assets:[15]

    Utilities, above ground and underground
    Water treatment (1,800 federal reservoirs and 1,600 municipal waste-
        water facilities)
    Well fields (water and oil)
    Oil and gas

Energy and nuclear (104 commercial nuclear power plants)
Government buildings (3,000 government owned and operated)
Government officials
Informational resources/infrastructure
Landmarks (5,800 historic buildings)
Skyscrapers (460)
Transportation: land, air, and sea (5,000 airports, 120,000 miles of railway, 300 inland/coastal ports, 590,000 highway bridges)
Banking and financial institutions (26,600 FDIC-insured institutions)
Schools
Military bases or personnel
Private-sector defense contractors
Law enforcement buildings or personnel
International corporations
Shopping areas
Sports arenas
Sporting events
Special or symbolic events
Media spectacles
Annual special events, e.g., boat and automobile shows, art festivals
Symbols of capitalism
Judicial facilities
Items associated with dates of significance
Cellular telephone tower sites
Agriculture (1,920,000 farms)
Postal and shipping sites (137 million delivery sites)
Chemical industry (66,000 chemical plants)
Pipelines (2 million miles of pipeline)
Public health and emergency services (5800 registered hospitals)
Religious institutions
Air- and seaports
Bridges and dams (80,000 dams)
Amusement parks

When identifying potential targets, law enforcement agencies need to coordinate with other government entities or private-sector groups that work directly with the areas of concern. Protection of infrastructures and assets "requires coordinated action on the part of federal, state, and local governments; the private sector; and concerned citizens across the country."[15] The lion's share of these assets are owned and operated by the private sector. An example of this coordination would be the identification of a water-pumping station. A law enforcement agency may see the need to identify and secure only the pumping station, but an employee of the water department may have additional concerns, such as the need for electricity to operate the pump, which may be overlooked and lead to extensive flooding.

Mass transit systems are targets that present a challenge for law enforcement. Bus and rail systems are mobile, cover an enormous area, and travel through densely populated regions. This makes them attractive soft targets due to their accessibility and often unsecured nature. For this reason, buses have been popular targets for terrorist groups for years in such places as Israel. In the United States it would be virtually impossible to guard and secure every bus and rail system with law enforcement personnel. GIS can help fill the void by identifying potential weaknesses or high-risk areas that may appear attractive to potential terrorists. Soft government targets such as mass transit may be selected for acts of sabotage or violence in response to government actions such as war. However, soft targets are not always chosen. Hard targets are also selected for the impact that will be felt by the victim country.

Terrorists often select targets in order to make a statement. In addition, they want to minimize exposure and maximize casualties. Security measures at a facility or site should not be used as a variable when deciding whether or not to identify a location. Terrorists are not fearful of maximum security, as shown by the bombings of the Khobar Towers in Saudi Arabia, the USS *Cole* in Yemen, and embassies throughout the world. Once identified, maps, just like any other intelligence product, are of little value if they are not disseminated and used.

Dissemination of intelligence

Intelligence has no value if it is not disseminated. No matter how good the analysis and intelligence are, if management and other government officials do not review, consider, and respond to it with open minds and in a timely manner, it will be of no use. We will only hear, after the fact, anecdotal testimonials of warnings that were made but ignored. Past history demonstrates this to be true, as illustrated by three devastating events in the history of the United States: the bombing of Pearl Harbor (December 7, 1941), the World Trade Center attack (September 11, 2001), and the Columbia shuttle disaster (February 1, 2003). The signs, and possibly some documentation, were allegedly present. Information was gathered and reviewed but not acted upon. This demonstrates the need for accurate, timely, and verifiable intelligence. Information should not be ignored because it lacks any of these three conditions (accurate, timely, and verifiable), but an open mind must be kept to all possible scenarios.

In November 2001, the U.S. Attorney General reported that sharing information with all government employees is critical in order to prevent and disrupt terrorist acts. Many law enforcement agencies traditionally disseminated intelligence information based on "need" to certain segments of the force. With homeland security, everyone shares in the need for information. There are some instances when intelligence must be restricted, but on many occasions there is no reason for these constraints.

In the Antiterrorism Act of 1996, the FBI was the agency charged with gathering terrorist information. During the same year, the FBI Counterterrorism Center was established to combat terrorism on three fronts: international, domestic, and countermeasures relating to both. Joint task forces also play a role in the nation's response to terrorism. As of 2003, FBI director Robert Mueller reported that there were 56 Joint Terrorism Task Forces (JTTFs) in operation within the United States.[16] The JTTFs are the conduits used by many local and state law enforcement agencies to introduce the information or intelligence that they harvest. Questions remain whether they will be the sole conduits or if regional-level task forces should be used much like a chain of command. There are two other avenues for disseminating information, and it will depend on the state as to which, if any, are utilized. They are offices of statewide intelligence and designated state homeland security units. On the White House Web site a map with a link to a contact name, telephone number, or e-mail address for each state and territory in the Union is provided. This information has been compiled into a reference list in Appendix F.

Commonly used analytical reports

Regardless of the venue, it is critical that information be reported and disseminated immediately. Many styles of analytical reports have been commonly used in the past several years. There is no need to reinvent the wheel just because it now deals with terrorism or organized hate, and analysts should stay with proven methods.

Outlined below are various types of analytical reports. Each has a place in the analytical world and should be applied accordingly:

Assessments — Threat and vulnerability assessments are two of the more common.

Briefings — These reports are not case studies, but rather are designed to provide a summary overview of the case in question. They are usually delivered to command staff members and address only the basic facts.

Bulletins — These short reports are often in the form of "be on the lookout" (BOLO), identifying areas of concern and wanted subjects. They are direct and concise.

Chronological reports — These are commonly referred to as timelines and include confirmed and unconfirmed information, noted accordingly.

Commodity flowcharts — These are used to track the flow of currency and goods. A separate chart is often done for each item.

Event flowcharts — These charts come in different styles, two of which were described earlier, and are used to visually depict a series of events or occurrences. Only a summary of the event is noted.

Frequency distribution lists — Uses a table of numbers, indicating the number of event occurrences. These events are often analyzed and weighted with respect to a case.

Link analysis — This method is used to identify and establish interrelationships among activities, events, individuals, corporations, finances, and telephone records by visual means.

Maps — These are also referred to as spatial analysis, spatial referencing, and geographic distribution analysis. The potential use of geographical information is virtually endless and includes the use of orthophotography and satellite imagery.

Matrix charts — These charts are used to identify connections or relationships among people and organizations using a series of grids and symbols.

Net worth analysis —Also referred to as financial analysis reports. These documents show the financial affairs of the target in question as well as its assets and expenses.

Profiles — These are comprehensive reports on an individual, group, or corporation, and include virtually every aspect of their existence, including behavior.

Statistical reports — These reports are often used for comparative purposes and aid management in identifying shifts in activity.

Strategic reports — These reports are often used to monitor, track, and project long-range activities.

Tactical reports — These reports are designed to meet the immediate needs of a case and are used by management in developing operational and deployment strategies.

Telephone and toll record analysis — These reports are often done with the assistance of complex computer programs that establish links, track incoming and outgoing calls, and aid in identifying locations.

Warnings — These are used to forecast or predict the occurrences of future behavior based on validated and corroborated threat analysis information.

One report being produced by the federal government is the FBI Intelligence Bulletin. According to FBI director Robert Mueller, "a new FBI Intelligence Bulletin is sent to more than 17,000 law enforcement agencies virtually every week."[16] The question that should be posed to members of an agency is how many people have seen this bulletin or even know it exists? It is commendable that a bulletin is being prepared and disseminated, but if it is not reaching personnel beyond the command staff, how much value is there in producing it? The FBI has done its part. A check of several personnel working in analytical units in a large metropolitan area revealed that no one had ever seen this document or even knew of its existence. These are the employees who will be asked to analyze matters surrounding homeland security. Dissemination practices have to be direct, concise, and reach those in the trenches.

Special requests for dissemination, such as "for internal use only" or "in-house distribution" should be avoided. Once a document is disbursed, it is no longer under the sender's control. It must be assumed that every document will end up in court, be subject to public record laws, or innocently distributed out of the sender's intended circle. There is also the chance that the information may be leaked to individuals without clearance.

When preparing a report, questions should be answered, not created. The reader of the document should be able to clearly understand the content of the report and not need to return to the preparer for further clarification. Documents should include the preparer's name or initials, date prepared, source or sources of the data used to compile the report, a document identification number, and if there have been any revisions these should also be noted. For every document there should be supporting documents. Analysts must log requests as they come in, document actions taken, and maintain copies of all analytical subproducts (queries). When compiling these records, it is important to maintain their true form as they evolve. Storage of these records, whether manual or electronic, is an issue dependent on public record laws of a jurisdiction. In some locales, storing records on a local unsecured personal computer may subject the entire case to public review. This can lead to the leakage of intelligence through completely legal means. Caution has to be used at every step. Nothing should be taken for granted.

Dissemination of the report is what the analyst is working toward. Therefore, it is important that the proper personnel be on the receiving end. Within an agency, the two most common methods of dissemination are photostatic copies or electronic mail (e-mail). Use of e-mail poses a whole new set of concerns. When distributing documents via e-mail, the size of the document is important. If it is difficult for the recipient to access the information, they may delete it. Another consideration is the use of electronic tracking and expirations. Electronic tracking provides assurance that the document was received and opened. Intelligence reports should never be typed directly into an e-mail. Analysts should prepare an independent document and insert it as an attachment. This will aid in diverting improper viewing. Expiration dates should be established when disseminating information electronically. These help ensure that information is reviewed in a timely manner and that information is not reviewed for possible action after it is no longer valid.

Chapter concepts

1. Information is transformed into intelligence. It is important to use various sources in order to develop a group's modus operandi, e.g., capabilities, history, statements, and intentions, causes, and motivations.
2. When investigating terrorist and organized hate groups, it is essential that the components of a group or organization profile and the components of an offender profile be analyzed thoroughly.
3. Various nontraditional resources for analytical consideration are available. When analyzing these resources, tunnel vision can be avoided through the use of the Macro–Micro–Macro continuum.

4. The role of threat and vulnerability assessments in homeland security is discussed. These assessments need to be current and conducted via partnering with the private sector.
5. Valuable insight can be gained through the use of spatial referencing and analysis and through identifying potential targets.
6. Commonly used analytical reports are described. The ways intelligence is disseminated are discussed.

References

1. Heymann, P.B., *Terrorism and America: A Commonsense Strategy for a Democratic Society*, MIT Press, Cambridge, MA, 1998, p. 25.
2. Hoffman, B., Countering the new terrorism, in *Terrorism Trends and Prospects*, Lesser, I.O., Ed., RAND, Santa Monica, CA, 1999, p. 25.
3. The Smoking Gun, Bin Laden's Terrorism Bible, http://thesmokinggun.com/archive/jihadmanual.html, Terrorism 101: A How-To Guide (February 27, 2003).
4. Gottlieb, S., Arenberg, S., and Singh, R., *Crime Analysis: From First Report to Final Analysis*, Alpha Publishing, Montclair, CA, 1994, p. 59.
5. Sweeney, W.J., *Intelligence Analyst's Source Book*, Alpha Group Center, May 2002, photocopy.
6. Franklin, R.A., The Hate Directory: Hate Groups on the Internet, http://www.bcpl.net/~rfrankli/hatedir.html, January 15, 2003, Release 7.1.
7. Cooper, J., Nelson, E., and Ronczkowski, M., Tactical/investigative analysis of targeted crimes, in *Advanced Crime Mapping Topics*, National Law Enforcement and Corrections Technology Center, Denver, CO, 2002, p. 32.
8. Heuer, R.J., Jr., *Psychology of Intelligence Analysis*, Center for the Study of Intelligence, Central Intelligence Agency, 1999, Chap. 8, p. 2.
9. International Association of Chiefs of Police Project Response, Leading from the Front: Law Enforcement's Role in Combating and Preparing for Domestic Terrorism, IACP, Alexandria, http://www.theiacp.org, Feb. 28, 2003, p. 8.
10. United States General Accounting Office, Homeland Security Key Elements of a Risk Management Approach, Decker, R.J., Oct. 12, 2001, p. 6.
11. United States General Accounting Office, Homeland Security, p. 3.
12. United States General Accounting Office, Homeland Security, p. 5.
13. Federal Interagency Coordinating Committee on Digital Cartography, Geographic Information Systems, 1988.
14. Federal Geographic Data Committee, Homeland Security and Geographic Information Systems, http://www.fgdc.gov/publications/homeland.html, Mar. 12, 2003.
15. President, Report, The National Strategy for The Physical Protection of Critical Infrastructures and Key Assets, White House, February 2003, p. vii.
16. Mueller, R.S., III, Teamwork is our future, *The Police Chief*, January 2003, p. 8.

chapter seven

The threat: the future is here today — learning from the past

Bombings, or what are referred to today as improvised explosive devices (IEDs), are nothing new. "Traditional" bombs have been, and will likely continue to be, the leading weapon of terrorists and extremists alike. Much talk and law enforcement focus today has centered on chemical, biological, and nuclear attacks. Although these possibilities should not be overlooked, analysts must look for the SKRAM components outlined in Chapter 4, as well as the fact that terrorists learn from their predecessors. One of the more common skill sets in the world of terrorism centers on manmade IEDs.

Tactics among the majority of some of the largest terrorist organizations, or their spin-offs, of the past century, e.g., IRA and PLO, have demonstrated the consistent use of IEDs in their attacks. Perhaps the biggest difference over the past century has been the refinement or capacity in which attacks are done. For instance, vehicles instead of packages have been packed with explosives by the IRA in their attacks. This method has been taken further by groups such as Hezbollah through the use of truck bombs. Suicide bomb vests can carry a limited amount of explosive, but car and truck bombs can carry thousands of pounds. What method of transportation will be used or attacked next? This question will depend largely on the SKRAM variables of the individuals involved and the group's desire to make a larger statement.

Transportation targeted

Modes of transportation have been either the target of terrorist attacks or used to facilitate attacks for over a century. One of the first examples of this is the attacks on Alexander II, Czar of Russia. Leaders of Narodnaia Volia decided to assassinate Czar Alexander. Their initial plan was to blow up the Czar's train. They split into two groups and, disguised as shopkeepers, rented two buildings along the Imperial route. The explosion on the railway from Livadia to Moscow never materialized because they missed the Czar's train.

Narodnaia Volia, more commonly referred to as the "The Peoples Will" or "Will of the People," a precursor to the Socialist Revolution Party, originated in Russia during the fall of 1879. Members of this organization were ultimately responsible for the death of Czar Alexander II. In 1881, after several unsuccessful attempts, a member of the People's Will assassinated the czar with a hand-thrown bomb. On March 1, 1881, the czar was returning by horse-drawn carriage to the Winter Palace. When he reached Catherine Quay, two bombs were thrown by a member of the People's Will. The first bomb was unsuccessful, but the second bomb satisfied the populists' objective. The czar died a short time later. This event can be seen as a precursor of attacks on modes of transportation.

Transportation and terrorism

According to the Terrorism Knowledge Base Web site, between January 1, 1968, and January 1, 2006, there were 988 terrorist incidents targeting transportation that were committed by 95 terrorist groups worldwide.[1] Transit systems are common terrorist targets. These numbers are just an example of incidents that highlight the fact that transit vehicles are a target of choice for many terrorists. Terrorism waged against transit systems allow the terrorists to meet their prime objectives easily and with a high likelihood of casualties. Millions of people pass through transit facilities every day, and in some locations it is the primary mode of transportation. Besides the volumes of people passing through, transit systems are potential targets because they provide:

- Easy access — systems are hard to secure
- Large concentrations of people in vehicles, trains, and terminals
- A vital component of the economic and social infrastructure
- Service disruption that could affect millions of people
- A target-rich environment

Although people seem fearful, almost paranoid, over chemical, biological, and radiological threats, bombs in the form of IEDs are the most common. Finding an IED in a transit attack is a much more likely scenario than finding anything else. Surface transportation systems cannot be protected as easily as airplanes. Trains, buses, subways, and light rail systems must remain readily accessible, convenient, and inexpensive for the traveling public. Therefore, they make attractive targets.

In the United States, use of Transportation Security Administration (TSA) officials at airports throughout the country was an effort to standardize and solidify air security. However, for every pro there is a con. Just like with cyber security, there is no foolproof means of security. Terrorists are calculating and patient in preparing for attacks. Although TSA performs admirably, there are still weaknesses that can be exploited. The same can be said about any form of transportation, regardless of which agency protects it. There are many transportation system vulnerabilities largely because most fixed transportation infrastructure lies unguarded.

Few countries in the world have weakness exploited and have fallen prey to more attacks on transportation than the United Kingdom, primarily London. The primary foe, the Irish Republican Army (IRA), is widely known for their attempts, hoaxes, or direct terrorist attacks on buses and railways.

The IRA campaign against transportation

In the modern era of terrorism, the IRA can be construed as leading the way in attacks against surface transportation. According to a Mineta Transportation Institute report in 2001, between 1972 and 2000 the IRA exported their terrorist acts to the British mainland targeting surface transportation in England at least 45 times.[2]

- The focus of attacks was on the rail system but buses on the mainland were not immune.
- From 1991 to 1999 alone, 81 explosive devices, 6,589 bomb threats and 9,430 suspicious objects. Security measures implemented during the campaign reduced threats and incidents and effectively reduced "ordinary" crimes such as robbery and vandalism, too.
- Of the 81 explosive devices that were placed at transport targets, 79 were hand-placed time bombs. Fifty percent of them did not work as intended. Altogether, three people were killed by IRA bombs on the rail system.
- In all, 17 persons killed, 200 injured between 1991 and 1999.

However, the IRA is not the only terrorist organization to target transportation. Many have learned from their tactics and continue to exploit the ease of utilizing and targeting surface transportation in terrorist endeavors. Another country that has experienced a significant number of attacks against transportation is India. Between 1920 and 2000 India had the most fatalities as a result of attacks on modes of transportation, with more than twice as many attacks as most countries.

Planes, trains, and automobiles — but there are more

Modes of transportation pose difficulties for law enforcement personnel dealing with terrorism. Virtually everyone in the world uses, or is likely to use, a mode of motorized transportation. Dependency, accessibility, and reliability of transportation create unique opportunities for terrorists to exploit weaknesses. Everything from rescue vehicles, taxis, limousines, trucks, and motorcycles often gain, or can gain, immediate access to a number of venues in the United States or abroad.

Transportation attacks are a grave concern to most investigators dealing with terrorism. On July 18, 2002, the FBI formally created the National Joint

Terrorism Task Force (NJTTF) to act as a conduit for information. In an April 2004 federal report, it was noted that the NJTTF works with the FBI's Office of Intelligence to coordinate inter-agency intelligence-gathering initiatives dealing with transportation, such as:[3]

Foreign flight crew vetting
Maritime threat project
Operation dry dock
Agricultural aviation threat project

It is evident that transportation and terrorism is and will continue to be a concern in the United States and abroad.

United States: terrorism and transportation

Besides unattended IEDs, there have been numerous terrorist attacks against various forms of transportation in the United States. Most were classified and handled as crimes. According to Dunham of the Anser Institute, during the early 1990s the United States experienced several attacks on public transportation, including a 1992 attack in which someone left a hand grenade on a railroad station platform in Chicago.[4] He also noted other attacks that were reviewed by researchers in Florida. Based on a 2002 study conducted by researchers at the University of South Florida, there is a history with regard to major violent attacks on mass transportation in the United States, some of which are outlined below.[5]

- August 6, 1927: Two bombs explode in two New York City subway stations. The bombs injured many persons, one of them, it was believed, fatally.
- December 7, 1993: Armed gunman, Colin Ferguson, kills 6 and injures 17 passengers aboard a Long Island Railroad train during rush hour.
- December 15 and 21, 1994: Edward Leary explodes two homemade bombs on the New York City subway system, injuring 53 people, in an apparent attempt to extort money from the New York Transit Authority.
- October 9, 1995: "Sons of the Gestapo" sabotage Amtrak's Sunset Limited train, causing a derailment in the Arizona desert, killing one and injuring 65 others.

Although these incidents may have been lost in the annals of law enforcement history, they should be reviewed by entities working terrorism in order to learn from the past. Americans inherently have short memories. This is probably why U.S. citizens are unaware of the aforementioned events and were in utter disbelief that the hijacking of aircrafts could originate from their own country and further dismayed by the use of them as bombs. Short memories and lack of historical knowledge may be the reason for the disbelief. September 11, 2001, wasn't the first or even the second attack on New York City and it certainly wasn't the first hijacking or multiple hijacking to take place. Planes, trains, automobiles, and even bicycles have been used in numerous terrorist attacks. Just remember that the mode of transportation has not always been motorized. Just like the attack on Czar Alexander II, there have been carriage or cart attacks, even in the United States.

One of the first cart attacks in the United States occurred on September 16, 1920, at the corner of Wall and Broad streets, the hub of American capitalism. Just after noon, as workers poured onto the street for their lunchtime breaks, a horse-drawn cart exploded into the crowd. The people believed to be responsible, for this yet unsolved event, were members of Bolshevist or anarchist movements. Such an event today would lead to these members or groups to be designated as terrorists.

To New Yorkers and to Americans in 1920, the death toll of over 30 people from the blast seemed incomprehensible. When Americans in 1920 heard of the carnage on Wall Street, many believed they had encountered a type of violence never before seen. There had been bomb explosions before at Chicago's Haymarket Square in 1886 and at the Los Angeles Times building in 1910, but they were attributed to specific labor movements. The blast on Wall Street, by contrast, seemed to be purely symbolic, designed to kill as many innocent people as possible in an assault on American power.

Symbolic government targets

There are many venues that can be considered symbolic for potential attack, many of which have involved a mode of transportation. One of the more common symbolic targets has been that of western government facilities outside their respective country. Over the decades many government building, embassies, and official residences have been the target of many terrorist-related attacks. Arguably, the United States' facilities have been perhaps one of the more attractive targets of terrorists and terrorist organizations. Diplomatic installations have been well documented and targeted in Africa, but they are not an anomaly. Between 1987 and 1997, according to information from an after-action report on the African embassy bombings, there were over 230 attacks on U.S. diplomatic and consulate installations throughout the world. The majority of the attacks took place in the late 1980s and the weapons of choice were bombs and rocket attacks. Diplomatic installation attacks took place on virtually every continent. Countries such as Spain, Peru, Dominican Republic, South Korea, Ecuador, Columbia, Italy, Pakistan, Australia, Serbia, and Algiers have all experienced and seen the carnage that can be achieved through pure hatred targeting symbolic facilities.

There have also been attacks that symbolically mentioned or were focused on government issues. These attacks have come in a variety of ways but quite often the common variable that they share is a mode of transportation.

Figure 7.1 757 Aircraft commonly used throughout the world.

Notable terrorist cases and attacks with a transportation nexus other than 9/11

Aviation (Figure 7.1)

In 2003, United States Secretary of State Colin Powell noted that one of the greatest threats to aviation was the use of man-portable air defense systems (MANPADS). Use of MANPADS against civilian aircraft came to the forefront in November 2002 in an attack against an Israeli Air Arikia Boeing 757 as it departed Kenya. This event is not limited to those outside the United States. In 2003 a criminal complaint was filed in New Jersey against Hemant Lakhani for import and transfer of a shoulder-fired surface-to-air-missile (Figure 7.2). Although the use and range of MANPADS make them an attractive weapon for a potential terrorist, they have not been shown to be the preferred tactic. Bombs and hijackings have largely been the methods of attack.

According to James Poland, statistics on explosions aboard aircraft between 1949 and 2001 demonstrated that 80 aircraft were damaged or destroyed as the result of an explosive device. During the same time frame, the United States recorded the damage or destruction of 15 aircraft.[6]

PFLP — The masters of airplane hijacking

The Popular Front for the Liberation of Palestine (PFLP) was founded on December 11, 1967, by Dr. George Habash, a Palestinian Greek Orthodox Christian, when it broke away from the Arab Nationalist Movement. The PFLP forged international relationships, even on the operational level, with the Japanese Red Army and the Lod Airport Attack on May 30, 1972, and with the Baader Meinhof Gang in Germany and the Air France hijacking to Entebbe in 1976. The organization quickly specialized in showcase, large-scale terrorist operations beginning on July 23, 1968, with a hijacking to Algeria of an El Al flight en route from Rome to Tel Aviv. The PFLP quickly switched to non-Israeli carriers, including the simultaneous triple hijacking of TWA, Swissair, and Pan-Am aircraft to Jordan on September 6, 1970. In a media spectacle, the three aircraft were emptied of passengers and blown up as cameras rolled.

UNITED STATES DISTRICT COURT
DISTRICT OF NEW JERSEY

ORIGINAL FILED

AUG 1 1 2003

UNITED STATES OF AMERICA	:	**CRIMINAL COMPLAINT** SUSAN D. WIGENTON U.S. MAG. JUDGE
	:	
v.	:	
	:	
HEMANT LAKHANI,	:	
a/k/a "Hemad Lakhani"	:	Mag. No. 03-7106

I, James J. Tareco, being duly sworn, state the following is true and correct to the best of my knowledge and belief.

Count One

From in or about December, 2001, to on or about August 12, 2003, in the District of New Jersey and elsewhere, defendant HEMANT LAKHANI, a/k/a "Hemad Lakhani," did knowingly and willfully attempt to provide material support and resources, and to conceal and disguise the nature, location, source, and ownership of material support and resources, intending that they were to be used in preparation for, and in carrying out, a violation of Title 18, United States Code, Sections 32, 2332a, and 2332b.

In violation of Title 18, United States Code, Sections 2339A and 2.

Count Two

From in or about December, 2001, to on or about August 12, 2003, in the District of New Jersey and elsewhere, defendant HEMANT LAKHANI, a/k/a "Hemad Lakhani," did knowingly and willfully engage and attempt to engage in the business of brokering activities with respect to the import and transfer of a foreign defense article, namely a shoulder-fired surface-to-air-missile of foreign origin, which was a non-United States defense article of a nature described on the United States Munitions List, without having first registered with and obtained from the Department of State's Directorate of Defense Trade Controls a license for such brokering or written authorization for such brokering.

In violation of Title 22, United States Code, Section 2778(b)(1) and (c), Title 22, Code of Federal Regulations, Sections 121.1, 127.1(d), 129.3, 129.6 and 129.7, and Title 18, United States Code, Section 2.

I further state that I am a Special Agent of the Federal Bureau of Investigation and that this complaint is based on the following facts:

SEE ATTACHMENT A

continued on the attached pages and made a part hereof.

James J. Tareco, Special Agent
Federal Bureau of Investigation

Sworn to before me and subscribed in my presence,
August 11, 2003 in Essex County, New Jersey

HONORABLE SUSAN D. WIGENTON
UNITED STATES MAGISTRATE JUDGE

Signature of Judicial Officer

Figure 7.2 2003 Criminal complaint against Hemant Lekhani.

Pan Am 103

Pan American World Airways (Pan Am) flight number 103, traveling from London's Heathrow Airport to New York's John F. Kennedy International Airport exploded on December 21, 1988, while at 31,000 feet, killing 270 people. The aircraft, a Boeing 747-121 with registered tail number N739PA, and named "Clipper Maid of the Seas," was blown up as it flew over Lockerbie, Dumfries, and Galloway, Scotland, when 12 to 16 oz (340 to 450 g) of Semtex-H plastic explosive was detonated in its forward cargo hold, triggering a sequence of events that led to the rapid destruction of the aircraft. Two Libyan intelligence officers were eventually charged with the incident. However, some speculate that there may have been ties to the PFLP-GC.

Pre incident indicators

In the subsequent investigation dubbed Operation Autumn Leaves, and headed in the United States by the FBI, several motives were considered. There were two primary motives publicly speculated. The first was the April 1986 bombing of Tripoli and Benghazi on April 15–16, 1986, by U.S. warplanes. The bombings were allegedly done in retaliation for the bombing 10 days earlier of a Berlin nightclub used by U.S. soldiers, which had killed three and injured 230. The second was the July 1988 downing of Iran Air 655, a passenger jet incorrectly identified by an American warship, the USS *Vincennes*, as a hostile military aircraft.

According to Simonsen and Spindlove, the intelligence community had received warnings of troubles in Europe. A total of nine security bulletins that could have had relevance to the Pan Am incident were issued between June and December 1988. One bulletin even described how a Toshiba radio cassette player and a barometric trigger could be used as a bomb.[7] West German police authorities had recovered a similar device in a vehicle belonging to a member of the PFLP-GC.

Richard Reid

On December 22, 2001, Richard Reid an Islamic convert, also known as the shoe bomber, boarded American Airlines flight number 63, a Boeing 767-300 aircraft, en route from Paris to Miami. While in flight he attempted to ignite the fuse of bomb (plastic explosives) concealed in the heel of his shoe and was subsequently arrested. Following his nine-count indictment (Figure 7.3) and being found guilty, Reid openly stated that he was an Islamic fundamentalist and an enemy of the United States, similar to al-Qaeda. Reid was fined and sentenced to 110 years in prison.

Maritime

The legal issues related to maritime security, in particular hijackings and piracy, are convoluted and complex. International maritime laws only

UNITED STATES DISTRICT COURT
DISTRICT OF MASSACHUSETTS

UNITED STATES OF AMERICA)
)
v.   )
)
RICHARD COLVIN REID,   )
a/k/a ABDUL-RAHEEM,   )
a/k/a ABDUL RAHEEM, ABU   )
IBRAHIM   )
)
)
)
)
)
)
)
)
)
)
)
)
)
)
)
)
)
)
)
)
)
)

CRIMINAL NO. : 02-10013-W6Y

VIOLATIONS:
18 U.S.C. §2332a(a)(1)
(Attempted Use of a Weapon of
Mass Destruction).
18 U.S.C. §2332
(Attempted Homicide)
49 U.S.C. §§46505(b)(3) and (c)
(Placing Explosive Device on
Aircraft)
49 U.S.C. §46506(1) and 18 U.S.C.
§1113
(Attempted Murder)
49 U.S.C. §46504
(Interference with Flight Crew
Members and Attendants)
18 U.S.C. §§32(a)(1) and (7)
(Attempted Destruction of
Aircraft)
18 U.S.C. §924(c)
(Using Destructive Device During
and in Relation to a Crime of
Violence)
18 U.S.C. §1993(a)(1) & (8)
(Attempted Wrecking of Mass
Transportation Vehicle

INDICTMENT

COUNT ONE: (18 U.S.C. §2332a(a)(1) -- Attempted Use of Weapon
of Mass Destruction)

The Grand Jury charges that:

1.   At all times relevant to this count brought under Title
18, United States Code, Chapter 113B--Terrorism, Al-Qaeda was a
designated foreign terrorist organization pursuant to 8 U.S.C.
§1189.

2.   At various times relevant to this count, Richard Colvin
Reid received training from Al-Qaeda in Afghanistan.

Figure 7.3 Nine-count indictment against Richard Reid.

recognize piracy if the vessel is in international waters. Should the vessel
be within the territorial waters of a country that country is then responsible
for pursuing and investigating the incident, usually under the crime of
robbery. Other issues arise when you consider that many vessels that
regularly traverse a country's waterways are often registered and bear the
flags of other lands. (Figure 7.4.)

Figure 7.4 Cruise liners carry thousands of people and make attractive targets for terrorists.

Crews of cargo and passenger vessels emanate from many countries, and the ships are flagged in various lands throughout the world, all of which pose security difficulties. Although there has been much focus on passenger vessels, due to obvious reasons, it may be the use of cargo containers that poses a great risk to national security. These ships often arrive from countries with less than stellar security measures in place as well as coming from what many consider to be shallow draft ports. It is these ports that cannot accommodate many of today's secure and modern vessels; therefore, older less secure vessels are used. With thousands of cargo ships arriving in the United States alone each year, law enforcement should be cognizant of the hazardous possibilities that may lie within one, or more, of the 4,000 steel 40-foot containers. Officials at many ports utilize what is referred to as a gamma ray device to scan containers. However, it is highly unlikely that more than 5 percent of the containers arriving in the United States are scanned. Besides the shear volume of containers arriving, one must remember that these containers are then loaded on the backs of trucks and often driven through the heart of many cities.

According to a report from the International Maritime Bureau (IMB), a total of 23 vessels were hijacked in 2005, the highest in four years, and 440 crewmembers were taken hostage, the highest number since IMB started compiling statistics in 1992. They further noted that the number of reported piracy attacks for 2005 fell from 329 in 2004 to 276 in 2005, the lowest recorded figure in six years. It was also noted that locations such as Somalia, Iraq, Tanzania, and Vietnam reported increases in piracy.

In spite of accounting for nearly 30 percent of all reported attacks, figures for Indonesia showed a drop from 94 reported attacks in 2004 to 79 attacks in 2005. Attacks in the Malacca Straits fell from 38 in 2004 to 12 attacks in 2005. Malaysia, Thailand, Brazil, Venezuela, Colombia, Haiti, Nigeria, and Guinea also all recorded a fall in the number of reported piracy and armed robbery attacks.[8]

Many of the aforementioned vessels targeted in the referenced statistics were largely cargo and goods-carrying ships. The rise in maritime criminal activity and the potential for a catastrophic attack on passenger ships has been creating much debate about how vulnerable cruise ships, a virtual floating city, may be to attack. With the size of vessels growing and the exponential increase in cruising passengers, there should be concern. Some cruise ships carry a crew of 1,000 and approximately 3,000 passengers. Even military vessels have not been void of attacks from terrorists. Should a cruise or military ship fall prey to a terrorist attack in the future it won't be the first.

Achille Lauro

On October 7, 1985, a well publicized cruise ship, *Achille Lauro*, was pirated with all aboard held hostage by four heavily armed Palestinian terrorists off the coast of Egypt. The hijackers were members of the Palestine Liberation Front (PLF), which broke away from the PFLP-GC in the late 1970s and later split again into pro-PLO, pro-Syrian, and pro-Libyan factions. The pro-PLO faction was led by Muhammad Abbas (aka Abu Abbas), the leader of the hijackers, and was based in Baghdad prior to Operation Iraqi Freedom.

The Italian cruise ship *Achille Lauro* was on a 12-day Mediterranean cruise and carrying about 680 passengers and a mostly Italian and Portuguese crew of about 350.

The hijackers demanded that Israel free 50 Palestinian prisoners. During the siege the terrorists killed a disabled Jewish-American tourist, 69-year-old Leon Klinghoffer, and threw his body overboard with his wheelchair. After a two-day drama, the hijackers surrendered in exchange for a pledge of safe passage.

The hijackers boarded an Egyptian jet and attempted to fly to freedom when U.S. Navy F-14 jet fighters intercepted it and forced it to land in Sicily, Italy. The terrorists were taken into custody by Italian authorities.

USS Cole

On October 12, 2000, the United States Naval destroyer *Cole* was attacked by a small boat loaded with explosives while in port in Yemen. As part of the USS George Washington Battle Group, the USS *Cole* was in transit from the Red Sea to a port in Bahrain when the ship stopped in Aden for routine refueling. Yemen was the Defense Fuel Support Point that had been open just over a year when the attack occurred.

According to a CRS Report for Congress, prior to arriving in Aden, the ship's crew had filed a required force-protection plan and was at a heightened state of readiness. The condition of readiness included steps that were specifically intended to provide protection against attack by small boats.[9]

The USS *Cole* had just completed mooring operations at 9:30 a.m. and began the refueling process, which started at 10:30 a.m. At 11:18 a.m. local Bahrain time, a small boat approached the port side of the destroyer and detonated an explosion that caused a 40-foot by 40-foot gash in the port side of the *Cole*. It was reported that two suicide bombers aboard the boat were seen standing at attention just before the blast that killed 17 of the USS *Cole*'s 320 sailors and injured 39 others.

The FBI investigated a report out of London that a Yemeni Islamic group, the Jaish-e-Mohammed (Mohammed's Army) and the Aden-Abyan Islamic Army, both with ties to or off-shoots of Islamic Jihad, had claimed responsibility for the attack. The individuals responsible are also an alleged part of bin Laden's network of terror — al-Qaeda.

Attacks against military targets either by land, sea, or air are not new. Nearly all the Islamic terrorist groups have expressed one thing in common: They want all U.S. and Western forces out of the Middle East, which they consider to be holy Muslim land.

Buses and trains/railways

As alluded to earlier in this chapter, buses and railways (Figure 7.5 and Figure 7.6) have been and will probably continue to be targets of terrorists. Accessibility and ease of boarding, with little or no screening, make them attractive assets for the terrorist to breach and exploit.

Although many jurisdictions have laws that forbid the carrying or introduction of weapons such as guns and knives on board mass transit, the fact remains that little is done to prevent it. Furthermore, one does not require a gun, knife, or even explosive to overtake a mode of transportation. An item that has little regulation and is largely not prohibited on public transportation is the paintball marker also known as a paintball gun. These devices are used by the law enforcement and military communities in many training exercises due to their ability to simulate real life scenarios. They have even been used by jihad followers. In 2000 and 2001 nine individuals with terrorist ties conducted military style training with these devices in preparation for holy war in Fredericksburg, Virginia. Randall (Ismail) Royer, an American citizen who converted to Islam and a former alleged official of the Council on American-Islamic Relations (CAIR), and the other men are believed to be linked to the Pakistan-based religious organization, Lashkar-e-Taiba (Tayyiba), a Kashmir separatist group that the United States designated a terrorist organization in 2001. With paintball markers, a form of compressed gas, e.g., dive tank, and a case of paintballs (2,000 balls), or more, it would not be difficult for a terrorists to commandeer a mode of transportation. Should the paintballs be frozen and fired at an unprotected individual there is a chance that the attack could be deadly. Based on the aforementioned it is important for the law enforcement to remain cognizant of opportunities beyond conventional weaponry.

Israel Bus 405

On July 6, 1989, a fanatical follower of Hamas, Abd Al-Hadi Hganayem, boarded bus number 405 from Tel Aviv to Jerusalem after allegedly checking to confirm no Arabs were on board. The bus was filled with passengers and nine Israeli soldiers. Just before reaching the ravine at the village of Abu Gosh, the suspect rose up and reached the driver seat and chanted loudly

Figure 7.5 Buses and vans can carry hundreds of pounds of explosives. The three vehicles pictured here could pose a great danger to this airport terminal.

Figure 7.6 Trains have been attractive targets for terrorists for years.

"Allah akbar, Allah akbar" as he forced the bus over the cliff. Sixteen passengers, including one American, were killed and nearly another 30 injured.

London 2005

On July 7, 2005, four explosions occurred in Central London between 8:51 a.m. and 9:47 a.m. (local time) using IEDs, three detonated on trains and one on a red double-decker bus by four suicide bombers.

According to the Terrorism Knowledge Base (TKB), the three train blasts occurred within moments of each other and the bus bombing happened about an hour after the first three. One of these attacks targeted a train on the Piccadilly line, on train 311 traveling south from Kings Cross station to Russell Square at 8:50 a.m. One bomber, identified as Jamaican-born Germaine Lindsay, detonated his explosives in the first car of the train near a set of double doors. The blast was strong enough to cause major damage to the second carriage of the train as well. Twenty-six passengers, plus the bomber were killed in this attack. Because the train runs deep into the ground at this point of the line, it took rescue workers days to remove all the bodies from the wreckage. All four attacks occurred at the height of rush hour and on the same day that the G8 summit was scheduled to begin in Scotland.[10]

Initially the blasts claimed 55 lives: 26 at Kings Cross, 13 died on the bombed bus at Tavistock Square, and the attacks at Edgware and Aldgate each killed six people. London officials investigated a Pakistani and al-Qaeda connection that three of the four bombers visited Pakistan and the fourth purportedly toured Afghanistan before the attacks. One of the suspects, Germaine Lindsay, was known to another terror suspect in America, Iyman Faris.

Tokyo 1995

On March 20, 1995, members of the Japanese religious cult Aum Shinrikyo released sarin (nerve gas) on Tokyo's subway system, killing 12 persons and making over 5,000 thousand ill. It was the first large-scale use of a poison gas by a nongovernmental group and, although Aum Shinrikyo previously had not been identified as a terrorist group in the traditional sense of that term, the incident was promptly labeled an act of terrorism.

Tokyo's Subway System.   Arguably the most comprehensive metro system in the world, Tokyo's first line opened in 1927 during the capital's rapid urbanization and today operates 21 lines owned by two principal operating companies. In addition to the subway, a number of monorail, tram, and private lines also serve the city. Tokyo's vast subway network comprises two separate subway systems. According to the Mineta Transportation Institute, the Teito Rapid Transit Authority (TRTA) is the older and larger system. It began operations in 1927 and currently runs 1,677 motor cars and 536 trailer cars over eight lines with a total mileage of 154.6 kilometers (96 miles). Three of its lines Marunouchi, Hibiya, and Chiyoda were the targets of the 1995 chemical attack. The second system, the TOEI, is run by the municipal government. It operates 524 cars on four lines with a total mileage of 40 miles. In addition, Japan Rail operates an extensive commuter network, and the adjoining city of Yokohama has two of its subway lines.[11]

Public transportation is vital in the huge metropolitan area of Tokyo. Millions use it daily; encouraged by the fact that the majority of Japanese companies pay the full travel costs of their employees. Without its subways, the city would stop. During peak hours the subways are fantastically overcrowded, with station staff sometimes literally pushing passengers into the cars. This too may have been a factor on March 20. The attack took place at the height of the morning rush hour, when passengers are accustomed to boarding the trains rapidly, without necessarily heeding what is going on. This not only provided concealment for the attackers, but also meant that even as ill passengers were stumbling off the contaminated coaches, new passengers were shoving their way on board. Within minutes, more than a thousand people had been exposed to the poison gas left behind by members of Aum Shinrikyo.

Aum Shinrikyo.   The base of operations for the Aum Shinrikyo cult is primarily in Japan, their home country, but the cult is said to have had operations and followings overseas in countries such as the United States, Australia, Russia, Germany, Taiwan, Sri Lanka, and the former Yugoslavia.

Aum Shinrikyo (Supreme Truth) began operating as a religious organization in July 1987, having been founded as the Aum Shinsen no Kai organization in 1984. The head of the cult was Chizuo Matsumoto, also known as Shoko Asahara, a partially blind, charismatic former acupuncturist. He is currently incarcerated on death row in Japan. Shoko Asahara faced 27 murder counts in 13 separate indictments. The prosecution argued that Asahara gave orders to attack the Tokyo subway in order to overthrow the government and install himself the position of king of Japan. He developed his group and organized it along quasi-government lines, with its own ministries and departments, all under the Supreme Leader Asahara. The empire included a diverse business conglomerate bringing the cult an estimated net worth in the billions. In August 1989, the cult formed its own political organization, the Shinri Party, which contested the 1990 general election. None of the 25 candidates won seats.

Pre-incident indicators.   Much of the cult's intrinsic paranoia reflected the hypochondriac paranoid fantasies of its supreme leader, who claimed that he and his followers were themselves being attacked by chemical weapons. The group published its own magazine/paper and made continuous threats against the Japanese government, as well as others. To battle against its numerous enemies and to prepare for its role in the fantastical future imagined by its members required that the cult obtain the most advanced weapons of mass destruction and various assault weapons such as the AK-47 rifle. The weapons of mass destruction component required scientists, technicians, secret laboratories, front companies, a covert arms acquisition program, international connections, and huge sums of cash. Aum allegedly spent upwards of $10 million on the development of biological agents. In October 1992, Aum leader Shoko Asahara and 40 followers went to Zaire, ostensibly to help treat Ebola victims but the real intention for the group, determined in 1995, was to obtain virus samples for a biological weapon. Prior to the 1995 subway attack, Aum had sprayed botulinum toxin over Tokyo several times in 1990 and conducted similar activities with anthrax spores in 1993. It was Aum's escalating attacks and criminal efforts that brought them to the attention of law enforcement prior to their big sarin attack.

Although stripped of its legal status and tax privileges as a religious organization, following the poison gas attack in Tokyo, Aum Shinrikyo revived its activities in early 1997. The group raised and continues to raise funds through an array of sources. Two of their more common business methods have been the selling of cheap computers and the attendance of individuals at their seminars. They also raise funds from their membership.

Highlights of Aum in other countries

United States
- In 1987 the cult started a company in New York by the name Aum USA Company.
- In 1993 two Aum members attended flight school in Dade county Florida.
- In 1994 Aum developed a business relationship with an export business in California.
- Early in 1995 members of Aum inquired about survival equipment at a trade show in Nevada.

Australia
- Records confirm that Aum was in Australia from April 1993 to October 1994.
- Aum formed two companies in Australia: Clarity Investments and Maha Posya.
- Aum purchased a 500,000-acre sheep farm.
- The Australian Justice Minister stated that Aum members tested sarin gas in Australia before the Tokyo attack.

Taiwan
- The presence of Aum in Taiwan was primarily business oriented.
- Aum established a company in Taiwan in June 1993 by the name of Dai Hanei (Great Prosperity) as a purchasing agent, supposedly for the purchase of computer parts.

Sri Lanka
- Relatively little is known about Aum's activities in Sri Lanka.
- The cult reportedly owns considerable assets there including a tea plantation that Aum began operating in 1992.

Aum Today.   Although the group's founding father is incarcerated, it still exists. Today it is under the leadership of Fumihiro Joyu. At his release on December 29, 1999, Joyu became the de facto head of the organization. As a result of being Aum Shinrikyo's spokesperson, Joyu was arrested and tried for libel for publicly naming a third party as responsible for the sarin gas attack. Under his leadership, the group has changed its name to Aleph, the first letter of the Hebrew alphabet, which means to start anew, and has an estimated membership/following of 65,000. Although membership has been declared illegal in Russia, it has been suggested that approximately two-thirds of the group's followers live in Russia.

Madrid 2004

On March 11, 2004, citizens of Spain experienced one of the largest and deadliest terrorist attacks on their soil, which killed nearly 200 and injured hundreds more (Figure 7.7). Between 7:30 a.m. and 7:45 a.m. local time, ten explosive devices were detonated in four trains along the C-2 commuter train line, which runs through Madrid, Spain. The total number of IEDs that were planted was 13 (backpacks or sports bags). Ten detonated on the trains, and the Spanish National Police explosives detonation team detonated the remaining three.

The bombs were allegedly placed in passenger cars on four Madrid-bound trains. The suspected terrorists boarded the trains outside Madrid during the morning rush hour and between 7:00 a.m. and 7:15 a.m. planted the explosive devices. The devices were set to explode 35 minutes after being placed on the trains and were located and detonated in such a

Figure 7.7 Madrid train bomb blast, March 11, 2004.

manner to maximize casualties. Estimates are that up to 700 people were on each of the trains, with an average of 100 people in each of the passenger cars. In addition, it was theorized that the devices were set to explode at or near the railway stations. Three of the four trains were near or at the station when the explosions took place but the fourth was behind schedule and was outside the station area.

The first explosives, a total of three, detonated at 7:39 a.m. on a commuter train that had already arrived at the Madrid Atocha Train station, with 34 deaths. The second explosion occurred at 7:42 a.m., on a commuter train that was running two minutes behind schedule. This train was actually moving into the main station, and was approximately 500 meters away from the first. The train came to a halt near the C/Tellez, as four bombs exploded causing 64 deaths. The third train, with two bombs detonating at 7:42 a.m., was approximately 1000 meters from train #2, at the Pozo del Tio Raimundo station. This was the bloodiest, with at least 67 deaths. Finally, the fourth train was several hundred meters away at the Sta. Eugenia station, where one bomb exploded at 7:42 a.m., causing 16 deaths. Three further explosive devices hidden in backpacks were destroyed in police-controlled explosions. Open sources report that the IEDs had been planted to hit emergency services as they arrived on the scene.

Operational factors. After investigators began their initial investigation, Spanish authorities suspected the Basque Separatist Nation, also known as ETA, was involved due to prior threats against the railway and the pending national election. As the investigation developed it became evident that ETA, if involved directly or indirectly, was not the principal party responsible for this catastrophic event. The investigation ultimately led to the identification of primarily Moroccan Islamic extremists who had immigrated to Spain. The authorities surmised that the members of the cell responsible for the attack were associated with the Moroccan Islamic Combatant Group or an offshoot of Salafiya Jihadia who shared ideology with al-Qaeda.

Within approximately one month Spanish authorities arrested, detained, and questioned hundreds of individuals. They arrested and brought charges against 18 individuals of whom 14 were of Moroccan descent. Several suspects, including the alleged mastermind, blew themselves up when Spanish authorities went to their apartment.

There were reportedly few operational or pre-incident indicators of the attack such as surveillance. Osama bin Laden had threatened Spain for its role in the war on terror in the months prior to the attack. Cell members appear to have operated independently and supported their activities through criminal acts such as illegal narcotics. The explosive devices detonated by the suspects were made of sports type bags, Goma-2 ECO explosives (gelatin dynamite), bolts and nails, and were activated by a modified cell phone. It was learned that the explosives and detonators used were obtained by theft with the assistance of a Spaniard with ties to the mining community and they were transported in a stolen van. It appears that the terrorists made use of local and readily available material in developing their plot.

Strategically there were a few pre-incident indicators including previous threats, knowledge of extremist Islamic activity, prior knowledge of railway attempts from a known terrorist group in the country, and the pending national election. Although likelihood of mass casualties was an obvious target, it appears that a second event, the national elections, may have played a dramatic role. It has been speculated that this event single-handedly changed the Spanish political landscape when the incumbent party lost the election.

Trucks, cars, vans, taxis, limos, and rescue vehicles

This section encompasses most forms of day-to-day transportation (Figure 7.8). These modes of transportation are plentiful and have a common denominator — the ability to gain access to a location with little questioning. They also have the ability to carry hundreds to thousands of pounds of explosives. Truck bombs have been used to attack U.S. targets for at least 20 years. In recent years there has been some focus on taxis and rescue vehicles. Taxis may have gained focus due to the large number of foreign nationals who operate them. It would be hard to find a law enforcement member who would question or even stop a rescue vehicle. However, consideration should be given to limousines. These vehicles often have more access to facilities such as airports and corporate offices. Limousines are also rarely encountered by law enforcement officials. Many cases have a nexus to common forms of transportation, some of which are enumerated in Chapter 4.

Use of a vehicle as a bomb delivery system is not new. One of the first groups to exploit this and use it to their advantage, in the amount of devastation that they could achieve, was the Irish Republican Army. According to Poland there have been the following methodologies used by terrorists and criminal bombers in the use of vehicle bombs.[12]

1. Placing the explosive materials on or in the car to kill the occupants
2. Use of the vehicle as a launching system
3. Use of the vehicle as a booby trap or antipersonnel device to ambush personnel
4. Use of a hostage for the transportation or delivery of explosives
5. Use of the vehicle as a fragmentation device when detonating a large quantity of explosives
6. Use of multiple vehicle bombs in a coordinated strike
7. Use of the vehicle in a suicide attack

There is little doubt in the potential of using a vehicle as a bomb. They have been, and will likely continue to be, used to deliver devastating blows to government and military targets just like in Oklahoma City and Saudi Arabia.

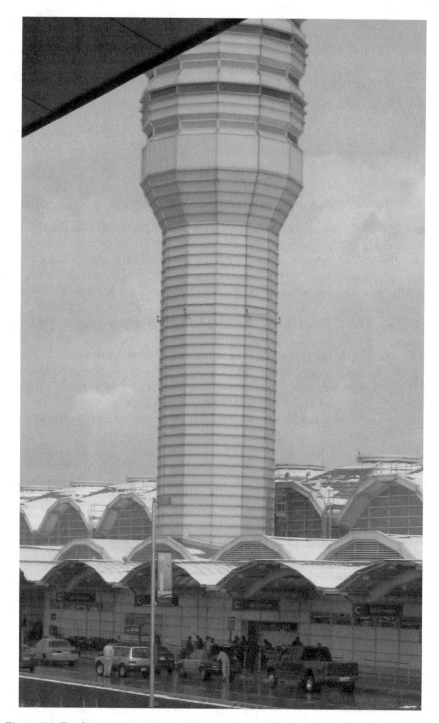

Figure 7.8 Trucks, taxis, SUVs, and cars are potential hazards. Note how many are within yards of an air traffic control tower, using public access.

Khobar Towers

On June 25, 1996, a fuel truck converted into a bomb estimated to be a "yield" of more than 20,000 pounds of TNT-equivalent explosives killed 19 U.S. military service members and injured an additional 500 service members housed at Khobar Towers. It also injured many Saudi Arabian citizens and third-country nationals (TCNs), and severely damaged or destroyed a significant amount of property. The blast formed a crater that was between 15 and 35 feet deep and approximately 55 to 85 feet wide. This was the second bombing in Saudi Arabia in less than a year. The first terrorist attack occurred on November 13, 1995. Five Americans were killed when terrorists exploded a much smaller bomb (estimated to be between 200 and 250 pounds of TNT-equivalent explosives) in front of the office of the Program Manager of the Saudi Arabian National Guard.

The bombing of Khobar Towers on June 25, 1996, was a hideous act of terrorism. An Air Force security policeman spotted suspects backing up what appeared to be a cylindrical-shaped sewage truck perpendicular to the north perimeter fence, near Building 131, outside the American sector of the Khobar Towers complex (Khobar Towers also housed British, French, and Saudi military forces). After noticing two men run from the truck and jump into a waiting car, which then sped away, the security police immediately ordered personnel to begin evacuating the building. The evacuation was conducted using a floor-by-floor notification system. Within four minutes of spotting the truck, the bomb detonated.

At Khobar Towers, Saudi Arabia, the host nation, exercised sovereignty both inside and outside the complex. Saudi Arabia did not permit the United States latitude in its activities within the installation, but permanent physical improvements, such as even the construction of a wall, or modifications to buildings, required Saudi approval. Internal security was a shared responsibility between the United States, coalition forces, and the Saudi Arabian military police. Security outside the fence was the responsibility of the Saudis.

Pre-incident indicators. Ten suspicious incidents, including four of possible surveillance, were reported by military personnel in April, May, and June 1996. These incidents were subsequently reported in summary form in the June 17, 1996, issue of the *Military Intelligence Digest*, which stated that the incidents led to increased security measures. Many were during the period of the Hajj. These incidents were investigated by the Saudi military and local police. None indicated an attack on Khobar Towers was imminent. These suspicious incidents near the Khobar Towers in the Spring of 1996 were also thoroughly evaluated by the entire military chain of command.

There were prior incidents even though the military had hardened and secured the facility on numerous occasions. These incidents included one possible threat indicator when a suspect rammed a Jersey barrier on the east perimeter of the facility. It was reported to Saudi authorities. There were four incidents of possible surveillance, which were reported to local Saudi authorities for further investigation. These occurred on April 1, 4, 17, and

25, 1996, and all involved reports, by military personnel, of Middle Eastern men driving by or parked and observing the compound. Of the five remaining incidents, two were inconclusive and three were completely discounted.

The military staff discussed these incidents with the Saudis, who did not view them as threatening. They attributed the incidents of possible surveillance to natural curiosity on the part of the Saudi populace about the activities of Americans inside the perimeter. Just outside the northern perimeter of Khobar Towers is a parking lot that was used by people visiting a nearby mosque. It also serviced a recreational area. During the month-long period of the Hajj, it was not unusual for many people to congregate in this area in the evenings. Most of the reported incidents took place during this time, and this may have caused the Saudi police to dismiss them as non-threatening. The Saudis said they had undercover security personnel in the area and they were not concerned.

Embassy — Nairobi, Kenya

On August 7, 1998, at approximately 10:30 a.m. local time, terrorists driving in a truck detonated a large bomb in the rear parking area, near the ramp to the basement garage, of the American Embassy in Nairobi. A total of 213 people were killed, of whom 44 were American Embassy employees (12 Americans and 32 Foreign Service national employees). Twenty-two embassy employees were seriously injured. An estimated 200 Kenyan civilians were killed and 4,000 were injured by the blast in the vicinity of the embassy.

The security systems and procedures relating to actions taken in Nairobi appear to have been to some extent adequate. The fact that the suicide bomber failed in his attempt to penetrate the embassy's outer perimeter, thanks to the refusal of local guards to open the gates is a testament to this. In Dar es Salaam, the suicide bomber likewise failed to penetrate the perimeter, apparently stopped by a blocked entry point by an embassy water truck.

Embassy — Dar es Salaam, Tanzania

On the morning of Friday, August 7, 1998, a truck laden with explosives drove up Laibon Road to one of the two vehicular gates of the U.S. Embassy in Dar es Salaam. According to physical evidence and reports from persons on the scene just prior to the bombing, the truck was unable to penetrate the perimeter because it was blocked by an embassy water tanker. Faced with being unable to breach the interior perimeter, the suicide bomber detonated his charge at 10:39 a.m. at a distance of about 35 feet from the outer wall of the chancery.

The bomb attack killed more than 10 people and another 85 people were injured. No Americans were among the fatalities, but many were injured, two of them seriously. The chancery suffered major structural damage and was rendered unusable, but it did not collapse. No one inside the chancery was killed, in part due to the strength of the structure and in part to simple luck. A number of third-country diplomatic facilities and residences in the immediate vicinity were also severely damaged, and several American Embassy residences were destroyed, as were dozens of vehicles. The American Ambassador's residence, a thousand yards distant and vacant at the time, suffered roof damage and collapsed ceilings.

Pre-incident indicators. There were no credible intelligence reports that provided an immediate or tactical warning of the August 7 bombings. A number of earlier intelligence reports cited alleged threats against several U.S. diplomatic and other targets, including the embassies in Nairobi and Dar es Salaam. All of these reports were disseminated to the intelligence community and to appropriate posts abroad, but were largely discounted because of doubts about the sources. Other reporting, while taken seriously, was imprecise, changing, and nonspecific as to dates, diminishing its usefulness. Indeed, for eight months prior to the August 7 bombings, no further intelligence was produced to warn the embassies in Nairobi and Dar es Salaam.

While there was never an indication of when or how the U.S. embassies in Nairobi, Kenya, and Dar es Salaam, Tanzania would be attacked, there was mounting intelligence to suggest that the embassies were not adequately secure and were potentially targets of terrorist plots. Consequently, while certain threats were identified and intelligence had been collected and disseminated in some cases, they were often discounted before reaching high-level officials and determined to be unfounded.

In the summer of 1997, CIA identified Wadih el-Hage as a key figure in al-Qaeda's leadership in Kenya. In August, 1997, the Kenyan police, CIA, and FBI raided el-Hage's house in Nairobi, downloaded files from his computer, and confiscated a number of written correspondences. He was extensively questioned three times by the FBI, but the documents from his home were not translated because of the unavailability of Arab-speaking staff and the low priority given their contents.[13]

In examining the circumstances of these two bombings, the Accountability Review Boards for Nairobi and Dar es Salaam determined that the security systems and procedures for physical security at the embassies were generally met and, in some cases, exceeded the systems and procedures prescribed by the Department of State for posts designated at the medium or low threat levels. However, these standard requirements had not sufficiently anticipated the threat of large vehicular bomb attacks and were inadequate to protect against such attacks. For example, neither the embassy in Nairobi nor the one in Dar es Salaam met the department's standard for a 100-foot setback/standoff zone. Both were "existing office buildings" occupied before this standard was adopted, so a general exception was made — a weakness that was exploited.

Bicycles

In the significant date list highlighted in Chapter 4 there was probably one event that went largely unnoticed. The event was on July 23, 2001, and involved the use of a bicycle as a bomb that killed seven in Kashmir.

Figure 7.9 Bicycles are a common form of transportation and are allowed in buildings and mass transit systems.

On December 10, 2004, 11 persons, including two army personnel, were killed and 26 others sustained injuries when a bomb attached to a bicycle exploded at Quetta in the Baluchistan province of Pakistan. Fifteen members of the Frontier Corps and Baluchistan Reserve Police personnel were injured by a remote-controlled bicycle bomb in the southwest city Quetta when they passed by.

These are just examples direct attacks that have taken place using bicycles (Figure 7.9). This mode of transportation has also been used in several suicide attacks. Between 1996 and 2000 there were at least three suicide bombing attacks in Sri Lanka by members of LTTE.

Bicycle frames are often made of hollow aluminum tubing, which can be packed with explosives. Many have saddle bags that can carry a fair amount of explosive material. Law enforcement personnel often x-ray and inspect bags, but the bicycle often goes without inspection. In many large metropolitan areas bicycles are allowed into buildings and on trains and buses. This weakness can be exploited by the terrorist and should not be overlooked in analysis or threat and vulnerability assessments.

The sheer magnitude of possibilities with regard to the use of transportation will prove to be a formidable challenge for law enforcement. The use of vehicle-borne improvised explosive devices (VBIED) will be the likely scenario encountered. There are, however, some situations that may afford personnel the opportunity to gain insight into a group's activities or even thwart a future attack with regard to transportation. Outlined below are some situations that may serve as pre-incident indicators:

- Person renting a vehicle is nervous, overly private, or does not appear to have a demonstrated need
- Vehicles parked for extended period of times at government, military, or other high-risk targets
- Inquiries about vehicle modifications, payload capabilities, or speed
- Desire to pay by cash and the need to get a deposit back without delay
- Theft of delivery, military, cargo, or civil service vehicles
- Inquiries about deliveries including timeline and routes
- Theft or purchase of paint, decals, or lighting equipment that can be used to modify a vehicle to appear as an emergency, delivery, or security vehicle

Incidents such as those noted above may come via law enforcement reports or even anonymous tips called into police departments. These events should be taken seriously and reviewed in the analytical process.

Summary of recent transportation targets

Between 1997 and 2000 there were over 110 terrorist incidents targeting buses, bus depots, or bus stops (Figure 7.10). During this same time period the second target of choice appears to be railways. There were at least 65 train- or railway-related terrorist attacks throughout the world in the three-year time span. It is apparent that no one single country is immune from these attacks. Some of the more prevalent countries experiencing attacks on transportation have been:

Figure 7.10 The power and devastation of a bomb that was brought on a bus.

- Israel
- India
- Tajikistan
- Germany
- Guatemala
- Pakistan
- Russia
- Georgia
- Philippines
- Sri Lanka
- United Kingdom

Regardless of the location, there have been several methods of attacks used on transportation. Everything from hijacking, handgun attacks, and bombings has been used to commit the majority of terrorist incidents involving transportation. One method that receives much attention is that of the suicide or homicide bomber.

Use of suicide bombers

Although not the staple in the terror repertoire, suicide bombing demonstrates how no one is safe, and how easily a terrorist can penetrate locations and create death and destruction (Figure 7.11). Islamic fundamentalist suicide bombers are discussed and highlighted on most modern media outlets as the main perpetrators of suicide attacks. Prior to the satellite and 24-hour cable explosion, suicide bombers were committing their atrocities throughout the world in regions outside the Middle East. According to Hudson, the unrivaled

Figure 7.11 Hamas suicide bombers.

world leaders in terrorist suicide attacks are not the Islamic fundamentalists but are the Tamil Tigers of Elam in Sri Lanka also known as LTTE. LTTE are extremely committed and so dedicated to carrying out their mission that they carry cyanide capsules to avoid capture. In the wake of the Ghandi assassination, no fewer than 35 LTTE operatives committed suicide rather than be questioned by authorities.[14] One of the more notable attacks against a western country was the April 1983 U.S. Embassy in Beirut when a suicide bomber detonated a van, killing 63 people. According to the U.S. Army, there have been at least 300 separate suicide terrorist attacks worldwide since the Beirut attack. However, this report notes that suicide terrorism has been on a continuous decline over the past 20 years.[15]

Who are the bombers and their groups?

Without little debate, most would argue that the leaders in suicide bombing today are members of Hamas in Palestine. An Israeli media outlet in late 2001 reviewed the makeup of 100 Palestinian suicide bombers and they noted the following.[16] Of the 100 suicide bombers, 75 were killed while perpetrating 67 different missions. In several attacks, like the one at Beit Lid in 1995, several suicide bombers participated in the same mission. The other 25 bombers were either intercepted by Israeli or Palestinian security forces before carrying out their attack or were captured after their explosives failed to detonate. Seven of the 30 suicide bombers sent on missions during the past year were arrested. Outlined below are some characteristics or traits:

- 66 belonged to Hamas, 34 were members of Islamic Jihad
- 67 were between the ages of 17 to 23 and most of the others were also under the age of 30
- 54 came from Gaza, 45 from the West Bank, and one was an Israeli Arab; the Israeli Arab, who carried out the attack in Nahariya in September, 2001, was also an exception in his advanced age — 53
- 23 had elementary education, 31 were high school graduates, and 46 had higher education
- 86 were unmarried and 14 were married

According to Martin, approximately 125 suicide bombings were carried out between 2001 and 2004, with 53 of these attacks occurring in 2002.[17] He noted that there was a marked increase in the number of females being used to carry out suicide missions. One of the more well known female suicide bombers is Wafa Idriss. Wafa was a nurse with the Red Crescent, the Palestinian version of the Red Cross. On January 27, 2002, the 28 year-old nurse walked into a shopping district on Jerusalem's Jaffa Road and detonated a bomb, killing herself as well as an Israeli, and injuring 150 others. In the Palestinian community Idriss became a celebrity and was worshipped

Figure 7.12 Female suicide bomber garment.

to the point that on July 24, 2003, Palestinian television broadcasted a glorious celebration of her life including an orchestra and song. Since her detonation in 2002 through the end of 2004 there were at least eight other Palestinian women who have carried out suicide missions. These missions are not limited to Palestinian women. In November 2005 a Belgian-born convert to Islam, Muriel Degauque, became the first European woman suicide bomber, killing herself in Iraq. An example of a female suicide garment is a "bra bomb" (Figure 7.12).

Use of females in attacks should not come as a surprise. Terrorists do their homework and, just like law enforcement should look to anticipate behaviors, they have found a well-noted weakness. Law enforcement personnel focus on men, as do military personnel. Terrorists have exploited this for nearly a half of a century, and it was noted in the film *Battle of Algiers*, a movie about the FLNs success over the French in the Algerian war for independence in the late 1950s.

When examining the use of suicide terrorism from a group perspective, the U.S. Army noted that there are several reasons that this tactic is employed by a group. Outlined below are some of these reasons:[18]

1. Suicide attacks can result in large casualities and extensive damage.
2. Success of the suicide mission is almost guaranteed once the attacker departs for the operation.
3. Suicide attacks usually have a large psychological effect on the public due to the sense of helplessness.
4. Suicide attacks are relatively inexpensive, yet very effective. Estimates are that it can cost as little as $150 to conduct a suicide attack.
5. Suicide attacks often result in large donations to support the cause of the group.
6. Suicide attacks are normally less complicated than other types of operations.
7. The use of suicide terrorism presents minimal security risks to the group.
8. Media coverage of a suicide attack is almost guaranteed.

What can you look for?

Security or precautionary measures will not be sufficient in combating the potential problem posed by the suicide bomb threat. This was evident in the 2005 London attacks. Without a doubt, these types of events will continue to occur. Despite the shared willingness to die for their beliefs, there is no one unique profile for a suicide bomber that law enforcement can look for. However, suicide bombers do not act by themselves. There are handlers, motivators, spiritual advisors, and logistical and operational supporters. Someone must recruit and train these individuals. James Poland suggests that by taking proactive measures it may be possible to interdict future suicide attacks. He suggests the following proactive measures:[19]

1. Family members may notice a change in the son or daughter's behavior patterns.
2. Successful counterstrategy requires comprehensive intelligence of the recruitment, selection, and training of the suicide bomber.
3. The person who recruits the potential suicide bomber usually follows that person throughout their military-type training and spiritual awakening.
4. Operational groundwork for the attack includes preparation of the explosive device, locating a safe house, and the transport of the bomber and explosives to the target.
5. Organizations that support and create an atmosphere for the use of suicide attacks must be identified.

Just like identifying a terrorist in a crowd, you will not be able to readily identify a suicide bomber. However, clothing is perhaps the most outwardly present observation. Items such as baggy clothes, clothing not consistent with the weather, and presence of heavy bags may give visual clues.

There are at least 15 terrorist organizations, including Hamas, Hezbollah, PIJ, and PKK, in at least 12 different countries that have utilized suicide terrorists, so there is no one clear cut profile with which to work. However, according to Ganzor, there are some characteristic traits that have been observed in Middle Eastern suicide bombers. In the Anti-Defamation League publication, *Countering Suicide Terrorism*, Ganzor noted the following common characteristics of suicide bombers:[20]

1. Young — usually from 18 to 27 years of age.
2. Usually not married, unemployed, and from a poor family.
3. Usually the shahid completed high school.
4. Most were devoted students in the Islamic fundamentalist education centers in Gaza and in the West Bank directed and financed by Hamas.
5. Some of the shahids arrested by Israel in the past expressed the desire to avenge the death or injury of a relative or close friend at the hands of Israel.

Most suicide bombers feel a sense of patriotism and are promised eternal life in paradise, 72 virgins, and the privilege to promise life in heaven to 70 relatives. They may also believe that the social and economic status of their family may improve. The latter belief is realized when, as the Iraqi government once did, thousands of dollars were paid to the families of the suicide bomber.

Homegrown terror — learning from others

There have been numerous individuals that could be classified as extremists or terrorists, both born and naturalized, who have roots in the United States. This is hard for some to believe or acknowledge, but none the less, it is true. Not every terrorist emanates from Europe, South America, Asia, or the Middle East. What is even tougher to comprehend is the fact that many of these individuals adopt the ideology of some of the most radical/extremist religion-based groups. We can comprehend that a citizen can belong to a "domestic terrorist group" but cannot fathom that he or she would join a "foreign terrorist group." This is a naïve approach. Terror is not restricted to a single country of origin. Just ask your self one question. If you wanted to pull off an attack in a country, is it better to be a foreigner and try to assimilate into society or find someone who is a citizen, familiar with the surroundings and who "fits in"? Terrorists are not always from a particular ethnicity or culture. Just as terrorists from other lands may conduct operations in the United States, it is important to note that American citizens have supported terrorist operations abroad. An example of this would be Jaber Elbaneh, a U.S. citizen who was in custody in Yemen prior to escaping from prison with 23 other terrorists, and is wanted in Buffalo (Lackawanna), New York for a 2003 charge of providing material support to a terrorist organization. Others, who were not originally Muslims, have taken part in terrorist activities.

Outlined below is a sample of some of the more notable Americans who fought for the "enemy" or against members of the Western World:

> Clement Rodney Hampton-El (aka Dr. Rashid): A former New Jersey hospital technician, Hampton-El was wounded while fighting with Mujahideen fighters in Afghanistan in 1988. Hampton-El eventually returned to the United States. It has been alleged that he became a bomb expert and had ties to Ramzi Yousef and Sheikh Omar Abdel Rahman. Clement Rodney Hampton-El was convicted of conspiring to blow up New York City landmarks in a 1993 terror plot linked to the World Trade Center bombing in February of that year.
>
> John Walker Lindh: An American citizen born in Washington, D.C. and lived in Marin County, California, was captured in 2001 while fighting for the Taliban in Afghanistan.
>
> Adam Gadahn: Born in California and raised in Riverside County, Gadahn is suspected of being a member of al-Qaeda and is being investigated

for being a spokesperson in video tapes from al-Qaeda against America. He is allegedly affiliated with the Wahhabi organization, the Islamic Society of North America (ISNA).

Iyman Faris: A truck driver from Ohio, was born in Kashmir and entered the United States in the early 1990s, and became a citizen in the late 1990s. In 2003, Faris pled guilty to providing support to al-Qaeda. Faris allegedly met Khalid Sheikh Mohammad in 2002 and knows a suspect from the 2005 London bombings.

Jose Padilla: Born in Brooklyn, New York, Padilla, a street gang member, converted to Islam while in prison. He was arrested in Chicago in 2002 after traveling throughout the Middle East.

Expanded details

Iyman Faris

Iyman Faris, also known as Mohammed Rauf, a naturalized U.S. citizen, was born in Kashmir in 1969. He lived in Ohio and was employed as a truck driver. Faris pled guilty in May 2003 for casing a New York City bridge and providing material support for al-Qaeda. Faris admitted to traveling to a training camp in Afghanistan in late 2000, where he was introduced to Osama bin Laden (Figure 7.13). He also admitted that during a meeting in late 2000, one of bin Laden's men asked him about "ultralight" airplanes, and said al-Qaeda was looking to procure an "escape airplane." Faris admitted that about two months later, he performed an Internet search at a cafe in Karachi, Pakistan, and obtained information about ultralights, which he turned over to a friend for use by al-Qaeda.

During a visit to Karachi in early 2002, he was introduced to a senior operational leader in al-Qaeda. A few weeks later, the operational leader asked what he could do for al-Qaeda. Faris said he discussed his work as a truck driver in the United States, his trucking routes and deliveries for airport cargo planes. The al-Qaeda leader said he was interested because cargo planes would hold "more weight and more fuel."

The al-Qaeda leader spoke with Faris about destroying a bridge in New York City by severing its suspension cables, and tasked Faris with obtaining the equipment needed for that operation. The leader also explained that al-Qaeda was planning to derail trains, and asked Faris to procure the tools for that plot as well.

Jose Padilla — aka The Dirty Bomber

It is unclear whether Jose Padilla, also known by his adopted Muslim name Abdullah al Muhajir, was using his gang affiliation to sponsor terrorism. Padilla, an admitted Latin Disciple gang member, was arrested at Chicago's O'Hare Airport as an associate member of the al-Qaeda terrorist network (Figure 7.14). The FBI reported that Padilla had changed his name, converted to Islam, and trained with the terrorist network after his last release from prison.

IN THE UNITED STATES DISTRICT COURT FOR THE

EASTERN DISTRICT OF VIRGINIA

Alexandria Division

UNITED STATES OF AMERICA	)	
	)	
v.	)	CRIMINAL NO.
	)	
IYMAN FARIS,	)	
a/k/a Mohammad Rauf,	)	
	)	
Defendant.	)	

STATEMENT OF FACTS

Should this matter proceed to trial, the United States would prove the following beyond a reasonable doubt:

1. The defendant, Iyman Faris, a/k/a Mohammed Rauf, was born in Kashmir on June 4, 1969. The defendant entered the United States in May 1994 and became a United States citizen in December 1999. Defendant has been employed as an independent truck driver for several years.

2. In late 2000, the defendant traveled with a long-time friend, hereafter referred to as conspirator-1 (C-1), from Pakistan to Afghanistan. (The defendant has known C-1 since the Soviet/Afghanistan war in the mid-1980's and has maintained a friendly relationship with him since that time.) After arriving in Afghanistan with C-1, the defendant was introduced to Osama bin Laden at an al Qaeda training camp. The camp had numerous tents and buildings, and there were several men present who wore black scarves and carried weapons. Since at least this meeting, the defendant knew that Osama bin Laden and C-1 were senior leaders in al Qaeda. The defendant understands C-1 to be Osama bin Laden's "right foot" – a man who serves a critical leadership role in providing supplies and materials needed by al Qaeda.

3. During this meeting in late 2000, one of Osama bin Laden's men asked the defendant

Figure 7.13 *United States v. Iyman Faris*, Statement of Facts.

While street gangs are known for causing havoc on city streets through acts of "crime," Padilla was set to inflict major damage by conspiring to build and detonate a "dirty bomb" in the United States according to the FBI.

William Morgan — Cuban Revolutionary

The aforementioned individuals were not the first and certainly won't be the last. One of the first modern era Americans to have left the United States

UNITED STATES DISTRICT COURT
SOUTHERN DISTRICT OF FLORIDA

CASE NO. 04-60001-CR-COOKE (s) (s) (s) (s) (s)
18 U.S.C. § 956(a)(1)
18 U.S.C. § 371
18 U.S.C. § 2339A
18 U.S.C. § 922(g)(5)(B)
18 U.S.C. § 1001(a)
18 U.S.C. § 1621(1)
18 U.S.C. § 1505
18 U.S.C. § 924(d)(1)
18 U.S.C. § 2
21 U.S.C. § 853

UNITED STATES OF AMERICA

v.

ADHAM AMIN HASSOUN,
a/k/a "Abu Sayyaf,"
MOHAMED HESHAM YOUSSEF,
a/k/a "Abu Turab,"
KIFAH WAEL JAYYOUSI,
a/k/a "Abu Mohamed,"
KASSEM DAHER,
a/k/a "Abu Zurr," and
JOSE PADILLA,
a/k/a "Ibrahim,"
a/k/a "Abu Abdullah the Puerto Rican,"
a/k/a "Abu Abdullah Al Mujahir,"

Defendants.

_____/

FILED by _____ D.C.
MAG. SEC.

NOV 17 2005

CLARENCE MADDOX
CLERK U.S. DIST. CT.
S.D. OF FLA. · MIAMI

SUPERSEDING INDICTMENT

The Grand Jury charges that:

INTRODUCTION

At times material to this Superseding Indictment:

Figure 7.14 Indictment of Jose Padilla, aka Abdullah al Muhajir.

to fight for someone else's beliefs was a man from Toledo, Ohio, William Alexander Morgan. Described by some as a troubled person; expelled from several schools, arrested, and removed from the U.S. Army, he was a recruiter's ideal candidate. According to the *Toledo Blade*, Morgan left his hometown to fight alongside Fidel Castro and Che Guevara and Castro's revolutionary forces in 1957. In Cuba he was the Yanqui Comandante who was promoted to the rank of major. He was described as a charismatic tough man who stunned his family by leaving his home in Toledo to join the revolutionary forces — a soldier of fortune who vowed to fight for "freedom and democracy."[21]

Leading a band of young guerillas, he captured the town of Cienfuegos in 1958 in one of the last battles of the revolution. He was celebrated by many for his actions. However, his celebrity status diminished and he was eventually executed by Castro's government in March 1961.

Besides learning from others, individuals obtain and learn their ideology in many ways. One of the more prevalent is through radical or extremist teachings, some of which occur locally. Long-standing extremist-based groups are located in the United States.

Cases for groups found in the United States and abroad

Lackawanna Six

The Lackawanna Six, also known as the Buffalo Six, is a group of Yemeni-Americans, born and raised in the United States, who were charged with providing material support to al-Qaeda. They allegedly traveled to Pakistan and to Afghanistan in early 2001. They were arrested in the Buffalo area in late 2002. In 2003, they pled guilty to the charges and were subsequently sentenced.

Portland Seven

The group that came to be known in the media as the Portland Seven was a group of American Muslims from the Portland, Oregon area. In October 2002, the FBI began an operation that attempted to close down the suspected terrorist cell. The seven individuals were allegedly attempting to join al-Qaeda forces in their fight in Afghanistan after 9/11.

Northern Virginia

In Northern Virginia, 11 men were indicted for conspiring to violate the Neutrality Act and firearm laws based on their participation in military-style training, including the use of paintballs, in the United States. Several of the defendants traveled to Lashkar-e-Taiba (LET) terrorist training camps in Pakistan in preparation for conducting violent jihad in Kashmir and elsewhere.

IAP

Characterized by investigative reporter and terrorism expert Steven Emerson as Hamas' primary voice in the United States, the Islamic Association for Palestine (IAP) has established its North American Headquarters in Bridgeview, Illinois. In Emerson's documentary *Jihad in America*, the IAP was based and situated in Richardson, Texas. The IAP has been investigated by Emerson for their alleged ties to the first World Trade Center Bombing. Emerson questioned a representative of the IAP as to their support for

Hamas and their dislike for Jews. In this interview there is little doubt of the representative's deception and attempt to avoid the truth. Emerson even noted in his February 1998 statement before the Senate Judiciary Committees Subcommittee on Terrorism, Technology, and Government Information that the IAP is a vehicle to recruit and train terrorist to attack the Israelis. Prior to being taken down, the IAP Web site proudly displayed an Israeli flag surrounded by a circle with a line through it and proclaimed "Jews Against Zionism."

The IAP was founded in 1981 by Mousa Mohammed Abu Marzook, a founder of the Holy Land Foundation, which was shut down due to its financial ties to terrorism. He is now an alleged political leader of Hamas and is located in Syria. A protégé of Marzook is Rafeeq Jaber, as of January 2006 the current president of the IAP. He is also a founder of the national office of the Council on American Islamic Relations (CAIR) and a board member of the Mosque Foundation, also located in Bridgeview. The Mosque Foundation has been the focus of investigations for nearly 10 years for their alleged involvement related to raising funds for Palestinian terrorist organizations, primarily Hamas and the Muslim Brotherhood. Activities, financial and otherwise, of several members of the Bridgeview mosque and the Mosque Foundation, have brought this small town into the forefront of some of the more significant terrorist events and terrorist groups.

Situated in the Village of Bridgeview, Illinois, is a mosque with over 2,000 prayer attendees that has been on the terrorist-related radar screen of federal authorities for more than a decade. Over the past several years, United States government officials have taken legal action against a number of former officials and other prominent members of the Bridgeview mosque for funding and participating in terrorist organizations, primarily Hamas affiliated. Membership of the mosque has allegedly poured hundreds of thousands of dollars into three charities that were closed shortly after 9/11 for financing terrorism: Global Relief Foundation, the Holy Land Foundation, and the Benevolence International Foundation.

On February 8, 2004, the *Chicago Tribune* published an investigative report titled "Struggle for the Soul of Islam, Hard-Liners Won Battle for Bridgeview Mosque." This article provides explicit insight into one of the United States' largest Palestinian communities located in Cook County, Illinois — Bridgeview. Radical aspects of some of the membership as well as the aggressive fundraising efforts were highlighted.

Reporters and everyday citizens appear to have more insight into events that occur in this small village, Bridgeview, whose motto is "A Well Balanced Community," than local authorities who appear to view the aforementioned concerns as a matter for federal authorities. These local officials may also be concerned with political repercussions in a town whose political base once emanated from European decent and is now seen by some as "little Palestine." These officials are not alone in this mentality. Several small communities have experienced the reaches of radical, extreme, and terror groups and they are totally unaware, fearful, or refuse to acknowledge it. At present there is an active group in the United States, Jamaat al-Fuqra, which has extended its physical reaches in the same aggressive manner as the IAP. Jamaat al-Fuqra has continued to stretch its reach across the United States, including extreme rural communities.

Jamaat al-Fuqra and the Muslims of America

Jamaat al-Fuqra (JUF), also referred to as al-Fuqra, and µl-Faqra (The Poor, The Impoverished, and Community of the Poor), is a Sufi Islamic extremist sect consisting of predominately African American Muslims. Pakistani cleric Sheikh Mubarik Ali Gilani founded JUF in 1980 in Brooklyn, New York, but Gilani currently allegedly resides in the outskirts of Lahore, Pakistan. The group allegedly seeks to purify Islam through violence and was banned by the U.S. Department of State in 2000. Some refer to the group as Muslims of America (MOA). However, JUF and MOA are not necessarily one and the same. Members of JUF are not necessarily members of MOA and vice versa. MOA is a tax exempt, nonprofit organization registered in various locations in the United States, Caribbean, and Canada and may be used as a "front" for JUF activities. Both groups strictly adhere to the teachings, guidance, and orders of Sheikh Mubarik Ali Gilani from his base in Pakistan. Gilani is also the person that Daniel Pearl was seeking to visit and interview when he was abducted and murdered.

MOA is estimated to have as few as 3,000 and as many as 12,000 members in the United States alone who live on or around over two dozen rural compounds called "jamaats," or villages. These are located in over 10 locations across the United States: Coldwater, Michigan; Hancock, New York (alleged headquarters known as Islamberg); Jetersville, Meherrin, and Red House, Virginia; Commerce, Georgia; York, South Carolina (known as Islamville); Dover, Tennessee; Sweeny, Texas; Reidsville, North Carolina; and Fresno, California. MOA members have reportedly assimilated into society and hold positions in the public and the private sector. However, assimilating may not be that far of a stretch since the group has focused efforts on recruiting black men and women from within the community. Several of the men have reportedly been brought to Pakistan by Gilani for the purposes of training.

Coming to the attention of law enforcement

MOA and JUF were virtually unknown names to many in the law enforcement community during their first 10 years of existence. However, in the late 1980s the Colorado Attorney General's Office successfully prosecuted five members of JUF between 1993 and 1994. The investigation was initiated by Colorado Springs detectives who were investigating a series of burglaries. During subsequent investigations by Colorado law enforcement in the late 1980s, personnel discovered documents containing surveillance photos of many potential "targets." These included U.S. military installations such as Buckley Air Force Base in Denver, Rocky Mountain Arsenal in Commerce

City, the U.S. Air Force Academy in Colorado Springs, two Wyoming National Guard armories in Cheyenne, and Cheyenne's Warren Air Force Base. They also located and seized a large weapons cache including bomb-making materials, explosives, military training manuals, and an array of "how to" publications.

The most damning items that helped secure the prosecutions were several workers' compensation claims, which led to a full-scale fraud investigation. This investigation revealed that members had defrauded the State of Colorado of approximately $350,000 over an eight-year period.[22]

The JUF and MOA today

Gilani currently lives in the outskirts of Lahore, Pakistan. While in Pakistan Gilani allegedly seeks to carry out a self-declared policy of jihad or holy war against enemies of the group. These include but are not limited to Muslims with whom they disagree, such as those in India who support the creation of an Islamic state in Kashmir, Hindus, Hare Krishna, Israel, the Jewish Defense League, and the Nation of Islam.

Educating, recruiting, and funding

Gilani controls JUF and Muslims of America, which allegedly has six branch offices in U.S. cities and Toronto, Canada. The International Quranic Open University, Inc., established in 1982 and operated by MOA, is their primary educational facility. The university has the alleged support of Pakistani authorities and is suspected of having ties to Pakistan's Inter-Services Intelligence Directorate (ISID).

Reflecting the doctrines of the organization, members of JUF refer to themselves as "Soldiers of Allah." They seek to recruit and expand their operations. One of the more prevalent recruiting grounds has been through the prison system. Many members of JUF have been convicted of criminal acts and have spent time in jails and prisons. Once released from incarceration, select members are welcome to live on one of the organization's remote rural compounds. However, recidivism appears not to dissipate once they join the group or move to a compound. There have been numerous criminal acts attributed to members of JUF and MOA over the past 25 years, many in the United States, including fire bombings and murders/assassinations. It is the criminal acts that appear to be funding much of the organizations activities including narcotics. There are also alleged nonprofit operations, educational initiatives, and businesses such as a security company.

JUF and MOA appear to have been around for over two decades and show no signs of being eliminated, and it is incumbent upon today's law enforcement community to be aware of their activities, as well as other similar groups. Even though JUF and MOA seem to be thriving in North America, they are not and will not be the last case of suspicion to come to the attention of law enforcement in North America or abroad.

FILED
CHARLOTTE, N. C.

UNITED STATES DISTRICT COURT
WESTERN DISTRICT OF NORTH CAROLINA
CHARLOTTE DIVISION

JUL 3 1 2000

U. S. DISTRICT COURT
W. DIST. OF N. C.

UNITED STATES OF AMERICA)

v.)

DOCKET NO. *3:00 CR-147-mu*

BILL OF INDICTMENT

1. MOHAMAD YOUSSEF HAMMOUD)
   a/k/a Ali A. A. Abousaleh)
   a/k/a Ali A. A. Albousaleh)
2. BASSAM YOUSSEF HAMOOD)
   a/k/a Bassem Hammoud)
   a/k/a Bassam Hammoud)
3. CHAWKI YOUSSEF HAMMOUD)
4. MOHAMAD ATEF DARWICHE)
   a/k/a Mohamad Darwich)
5. ALI HUSSEIN DARWICHE)
   a/k/a Ali Hussein Darwich)
6. ALI FAYEZ DARWICHE)
   a/k/a Ali Darwich)
   a/k/a Ali Darwieh)
7. SAID MOHAMAD HARB)
   a/k/a Mustapha Harb)
   a/k/a Ahmad Al Alquam)
   a/k/a Mohamad Dbouk)
8. ANGELA GEORGIA TSIOUMAS)
   a/k/a Angie Tsioumas)
9. MEHDI HACHEM MOUSSAOUI)
   a/k/a Mehdi Moussoui)
   a/k/a Mehdi Masawi)
10. FATME MOHAMAD HARB)
    a/k/a Fatima Harb)
    a/k/a Fahtme Harb)
11. SAMIR MOHAMAD ALI DEBK)
    a/k/a Samir Depk)
12. HAISSAM MOHAMAD HARB)
    a/k/a Mohamad Dbouk)
13. TERRI JEANNE PISH)
14. TONIA YVONNE MOORE)
15. JESSICA YOLANDA FORTUNE)
)
)
)

Violation(s): 8 U.S.C. § 1324(a)(1)(A)(v)(I)
               8 U.S.C. § 1325(c)
               18 U.S.C. § 201(b)(1)
               18 U.S.C. § 371
               18 U.S.C. § 982
               18 U.S.C. § 1546(a)
               18 U.S.C. § 1956(h)
               18 U.S.C. § 2342

Figure 7.15 Charlotte Hezbollah cell; *United States v. Mohamad Hammoud et al.* Bill of Indictment.

Other notable cases

Charlotte Hezbollah case

Iredel County, North Carolina, appears to be a location far from the war on terror. However, in early 1995 it became the epicenter of one of the largest terrorist-related cases in the United States against members of Hezbollah (Figure 7.15). This case would also be one of the first tests of the 1996 enacted 18 U.S.C. (2339B), which prohibits providing material support and resources to designated foreign terrorist organizations.

What was dubbed by some as Operation Smokescreen, was initiated by Deputy Sheriff Robert Fromme who was working an off-duty detail for J.R. Tobacco in Statesville, North Carolina, for the purpose of apprehending shoplifters. His observations would eventually lead to a 4-year investigation, involvement of over 15 local, state, federal, and international law enforcement agencies, and the arrest and conviction of more than 25 individuals.

Birth of the cell

Cell leader Mohamad Hammoud from Beirut, along with two relatives, entered the United States in 1992 after he purchased fraudulent U.S. visas in Venezuela after several attempts to obtain a visa in Syria through the U.S. Embassy. Once detained at JFK International Airport in New York, Hammoud claimed asylum, which was eventually denied in late 1993. He was ordered deported and then filed an appeal. In an attempt to remain in the United States while his appeal was pending, Hammoud entered into three fraudulent marriages between 1994 and 1997. During his efforts, which were found to be based on fraudulent documents, Hammoud was ordered to be deported at least once. Mohamad's brother, Chawki, and other relatives that were involved in the cell, engaged in similar behavior. The behavioral patterns of the cell members led them into entering into several bogus marriages. They even paid for at least one Charlotte, North Carolina man to travel to Lebanon for a marriage and bribery of an embassy official in Cyprus.

Once in the United States, cell members moved quickly to establish residency in the Charlotte area in modest rented apartments and took menial jobs including working at a pizza place. However, there was a need to assimilate into society and avoid detection by law enforcement officials. The cell's subjects assumed identities and established others in efforts to avoid officers, further criminal activity, and pursue initiatives designed to fund their operations. One of the codefendants, Said Harb, testified that he had many identities and made at least $150,000 per identity. It would ultimately be the cell's criminal activity that would be the basis for their demise.

Making the case. After establishing their base in the United States, Hammoud's cell resorted to credit card schemes and cigarette smuggling in order to raise millions of dollars. Deputy Fromme initially observed what he thought were "Hispanic" men driving vans with out-of-state license plates and making large purchases with cash. His keen observation would lead to an investigation of a core group of eight Charlotte residents, including Hammoud, and the fact that they had purchased nearly $8 million worth of cigarettes. The profits reaped from their efforts were in the neighborhood of $2 million. These profits were eventually laundered through fraudulent shells and alias names, as well as reinvested into the cigarette smuggling operation.[23]

The smuggling efforts were made attractive by the $7.00 per carton of cigarettes tax mark-up in Michigan compared to North Carolina. Expenses associated with the delivery of the cigarettes included rental vehicles, gas, and hotels, which were charged on credit cards. The profits derived from the cell's criminal activity enabled them to live large beyond their apparent means and to purchase many questionable items such as laser range finders and aviation software.

Law enforcement personnel ultimately did what they do best, investigate crime. There were many crimes that were available for investigation including fraud, visa violations, cigarette smuggling, stolen property, immigration violations, bribery, money laundering, bank fraud, and racketeering. In investigating the criminal activities of the group, law enforcement personnel employed traditional investigative techniques:[23]

- Physical surveillance
- Search warrants, subpoenas, and seizures
- Cultivation of witnesses
- Analysis of telephone records
- Analysis of financial records
- Pen registers and pole cameras

Investigators also found and reviewed correspondence indicating various members' involvement, books and pamphlets, and receipts, some with direct links to Hezbollah and its leadership. The aforementioned, coupled with cooperative police work such as that from their counterparts in Canada, and the execution of 18 search warrants in July 2000, enabled investigative personnel to put the puzzle together and successfully prosecute cell members.

After a five-week trial Hammoud was found guilty on all charges and sentenced to 155 years in prison.

Bali case

One of the locations in the world that has seen a rise in terrorism activities has been Indonesia. On August 6, 2003, a car bomb exploded outside a J.W. Marriot Hotel in Jakarta, killing 12, and on September 9, 2004, a truck packed with explosives detonated outside the Australian Embassy in Jakarta, killing 11 people. A second location in the region to feel the rage of terrorists has been Bali. Most recently, on October 1, 2005, bombs exploded near three restaurants, killing four people. However, the case we will focus on is the one that occurred on October 12, 2002, which killed over 200 people at Sari Club and Paddy's Bar in Kuta (Figure 7.16). The 2005 nightclub bombings were the seventh major bombing in the region in a three-week time span. Indonesian police attributed the 2005 attack to the men behind the 2002 attack.

On October 12, 2002, a car bomb exploded outside the Sari nightclub in Bali, a popular tourist island in Indonesia. The attack was attributed to Jemaah Islamiah (JI), an Indonesian terrorist group with aims of creating an Islamic state composed of parts of Indonesia, Malaysia, and the Southern Philippines. However, according to U.S. and Asian intelligence authorities the attack was connected to al-Qaeda.

Figure 7.16 Sari nightclub in Bali after car bomb explosion, October 12, 2002.

Case specifics.   In February 2002, a meeting was held in Thailand between the operational chief of JI, Nurjaman Riduan Ismuddin, also known as Hambali, and several other men including one known as Mukhlas, where the topic of bringing jihad to South East Asia was discussed. In April of the same year Mukhlas returned home to the village of Tenggulun in Indonesia's East Java province to begin planning the attack with his younger brother Amrozi, when they allegedly decided to target Bali. Five months later Amrozi reportedly bought the chemicals and van necessary for the attack. It has been suggested by some in the law enforcement community that the 2002 attack cost the terrorists somewhere in the neighborhood of just $30,000.

On October 12, 2002, a suicide bomber with a backpack bomb detonated himself inside Paddy's bar. A few minutes later, a van parked outside the Sari Club exploded. The combined explosions killed over 200 people. A few miles away, a bomb exploded at the U.S. consulate about a minute after the van exploded. However, no one was injured. Seven days later, the purported radical spiritual leader of Jemaah Islamiah, Abu Bakar Bashir, was arrested by police.

A short time later on November 5, Amrozi was arrested in East Java where he confessed to owning the van responsible for the blast and also for buying the explosives used. He implicated his brother Mukhlas in the ownership of the van. Three days later al-Qaeda claimed responsibility for the Bali attacks.

Hambali, the purported organizer of the Bali bombings was detained in Thailand by the U.S. government in August 2003. Hambali was also believed to have been involved in the 2003 J.W. Marriot Hotel bombings in

Jakarta, as well as being a close associate of Khalid Sheikh Mohammed, the mastermind of the 9/11 attacks on America.

Throughout this chapter several examples, such as the indictments that were illustrated, have been cited and illustrate what law enforcement will likely see again, only with different players. Access to such documents may make interesting reading and research for books such as this, but law enforcement must remember its potential impact on future terrorists. What value do "clearances" have if many aspects of a case are widely available through Freedom of Information Act or Sunshine Law requests? While you may not be able to legally seal every document, you must remain cognizant of what others can obtain and even learn from in the future.

Chapter concepts

1. Modes of transportation have been used in terrorist attacks for over a century.
2. Transit systems are targets because they provide easy access, large concentrations of people, are vital to the economy, service disruption could affect millions, and are a target-rich environment.
3. Aviation has been targeted by terrorists for decades. The masters of airline hijacking have been the PFLP terrorist group.
4. Transportation, especially buses and railways, have been targeted by terrorists for decades in an attempt to demonstrate that everyday citizens are not safe.
5. Most terrorist attacks involving transportation had pre-incident indicators prior to the actual attacks.
6. Suicide attacks have been largely used by LTTE and Hamas. A method to identify suicide bombers is not available but there are potential indicators to identify.
7. Home-grown terrorists are a concern. There have been several from the United States including Faris, Padilla, Hampton-El, and Lindh.
8. There are groups that may pose a concern for law enforcement today in the United States, e.g., IAP, JUF, and MOA.

References

1. Terrorism Knowledge Base, http://www.tkb.org/GroupTargetModule.jsp, National Memorial Institute for the Prevention of Terrorism (26 February 2006).
2. Jenkins, B.M., and Gersten, L.N., *Protecting Public Surface Transportation Against Terrorism and Serious Crime: Continuing Research on Best Security Practices*, Mineta Transportation Institute, September 2001, pp. 25–27.
3. U.S. Department of Justice Federal Bureau of Investigations, The FBI's Counterterrorism Program Since September 2001, Report to the National Commission on Terrorist Attacks Upon the United States (14 April 2004), pp. 14–15.
4. Dunham, S., http://www.homelandsecurity.org/newjournal/articles/dunhammasstransit.htm, Mass Transit Defends Itself Against Terrorism, Homeland Security Institute, March 2002 (12 March 2006).

5. National Center for Transit Research, Public Transportation Anti-Terrorism Research Guide, Center for Urban Transportation Research University of South Florida, April 2002, p. 5.

6. Poland, J.M., *Understanding Terrorism Groups, Strategies, and Responses* 2nd ed., Prentice Hall, Upper Saddle River, NJ, 2005, p. 202.

7. Simonsen, C.E. and Spindlove, J.R., *Terrorism Today The Past, the Players, the Future*, 2nd ed., Prentice Hall, Upper Saddle River, NJ, 2005, p. 371.

8. ICC Commercial Crime Services, http://www.icc-ccs.org/main/news.php?news-id=63, International Chamber of Commerce, 31 January 2006 (12 March 2006).

9. Perl, R., and O'Rourke, R., Terrorist Attack on USS *Cole*: Background and Issues for Congress, CRS Report for Congress, 30 January 2001, p. 2.

10. Terrorism Knowledge Base, http://www.tkb.org/Incident.jsp?incID=24394, Abu Hafs Al-Masri Brigade and Secret Organization of Al-Qaeda in Europe Attacked Transportation Target (July 7, 2005, United Kingdom), MIPT, (11 March 2006)

11. Jenkins, B.M. and Gersten, L.N., *Protecting Public Surface Transportation*, pp. 49–51.

12. Poland, J.M., *Understanding Terrorism Groups*, p. 192.

13. Wikipedia, http://en.wikipedia.org/wiki/1998_U.S._embassy_bombings #Pre-bombing_intelligence, 1998 United States embassy bombings, (4 March 2006).

14. Hudson, R., *The Sociology and Psychology of Terrorism: Who Becomes a Terrorist and Why?*, Federal Research Division, September 1999, p. 29.

15. Deputy Chief of Staff for Intelligence, Suicide Bombing in the COE, U.S. Army Training and Doctrine Command, Handbook No. 1.03, August 2005, p. 2-I4.

16. Harel, A., http://www.haaretzdaily.com/hasen/pages/ShArt.jhtml?itemNo= 80841, Haaretz Daily, 10, August 2001 (11 March 2006).

17. Martin, G., *Understanding Terrorism* 2nd ed., Sage Publishing, Thousand Oaks, 2006, pp. 366–367.

18. Deputy Chief of Staff for Intelligence, Suicide Bombing in the COE, U.S. Army Training and Doctrine Command, Handbook No. 1.03, August 2005, p. III-1–2.

19. Poland, J.M., *Understanding Terrorism Groups*, p. 225.

20. Ganzor, B., *Countering Suicide Terrorism*, The Anti-Defamation League and The International Policy Institute for Counter Terrorism, 2002, p. 146.

21. Sallah, M.D., http://www.latinamericanstudies.org/cuban-rebels/morgan.htm, *Toledo Blade*, March 3, 2002 (25 February 2006).

22. Colorado Department of Law, http://www.ago.state.co.us/pr/121001_link.cfm, Information Regarding Colorado's Investigation and Prosecution of Members of Jamaat Ul Fuqra (11 March 2006).

23. Broyles, D.S., and Rubio, M., A Smoke Screen for Terrorism, The United States Attorney's Bulletin, Executive Office for United States Attorneys, Volume 52, Number 1, January 2004, p. 33.

chapter eight

What the future may hold

Law enforcement is heading for uncharted waters. Beyond dealing with criminal activity and enforcing state statutes, law enforcement personnel are at the time of this writing in the throes of war with a frontline that has no defined latitude or longitude. The enemy is often faceless and leaderless. What will the future hold? Although no one can predict the future, one certainty is that technology will be at the forefront. International and domestic terrorist groups are here to stay, but they will no longer be treated as two distinct factions. There are no boundaries with terrorists or organized hate groups. Law enforcement has embarked on a new frontier that cannot be disregarded and appears to be endless. Times have changed and so must law enforcement.

Chances are that the greatest terrorist impact will come from technology or science, such as cyber- or bioterrorism, rather than from conventional bombs. However, do not underestimate the importance of conventional bombs or improvised explosive devices to the traditional terrorist. Of the tens of thousands of terrorist incidents, based on tactics, from 1968 through 2005, the number one tactic is bombing, coming in around at just fewer than 60 percent. No matter what the source of the impact, agencies are cautioned against a simplistic approach. History has demonstrated that most terrorist attacks are events that are planned, often over the course of months and years. Therefore, we must use extreme caution when gathering information and must avoid overlooking any seemingly harmless aspect of situations or events presented. The smallest, seemingly meaningless, communication, transmission, purchase, or inquiry could be the missing component that links events. Agencies should take this information into account as well as all the categories mentioned in previous chapters when developing their database structures. Relegating minor items to a "comments" section or omitting them altogether may have adverse effects in the future. Also, database managers should include information on the various forms of terrorism, especially cyber and biological.

Foreign-based terrorist influence

The influence of foreign-based terrorist organizations is here to stay, and al-Qaeda is not the only one. Outlined below is the official list of foreign terrorist organizations as identified by the U.S. Department of State:

17 November
Abu Nidal Organization (ANO)
Abu Sayyaf Group (ASG)
Al-Aqsa Martyrs' Brigade
Ansar al-Islam (AI)
Armed Islamic Group (GIA)
Asbat al-Ansar
Aum Shinrikyo (Aum)
Basque Fatherland and Liberty (ETA)
Communist Party of Philippines/New People's Army (CPP/NPA)
Continuity Irish Republican Army (CIRA)
Gama'a al-Islamiyya (IG)
Hamas
Harakat µl-Mujahidin (HUM)
Hezballah (or Hizballah)
Islamic Movement of Uzbekistan (IMU)
Jaish-e-Mohammed (JEM)
Jemaah Islamiya Organization (JI)
Al-Jihad (AJ)
Kahane Chai (Kach)
Kongra-Gel (KGK)
Lashkar e-Tayyiba (LT)
Lashkar i Jhangvi (LJ)
Liberation Tigers of Tamil Eelam (LTTE)
Libyan Islamic Fighting Group (LIFG)
Mujahedin-e Khalq Organization (MEK)
National Liberation Army (ELN)
Palestine Liberation Front (PLF)
Palestinian Islamic Jihad (PIJ)
Popular Front for the Liberation of Palestine (PFLP)
Popular Front for the Liberation of Palestine-General Command (PFLP-GC)
Al-Qaeda
Real IRA (RIRA)
Revolutionary Armed Forces of Colombia (FARC)
Revolutionary Nuclei (RN)
Revolutionary People's Liberation Party/Front (DHKP/C)
Salafist Group for Call and Combat (GSPC)
Shining Path (SL)
Tanzim Qa'idat al-Jihad fi Bilad al-Rafidayn (QJBR)
United Self-Defense Forces of Colombia (AUC)

Appendix D lists the U.S. State Department's officially recognized foreign-based terrorist groups in the world that are full of hate and have no limitations in their pursuit of fulfilling their beliefs. Investigators and analysts should not be lulled into thinking that these are the only groups or factions dedicated to terrorism. It is merely the officially recognized listing.

Groups, movements, and ideologies with a presence in the United States

Many groups have had a presence, a following, or have conducted business in the United States. According to the U.S. State Department's designated foreign terrorist organization list for 2002, several groups have a confirmed presence in the United States:

1. al-Qaeda, Arabic for "the base" or "the formula," depending on the translation (worldwide), an Islamic extremist organization that opposes "non-Islamic" regimes and that has been linked to bombings throughout the world against U.S. government interests. An argument exists that although this is often classified as a group, that al-Qaeda is more of a movement or an ideology when compared to others.
2. al-Gama'a al-Islamiyya (Egypt), an Islamic extremist group responsible for attacks on tourists in Egypt.
3. Hezbollah (Lebanon), an Islamic extremist group linked to the Iranian government and responsible for suicide truck bombings against U.S. interests.
4. Kahane Chai (Israel and the West Bank), a Jewish extremist group seeking to continue the founder's rejectionist agenda.
5. Hamas, a Palestinian fundamentalist group, an offshoot of the Muslim Brotherhood that came into existence in 1987, is another group with an alleged presence in the United States.

Despite the reference to the State Department's designated foreign terrorist listing, law enforcement personnel should not become complacent and merely focus on these or any one group for that matter. Many members of groups have splintered away and the groups themselves have morphed their ideology into one some may consider to be another group or faction. The fact remains that several groups, or remnants of the group, i.e., active members, do remain within the United States. Groups such as the IRA, PKK, LTTE, and Jamaat al-Fuqra do have a presence within many countries even though they are not on an "official" listing.

Although Appendix D outlines sufficient details on the groups noted above, more in-depth detail is warranted. Therefore, three of the more prevalent, intentionally excluding al-Qaeda, which is viewed more as a movement, are outlined below.

Hezbollah

Hezbollah, or Hizbollah, has continued to extend its international reach over the last quarter of a century. Arabic for the Party of God, Hezbollah is a pro-Iranian, Shi'ite, terrorist organization that grew out of the Iranian Revolution and the Iranian Revolutionary Guard between 1979 and 1982. There are several names associated with Hezbollah including Islamic Jihad, Revolutionary Justice Organization, and the Organization of the Oppressed on Earth.

Since its inception Hezbollah has become a sophisticated military and political network that reaches beyond Iran and Lebanon to virtually every continent in the world. With a multi-million dollar annual budget, with funding from Iran and Syria as well as illicit activities and donations, Hezbollah has become a formidable foe for any one government to address. The complexity of Hezbollah is evident in their hierarchal structure, which is comparable to a stand-alone government. Governed by a Secretary General, they have several councils with distinct areas of responsibility consisting of executive, judicial, political, and jihad (military).

al-Gama'a al-Islamiyya

Organized in 1973 in the Upper Nile regions of Al-Minya, Asyu't, Qina, and Sohaj in Egypt, al-Gama'a al-Islamiyya came into being and became an active militant group in the late 1970s. Also known as the Islamic Group (IG), al-Gamma, or Jamaat al-Islamiyya, this group has been inspired by past generations of Egyptian Islamists mainly Sayyid Qutb (spelling varies) of the Muslim Brotherhood. Qutb's writings, *Signposts and Milestones*, are and continue to be inspirational to many followers. Therefore, law enforcement should review such literature and have a fundamental understanding of what the "enemy" may be following.

Around 1948–1949 Qutb studied in the United States (Greeley, Colorado) for at least six months, and his writings and views toward the United States were not favorable. Another leading voice associated with al-Gamma is Sheikh Omar abd al-Rahman who is also known as the blind Shiekh. He became widely known for his alleged affiliations with members of the first World Trade Center bombing in February 1993. Due to their ties to Afghanistan, there is also an alleged relationship with Osama bin Laden.

Hamas (Islamic Resistance Movement)

Created in late 1987 in Gaza by Sheikh Ahmad Yassin as a Palestinian off-shoot of the Muslim Brotherhood, it is dedicated to the victory of Islam and eradication of the State of Israel. An acronym, Hamas, Arabic for Islamic Resistance Movement, which means "zeal," is both a terrorist organization and a social/religious movement. As of 2006, it is now a political force to be reckoned with in Palestine.

Hamas allegedly receives millions of dollars in funding from Iran. They have also been recognized internationally for their fundraising ability, largely through alleged charities. To many Palestinians, Hamas members are not terrorists but liberators. Hamas-related activities have been identified in Illinois, Virginia, Michigan, Texas, and California. Two of the more notable Hamas affiliates in the United States are the Holy Land Foundation (HLF) and the Islamic Association for Palestine (IAP). The IAP currently notes its North American Headquarters to be in Bridgeview, Illinois.

Although the Tamil Tigers of Elam (LTTE) are associated with developing some of the first suicide vests and deploying suicide bombers, it is Hamas that has personified the use of suicide bombers. When analyzing approximately 545 terrorist incidents attributed to Hamas the overwhelming majority of attacks, nearly 85 percent, have targeted private citizens and property.

The Muslim Brotherhood Movement (Hizb al-lkhwan al-Muslimun)

Founded in Cairo, Egypt, between 1927 and 1928, the Muslim Brotherhood continues to have a tremendous following. It has allegedly been involved in Islamic revolutions in Egypt, Algeria, Syria, and the Sudan. Today, the Brotherhood, largely funded through Saudi Arabia, is banned in Egypt and has extended its reaches worldwide especially in Europe and North America through an array of organizations, many of which are student and youth based. The group is Sunni and doctrinally fundamentalist. There are many key or principal individuals associated with furthering the group's teachings and ideology. Among its alumni are Sayyid Qutb, Ayman Zawahiri (Osama bin Laden's deputy), and Omar Abdul Rahman.

Prior to individuals like Sayyid Qutb coming to the forefront and initiating many of his writings, the Muslim Brotherhood had a strong presence and leadership.

The Brotherhood was founded by Hassan Al-Banna (1906–1949), a modest man from northern Egypt who was a sheikh's son born during the fall of the Ottoman Empire, the demise of the Caliphate, and the rise of modernization/"de-Islamization" of Egypt and the Middle East (i.e., in social psychology a "cathexis" or significant emotional turning point for Islamic civilization). At the age of 12, Al-Banna became leader in his village of The Society for Moral Behavior and the Society for the Prevention of the Forbidden (*haram*). Al-Banna and other members imposed burdensome fines on Muslims who cursed their fellows and their families, or cursed in the name of religion. Al-Banna met his demise in February 1949 when he was shot by alleged secret agents of the Egyptian government shortly after he declared they were responsible for Arab weaknesses. Prior to his death the Brotherhood undertook what many would consider to be a radical form of Islam.

Wahhabiism

Salafism or Wahhabiism is a radical sect of Islam and is the ideological base of the Muslim Brotherhood. Salafis or Wahhabis claim to strictly follow the example of the Prophet and command a pure, unadulterated understanding of the Islamic religion. Al-Banna and co-founders of the Muslim Brotherhood were steeped in teachings of Muhammad Ibn Abdul al-Wahhab al-Tamimi (1703–1792), the leading scholar of Salafism or Wahhabiism, who was born in what is now Saudi Arabia. Wahhab was considered by many as a radical evangelist who believed Islam was corrupted by countless errors and innovations. He went as far as declaring most Islamic scholars, thinkers, and clerics as heretics. In 1736 he authored the "Book of Monotheism," which became a reference text for the Wahhabi movement. While accused of being devoid of intellectual creativity, Al-Wahhab nonetheless had some influence on the Brotherhood. Al-Wahhab taught that Islam had vanquished many earlier civilizations but had become corrupted by foreign influences and therefore had lost its sense of "unity" (*tawhid*). The concept of tawhid (unity of God) is the most important part of the Salafi ideology and most are fixated with the concept. From Al-Wahhab the term "Salafist" came into being, denoting a "pure" form of Islam believed to have been practiced by Muhammad and the early caliphs, the "al-salaf al-salihin." Based on Wahhabi thinking, modern Wahhabis have transformed their radical religious reform into a political force. They have drawn heavily on modernist notions of nationalism and Marxist conceptions of class struggle and world revolution. Many aspects of Islamic law are strict, e.g., it forbids the uprising against Muslim rulers. However, Wahhabbi doctrine allows scholars to declare leaders of countries like Egypt, Algeria, and Saudi Arabia as "unbelievers" in order to revolt against them. Scholars or "salafis" are the primary nodes in the network and are responsible for many of the negative practices and terrorism. Salafiyya is not a unified movement, and there exists no single Salafi sect. Since its initial beginnings, the Wahhabi sect continues to have a large following of believers, especially in North America. In addition, its beliefs are regularly practiced in Saudia Arabia and Qatar.

Wahhabi organizations in North America

Many organizations exist in North America. Outlined below are several of the most prevalent and widely known Wahhabi-based organizations believed to be in existence. Just like with any other religious belief, law enforcement personnel should exercise caution when performing analysis or drawing relational conclusions.

- Muslim World League (MWL), aka Rabita, founded in 1962, and based, in Saudi Arabia; headquarters in Herndon, Virginia; sister organization of the World Assembly of Muslim Youth
- World Assembly of Muslim Youth (WAMY), found in approximately 34 countries and based in Saudi Arabia; helps coordinate the work of domestic groups like the Muslim Student Association

- Muslim Student Association (MSA), established in 1963 by Muslim activists from the Muslim Brotherhood and Jamaat-e-Islami
- Islamic Society of North America (ISNA), established in 1981 by leaders of MSA
- North American Islamic Trust (NAIT), founded by the MSA
- Islamic Circle of North America (ICNA), founded in 1971; North American arm of Jamaat-e-Islami
- International Institute of Islamic Thought (IIIT), which was established in 1980 by leaders of ISNA and WAMY
- Council on American-Islamic Relations (CAIR), Islamic Association for Palestine (IAP), Mosque Foundation, and Holy Land Foundation (HLF), which were allegedly founded by or affiliated with Hamas
- Tabligi Jamaat ("Missionary Party, TJ"), which was founded in 1926 in India

In addition to these organizations, several terrorist organizations follow the Wahhabi beliefs. The groups below have some affiliations that would be considered Wahhabi, and some have been officially designated as terrorist groups.

- Al-Qaeda ("The Base" or "The Formula")
- Hizb ut-Tahrir (HT), founded in Jerusalem in 1953
- Jemaah Islamiya ("Islamic Party"); ties to the Bali nightclub bombing
- Hamas, created in 1987 as a spin-off of the Palestinian branch of the Brotherhood
- Islamic Jihad, Egyptian based and active since 1970
- Hezbollah ("Party of God"), formed in 1982 in Iran
- Ikhwan Al-Muslimin ("Muslim Brotherhood"), founded in Egypt in the late 1920s
- Al-Gama'a Al-Islamiyya ("The Islamic Group"), most powerful Egyptian group founded in 1970s
- Jamaat Al-Fuqra ("The Poor"), formed in Hancock, New York in 1980, with a base in Lahore, Pakistan. This group is also referred to as a cult by some. Many of its members are African-American (black) Muslim converts who are living in rural compounds, in several states, established by the organization.

With any successful and long-lasting group or organization there is often a strong physical presence who leads or a history of strong thinkers. Wahhabi is no different.

Wahhabi thinkers

Many movements have a charismatic ideologue to establish their base of thought and lead interpretations of material for others to follow. Outlined below are some of the leaders and thinkers associated with the Wahhabi movement.

1. Mohammed Ibn Abdul Wahhab
2. Osama bin Ladin
3. Abdul A'La Mawdudi – founded Jamaat-e-Islami in 1941 in Lahore, Pakistan – died in 1979
4. Sayyid Qutb (Syed Qutb) – chief ideologue of the Muslim Brotherhood after al-Banna's death in 1949 – *Milestones and Signposts* – executed in 1966
5. Nasir Al-Albani – author and not a religious scholar – died while under house arrest in Jordan in 1999
6. Abd Al-Aziz Ibn Abdullah Baz (aka Bin Baz) – Saudi who died in 1999 – material and pamphlets widely spread in United States and Canada

Another individual who can be considered a leader is Sheikh Mubarak Ali Gilani, who also calls himself the sixth Sultan Ul Faqr, and is the chief of Jamaat Al-Fuqra (JF). He currently resides in Lahore, Pakistan. Wall Street Journal reporter Daniel Pearl was allegedly on the way to meet Sheik Gilani in Pakistan when he was kidnapped and later killed. Mr. Pearl was investigating accusations that shoe-bomb suspect Richard C. Reid was one of Sheik Gilani's followers. It has been suspected that the 9/11 mastermind, Khalid Sheikh Mohammad (KSM), was responsible for Pearl's execution. It should be noted that KSM had attended Chowan College in 1983, a small Baptist school in Murfreesboro, North Carolina, before transferring to the North Carolina Agricultural and Technical State University and completing a degree in mechanical engineering in 1986. KSM joined the Brotherhood when he was approximately 16 years old, prior to coming to the United States.

The Muslim Brotherhood and its alleged affiliates are no different than virtually any other extremist or terrorist-based organization, foreign or domestic. They have shown the propensity to target and recruit society's youth in order to bring them to their way of thinking. The Brotherhood just appears to be a bit more discrete in its tactics and has successfully utilized various student associations to promote their agenda. KSM, Sayyid Qutb, and even suspected London bomber Magdy Asi el-Nashar, a chemical engineering student from North Carolina State University, all have had ties to American universities. Although there may be no direct confirmation of the aforementioned individuals to the Muslim Brotherhood while in the United States, one cannot dismiss the opportunities that may have existed for direct or indirect support.

Means of support

In addition to the deep-seated concern of the groups with confirmed and non-confirmed official presences in the United States, six countries have been officially designated by the U.S. Department of State as being sponsors of terrorism: Cuba (designated March 1982), Iran (designated January 1984), Libya (designated December 1979), Sudan (designated August 1993), North Korea (designated January 1988), and Syria (designated December 1979). Although these are the officially recognized states, there is a strong likelihood that other locales are associated with having terrorist bases. The potential for terrorist activities that threaten the security of the United States, its nationals, or allied nations, is greatly enhanced because of the states that sponsor terrorism. However, these countries cannot be handled by local or state law enforcement. This mission falls on the federal government and the military. The role of law enforcement is to provide detailed local information and intelligence to the appropriate authorities on domestic-related matters and on those that involve international groups. Cyberactivity is one component that will likely play key roles in future foreign-based terrorist endeavors and will be handled largely by law enforcement. The cyberworld provides a way for faceless operatives within terrorist organizations to attack key infrastructure systems from virtually anywhere in the world. Local law enforcement will likely encounter or investigate cyber-based operations dealing with terrorist recruiting, financing, and research.

Cyberterrorism

The U.S. infrastructure is fragile, even though it is perceived as secure. For every precaution in place, it is likely that there is an individual or group trying to compromise or access the system.

Technology growth has expanded the opportunities for penetrating vital commercial and financial computer systems and for disabling a national computer infrastructure. This can be characterized as a cyber or technical Pearl Harbor. Cyberterrorism will probably not have a body count associated with it, but it can cripple a nation, put corporations out of business, and cause huge financial loss. An example of financial loss was demonstrated in a survey of 611 companies doing business on the Internet in 2001. Results indicated that 83 percent of the companies experienced security breaches and 62 percent said there was some type of financial loss, with average damages of $47.8 million, compared to $26.6 million in 1999.[1] This is a drop in the bucket compared to the potential for disaster if an entity like the stock market were targeted.

The information listed above is for one country, the United States. A 2001 Dartmouth College Institute for Security Technology Studies report[1] reviewed four international cases. It demonstrated the correlation between conflict among countries and the rise in the number of Web site defacements that were experienced by one or both of the countries involved in physical conflicts.

The first case study examined the Pakistan/India/Kashmir region conflict. Pakistani hacker groups allegedly defaced hundreds of Indian Web sites between 1999 and the summer of 2001. By the end of summer in 2001, India experienced a 107 percent increase in the number of attacks compared to the entire year of 2000.

The second case study reviewed data from the Israel/Palestinian conflict. A strong connection was realized between Web site defacements and key physical events between February 2000 and April 2001. It was evident that during the height of sustained violence there was a dramatic spike in the number of cyber attacks in the form of Web defacements, denial of service, and use of worms and Trojan horses.

The third case reviewed was the Former Republic of Yugoslavia (FRY) and NATO conflict in Kosovo. During a NATO bombing campaign, hackers, allegedly employed by the FRY military, began a ping saturation campaign to keep legitimate users from accessing data. This was directed at servers hosting NATO's Web site and electronic mail traffic.

The final case study involved the United States and China spy plane incident. After a mid-air collision on April 1, 2001, between a U.S. spy plane and a Chinese fighter aircraft, an online campaign of mutual cyber attacks and defacements took place on both sides. Between April and May of that year, over 1,000 U.S. sites experienced denial of service attacks and defacements. Sites attacked included the White House, the Department of Energy, and the U.S. Air Force.

Although just four case studies were reviewed, there is strong evidence supporting the connection between events and cyber attacks. For law enforcement, this is another point to consider when identifying patterns or trends.

Defining cyberterrorism

Just as with every other component of terrorism, a working definition is needed for cyberterrorism. One of the first recognized working definitions came from the U.S. Air Force in the late 1970s. The problem associated with this definition was that it was broad-based and encompassed virtually anything dealing with information. Cyberterrorism was defined as "The use of information and information systems as weapons in a conflict where information and information systems are targets."[2]

Over time the above definition, although not incorrect, has been modified. The National Defense Agency expanded upon the U.S. Air Force's definition and can be readily modified to fit the needs of most law enforcement agencies. They define cyberterrorism as "Any action to deny, exploit, corrupt or destroy the enemy's information and its functions; protecting ourselves against those actions; and exploiting our own military information functions."[2] Although this definition mentions enemy and military information functions and war-like terms, it is just as applicable to law enforcement now that it is part of the war effort. Regardless of the definition, law enforcement must remain cognizant of local, state, and federal laws governing cyber crimes.

Spectrum of cyber conflict

The spectrum of cyber conflict can be used to help understand the scale of activity associated with the cyberworld. Few agencies routinely deal with incidents of cyber crime. This, coupled with the in-depth knowledge needed to investigate crimes of this magnitude, has greatly limited proactive investigations concerning cyber crimes. Much of what is publicly mentioned about proactive cyber crime investigations is centered on child pornography and sexual predators.

Tracking violations of law or computer intrusions currently rests with law enforcement, but this is not seen as a priority. Much of the information and evidence collection is done after the fact and is often left up to local law enforcement officials, or perhaps the FBI in the case of a large investigation. Unlike in the U.S. Army's Spectrum of Conflict, the military or Department of Defense (DOD) is not likely to participate in such actions. This is because many of the occurrences are of a domestic nature, and the traditional war-fighting military is prohibited from performing these duties. Its role is to provide national defense and to operate in an international theater.

Distinguishing between the two separate domains, domestic and international, requires coordination of the military and law enforcement, because cyber warfare provides for the ability to attack infrastructures vital to the national security from within or from outside the country. This is ironic, considering that the DOD has been the victim of numerous intrusion attempts since 1994. The total number of network attacks reported in 1994 throughout the DOD was 225. By 1999, the total reported events escalated to just over 22,000 and this number was anticipated to reach 24,000 by the end of 2001.[3] Examples of some of these attacks can be found in Figure 8.1, Figure 8.2, and Figure 8.3. Information shown in Figure 8.1 is from the year 2000 from the U.S. Army Web site, which was hacked by a 16-year-old from Poland who referred to himself as "Terrorist of the New Age." It was reported that the Army's Web site was "pinged" three times per second in 1999. Figure 8.2 shows the result of a hack in 1999 by a 17-year-old from England into the U.S. Navy Web site. Navy personnel reported that their Web site experienced a hack attempt every 23 seconds in 1999. Figure 8.3 shows a hack into the official Pentagon Web site.[4] Cyber vulnerability of the Armed Services "is magnified by the fact that 95 percent of all U.S. military traffic moves over civilian telecommunications and computer systems."[5]

Figure 8.1 Army (hacked Web screen). (Courtesy of Sergeant Sean Holtz. With permission.)

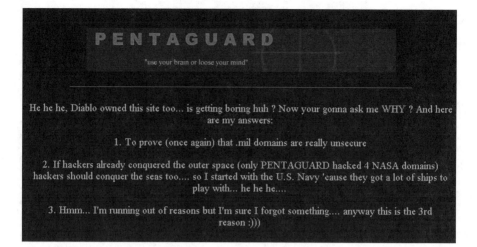

Figure 8.2 Navy (hacked Web screen). (Courtesy of Sergeant Sean Holtz. With permission.)

Figure 8.3 Pentagon (hacked Web screen). (Courtesy of Sergeant Sean Holtz. With permission.)

It has been stated that "Internet users now number 120 million — 70 million of them in the United States. An estimated 1 billion people — one-sixth of humanity — will be on-line by 2005, two-thirds of them abroad."[6] These staggering figures demonstrate the tremendous tasks ahead for law enforcement. Even though the number of attacks is dwarfed by the number of potential users, law enforcement must remain vigilant when investigating cyber attacks because just one computer hard drive can contain over 50 million pages of data.

One of the primary cyber crimes that exists and receives little media attention is often referred to as hacking. In 1998, the vulnerability of infrastructure systems was highlighted in an investigation into a Department of Energy laboratory that was shut down for a few weeks due to a breach of its systems by a hacker. Most hackers are thrill-seeking individuals driven to outdo each other with their unique abilities and who generally will not damage data or systems. They will make it known that they gained access and will leave their electronic signature or cyber tag. A cyberterrorist, on the other hand, will try to avoid detection through the use of a Trojan horse and phreaking (see Appendix I). This enables them to completely eliminate target records or systems while remaining anonymous and avoiding detection.

The spectrum of cyber conflict was discussed in a report prepared by a commanding member of the U.S. Air Force in 2001, and law enforcement's role was explained in detail. It was noted that the spectrum consists of "various forms of cyber attack such as hacking, hacktivism (a form of computer-based civil disobedience), espionage, terrorism, and information warfare."[3] The level of escalation as it relates to the spectrum that was detailed in the report is demonstrated in Figure 8.4. A dashed vertical line divides the spectrum in order to differentiate between unintentional and intentional actors. The activity to the left of this line is seen as that of individuals who may be largely unaware or do not truly understand the international ramifications of their actions. Activity to the right of the dashed line is viewed as that of people with motive and intention to inflict damage on national security interests.

Cyber crime on the spectrum is first on the level of escalation and is sometimes referred to as illegal exploration or hacking. Much of this activity comes in the form of illegal access into a company or government network system. Some hackers start out as outsiders who use various password attacks in order to gain access as a user of the network. Many begin as insiders, in the form of disgruntled or former employees. They will use known weaknesses in the system to gain further access as an administrator or super user. Once these privileges are attained, a hacker then can read or alter files, control a system, and insert a rogue code such as a virus to damage the infrastructure.

Hacktivism, the second step on the spectrum, is described as a form of electronic disobedience. The goal is to draw attention to a particular issue, such as human rights or political beliefs, by engaging in actions that are

Spectrum of Cyber Conflict

Figure 8.4 Spectrum of cyber conflict.

unusual in order to attract media attention. The motivation of a person committing an act of hacktivism differs from that of a hacker in that hacktivism represents a political motivation.

The next step on the spectrum is intentional actions in the form of cyber espionage. This may appear to be hacking, but in reality the mission of a cyber espionage attack is to avoid detection and to gather as much information as possible from the targeted system. With the ability to attack through cyber means, terrorist organizations have a new arena in which to commit their acts and to gather valuable information about those they see as the enemy. Many organizations, especially organized hate groups, are technologically savvy. They know how to use the systems to spread their messages, recruit, and attain illicit funds. The ability to commit acts of terrorism through nonlethal means, such as access to information, intelligence, and infrastructures, can cause detrimental effects on the general populous.

Reaching government infrastructures through cyberterrorism leaves only one step on the spectrum, cyber warfare. Cyber warfare is an intentional act designed to affect national security. It is an intensified extension of cyberterrorism.

No matter what level of the spectrum is used, law enforcement will be involved. However, military involvement will generally be limited to acts ranging from cyber espionage to cyber warfare, providing a third country is involved.

One way the law enforcement community may become involved is by being a victim of cyber crimes or hacking. For example, several agencies, including the Los Angeles Police Department, U.S. Department of Justice (DOJ), and

Figure 8.5 CIA (hacked Web screen). (Courtesy of Sergeant Sean Holtz. With permission.)

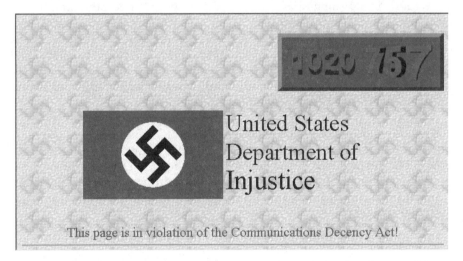

Figure 8.6 DOJ (hacked Web screen). (Courtesy of Sergeant Sean Holtz. With permission.)

the CIA were directly victimized in the past several years. Figure 8.5 illustrates an attack to the CIA Web site. Figure 8.6 is from the DOJ site, showing a symbol used by several organized hate groups. Hackers as well as terrorists are resilient, and no single government agency is immune to attack.

In order to enhance cyber security, law enforcement will need to partner with private-sector corporations. More than 80 percent of all information systems in this country are owned by the private sector.[7] Solutions for improving cyber security will require joint initiatives between government and private entities as well as an understanding of how to read what you are viewing. Everyone is likely to be somewhat familiar with the Internet. However, one common piece of the puzzle may come from the use of Internet protocol (IP) addresses and e-mail headers.

Using IP address and e-mails in analysis

Increasingly, analysts and investigators in agencies throughout the world are being asked to deal with complaints from citizens about crimes committed against them by others who have discovered how to victimize people over the Internet. An even greater concern is the amount of correspondence being sent through e-mails or other electronic means by terrorists or their organizations. Based on the aforementioned, it is essential that law enforcement personnel become aware of the terrorists' need to communicate in a covert manner and learn how to exploit this weakness and use it in their analysis.

Some Internet problems that might come your way

What is brought to your attention by someone might be an e-mail or a newsgroup posting. The problems with e-mails and newsgroup postings are that people can easily become offensive or even criminal. It is relatively easy to enclose, in a posting or an e-mail, vivid images of child pornography, for example, or to post a threat to a person's life. Issues that may arise from electronic communications are full of information that may be the missing piece to your puzzle. E-mails contain dates, times, machines, locations, and descriptors. Each of these may be what you will need to develop that association. Just don't forget these in your link analysis and databases. They are just as powerful as telephone numbers and addresses.

Chat rooms have their own problems, some of which are difficult for someone with little Internet experience to understand. Some of the most disgusting goings-on include pedophiles lurking in children's chat channels and children stumbling into adult-related chats. During recent events throughout the world, e.g., World Trade Organization (WTO), many anarchist based groups thrived on chat rooms. If anarchists can use them, why not terrorists?

Finding information in an e-mail

As with most police work, you know what has happened and to whom. All you need to do now is find out who did it — and prove it. It is amazing how much open source information is available if you know how to look for it. With electronic sources the opportunities to obtain information seem to be endless. The only obstacle is knowing how to harvest the information and remembering to incorporate it into your analysis.

Many terrorists today are technology experts. Use of mobile and satellite telephones, instant messaging, and e-mails are widely available and can be used by the terrorist to communicate. These electronic media provide new challenges to law enforcement. While law enforcement faces these challenges, terrorists continue to learn from the communication errors made by terror cells that have been discovered by law enforcement. Cells have gained insight into law enforcement's ability to trace telephone calls and e-mail correspondence. Therefore, they must embrace creative ideas such as sharing a common e-mail account. One subject would then create a message and leave it in the draft folder, instead of sending it over the Internet. A second subject would then sign in to the same account and read the message, thus reducing the opportunities of being discovered. Although this option can transpire, the more likely scenario is that of the e-mail being sent. However, many in the law enforcement profession are not versed in the information available in an email, outside of the text body, and how to retrieve it. Outlined below is some basic information that can be useful in exposing the information and other variables that can be used to develop relational links.

Generally, your investigation will start from one of three points: an e-mail address, a web address, or an IP address.

- e-mail address — xxxxx@xxxxxxx.com
- web address — http://xxxxxxxxx.xxxxxxx.com/~sbunting/ or http://125.175.13.92/~43253/ (the latter is expressed using an IP address instead of a domain name format; both interpret to mean the same address)
- IP address — 125.175.13.92 (IP address of copsrus.mytown.com)

E-mail addresses

If the information involves an e-mail or newsgroup posting, you should obtain a printed copy of it. But you also need a digital copy of what's on the machine, because it is only here that you can view what is called the "extended header" that reveals the IP address of the perpetrator. The IP address you will eventually use in your search warrant will disclose the name and address of the person using that account for criminal activity.

What is a header?

A header is a section of code that contains information about where the e-mail came from and how it reached its destination. It will contain the e-mail address of the originator and/or the computer the perpetrator was using.

Revealing extended headers in different e-mail programs varies by software product used. The majority of the more widely used packages provide sufficient information on their website or help menu to guide one through the process of viewing the e-mail's extended header. Other resources, primarily on the Internet, will be a valuable source of information in translating an e-mail header.

Here is what the typical header looks like. What you are looking for in the header is the IP address, sometimes conveniently identified as the "Originating IP." We can trace and track someone by sending a search warrant to the Internet service provider (ISP) with the date and time of the offending e-mail, along with the IP address of the bad guy's computer. Outlined below is a sample email header.

```
From - Mon Mar 19 08:17:17 2006

Return-Path: < wsmith@xxxxxxxxxxx.gov >

Received: from otma1.otm.xxxxxxxx.gov (votma1.xxxxxxxx.gov
[167.21.1.115])

by xxxxxxxx@xxxxxx.com (8.9.3/8.9.3) with ESMTP id NAA06271

for <xxxxxxxx@xxxxxx.com>; Thu, 15 Mar 2006 13:10:40 -0500
(EST)

Received: from flcjnetmail1. xxxxxxxx.gov (email.flcjnet.
xxxxxxxx.gov [172.20.66.11])

by otma1.otm. xxxxxxxx.gov (8.11.0/8.11.0) with ESMTP id
f2FIA7t28739

for < xxxxxxxx@xxxxxx.com>; Thu, 15 Mar 2006 13:10:07
-0500 (EST)

Received: from xxxxxxxxxxxxxxxx.gov [172.20.132.102] by
flcjnetmail1.xxxxxxxx.gov with ESMTP

(SMTPD32-5.05) id A8B32701AE; Thu, 15 Mar 2006 13:23:47
-0500

Received: by STATEGOV with Internet Mail Service
(5.5.1960.3)

id <FY66DSJT>; Thu, 15 Mar 2006 13:08:29 -0500

Message-ID: <777ED2AC6510D311BBB50000D11CB450167AAD@STAT-
EGOV>

From: William Smith wsmith@xxxxxxxxxxx.gov

To: "Jim Jones (E-mail)" xxxxxxxx@xxxxxx.com

Subject: Following My Brother

Date: Thu, 15 Mar 2006 13:08:28 -0500

MIME-Version: 1.0

X-Mailer: Internet Mail Service (5.5.1960.3)

Content-Type: text/plain

X-Mozilla-Status: 8003

X-Mozilla-Status2: 00000000
```

Headers also contain message identifiers. The Message-ID is a more or less unique identifier assigned to each message, usually by the first mail server it encounters. Also, the date section of the header will display a time. The time information displayed here (Date: Thu, 15 Mar 2001 13:08:28 -0500) is Greenwich Mean or World Time. This should be taken into consideration when performing temporal analysis. Do not forget that not every location in the world observes Daylight Savings Time and that machines are portable, which means that the time from a machine that originated in New York and is now in Los Angeles is likely to have a three-hour difference.

What is an IP address?

The reason you need a printout and a digital copy is that even when someone has gone to some lengths to hide their identity, there is sometimes a clue left behind. You may find the "IP address," which identifies a computer on the Internet. The IP address takes the form of a dotted-quad number, something like 128.175.13.92.

Understanding IP addresses

Which of the IP addresses above should be traced and how is this monstrosity read? Usually, the originating IP (in this case 172.20.132.102) is either called that, and/or is closer to the bottom of the stack, nearer to the actual body of the message.

It is important to note that this source IP address (172.20.132.102) will not resolve on the Internet as it is within a block of IP addresses that are "reserved" private IP addresses. They are used behind corporate firewalls and proxy servers. They access the outside world through a network address translation (NAT) service. To find where this IP address is located, you would have to contact the network administrator responsible for the IP address 167.21.1.115, which is a legitimate IP address and through which this private IP address passes on its way to the Internet.

Request for comments (RFC) 1918 describes IP addressing guidelines for private networks and for which Internet assigned numbers authority (IANA) has reserved for private networks. Several address ranges are reserved for "Special Use." These addresses all have restrictions of some sort placed on their use, and in general should not appear in normal use on the public Internet. They are

1. 10.0.0.0 to 10.255.255.255
2. 172.16.0.0 to 172.31.255.255
3. 192.168.00 to 192.168.255.255

According to the IANA, the above address blocks are reserved for use on private networks, and should never appear in the public Internet. There are hundreds of thousands of such private networks (for example home firewalls sometimes make use of them). The IANA has no record of who uses these address blocks. Anyone may use these address blocks within their own network without any prior notification to IANA.

The point of private address space is to allow many organizations in different places to use the same addresses, and as long as these disconnected or self-contained islands of IP-speaking computers (private intranets) are not connected, there is no problem. If you see an apparent attack, or spam, coming from one of these address ranges, then either it is coming from your local environment, or the address has been "spoofed."

Users are assigned IP addresses by Internet service providers (ISPs). ISPs obtain allocations of IP addresses from a local Internet registry (LIR) or national Internet registry (NIR), or from their appropriate regional Internet registry (RIR):

- AfriNIC (African Network Information Centre) — Africa Region
- APNIC (Asia Pacific Network Information Centre) — Asia/Pacific Region
- ARIN (American Registry for Internet Numbers) — North America Region
- LACNIC (Regional Latin-American and Caribbean IP Address Registry) — Latin America and some Caribbean Islands
- RIPE NCC (Réseaux IP Européens) — Europe, the Middle East, and Central Asia

The IANA's role is to allocate IP addresses from the pools of unallocated addresses to the RIRs according to their established needs. When an RIR requires more IP addresses for allocation or assignment within its region, the IANA makes an additional allocation to the RIR. Remember, it is quite possible that an IP address in an e-mail header could be fabricated. According to the IANA, e-mail protocols are not secure and anyone with the minor technical skills necessary can forge any part of an e-mail. Forgeries generally are difficult to identify. The IANA cannot locate the individuals who forge e-mail headers. In fact, return addresses can be spoofed right down to the packet level. (Just like in postal mail, one can put pretty much anything as a return address, but if there is a problem with the "to" address, the letter can't be delivered.) IP addresses can be spoofed in protocols other than e-mail, as well.

More about that IP address

The reason IP numbers are important is there are programs available on the Internet that translate these numbers into something approaching a readable language. You may get a web address or the details of an ISP.

You are likely to get an IP in an inquiry relating to Internet relay chat. People who "chat" can easily fake an e-mail address, but the IP is the only thing that can be relied upon, as it positively identifies the computer that the offender is connected through at the time of the offense.

It is very important, once you have traced the IP address back to the Internet service provider (ISP), to contact that provider as soon as possible. A chat is live, and there are few records of it, as ISPs tend not to keep records for very long (hours or possibly days). You will need to know the time and date of the offense (be careful with time zones — MST, EST, PDT, GMT, etc.). Armed with this information, the ISP should be able to identify which of their customers was accessing the Internet via that computer at that time.

No message, no extended header, no IP

If all you get on the bad guy is an e-mail address (no e-mail, no extended headers), then your next step is to find out to whom it belongs. One way to do that is to look it up in "the book." The Internet contains white pages that are the Internet equivalent of the phone book. If the address is not there, it doesn't necessarily mean that it doesn't exist, but it's worth a try.

It is important to note that there is no one-stop-shop place to search for a person's e-mail address to try to come up with a name.

Tracing an e-mail address to an owner

For e-mail investigations, providing the full e-mail headers is very helpful. However, this is not always available. If it is not available try changing the e-mail address to a web address, remove the xxxxx@ and replace it with www. You could well find the Web site of the user or the service provider. If you know the service provider, you can approach them for customer details.

Often, you can identify someone with as little as an e-mail address. If the person you are investigating has ever posted to a newsgroup, signed a guest book, participated in a mailing list or forum, chances are you, the investigator, can find out a lot of information about your subject with just an e-mail address. Here are some things you can try:

1. Go to http://www.google.com, click on Google Groups, and then select Advanced Groups Search. Here, you can search in one newsgroup, or search all newsgroups (thousands of them) by words in the subject of the posting, by message ID, or by author. Type the e-mail address that the subject is using in the author box. This should bring up any articles that he or she has posted. Pay close attention to this because often the author who has posted an article looking for teen boys, illegal weapons, or drugs will have also posted a few months prior trying to sell a peripheral or some other item. In this posting, he will have included a home telephone number, or an indication of what city he lives in. You may also find web page addresses, other e-mail addresses, an online resume, his work location, or something that will help you identify him or her.

2. Go to your favorite search engine and type in an e-mail address. This could show other places on the Internet that he has posted something using that e-mail address. Again, you may find a web page or some other important information.

3. If you do happen to find a web page, download it while you are there because it can be changed or deleted at anytime. There are a number of utilities you can use that will cache the web page with all its links intact so that offline you can browse them more easily, and save the digital evidence as you found it.

4. Go to www.freeality.com and do a reverse e-mail search, which could pop the subject's real name. You can also use this site to do other searches such as reverse phone number searches and address searches.

5. If you would just like to know where the subject's ISP is located, go to Internic.com and type in the domain name of the Web site or e-mail address. It will tell you to whom that domain is registered. This, of course, will not be of much help if the subject has a nation-wide ISP such as AOL, Compuserve, or Earthlink.

6. Go to www.search.com, a "meta" search engine, and type in a name or an e-mail address. If that e-mail address has been used to post anything to the Internet, you should get some hits.

Does your target have a web page?

If you have an e-mail address for your target, there is a chance that he or she could have a web page that could give you more information about the subject. Here are some things that may help you find their web page:

1. If you have an e-mail address of a person such as terrorist@once-uponatime.com, you could check for it by going to http://www.once-uponatime.com/~terrorist Of course you would replace the word onceuponatime with the name of the ISP he is using and the word terrorist with his username. The ~ character (found in the upper left hand side of your computer keyboard) indicates that the web site is likely put up by a person, not by an organization.

2. Here are some places that you can look for a home page:
   - If the person is using AOL, try going to http://members.aol.com/ username. Be sure to replace the word "username" with his or her screen name, or use the "Find" box here to search by screen name. Teknion Tracker also has a specialty area to search AOL web pages.
   - If the person is using an ATT account (user@worldnet.att.net) you can find out if he has a home page by going to http://home.att.net/ and searching for a member page or trying http://home.att.net/ ~username. Remember to replace the word "username" with the actual username of your suspect.
   - If the person is using an Earthlink (user@earthlink.net) you can find out if he has a home page by going to http://www.earthlink.net, and searching by username. Other national ISP accounts work pretty much the same way.

3. Once you find a web page, you may want to check the "source." Sometimes you'll find real name information in the top part of the HTML code. With your mouse, right click in the center of the page and go down to "view page source." If there is any personal information, it will be included in the meta tags near the top. Some subjects will also occasionally place passwords or instructions to operatives and co-conspirators in the HTML coding, and then alert them to come retrieve that information at a certain time and day, leaving law enforcement none the wiser. So you might want to check this area for unusual information.

A lot of the HTML coding will look like gibberish to you, but scan through it anyway. Not everything that appears in the source code appears on the screen, and it may be that, intentionally or otherwise, the author has left some clues there. A simple example is that if the subject wanted to send a covert message to someone, he could hide the message in the page by making the text the same color as the background. The message would be unreadable when viewing the page itself but clear as day in the source code. Try opening two viewers side-by-side and have one display the source code and the other one open to the visual interface. As you scroll through both you may observe discrepancies, if they are there.

You can also detect other things. Some of the code will give you a clue as to what software program and therefore what type of computer the offender was using, his geographic location, etc.

How do I trace a web address?

Get on the Internet and go to the site. Most sites contain details of the owner's life, hobbies, interests, location, phone, and the like. If the site does not contain the owner's details, it may provide some clue as to whom you are dealing with and where in the world they might be.

Go to a multiple DNS lookup engine such as http://www.bankes.com/ nslookup.htm or http://www.samspade.com and type in your web page address. It will tell you the ISP to contact and provide additional information. Two examples of information that was obtained from tracing web address data are illustrated in Figure 8.7 (Islamic Thinkers Society) and Figure 8.8 (Taliyah). The Islamic Thinkers Society New York City in (a group site that has been compared to al-Muhajiroun's, a radical group out of the United Kingdom) provides some definitive detail including when the site was last updated. The Taliyah site provides some insight as to what can be done in the electronic age from a prison cell, even death row. In the Taliyah site, enough information was gleaned to afford the opportunity to further expand open source information, which, as you can see, is quite detailed. When following sites such as these, it is important to note that the service providers may not be involved in a group's activities. Also, law enforcement should be cognizant of the use of country codes as noted in the Taliyah illustration.

■   Registrant:
    Domains by Proxy, Inc.

    DomainsByProxy.com
    15511 N. Hayden Rd., Ste 160, PMB 353
    Scottsdale, Arizona 85260
    United States

    Registered through: GoDaddy.com (http://www.godaddy.com)
    Domain Name: ISLAMICTHINKERS.COM
    Created on: 06-Oct-04
    Expires on: 06-Oct-06
    Last Updated on: 04-May-05

    Administrative Contact:
    Private, Registration ISLAMICTHINKERS.COM@domainsbyproxy.com
    Domains by Proxy, Inc.
    DomainsByProxy.com
    15511 N. Hayden Rd., Ste 160, PMB 353
    Scottsdale, Arizona 85260
    United States
    (480) 624-2599
    Technical Contact:
    Private, Registration ISLAMICTHINKERS.COM@domainsbyproxy.com
    Domains by Proxy, Inc.
    DomainsByProxy.com
    15511 N. Hayden Rd., Ste 160, PMB 353
    Scottsdale, Arizona 85260
    United States
    (480) 624-2599

    Domain servers in listed order:
    NS7.SECURE-DNS.NET
    NS8.SECURE-DNS.NET

Figure 8.7 Islamic Thinkers Society web address details.

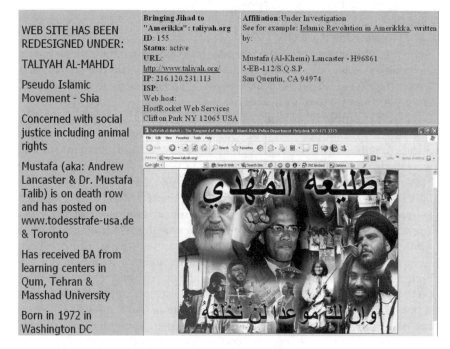

WEB SITE HAS BEEN REDESIGNED UNDER: TALIYAH AL-MAHDI Pseudo Islamic Movement - Shia Concerned with social justice including animal rights Mustafa (aka: Andrew Lancaster & Dr. Mustafa Talib) is on death row and has posted on www.todesstrafe-usa.de & Toronto Has received BA from learning centers in Qum, Tehran & Masshad University Born in 1972 in Washington DC	**Bringing Jihad to "Amerikka": taliyah.org** ID: 155 **Status:** active URL: http://www.taliyah.org/ IP: 216.120.231.113 ISP: Web host: HostRocket Web Services Clifton Park NY 12065 USA	**Affiliation:** Under Investigation See for example: Islamic Revolution in Amerikkka, written by: Mustafa (Al-Khemi) Lancaster - H96861 5-EB-112/S.Q.S.P. San Quentin, CA 94974

Figure 8.8 Taliyah web address details.

In the Web site noted in the illustration, the individual has been posting to a Web site located in Germany, thus the ".de" in the address. Furthermore, some sites that may appear to be overseas or in another country may actually be hosted from a web server located in a consulate or embassy right in your own back yard.

Bioterrorism and weapons of mass destruction (WMD)

Biological and chemical weapons and their uses are receiving a great deal of media attention. Attaining or making these WMD takes some level of expertise. Relatively few places in the world (approximately 17 states) have the people with the skills necessary to develop a biological weapon or possess the radioactive material necessary to develop a nuclear weapon.[8] Although opportunities appear limited and results unpredictable, chemical and biological materials should not be overlooked. A report by the CSIS in 2000, referring to biological agents such as anthrax and plague, noted that "Ounce for ounce, the lethality of these agents is many times that of chemical agents or nuclear weapons."[5] There are five general categories of WMD that can be used by analysts tracking materials and investigative leads:

Biological
Chemical
Explosive
Incendiary
Nuclear

WMD that fall into these categories come in many deadly forms and devices. In the United States, Title 18 of the U.S. Code covers the legislative description for many of the destructive devices used as WMD. A synopsis of what Title 18 encompasses is listed below.

Poison gas
Any weapon involving a disease organism
Any weapon designed to release radiation or radioactivity at a level dangerous to human life
Any destructive device as defined in Section 921 of this Title

The destructive devices as defined in Section 921 of Title 18 U.S.C. are as follows:

Any explosive, incendiary, or poison gas
Bomb
Grenade
Rocket having a propellant charge of more than four ounces
Missile having an explosive or incendiary charge of more than one-quarter ounce

Mine

Device similar to any of the devices described in the preceding clauses

Any type of weapon (other than a shotgun or a shotgun shell) which may be readily converted to expel a projectile ... with a bore of more than one-half inch in diameter

Any combination of parts ... from which a destructive device can be assembled

FBI data reveal over 10,000 bombings resulting in 355 deaths and over 3,000 injuries between 1990 and 1995. Based on FBI data calculations, approximately 70 percent of domestic terrorist incidents involve some type of explosives. Analysts need to be aware that explosive devices can be composed of a wide variety of materials. A comprehensive list of explosive materials as listed by the ATF that should be added to all databases is provided in Appendix E.

The numbers of chemical, biological, and nuclear attack incidents are not as startling as those of conventional explosives mentioned above. The Center for Non-Proliferation Studies, in a 2000 CSIS report, showed that in 1999 there were 175 reports of chemical, biological, and nuclear terrorism, 104 of which occurred in the United States. This was a dramatic increase over the database findings in February 2000 of a total of 687 incidents since 1900.[9] Definitive numbers are difficult to attain. The center uses the media as its source of information, and it was noted that apparent increases might be attributed to hoaxes and different reporting methods. Regardless of the true numbers, there definitely appears to be an increase in the use or the perceived use of these agents.

There are numerous biological agents that can be employed by terrorists. The U.S. Army Medical Research Institute of Infectious Diseases lists the following diseases and biological toxins as potentially suitable for introduction into the population by deliberate dispersal:[10]

Bacterial infections — anthrax, cholera, plague, tularemia, and "Q" fever

Viruses — smallpox, Venezuelan equine encephalitis, and viral hemorrhagic fevers

Biological toxins — botulinum, staphylococcal enterotoxin B, ricin, and T-2 mycotoxins

Chemical agents have been used in warfare for years, even by law enforcement in the form of riot-control agents. The following are among the commonly employed chemical agents:[10]

Nerve agents — Sarin (GB)

Vesicants — Mustard gas (HD, H), Lewisite (L)

Lung-damaging agents — Phosgene

Cyanide

Riot-control agents — CS and CN

Methods of exposure to the biological and chemical agents mentioned above include the following:

Absorption (through the skin)
Ingestion (swallowing or eating)
Inhalation (breathing)
Injection (usually through a hypodermic syringe)

The above chemical and biological concerns are critical components for analyzing materials and data, but a greater concern exists for the first responder. It is one thing to analyze information about WMD, but it is the first responders of the world who will encounter, usually unsuspectingly, chemical and biological agents. Therefore it is essential that information be made immediately available to them as it is discovered, and that they be properly trained in all aspects of this extremely dangerous situation.

Many how-to documents are available, some covering chemical and biological agents. In the previously mentioned terrorism training manual document seized in Manchester, England, "Military Studies in the Jihad against the Tyrants," several poisons were described in detail. Included in this compendium was information on extracts or derivatives of herbal and plant products that can be used to make substances such as ricin. Also included was the weight of each item needed, and symptoms that can result from exposure. One method of poisoning that was mentioned in this manual, which law enforcement personnel, especially those investigating deaths, should be aware of, is of poisoning from eating intentionally spoiled food. The method of spoiling food is explained in detail, including the symptoms and their timeline, and how to "cook" the poison. It is virtually a cookbook on the topic. The fact that this has been put into writing and made available to the general public means that law enforcement must consider it a method of bioterrorism.

When it comes to weapons of mass destruction there are variables that analysts can look for in order to expose potential weakness or to anticipate behavior. The key is to avoid looking for "destruction." Instead look for items associated with weapons of mass victimization: ideology, knowledge, management, audience, social distance, and symbolic value (IKMASS).

- Ideology — intellectual or theoretical structure of the organization
- Knowledge — tactical, technical, and strategic information within the group
- Management — rules, etc., of group — necessary to identify operational manager, e.g., Aum Shinrikyo
- Audience — important to know the group's message, where audience is located, and for what purposes the attack would be taking place
- Social distance — religious, ethnic, cultural, socioeconomic — analyze speeches to identify the aforementioned
- Symbolic value — both human and physical, e.g., Yucca Mountain project in Nevada

		VEHICLE DESCRIPTION	MAXIMUM EXPLOSIVE CAPACITY	LETHAL AIR BLAST RANGE	MINIMUM EVACUATION DISTANCE	FALLING GLASS HAZARD
V E H I C L E B O R N E I M P R O V I S E D	**E X P L O S I V E D E V I C E S**	COMPACT SEDAN	500 Pounds 227 Kilos (In Trunk)	100 Feet 30 Meters	1,500 Feet 457 Meters	1,250 Feet 381 Meters
		FULL SIZE SEDAN	1,000 Pounds 455 Kilos (In Trunk)	125 Feet 38 Meters	1,750 Feet 534 Meters	1,750 Feet 534 Meters
		PASSANGER VAN OR CARGO VAN	4,000 Pounds 1,818 Kilos	200 Feet 61Meters	2,750 Feet 838 Meters	2,750 Feet 838 Meters
		SMALL BOX VAN (14 FT BOX)	10,000 Pounds 4,545 Kilos	300 Feet 91 Meters	3,750 Feet 1,143 Meters	3,750 Feet 1,143 Meters
		BOX VAN OR WATER /FUEL TRUCK	30,000 Pounds 13,636 Kilos	450 Feet 137 Meters	6,500 Feet 1,982 Meters	6,500 Feet 1,982 Meters
		SEMI- TRAILER	60,000 Pounds 27,273 Kilos	600 Feet 183 Meters	7,000 Feet 2,134 Meters	7,000 Feet 2,134 Meters

Figure 8.9 Federal Bureau of Alcohol, Tobacco, and Firearms (ATF) bomb blast distance guide.

Just like the acronym for SKRAM, identification of IKMASS variables will keep investigators and analysts alike focused on weaknesses and behaviors. Law enforcement deals largely with victims not destruction and will excel by successfully analyzing those variables that can be verified, validated, and corroborated for the purpose of identifying a specific or grave threat.

Regardless of the threat, target, or tactic, one thing will more than remain consistent — bombs. Bombs have been the staple of nearly every terrorist group. Catchy acronyms and the meanings they represent are essential to understand. However, use of bombs has been and will likely continue to be the one weapon that law enforcement strive to identify in the future, either physically or in the elements needed to construct one. In response to this, Figure 8.9, a bomb blast distance guide, is provided as a reference for law enforcement and military personnel alike.

The past, present, and future

The focus of this book has been on circumstances surrounding the United States, but like many other subjects, law enforcement topics are applicable to other locales and nations. Past events have demonstrated the violence and hatred associated with terrorist and organized hate groups and have proved that rogue extremists know no borders. Thousands of events have taken place throughout the world over the past three centuries from which the law enforcement community can learn. Successful planning for the future requires an understanding of recent and distant past events. An example of this can be found in a 1999 Library of Congress Federal Research Division report that studied and analyzed terrorists and their organizations.[11] Events that were examined included the 1998 U.S. cruise missile attack against an al-Qaeda camp in Afghanistan, the use of nuclear suitcase bombs, and the bombing of one or more airliners with time bombs. Spectacular retaliation methods against Americans were proposed. Apparently, there were signs or some indicators present that elaborate methods of destruction existed, or these assumptions could not have been made two years before the 2001 deadly World Trade Center attack.

Current international terrorist threats against the United States and other countries can be divided into three categories:

1. State sponsors of terrorism
2. Formal terrorist organizations
3. Loosely affiliated rogue extremists

These three categories have been addressed in some manner throughout this book. Even though there is tremendous concern regarding international or foreign-based terrorists, law enforcement must also remain aware of the numerous domestic-based terrorist and organized hate groups. The greatest danger at present is the mixture of international and domestic terrorism. Hate and terrorism have no borders. Future considerations should be directed toward opening lines of communication and sharing data.

Plans for the future are evolving. The chances of having a national law enforcement database have been viewed as remote for years, but this is changing. If agencies are struggling simply to standardize methods and data entry within their own jurisdictions, can data be managed and overseen on a national level?

This is one question being answered today. Former U.S. Attorney General John Ashcroft unveiled the Gateway Information Sharing Project, a pilot program that integrates investigative data from federal, state, and local law enforcement agencies into one database. It will ultimately be accessible to all agencies participating via secure Internet. This program is the result of cooperation between numerous Illinois and Missouri local, county, and state agencies, the FBI, the U.S. Attorneys' offices of the Southern District of Illinois, and the Eastern District of Missouri St. Louis Joint Terrorism Task Force.

No matter what the future holds, the three components that cannot be overlooked are quality personnel, experience, and training. Training is probably the primary key to the future. The most important aspects to keep in mind are an understanding of the topic being analyzed, knowing what is being accomplished, and continually honing skills. Groups such as professional trade associations, private consultants, educators, and peers provide the best venues for future development.

Chapter concepts

1. Many foreign-based groups in the world are full of hate and are limitless in their pursuit of fulfilling their beliefs. Their influence is and will continue to be felt in the United States.
2. The Muslim Brotherhood's history and influence in the world have played an important role in the ideologies of terrorist groups like Hamas and al-Gamma.
3. There are many Wahhabi organizations in North America who play a role in the Islamic extremist movement.
4. The use of Internet protocol and electronic mail (e-mail) in analysis is essential in today's era of technology. The information that can be attained will likely aid in developing associations.
5. Cyber terrorism is one way that foreign-based terrorists will extend their reaches into other countries, and this will primarily be handled by law enforcement.
6. The spectrum of cyber conflict demonstrates the five levels that law enforcement will face: cyber crime, hacktivism, cyber espionage, cyber warfare, and cyberterrorism.
7. Weapons of mass destruction include biological, chemical, explosive, incendiary, and nuclear devices. Chemical agents pose significant threats, and exposure is caused by absorption, ingestion, inhalation, and injection.
8. Current international terrorist threats against the United States, as well as other countries, can be divided into three distinct categories: state sponsors of terrorism, formal terrorist organizations, and loosely affiliated rogue extremists.

References

1. Vatis, M.A., Cyber attacks during the war on terrorism: a predictive analysis, Institute for Security Technology Studies, Dartmouth College, Hanover, NH, September 22, 2001, pp. 5–9.
2. Holtz, S., *Cyber Terrorism*, Florida Atlantic University, Davie (February 19, 2003), photocopy.
3. Adkins, B.N., *The Spectrum of Cyber Conflict from Hacking to Information Warfare: What is Law Enforcement's Role?*, U.S. Air Force, April 2001, pp. vii, 1–2.
4. Holtz, S., Cyber Terrorism, Miami-Dade Police Department, Miami (March 14, 2003), presentation.
5. Cilluffo, F. et al., *Defending America in the 21st Century: New Challenges, New Organizations, and New Policies*, CSIS, Washington, DC, 2000, pp. 3–4.
6. Webster, W., and de Borchgrave, A., *Cybercrime … Cyberterrorism … Cyber-warfare … : Averting an Electronic Waterloo*, CSIS, Washington, DC, 1998, p. 3. http://www.csis.org/pubs/cyberfor.html (February 28, 2003).
7. RAND, Third Annual Report to the President and the Congress of the Advisory Panel to Assess Domestic Response Capabilities for Terrorism Involving Weapons of Mass Destruction, December 15, 2001, http://www.rand.org/nsrd/ terrpanel (February 28, 2003), p. 41.

8. Heymann, P.B., Dealing with terrorism: an overview, http://mitpress.mit.edu/journals/pdf/isec_26_03_24_0.pdf, Int. Security, 26, 3, Winter 2001/02, MIT (February 14, 2003), p. 24.

9. Cordesman, A.H., *Defending America: Redefining the Conceptual Borders of Homeland Defense*, CSIS, Washington, DC, 2000, p. 66.

10. IACP Project Response Team, Leading from the front: project response terrorism, International Association of Chiefs of Police, Alexandria, VA, p. 6.

11. Library of Congress Federal Research Division, The sociology and psychology of terrorism: who becomes a terrorist and why? http://www.loc.gov/rr/frd/terrorism.htm, September 1999 (March 7, 2003), pp. 1–53.

chapter nine

Conclusion

Many analysts began as clerical help and secretaries, working in back rooms and performing only administrative functions. Times have changed. They are now sought after and hired in large numbers. Their positions have come full circle and they are now recognized as professional and vital to many law enforcement organizations. International professional trade associations such as the International Association of Crime Analysts (IACA) and the International Association of Law Enforcement Intelligence Analysts (IALEIA) have made great strides in the preceding decade in the areas of training and sharing of practices, but one component, national certification, still eludes the associations. However, certification looms on the horizon and will greatly standardize practices of analysts worldwide.

Information access is another analytical area that has been addressed by some agencies. Analysts should be granted access to all pertinent case information. If analysts are restricted, the quality and type of intelligence obtained will be deficient. Communication is consistently mentioned as the number one key to successful intelligence. Limiting an analyst is essentially the same as censoring him. Proactively working together and sharing information is the answer to addressing future incidents and combating issues that threaten homeland security worldwide.

The modern era of terrorism has a relatively short but devastating past. The federal government has undertaken initiatives toward terrorism since at least 1972. In 1985, President Ronald Reagan gave a speech on terrorism in Chicago. He noted that if there is no reaction to terrorism, it will spread like a cancer. He was right, and now the cancer has reached our shores. During that same period the FBI and CIA created high-tech state-of-the-art antiterrorism centers with the focus on cogent intelligence. The federal government has established numerous intelligence centers throughout the United States since 1985, but not all focus on terrorism. Many were established in high drug-trafficking areas, and others in remote locales. How many are interconnected and share information? As learned in a post-9/11 world, the FBI and CIA collected in-depth intelligence on many groups but were prohibited by law from exchanging it. Reagan's speech is similar to today's rhetoric, that the terrorist scourge has hit home. The same "importance of intelligence and communication" speeches from nearly 20 years ago are being replayed now. This is supported by the conclusions drawn in the 2000 CSIS working group reports on homeland defense, that "U.S. homeland defense efforts have been reactive, disjointed, and focused on post facto consequence management."[1]

Technology is one way to overcome this. However, in order for technology to be effective there must be a set of national standards for each agency to follow. Law enforcement agencies are going to continue to purchase records management and CAD systems and develop proprietary databases designed to fit their needs and budgets, but with national standards the sharing of intelligence and data would be greatly enhanced. By establishing national standards, a designated agency such as the Department of Homeland Security has the opportunity to warehouse data from agencies throughout the nation. This could be achieved with little difficulty and minimal data conversion. The problem now being faced is that there are nearly 18,000 law enforcement agencies capturing data in 18,000 different formats. If we are ever to see continuous and effective sharing of information and intelligence, there must be national standards. Federal committees have been established in the arena of GIS. Effective standards, formal and informal, designed for use by programmers, cartographers, and analysts utilizing GIS, have made the sharing of GIS information routine among a wide variety of local, state, and federal agencies.

One method to effectively address information and intelligence sharing is by streamlining the process and consolidating resources into a "one-stop shop." The reorganization of the federal government's agencies under the Department of Homeland Security was perhaps the first step toward achieving this. One way to achieve a "one-stop shop" is to establish a national homeland security clearinghouse. Use of clearinghouses has proved to be an effective tool in law enforcement. In South Florida, a county-wide robbery clearinghouse was established 10 years ago to analyze and process information on nearly 10,000 robbery cases from over 30 different agencies. Since its inception, the clearinghouse has assisted in increasing the clearance rate well above the national average and decreasing the incidence of robbery. With the use of clearinghouses, detectives no longer have to rely on personal contacts and traveling around the county to check multiple databases. They have come to rely on the clearinghouse as their sole source of information and intelligence for coordinating countywide robbery-related events. By establishing a national homeland security clearinghouse, agencies throughout the country would be able to standardize practices, expedite the intelligence process, and rely on a single source rather than pass information through a wide range of local, county, state, and federal agencies, or individuals.

The public focus is still on excellent intelligence and information sharing, but little has been done to enhance the capabilities of routine law enforcement on this front. All the intelligence in the world cannot always prevent a tragedy. Only the proactive moves of those in charge, armed with quality intelligence, can help control possible future events. The U.S. intelligence machine is primarily geared toward threats from foreign attacks. That is where law enforcement comes in. Federal agents and the military cannot be everywhere, but with the entire law enforcement community working together for a common goal, the combined effort and force will be able to deter the actions of terrorist organizations. In order for law enforcement to help in the war on terrorism, it must have an understanding of the mission at hand.

Expanding horizons through media outlets

In order to help understand what has occurred and to gain insight, analysts and investigators must expand their horizons. One way to further this is by reviewing various news sources outside their respective country. Part of anticipating behaviors is the ability to identify the reality, and truths that are likely to be hidden, intentionally or unintentionally, published. Any investigator who has spent time perfecting interviews and interrogations will tell you that quite often there is some truth in any lie. Your job is to find it. Outlined below are some of the more prevalent Arabic/Islamic news Web sites. These sites provide information that may not be published in any other media outlet and help heighten law enforcement awareness.

Muslim/Arab Internet news sites and resources

http://www.ummahnews.com/	Ummah News
http://www.islam-online.net/	Islam Online
http://www.ibn.net/	Islamic Broadcasting Network
http://www.iviews.com/	Muslim and Arabic News Views
http://menareport.com/	Middle East News
http://www.musalman.com/	Muslaman
http://www.palestine-info.info/	Palestine Info Center
http://www.palestinemonitor.org	Palestine Monitor
http://english.planetarabia.com/	Planet Arabia
http://www.dawn.com	Dawn Newspaper
http://www.islamicnews.org/	International Islamic News Agency
http://www.middleeastwire.com/	Middle East News Online
http://www.informationtimes.com/	Information Times
http://www.q-news.com/	Q-News
http://www.ianaradionet.com/	IANA RadioNet
http://www.readmirror.com	Mirror International
http://ptimes.org/	Palestine Times
http://www.islamvision.org/	Islam Vision
http://kavkaz.org/	Kavkaz
http://www.mehrnews.com/	Mehr News
http://www.menareport.com/	North Africa Business report
http://www.megastories.com/attack/aip/ aipindex.shtml	Afghani Islamic Press

http://www.khilafah.com	Khilafah.Com Daily News
http://www.irna.com/en/	Islamic Republic News Agency (IRNA)
http://www.palestinechronicle.com	Palestine Chronicle
http://faridi.net/news	News from Pakistan
http://www.morojihad.com/	News from Mindanao
http://www.twf.org/News.html	The Wisdom Fund
http://www.vocfm.com	Voice of Cape - South Africa
http://www.arabia.com/english	Arabia.com
http://www.gulf-times.com	Gulf Times
http://www.gulf-news.com/	Gulf News Online
http://www.paknews.com	PAK NEWS
http://www.ahram.org.eg/weekly/	AL-AHRAM
http://www.jang.com.pk/thenews/	The International News (Pakistan)
http://www.islamicvoice.com	Islamic Voice Monthly Newsletter
http://www.milligazette.com/	Milli Gazette
http://www.salaam.co.uk/	Salaam
http://www.muslimviews.org	Muslim Views
http://www.muslimedia.com/	Muslim Media
http://www.mediamonitors.net/	Media Monitors
http://www.pmwatch.org	Palestine Media Watch
http://www.muslimthai.com	Muslim Thai News
http://www.arabnews.com/	Arab News
http://www.arabmediawatch.com/	Arab Media Watch
http://www.muslimobserver.com/	The Muslim Observer
http://www.nation-online.com/	The New Nation – Bangladesh
http://www.malaysiakini.com/	Malaysiakini
http://www.thisiscyberia.com/	Cyberia
http://www.al-moharer.com.au	Al-Moharer
http://pakobservercom.readyhosting.com	Pakistan Observer
http://www.newsofthegulf.com/	News of The Gulf
http://www.cairotimes.com/	Cairo Times
http://www.jang.com.pk/	The International News
http://www.ameinfo.com/press/	Middle East Business News
http://www.mediareviewnet.com/	Media Review Network
http://www.kashmirobserver.com/	Kashmir Observer
http://www.kmsnews.org/	Kashmir Media Service
http://www.ummah.org.uk/kashmir/index.htm	Jammu and Kashmir
http://www.greaterkashmir.com/	Greater Kashmir
http://www.ummah.org.uk/albayan/index.html	al-Bayan
http://www.1001sites.com/	Middle East Times
http://www.alb-net.com/index.htm	Kosova Crisis Center
http://www.kurdishmedia.com/	Kurdish Media
http://www.arabicnews.com/	ArabicNews.Com
http://www.jordantimes.com/	Jordan Times

http://www.alhewar.com/	Arabic and English Papers Online
http://www.sahafa.com/	Sahafa On-Line
http://www.quran.net/qnet/news	Several news outlets here
http://metimes.com/	Middle East Times - Egypt Edition
http://www.abdul.com/worldnews	99 news outlets here
http://news.pacificnews.org/news/	Pacific News Service
http://www.islam.org/media/ Network.HTM	More news outlets
http://www.muslimnews.co.uk	Muslims News
http://www.icna.com/main.shtml/	Islamic Circle of North America (news items)
http://www.arab.net/	ArabNet
http://members.aol.com/gnhbos/ arabnews.htm	Arabic Language News Outlets
http://www.alwafd.org/	Al-Wafd
http://www.aljazeera.net/	Al-Jazeera(Arabic)
http://english.aljazeera.net/	HomePage English version
http://www.asharqalawsat.com/	Asharqalawsat (Arabic)
http://www.sabiroon.org	Sabiroon
http://www.algeria-watch.org/	Algeria Watch

Awareness and an understanding of the topic are vital at all levels if law enforcement is to be successful in analysis, investigations, and proactive measures. Terrorism has been around for years. It may not be possible to eliminate it completely, but through comprehensive and thorough law enforcement efforts it can be controlled. Key to a successful endeavor is to maintain an awareness of current issues, have a fundamental understanding of the topic being faced, identify and exploit weaknesses, and be able to anticipate behavioral patterns. All the aforementioned will ultimately help prevent future catastrophic events and play an essential role in the war on terrorism. Other measures, such as table top exercises and on-the-job training scenarios, help ready personnel on an array of potential scenarios. However, one thing that tends be missing is the intelligence process. Scenarios and table tops do an excellent job in identifying weakness, equipment needs, and collaborative efforts among agencies, but most are designed to respond, react, and recover. Why not design and perform exercises that are proactive and based on intelligence. Lessons learned should not be void of the information and intelligence process.

Incidents and events, terrorist related or otherwise, do not occur in a vacuum. Traces and indicators are left by people and objects. With the use of databases, together with the ongoing collection of information and intelligence, terrorist groups can be located, assessed, traced, and their future activities predicted. Looking for and building the puzzle with SKRAM variables can assist in finding terrorist-related traces. You must be bold and locate pre-incident variables rather than analyzing past events. Anyone can analyze after the fact. Why wait when you can prevent an attack by being proactive?

Success and victory in the war on terrorism will be achieved by working together, and analysis and intelligence will likely be there too.

Reference

1. Cilluffo, F. et al., *Defending America in the 21st Century: New Challenges, New Organizations, and New Policies*, CSIS, Washington, DC, 2000, p. 9.

appendix a

Domestic-based terrorist organizations

Information comes from Jonathan R. White, *Terrorism: An Introduction*, Wadsworth Publishing, Florence, KY; MILNET Web site (http://www.milnet.com); SPLC Web site (http://www.splcenter.org); ADL Web site (http://www.adl.org); and the individual groups' Web sites.

1. **American Coalition for Life Activists:** Based in Oregon; founded by Andrew Burnett, a long-time antiabortionist activist whose group endorses the justifiable homicide of abortion clinic doctors
2. **Animal Liberation Front:** Support groups are based throughout North America; in 1993, the group reportedly planted arson or incendiary devices in four Chicago stores; based on its Web site, it does not condone violence, and membership only carries out direct action by whatever means necessary
3. **Army of God:** Highly militant antiabortion movement that believes God has given them the duty to kill abortionists; it allegedly claimed responsibility for a number of abortion clinic bombings in Georgia and Alabama; financially affiliated with Glory to Jesus Ministries in Virginia
4. **Aryan Nation (aka Aryan Republican Army and Aryan National Alliance):** Base of operation is located in Hayden Lake, Idaho; categorized as white supremacists, Christian Identity group; founded by Richard Butler in the mid-1970s; believe that it is its duty to populate the country with member's progeny through polygamy; allegedly seek to overthrow the American government using bank robberies as an end to their means; ideology follows Christian Identity, neo-Nazi, and paramilitary
5. **Branch Davidians:** Thought to be an extinct operation; during their height of operation, they had bases of operation in Utah and Texas; considered by some to be a form of a cult, they are primarily firearms protestors

6. **Christian Identity Movement:** Chapters are in approximately 18 states with an estimated 31 groups; alleged members were convicted of conspiracy to manufacture explosives; they are considered to be antiabortion and antibanking, and they depict Jews as biologically descended from Satan

7. **Citizens of the Republic of Idaho:** Based in St. Maries, Idaho; founded by Hari Heath; members do not believe in the bureaucracy of the U.S. courts and government; therefore, they created their own; considered to be relatively docile

8. **Colorado First Light Infantry:** Alleged members were charged with possessing and manufacturing illegal firearms; group publicly supports Timothy McVeigh's actions and the Oklahoma City bombing on April 19, 1995

9. **Colorado Militia:** Based in Aurora, Colorado; professed goals are those of weapons rights

10. **Covenant (aka Sword and Arm of the Lord):** Christian Identity group started in 1971 by James Ellison on the Arkansas/Missouri state line; based in Arkansas; considered to be a violent white supremacist group with close ties to members of the Ku Klux Klan

11. **Earth Liberation Front (ELF) (aka North American ELF):** Alleged members were linked to attacks against the U.S. Forest Service, logging companies, and bioengineering corporations; group is categorized as ecological activists

12. **Evan Mecham Eco-Terrorist International Conspiracy (EMETIC):** Formed in 1985; satirically uses the name of an Arizona governor; the group is known for spiking trees and various forms of sabotage

13. **Freeman:** Based in Montana; group members believe the U.S. legal system is not valid; supports an internal separatist government; alleged members were convicted for fraud and robbery; categorized as a right-wing group

14. **Ku Klux Klan:** Categorized as a white supremacy group established during the Civil War era, December 1865; the group is primarily active in the South but allegedly has membership in approximately 28 different states, with an estimated membership base of 5,500 to 6,000 in just over 100 different groups; subgroups go by various names including Invisible Empire, Knights of the Klu Klux Klan, United Klans of America, and the National Knights of the Ku Klux Klan

15. **Los Macheteros:** Marxist-Leninist group formed in 1976, but emerged publicly in 1978; it wants Puerto Rico to be an independent nation; name translation means "machete wielders" or "cane cutters"; Puerto Rican revolutionary group based in Puerto Rico and operating in several northeastern states including New York; members allegedly detonated explosives in New York and committed homicides; members are also known for their many publicly claimed robberies in the early 1980s, including one for $7.1 million in Connecticut

16. **Michigan Militia:** Formed in April 1994 by a firearm store owner named Norman Olson and real-estate agent Ray Southwell; categorized as a large weapons rights, survivalist, and militant antigovernment organization; no major illegal activity was directly traced to this group's membership; membership was reported as high as 12,000

17. **Militia of Montana (MOM):** Founded in February 1994 by John, David, and Randy Trochmann; categorized as a weapons rights and militant antigovernment organization; encourages members to arm themselves with guns and knives; no major illegal activity has been directly traced to this group's membership; paramilitary militia

18. **Mountaineer Militia:** Based in West Virginia; categorized as paramilitary, antigovernment, and weapons rights organization; alleged leader was convicted in August 1997 for conspiracy to engage in the manufacture of explosives

19. **National Alliance:** Founded by William Pierce, author of *The Turner Diaries*, in Hillsboro (Mill Point), West Virginia in 1974; categorized as a white supremacist and neo-Nazi organization; leader is Erich Gliebe

20. **North American Militia of Southwestern Michigan:** Categorized as a paramilitary, antigovernment, and weapons rights organization

21. **Patriot's Council:** Based in Minnesota; categorized as a violent antigovernment and tax protest organization; the group allegedly created ricin, a toxic nerve agent

22. **Phineas Priesthood:** Inspired by the book *The Vigilantes of Christendom* by Richard Hoskins; group membership opposes homosexuality, abortions, and interracial marriages; members have allegedly committed bank robberies and abortion clinic bombings

23. **Posse Comitatus:** Founded by Henry Beach in the early 1970s; name is Latin for power of the county; categorized as anti-Semitic and as a white supremacist organization; chapters were established in almost every state of the union and have had ties with the Arizona Patriots

24. **Reclaim the Seeds:** Categorized as an antibiotechnology organization; members allegedly claimed responsibility for a 2000 attack on crops at Seminis Vegetable Seeds Research Center and Davis campus of the University of California

25. **Republic of Texas:** Based in the Davis Mountains in West Texas; alleged leader is Richard McLaren; the organization contends that Texas was illegally annexed into the union in 1845 and that it remains an independent nation

26. **Southern California Minuteman:** Group is allegedly against the influx of illegal aliens into the U.S. from Mexico and has used snipers to control them

27. **The Order (aka The New Order):** Based in Oregon, Illinois, and Michigan; founded by the late Robert Mathews; categorized as a right-wing, white supremacist, neo-Nazi, racist, and anti-Semitic group; followed by and affiliated with such groups as the Silent Brotherhood and Strike Force II

28. **Viper Militia:** Based in Arizona; categorized as a paramilitary and antigovernment organization; allegedly had ties with Timothy McVeigh; trained to make illegal weapons and construct and detonate fertilizer bombs

29. **World Church of the Creator:** Founded in 1973 and headquartered in Riverton, Wyoming; also based in East Peoria, Illinois; alleged leader is Matt Hale; categorized as a white supremacist group

"Patriot" groups in the United States

The Southern Poverty Law Center's Intelligence Project identified 158 "Patriot" groups that were active in 2001. Of these groups, 73 were militias, two were "common-law courts," and the remainder fit into a variety of categories, such as publishers, ministries, and citizens' groups. By 2004 the number of militias was up to 52 and the number of "Patriot" groups was only 152, which was a decrease from 2003 where 171 were noted by the center. Generally, Patriot groups define themselves as opposed to the "New World Order" or advocate or adhere to extreme antigovernment doctrines. Groups listed here are not implied to advocate or engage in violence or other criminal activities, or be racist. The list was compiled from field reports, Patriot publications, the Internet, law enforcement sources, and news reports. Groups are identified by the city, county, or region where they are located. Within states, groups are listed alphabetically by place of origin.

Alabama
Alabama Committee to Get US Out of the United Nations, Birmingham

Alaska
Jefferson Party, Anchorage

Arizona
American Patriot Friends Network, Glendale
Sovereign Citizen Resource Center, Thatcher
Arizona Free Citizen's Militia, Tucson

Arkansas
Militia of Washington County, Fayetteville
Arkansas State Militia, Franklin County
Constitution Party, North Little Rock

California
California Militia, Brea
John Birch Society, Brea

State Citizens Service Center Research Headquarters, Canoga Park
Truth Radio, Delano
John Birch Society, Fountain Valley
Free Enterprise Society, Fresno
Second Amendment Committee, Hanford
John Birch Society, Laguna Hills
John Birch Society, Mission Viejo
John Birch Society, Newport Beach
John Birch Society, Oceanside
Southern California High Desert Militia, Oceanside
John Birch Society, Orange
John Birch Society, Riverside
John Birch Society, Santa Ana
Truth In Taxation, Studio City
Freedom Law School, Tustin

Colorado
American Freedom Network, Johnstown

Connecticut
Connecticut 51st Militia, Terryville

District of Columbia
American Free Press, Washington

Florida
Constitutional Guardians of America, Boca Raton
Citizens for Better Government, Gainesville
Constitution Party, Jupiter

Georgia
Militia of Georgia, Lawrenceville
Constitution Party, Woodstock

Idaho
Sons of Liberty, Boise
Police Against the New World Order, Kamiah

Illinois
Illinois State Militia, Addison
Southern Illinois Patriots League, Benton
Constitution Party, Springfield

Indiana
Old Paths Baptist Church, Campbellsburg
NORFED, Evansville
Indianapolis Baptist Temple, Indianapolis
Indiana Militia Corps 2nd Brigade, Northeast Indiana
Indiana Militia Corps 1st Brigade, Northwest Indiana
Indiana State Militia 14th Regiment, Owen County
Indiana Militia Corps 5th Brigade, Pendleton

Constitution Party, Shoals
Indiana Militia Corps 4th Brigade, Southeast Indiana
Indiana Militia Corps 3rd Brigade, Southwest Indiana

Iowa
Constitution Party, Randall

Kansas
Constitution Party, Wichita

Kentucky
Take Back Kentucky, Clarkson
Free Kentucky, Lebanon
Constitution Party, Louisville
Kentucky State Militia, Nicholasville
Kentucky Mountain Rangers, Smilax
Kentucky State Militia 9th Battalion, Western Kentucky

Louisiana
Common Law Defense Fund, Lafayette

Maine
Maine Militia, Belfast
Constitution Party, Spruce Head

Maryland
Southern Sons of Liberty, Citizens Militia of Maryland, Baltimore
Constitution Party, Taneytown
Save a Patriot Fellowship, Westminster

Michigan
Proclaim Liberty Ministry, Adrian
Michigan Militia Corps Wolverines, 3rd Division, Benzonia
Southern Michigan Regional Militia, Burton
St. Clair County Militia, Capac
Southern Michigan Regional Militia, Capac
Justice Pro Se, Dearborn
Michigan Militia, Detroit
Southern Michigan Regional Militia, Fowlerville
Michigan Militia Corps Wolverines, Kalamazoo
Southern Michigan Regional Militia, Monroe County
Michigan Militia, Inc., Redford
Southern Michigan Regional Militia, St. Clair
Lawful Path, Tustin

Minnesota
Minnesota Militia, St. Cloud
Constitution Party, St. Paul

Missouri
Missouri 51st Militia, Grain Valley
7th Missouri Militia, Granby

2nd Missouri Militia, Tuscumbia

Montana
Project 7, Kalispell
Militia of Montana, Noxon

Nevada
Center for Action, Sandy Valley

New Jersey
Constitution Party, Palmyra
New Jersey Committee of Safety, Shamong
New Jersey Militia, Trenton

New Mexico
New Mexico Liberty Corps, Albuquerque

New York
New York Patriot Militia, Slate Hill

North Carolina
United America Party, Zebulon

North Dakota
Constitution Party, Casselton

Ohio
Right Way L.A.W., Akron
Ohio Unorganized Militia Assistance and Advisory Committee,
    Ashtabula County
Ohio Unorganized Militia Assistance and Advisory Committee,
    Champaign County
True Blue Freedom, Cincinnati
Ohio Unorganized Militia, Columbiana County
Central Ohio Unorganized Militia, Columbus County
Ohio Unorganized Militia Assistance Advisory Committee,
    Darke County
Ohio Unorganized Militia Assistance and Advisory Committee,
    Delaware County
Central Ohio Unorganized Militia, Franklin County
E Pluribus Unum, Grove City
Ohio Unorganized Militia Assistance and Advisory Committee,
    Lebanon
Central Ohio Unorganized Militia, Madison County
Ohio Unorganized Militia Assistance and Advisory Committee,
    Montgomery
Ohio Unorganized Militia Assistance and Advisory Committee,
    Portage County
Ohio Unorganized Militia Assistance and Advisory Committee,
    Westerville

Oklahoma
Present Truth Ministry, Panama

Oregon
Emissary Publications, Clackamas
Southern Oregon Militia, Eagle Point
Freedom Bound International, Klamath Falls
Constitution Party, Portland
Embassy of Heaven, Stayton

Pennsylvania
American Nationalist Union, Allison Park
Pennsylvania 1st Unorganized Militia, Harrisburg
Constitution Party National Office, Lancaster

South Carolina
AWARE Group, Greenville
Constitution Party, Greenville

Tennessee
Militia of East Tennessee, Knox County
Constitution Party, Germantown

Texas
Texas Unified Field Forces, Alto
People's Court of Common Law, Arlington
13th Texas Infantry Regiment, Austin
Constitution Society, Austin
John Birch Society, Austin
Living Truth Ministries, Austin
Constitution Party, Brenham
13th Texas Infantry Regiment, Bryan
Buffalo Creek Press, Cleburne
13th Texas Infantry Regiment, Conroe
Citizens for Legal Reform, Dallas
Republic of Texas, Dallas
Texas Unified Field Forces, Duncanville
Republic of Texas, Fort Worth
Texas Unified Field Forces, Grimes County
Texas Unified Field Forces, Harleton
Texas Unified Field Forces, Harris County
Texas Unified Field Forces, Hill County
Republic of Texas, Houston
Texas Unified Field Forces, Hunt County
Texas Unified Field Forces, Huntington
Texas Unified Field Forces, Jackson County
Texas Unified Field Forces, Neches
Texas Unified Field Forces, Potter County

Texas Unified Field Forces, Red Rock
13th Texas Infantry Regiment, San Antonio
American Opinion Bookstore, San Antonio
Texas Unified Field Forces, Tom Green County
Republic of Texas, Victoria
Church of God Evangelistic Association, Waxahachie
Republic of Texas, White Oak

Vermont
Constitution Party, Quechee

Virginia
Virginia Citizens Militia, Roanoke
Constitution Party, Vienna

Washington
Jural Society, Ellensburg
Constitution Party, Tacoma
Yakima County Militia, Yakima County

Wisconsin
John Birch Society, Appleton
Constitution Party, Watertown

appendix c

Symbols of hate

White supremacists and other extremists have long been fond of signs, symbols, logos, and emblems, the meanings of which are not always obvious to the uninformed observer. Reproduced here with permission are some of the most popular symbols in current use on the Internet or in extremist publications, as displayed on the Southern Poverty Law Center's Web site (http://www.splcenter.org).

Ku Klux Klan Blood Drop

The blood drop is one of the Ku Klux Klan's best-known symbols. For Klan members, the drop represents the blood that Jesus Christ shed on the cross as a sacrifice for the white race.

The Night Rider

This depiction of the traditional robed Klansman on horseback signifies the Ku Klux Klan. Night riders originated in Ohio in the 1920s as a group of black-robed Klan terrorists who specialized in violent attacks on blacks and others.

ZOG

Zionist Occupied Government, a phrase used by anti-Semitic and white supremacist groups to denote the federal government. These groups believe the government is secretly controlled by Jews.

Nazi Swastika

Adopted in 1935 as the official emblem of Germany's Nazi Party, the swastika is now widely used by neo-Nazi, Skinhead, and other white supremacist groups. Dozens of variations on the swastika are common.

War Skins

This logo, incorporating a skull and crossbones, is used by the Skinhead followers of the neo-Nazi group White Aryan Resistance (W.A.R.).

Celtic Cross

Originally a symbol for the Celts of ancient Ireland and Scotland, the Celtic cross was adopted by many American white supremacist groups. In modern times, it was first used by the far-right National Front in England.

Thunderbolt

This is a Nazi symbol signifying the Schutzstaffel (SS), the elite military arm of Adolf Hitler's Third Reich. The SS supervised Nazi Germany's network of death camps.

National Alliance Life Rune

This is the official symbol of the neo-Nazi National Alliance, based in Hillsboro, West Virginia. Originally, it was a character from a Runic alphabet that signified life, creation, birth, rebirth, and renewal. Several Runic alphabets were used by the Germanic peoples between the 3rd and 13th centuries.

White Pride World Wide

Some groups incorporated this white supremacist slogan into the Celtic cross.

W.A.R. Swastika

The symbol used by the neo-Nazi group White Aryan Resistance (W.A.R.) incorporates the California-based group's acronym into a Nazi swastika.

Aryan Nations

This symbol is used by the neo-Nazi Aryan Nations, based in Hayden Lake, Idaho.

Crossed Hammers

Crossed hammers signify the many Skinhead groups that use the word "hammer" as part of their names. Such groups exist in Australia, Europe, and the United States, and many incorporate the crossed hammers into their own symbols.

Three-Bladed Swastika

This is a variation of the traditional swastika of Nazi Germany that is popular among some Skinhead and other white supremacist groups. It also has been used by some South African extremist groups.

Skinhead Skull and Crossbones

Many Skinhead groups use variations of this symbol, which incorporates the Celtic cross into a skull and crossbones.

Two forms of text labeling are also common and are listed below:

14 Words

This is shorthand for a slogan coined by David Lane, an imprisoned member of The Order, or Silent Brotherhood: "We must secure the existence of our people and a future for White children." The Order was a revolutionary neo-Nazi group responsible for the theft of millions of dollars in armored car heists and the murder of a Jewish radio talk show host in the 1980s.

88

This number, widely used by neo-Nazis and others, is shorthand for "Heil Hitler." H is the eighth letter of the alphabet, and so the abbreviation H.H. is translated as 88.

appendix d

Foreign-based terrorist organizations

The organization details listed here are from the U.S. Department of State. This report is now known as the Country Reports on Terrorism. These are not the only foreign-based terrorist organizations in existence; they are just the predominant and most active ones.

Abu Nidal Organization (ANO)

Other names

Fatah Revolutionary Council
Arab Revolutionary Brigades
Black September
Revolutionary Organization of Socialist Muslims

Description

International terrorist organization led by Sabri al-Banna. Split from the PLO in 1974. The group is made up of various functional committees, including political, military, and financial.

Activities

The group has carried out terrorist attacks in 20 countries, killing or injuring almost 900 persons. Targets include the United States, United Kingdom, France, Israel, moderate Palestinians, the PLO, and various Arab countries. Major attacks included the Rome and Vienna airports in December 1985, the Neve Shalom synagogue in Istanbul, the Pan Am flight 73 hijacking in Karachi in September 1986, and the City of Poros day-excursion ship attack in Greece in July 1988. The group is suspected of assassinating PLO deputy chief Abu Iyad and PLO security Chief Abu Hul in Tunis in January 1991.

ANO assassinated a Jordanian diplomat in Lebanon in January 1994 and was linked to the killing of the PLO representative there. The ANO has not attacked Western targets since the late 1980s.

Strength

A few hundred, plus a limited overseas support structure.

Location/area of operation

Al-Banna relocated to Iraq in December 1998, where the group maintains a presence. It has an operational presence in Lebanon in the Bekaa Valley and has several Palestinian refugee camps in coastal areas of Lebanon. It also has a limited presence in Sudan and Syria, among others, although financial problems and internal disorganization reduced the group's activities and capabilities. Authorities shut down the ANO's operations in Libya and Egypt in 1999. ANO has demonstrated the ability to operate over a wide area, including the Middle East, Asia, and Europe.

External aid

Has received considerable support, including safe havens, training, logistical assistance, and financial aid from Iraq, Libya, and Syria (until 1987), in addition to close support for selected operations.

Abu Sayyaf Group (ASG)

Description

The ASG is the most violent of the Islamic separatist groups operating in the southern Philippines. Some ASG leaders studied or worked in the Middle East and allegedly fought in Afghanistan during the Soviet war. The group split from the Moro National Liberation Front in the early 1990s under the leadership of Abdurajak Abubakar Janjalani, who was killed in a clash with Philippine police on December 18, 1998. His younger brother, Khadaffy Janjalani, replaced him as the nominal leader of the group, which is composed of several semiautonomous factions.

Activities

The ASG engages in kidnappings for ransom, bombings, assassinations, and extortion. Although from time to time it claims that its motivation is to promote an independent Islamic state in western Mindanao and the Sulu Archipelago, areas in the southern Philippines heavily populated by Muslims, the ASG now appears to use terror mainly for financial profit. The group's first large-scale action was a raid on the town of Ipil in Mindanao in April 1995.

In April of 2000, an ASG faction kidnapped 21 persons, including 10 foreign tourists, from a resort in Malaysia. Separately in 2000, the group abducted several foreign journalists, three Malaysians, and a U.S. citizen. On May 27, 2001 the ASG kidnapped 3 U.S. citizens and 17 Filipinos from a tourist resort in Palawan, Philippines. Several of the hostages, including one U.S. citizen, were murdered.

Strength

The ASG is believed to have a few hundred core fighters, and at least 1,000 individuals motivated by the prospect of receiving ransom payments for foreign hostages allegedly joined the group in 2000–2001.

Location/area of operation

The ASG was founded in Basilan Province and mainly operates there and in the neighboring provinces of Sulu and Tawi-Tawi in the Sulu Archipelago. It also operates in the Zamboanga Peninsula, and members occasionally travel to Manila and other parts of the country. The group expanded its operations to Malaysia in 2000 when it abducted foreigners from a tourist resort.

External aid

The ASG is largely self-financed through ransom and extortion. The group may receive support from Islamic extremists in the Middle East and South Asia. Libya publicly paid millions of dollars for the release of the foreign hostages seized from Malaysia in 2000.

al-Aqsa Martyrs Brigade

Description

The al-Aqsa Martyrs Brigade comprises an unknown number of small cells of Fatah-affiliated activists who emerged at the outset of the current Intifadah to attack Israeli targets. It aims to drive the Israeli military and settlers from the West Bank, Gaza Strip, and Jerusalem and to establish a Palestinian state.

Activities

The al-Aqsa Martyrs Brigade has carried out shootings and suicide operations against Israeli military personnel and civilians and killed Palestinians whom the group believed were collaborating with Israel. At least five U.S. citizens, four of them dual Israeli-U.S. citizens, were killed in these attacks. The group probably did not attack them because of their U.S. citizenship. In January 2002, the group claimed responsibility for the first suicide bombing carried out by a female.

Strength

Unknown.

Location/area of operation

The al-Aqsa Martyrs Brigade operates mainly in the West Bank and claimed attacks inside Israel and the Gaza Strip.

External aid

Unknown.

Armed Islamic Group (GIA)

Description

An Islamic extremist group, the GIA aims to overthrow the secular Algerian regime and replace it with an Islamic state. The GIA began its violent activities in early 1992 after Algiers voided the victory of the Islamic Salvation Front (FIS) — the largest Islamic party — in the first round of legislative elections in December 1991.

Activities

The GIA is responsible for frequent attacks against civilians, journalists, and foreign residents. In the last several years the GIA conducted a terrorist campaign of civilian massacres, sometimes wiping out entire villages in its area of operations and frequently killing hundreds of civilians. Since announcing its terrorist campaign against foreigners living in Algeria in September 1993, the GIA killed more than 100 expatriate men and women — mostly Europeans — in the country. The GIA uses assassinations and bombings, including car bombs, and is known to kidnap victims and slit their throats. The GIA hijacked an Air France flight to Algiers in December 1994. In late 1999, several GIA members were convicted by a French court for conducting a series of bombings in France in 1995.

Strength

Precise numbers are unknown — probably around 200.

Location/area of operation

Algeria and France.

External aid

Algerian expatriates and GSPC members abroad, many of whom reside in Western Europe, provide financial and logistical support. In addition, the Algerian Government has accused Iran and Sudan of supporting Algerian extremists.

'Asbat al-ansar

Description

'Asbat al-Ansar — the Partisans' League — is a Lebanon-based, Sunni extremist group composed primarily of Palestinians, which is associated with Osama Bin Ladin. The group follows an extremist interpretation of Islam that justifies violence against civilian targets to achieve political ends. Some of those goals include overthrowing the Lebanese Government and thwarting perceived anti-Islamic influences in the country.

Activities

'Asbat al-Ansar has carried out several terrorist attacks in Lebanon since it first emerged in the early 1990s. The group carried out assassinations of Lebanese religious leaders and bombed several nightclubs, theaters, and liquor stores in the mid-1990s. The group raised its operational profile in the year 2000 with two dramatic attacks against Lebanese and international targets. The group was involved in clashes in northern Lebanon in late December 1999, and carried out a rocket-propelled grenade attack on the Russian Embassy in Beirut in January 2000.

Strength

The group commands about 300 hundred fighters in Lebanon.

Location/area of operation

The group's primary base of operations is the 'Ayn al-Hilwah Palestinian refugee camp near Sidon in southern Lebanon.

External aid

The group probably receives money through international Sunni extremist networks and Bin Ladin's al-Qaeda network.

Aum Supreme Truth (Aum)

Other names

Aum Shinrikyo

Description

A cult established in 1987 by Shoko Asahara, the Aum aimed to take over Japan and then the world. Approved as a religious entity in 1989 under

Japanese law, the cult ran candidates in a Japanese parliamentary election in 1990. Over time, the cult began to emphasize the imminence of the end of the world and stated that the United States would initiate Armageddon by starting World War III with Japan. The Japanese government revoked its recognition of the Aum as a religious organization in October 1995, but in 1997 a government panel decided not to invoke the Anti-Subversive Law against the cult, which would have outlawed them. A 1999 law gave the Japanese government authorization to continue police surveillance of the cult due to concerns that Aum might launch future terrorist attacks. Under the leadership of Fumihiro Joyu, the Aum changed its name to Aleph in January 2000, and claimed to have rejected the violent and apocalyptic teachings of its founder. (Joyu took formal control of the organization early in 2002 and remains its leader.)

Activities

On March 20, 1995, Aum members simultaneously released the chemical nerve agent sarin on several Tokyo subway trains, killing 12 persons and injuring up to 6,000. The group was responsible for other mysterious chemical accidents in Japan in 1994. Its efforts to conduct attacks using biological agents have been unsuccessful. Japanese police arrested Asahara in May 1995, and he remained on trial facing charges in 13 crimes, including 7 counts of murder, at the end of 2001. Legal analysts say it will take several more years to conclude the trial. Since 1997, the cult has continued to recruit new members, engage in commercial enterprise, and acquire property, although it scaled back these activities significantly in 2001 in response to public outcry. The cult maintains an Internet home page. In July 2001, Russian authorities arrested a group of Russian Aum followers who planned to set off bombs near the Imperial Palace in Tokyo as part of an operation to free Asahara from jail and then smuggle him to Russia.

Strength

The Aum's current membership is estimated at 1,500 to 2,000 persons. At the time of the Tokyo subway attack, the group claimed to have 9,000 members in Japan and up to 40,000 worldwide.

Location/area of operation

The Aum's principal membership is located only in Japan, but a residual branch comprising an unknown number of followers surfaced in Russia.

External aid

None.

al-Gama'a al-Islamiyya

Other names

Islamic Group (IG)

Description

Egypt's largest militant group; has been active since the late 1970s. The group appears to be loosely organized, with an external wing with supporters in several countries worldwide. The group issued a cease-fire in March 1999, but its spiritual leader, Shaykh Umar Abd al-Rahman, sentenced to life in prison in January 1996 for his involvement in the 1993 World Trade Center bombing and incarcerated in the United States, rescinded his support for the cease-fire in June 2000. The Gama'a has not conducted an attack inside Egypt since August 1998. A senior member signed Osama Bin Ladin's fatwa in February 1998 calling for attacks against the United States. The group unofficially split into two factions: one that supports the cease-fire led by Mustafa Hamza, and one led by Rifa'i Taha Musa, calling for a return to armed operations. Taha Musa in early 2001 published a book in which he attempted to justify terrorist attacks that would cause mass casualties. Musa disappeared several months thereafter, and there are conflicting reports as to his current whereabouts. The group's primary goal is to overthrow the Egyptian government and replace it with an Islamic state, but disaffected IG members, such as those potentially inspired by Taha Musa or Abd al-Rahman, may be interested in carrying out attacks against U.S. and Israeli interests.

Activities

The group conducted armed attacks against Egyptian security and other government officials, Coptic Christians, and Egyptian opponents of Islamic extremism before the cease-fire. From 1993 until the cease-fire, al-Gama'a launched attacks on tourists in Egypt, most notably the attack in November 1997 at Luxor that killed 58 foreign tourists. Also, the group claimed responsibility for the attempt in June 1995 to assassinate Egyptian President Hosni Mubarak in Addis Ababa, Ethiopia. The Gama'a never specifically attacked a U.S. citizen or facility but has threatened U.S. interests.

Strength

Unknown — but at its peak, the IG probably commanded several thousand hard-core members and a like number of sympathizers. The 1999 cease-fire and security crackdowns following the attack in Luxor, Egypt in 1997, and more recently security efforts following September 11, probably resulted in a substantial decrease in the group's numbers.

Location/area of operation

The IG operates mainly in the Al-Minya, Asyu't, Qina, and Sohaj governor-ates of southern Egypt. The group also appears to have support in Cairo, Alexandria, and other urban locations, particularly among unemployed graduates and students. It has a worldwide presence, including in the United Kingdom, Afghanistan, Yemen, and Austria.

External aid

Unknown — but the Egyptian government believes that Iran, Bin Ladin, and Afghan militant groups support the organization. The group may also obtain some funding through various Islamic nongovernmental organizations.

Communist Party of the Philippines (CPP), New Peoples' Army (NPA)

Description

The military wing of the Communist Party of the Philippines (CPP), the NPA is a Maoist group formed in March 1969 with the aim of overthrowing the government through protracted guerrilla warfare. The chairman of the CPP's Central Committee and the NPA's founder, Jose Maria Sison, directs all CPP and NPA activity from the Netherlands, where he lives in self-imposed exile. Fellow Central Committee member and director of the CPP's National Democratic Front (NDF) Luis Jalandoni also lives in the Netherlands and has become a Dutch citizen. Although primarily a rural-based guerrilla group, the NPA has an active urban infrastructure to conduct terrorism and uses city-based assassination squads. The NPA derives most of its funding from contributions of supporters in the Philippines, Europe, and elsewhere, and from so-called "revolutionary taxes" extorted from local businesses.

Activities

The NPA primarily targets Philippine security forces, politicians, judges, government informers, former rebels who wish to leave the NPA, and alleged criminals. The group opposes any U.S. military presence in the Philippines and attacked U.S. military interests before the U.S. base closures in 1992. Press reports in 1999 and in late 2001 indicated that the NPA is again targeting U.S. troops participating in joint military exercises as well as U.S. Embassy personnel. The NPA claimed responsibility for the assassi-nation of congressmen from Quezon (in May 2001) and Cagayan (in June 2001) and many other killings.

Strength

The strength of the NPA is slowly growing and is now estimated at over 10,000.

Location/area of operations

The NPA operates in rural Luzon, Visayas, and parts of Mindanao. It has cells in Manila and other metropolitan centers.

External aid

Unknown.

Euzkadi Ta Askatasuna (ETA)

Other names

Basque Fatherland and Liberty

Description

ETA was founded in 1959 with the aim of establishing an independent homeland based on Marxist principles in the northern Spanish Provinces of Vizcaya, Guipuzcoa, Alava, and Navarra, and the southwestern French Provinces of Labourd, Basse-Navarra, and Soule.

Activities

The group is primarily involved in bombings and assassinations of Spanish government officials, security and military forces, politicians, and judicial figures. ETA finances its activities through kidnappings, robberies, and extortion. The group killed more than 800 persons and injured hundreds of others since it began lethal attacks in the early 1960s. In November 1999, ETA broke its "unilateral and indefinite" cease-fire and began an assassination and bombing campaign that killed 38 individuals and wounded scores more by the end of 2001.

Strength

Unknown — the ETA may have hundreds of members, plus supporters.

Location/area of operation

The group operates primarily in the Basque autonomous regions of northern Spain and southwestern France, but also bombed Spanish and French interests elsewhere.

External Aid

The ETA has received training at various times in the past in Libya, Lebanon, and Nicaragua. Some ETA members allegedly received sanctuary in Cuba, while others reside in South America.

Hamas (Islamic Resistance Movement)

Description

Formed in late 1987 as an outgrowth of the Palestinian branch of the Muslim Brotherhood. Various Hamas elements used political and violent means, including terrorism, to pursue the goal of establishing an Islamic Palestinian state in place of Israel. Hamas is loosely structured, with some elements working clandestinely and others working openly through mosques and social service institutions to recruit members, raise money, organize activities, and distribute propaganda. Hamas' strength is concentrated in the Gaza Strip and a few areas of the West Bank. Hamas has also engaged in peaceful political activity, such as running candidates in West Bank Chamber of Commerce elections and winning a majority in the 2006 Palestinian general elections.

Activities

Hamas activists, especially those in the Izz el-Din al-Qassam Brigades, have conducted many attacks — including large-scale suicide bombings — against Israeli civilian and military targets. In the early 1990s they also targeted Fatah rivals and began a practice of targeting suspected Palestinian collaborators, which continues. There was increased operational activity in 2001 during the Intifadah. Numerous attacks against Israeli government interests were claimed. The group has not targeted U.S. interests and continues to confine its attacks to Israelis inside Israel and the territories.

Strength

There are an unknown number of hardcore members and tens of thousands of supporters and sympathizers.

Location/area of operation

The group operates primarily on the West Bank, Gaza Strip, and Israel. In August 1999, Jordanian authorities closed the group's political bureau offices in Amman, arrested its leaders, and prohibited the group from operating on Jordanian territory. Hamas leaders are also present in other parts of the Middle East, including Syria, Lebanon, and Iran.

External aid

The group receives funding from Palestinian expatriates, Iran, and private benefactors in Saudi Arabia and other moderate Arab states. Some fundraising and propaganda activities take place in Western Europe and North America.

Harakat ul-Mujahidin (HUM)

Description

The HUM is an Islamic militant group based in Pakistan that operates primarily in Kashmir. It is politically aligned with the radical political party, Jamiat-i Ulema-i Islam Fazlur Rehman faction (JUI-F). Long-time leader of the group, Fazlur Rehman Khalil, stepped down as HUM emir in mid-February 2000, turning the reins over to the popular Kashmiri commander and his second-in-command, Farooq Kashmiri. Khalil, who was linked to Bin Ladin and signed his fatwa in February 1998 calling for attacks on U.S. and Western interests, assumed the position of HUM Secretary General. HUM operated terrorist training camps in eastern Afghanistan until Coalition airstrikes destroyed them during fall 2001.

Activities

The group conducted a number of operations against Indian troops and civilian targets in Kashmir. It is linked to the Kashmiri militant group al-Faran that kidnapped five Western tourists in Kashmir in July 1995: one was killed in August 1995 and the other four reportedly were killed in December of the same year. The HUM is responsible for the hijacking of an Indian airliner on December 24, 1999, which resulted in the release of Masood Azhar — an important leader in the former Harakat µl-Ansar imprisoned by the Indians in 1994 — and Ahmad Omar Sheikh, who was arrested for the abduction/murder in January–February 2001 of U.S. journalist Daniel Pearl.

Strength

The HUM has several thousand armed supporters located in Azad Kashmir, Pakistan, and India's southern Kashmir and Doda regions. Supporters are mostly Pakistanis and Kashmiris and also include Afghans and Arab veterans of the Afghan war. Supporters use light and heavy machine guns, assault rifles, mortars, explosives, and rockets. HUM lost a significant share of its membership in defections to the Jaish-e-Mohammed (JEM) in 2000.

Location/area of operation

Although based in Muzaffarabad, Rawalpindi, and several other towns in Pakistan, members conduct insurgent and terrorist activities primarily in Kashmir. The HUM trained its militants in Afghanistan and Pakistan.

External aid

The group collects donations from Saudi Arabia and other Gulf and Islamic states, as well as from Pakistanis and Kashmiris. The HUM's financial collection methods also include soliciting donations from magazine ads and pamphlets. The sources and amount of HUM's military funding are unknown. In anticipation of asset seizures by the Pakistani Government, the HUM withdrew funds from bank accounts and invested in legal businesses, such as commodity trading, real estate, and production of consumer goods. Its fundraising in Pakistan was constrained since the government clamped down on extremist groups and froze terrorist assets.

Hizballah (Party of God)

Other names

> Islamic Jihad
> Revolutionary Justice Organization
> Organization of the Oppressed on Earth
> Islamic Jihad for the Liberation of Palestine

Description

Formed in 1982 in response to the Israeli invasion of Lebanon, this Lebanon-based radical Shi'a group takes its ideological inspiration from the Iranian revolution and the teachings of the Ayatollah Khomeini. The Majlis al-Shura, or Consultative Council, is the group's highest governing body and is led by Secretary General Hassan Nasrallah. Hizballah (alternately spelled Hezbollah) formally advocates ultimate establishment of Islamic rule in Lebanon and liberation of all occupied Arab lands, including Jerusalem. It expressed as a goal the elimination of Israel. The group expressed its unwillingness to work within the confines of Lebanon's established political system; however, this stance changed with the party's decision in 1992 to participate in parliamentary elections. Although closely allied with and often directed by Iran, the group may have conducted operations that were not approved by Tehran. While Hizballah does not share the Syrian regime's secular orientation, the group has been a strong tactical ally in helping Syria to advance its political objectives in the region.

Activities

The group is known or suspected to have been involved in numerous anti-U.S. terrorist attacks, including the suicide truck bombings of the U.S. Embassy in Beirut in April 1983, the U.S. Marine barracks in Beirut in October 1983, and the U.S. Embassy annex in Beirut in September 1984. Three members of Hizballah — 'Imad Mughniyah, Hasan Izz-al-Din, and Ali Atwa — are on the FBI's list of 22 Most Wanted Terrorists for the 1985 hijacking of TWA Flight 847, during which a U.S. Navy diver was murdered. Elements of the group were responsible for the kidnapping and detention of U.S. and other Western hostages in Lebanon. The group also attacked the Israeli

Embassy in Argentina in 1992 and is suspect in the 1994 bombing of the Israeli cultural center in Buenos Aires. In fall 2000 it captured three Israeli soldiers in the Shabaa Farms and kidnapped an Israeli noncombatant whom it may have lured to Lebanon under false pretenses.

Strength

There are several thousand supporters and a few hundred terrorist operatives.

Location/area of operation

The group operates in the Bekaa Valley, the southern suburbs of Beirut, and southern Lebanon. It has established cells in Europe, Africa, South America, North America, and Asia.

External aid

The group receives substantial amounts of financial, training, weapons, explosives, political, diplomatic, and organizational aid from Iran and received diplomatic, political, and logistical support from Syria.

Islamic Movement of Uzbekistan (IMU)
Description

This is a coalition of Islamic militants from Uzbekistan and other Central Asian states opposed to Uzbekistani President Islom Karimov's secular regime. Before the counterterrorism coalition began operations in Afghanistan in October 2001, the IMU's primary goal was the establishment of an Islamic state in Uzbekistan. If IMU political and ideological leader Tohir Yoldashev survives the counterterrorism campaign and can regroup the organization, however, he might widen the IMU's targets to include all those he perceives as fighting Islam. The group's propaganda has always included anti-Western and anti-Israeli rhetoric.

Activities

The IMU primarily targeted Uzbekistani interests before October 2001 and is believed to have been responsible for five car bombs in Tashkent in February 1999. Militants also took foreigners hostage in 1999 and 2000, including four U.S. citizens who were mountain climbing in August 2000, and four Japanese geologists and eight Kyrgyzstani soldiers in August 1999. Since October the coalition captured, killed, and dispersed many of the militants who remained in Afghanistan to fight with the Taliban and al-Qaeda, severely degrading the IMU's ability to attack Uzbekistani or Coalition interests in the near term. IMU military leader Juma Namangani apparently was killed during an air strike in November. At year's end, Yoldashev remained at large.

Strength

Militants probably number under 2,000.

Location/area of operation

Militants are scattered throughout South Asia and Tajikistan. The area of operations includes Afghanistan, Iran, Kyrgyzstan, Pakistan, Tajikistan, and Uzbekistan.

External aid

The coalition has support from other Islamic extremist groups and patrons in the Middle East and Central and South Asia. IMU leadership broadcasts statements over Iranian radio.

Jaish-e-Mohammed (JEM)

Other names

Army of Mohammed

Description

The Jaish-e-Mohammed (JEM) is an Islamic extremist group based in Pakistan that was formed by Masood Azhar upon his release from prison in India in early 2000. The group's aim is to unite Kashmir with Pakistan. It is politically aligned with the radical political party, Jamiat-i Ulema-i Islam Fazlur Rehman faction (JUI-F). The United States announced the addition of JEM to the U.S. Treasury Department's Office of Foreign Asset Control's (OFAC) list (which includes organizations that are believed to support terrorist groups and have assets in U.S. jurisdiction that can be frozen or controlled) in October and the Foreign Terrorist Organization list in December. The group was banned and its assets were frozen by the Pakistani government in January 2002.

Activities

The JEM's leader, Masood Azhar, was released from Indian imprisonment in December 1999 in exchange for 155 hijacked Indian Airlines hostages. The 1994 HUA kidnappings by Omar Sheikh of U.S. and British nationals in New Delhi and the July 1995 HUA/Al Faran kidnappings of Westerners in Kashmir were two of several previous HUA efforts to free Azhar. The JEM on October 1, 2001, claimed responsibility for a suicide attack on the Jammu and Kashmir legislative assembly building in Srinagar that killed at least 31 persons, but later denied the claim. The Indian government publicly implicated the JEM along with Lashkar-e-Tayyiba for the December 13, 2001, attack on the Indian Parliament that killed 9 and injured 18.

Strength

The JEM has several hundred armed supporters located in Azad Kashmir, Pakistan, and in India's southern Kashmir and Doda regions, including a large cadre of former HUM members. Supporters are mostly Pakistanis and Kashmiris and also Afghans and Arab veterans of the Afghan war. The group uses light and heavy machine guns, assault rifles, mortars, improvised explosive devices, and rocket grenades.

Location/area of operation

The group is based in Peshawar and Muzaffarabad, but members conduct terrorist activities primarily in Kashmir. The JEM maintained training camps in Afghanistan until the fall of 2001.

External aid

Most of the JEM's cadre and material resources were drawn from the militant groups Harakat μl-Jihad al-Islami (HUJI) and the Harakat μl-Mujahedin (HUM). The JEM had close ties to Afghan Arabs and the Taliban. Osama Bin Ladin is suspected of providing funding to the JEM. The JEM also collects funds through donation requests in magazines and pamphlets. In anticipation of asset seizures by the Pakistani government, the JEM withdrew funds from bank accounts and invested in legal businesses such as commodity trading, real estate, and production of consumer goods.

al-Jihad

Other names

> Egyptian Islamic Jihad
> Islamic Jihad
> Jihad Group

Description

This is an Egyptian Islamic extremist group active since the late 1970s. al-Jihad merged with Bin Ladin's al-Qaeda organization in June 2001, but may retain some capability to conduct independent operations. The group continues to suffer setbacks worldwide, especially after the September 11, 2001 attacks. The primary goals are to overthrow the Egyptian government and replace it with an Islamic state and attack U.S. and Israeli interests in Egypt and abroad.

Activities

The al-Jihad specializes in armed attacks against high-level Egyptian government personnel, including cabinet ministers, and car bombings against official U.S. and Egyptian facilities. The original Jihad was responsible for the assassination in 1981 of Egyptian President Anwar Sadat. They claimed responsibility for the attempted assassinations of interior minister Hassan al-Alfi in August 1993 and prime minister Atef Sedky in November 1993. The al-Jihad has not conducted an attack inside Egypt since 1993 and has never targeted foreign tourists there. In 1995 the group was responsible for the Egyptian Embassy bombing in Islamabad; in 1998, a planned attack against the U.S. Embassy in Albania was thwarted.

Strength

Not known but probably has several hundred hard-core members.

Location/area of operation

The al-Jihad operates in the Cairo area but most of its network is outside Egypt, including Yemen, Afghanistan, Pakistan, Lebanon, and the United Kingdom, and its activities for several years have been centered outside Egypt.

External aid

Unknown, but the Egyptian government claims that Iran supports the al-Jihad. Its merger with al-Qaeda boosts Bin Ladin's support for the group. The group may obtain some funding through various Islamic nongovernmental organizations, cover businesses, and criminal acts.

Jemaah Islamiya Organization (JI)

Description

Jemaah Islamiya is an Islamic extremist group with cells operating throughout Southeast Asia. Recently arrested JI members in Singapore, Malaysia, and the Philippines revealed links with al-Qaeda. The JI's stated goal is to create an Islamic state comprising Malaysia, Singapore, Indonesia, and the southern Philippines. Three Indonesian extremists, one of whom is in custody in Malaysia, are the reputed leaders of the organization.

Activities

The JI began developing plans in 1997 to target U.S. interests in Singapore, and in 1999 conducted videotaped casings of potential U.S. targets in preparation for multiple attacks in Singapore. A cell in Singapore acquired 4 tons of ammonium nitrate, which has not yet been found.

In December 2001, Singapore authorities arrested 15 Jemaah Islamiyah members, some of whom had trained in al-Qaeda camps in Afghanistan, who planned to attack the U.S. and Israeli embassies and British and

Australian diplomatic buildings in Singapore. Additionally, the Singapore police discovered forged immigration stamps, bomb-making materials, and al-Qaeda-related material in several suspects' homes.

Strength

Exact numbers are unknown, but press reports approximate that the Malaysian cells may comprise 200 members.

Location/area of operation

The JI has cells in Singapore and Malaysia. Press reports indicate the JI is also present in Indonesia and possibly the Philippines.

External aid

Largely unknown, probably self-financed; possible al-Qaeda support.

Kach and Kahane Chai

Description

Their stated goal is to restore the biblical state of Israel. Kach (founded by radical Israeli-American rabbi Meir Kahane) and its offshoot Kahane Chai, which means "Kahane Lives" (founded by Meir Kahane's son Binyamin following his father's assassination in the United States), were declared to be terrorist organizations in March 1994 by the Israeli Cabinet under the 1948 Terrorism Law. This followed the groups' statements in support of Dr. Baruch Goldstein's attack in February 1994 on the al-Ibrahimi Mosque — Goldstein was affiliated with Kach — and their verbal attacks on the Israeli government. Palestinian gunmen killed Binyamin Kahane and his wife in a drive-by shooting in December 2000 in the West Bank.

Activities

The groups organize protests against the Israeli Government and harass and threaten Palestinians in Hebron and the West Bank. They have threatened to attack Arabs, Palestinians, and Israeli government officials. The groups vowed revenge for the death of Binyamin Kahane and his wife.

Strength

Unknown.

Location/area of operation

These groups have Israel and West Bank settlements, particularly at Qiryat Arba' in Hebron.

External aid

They receive support from sympathizers in the United States and Europe.

Kurdistan Workers Party (PKK)

Description

This party was founded in 1974 as a Marxist-Leninist insurgent group primarily composed of Turkish Kurds. The group's goal is to establish an independent Kurdish state in southeastern Turkey, where the population is predominantly Kurdish. In the early 1990s the PKK moved beyond rural-based insurgent activities to include urban terrorism. Turkish authorities captured Chairman Abdullah Ocalan in Kenya in early 1999; the Turkish State Security Court subsequently sentenced him to death. In August 1999, Ocalan announced a "peace initiative," ordering members to refrain from violence and withdraw from Turkey and requesting dialogue with Ankara on Kurdish issues. At a PKK Congress in January 2000, members supported Ocalan's initiative and claimed the group now would use only political means to achieve its new goal, improved rights for Kurds in Turkey.

Activities

The group's primary targets have been Turkish government security forces in Turkey. The group conducted attacks on Turkish diplomatic and commercial facilities in dozens of West European cities in 1993 and again in spring 1995. In an attempt to damage Turkey's tourist industry, the PKK bombed tourist sites and hotels and kidnapped foreign tourists in the early to mid-1990s.

Strength

PKK has approximately 4,000 to 5,000 members, most of whom currently are located in northern Iraq. The group also has thousands of sympathizers in Turkey and Europe.

Location/area of operation

PKK operates in Turkey, Europe, and the Middle East.

External aid

The PKK received safe haven and modest aid from Syria, Iraq, and Iran. Damascus generally upheld its September 2000 antiterror agreement with Ankara, pledging not to support the PKK.

Lashkar-e-Tayyiba (LT)

Other names

Army of the Righteous

Description

The LT is the armed wing of the Pakistan-based religious organization, Markaz-ud-Dawa-wal-Irshad (MDI) — a Sunni anti-U.S. missionary organization formed in 1989. The LT is led by Abdul Wahid Kashmiri and is one of the three largest and best-trained groups fighting in Kashmir against India; it is not connected to a political party. In October 2001 the United States announced the addition of the LT to the U.S. Treasury Department's Office of Foreign Asset Control's (OFAC) list — which includes organizations that are believed to support terrorist groups and have assets in U.S. jurisdiction that can be frozen or controlled. The group was banned, and its assets were frozen by the Pakistani government in January 2002.

Activities

The LT has conducted a number of operations against Indian troops and civilian targets in Kashmir since 1993. The LT claimed responsibility for numerous attacks in 2001, including a January attack on Srinagar airport that killed five Indians along with six militants, an attack on a police station in Srinagar that killed at least eight officers and wounded several others, and an attack in April against Indian border security forces that left at least four dead. The Indian government publicly implicated the LT along with JEM for the December 13, 2001, attack on the Indian Parliament building.

Strength

The LT has several hundred members in Azad Kashmir, Pakistan, and in India's southern Kashmir and Doda regions. Almost all LT cadres are foreigners — mostly Pakistanis from seminaries across the country and Afghan veterans of the Afghan wars. Goup members use assault rifles, light and heavy machine guns, mortars, explosives, and rocket-propelled grenades.

Location/area of operation

The LT was based in Muridke (near Lahore) and Muzaffarabad. The LT trains its militants in mobile training camps across Pakistan-administered Kashmir and trained in Afghanistan until fall 2001.

External aid

The group collects donations from the Pakistani community in the Persian Gulf and United Kingdom, Islamic NGOs, and Pakistani and Kashmiri businessmen. The LT also maintains a Web site (under the name of its parent organization Jamaat ud-Daawa), through which it solicits funds and provides information on the group's activities. The amount of LT funding is unknown. The LT maintains ties to religious and military groups around the world, ranging from the Philippines to the Middle East and Chechnya through the MDI fraternal network. In anticipation of asset seizures by the Pakistani government, the LT withdrew funds from bank accounts and invested in legal businesses such as commodity trading, real estate, and production of consumer goods.

Lashkar i Jhangvi

Description

This group is a military wing of the Sipah-i-Sahaba-i-Pakistan, a Sunni-Deobandi terrorist outfit. Lashkar i Jhangvi means "army of Jhang," a region in Pakistan. Lashkar i Jhangvi (LJ) is an extremist organization that emerged in 1997.

Activities

While LJ initially directed most of its attacks against the Pakistani Shia Muslim community, it also claimed responsibility for the 1997 killing of four U.S. oil workers in Karachi. Lashkar i Jhangvi also attempted to assassinate then Pakistani prime minister Nawaz Sharif in 1999. The group is also responsible for the January 2002 kidnapping and killing of U.S. journalist Daniel Pearl and a March 2002 bus bombing that killed 15 people, including 11 French technicians. Lashkar i Jhangvi have been tied to the Islamabad Protestant church bombing in Karachi in March 2002, in which two U.S. citizens were killed. In July 2002 Pakistani police arrested four Lashkar i Jhangvi members for the church attack.

Strength

Membership numbers are unknown. LJ has ties to al-Qaeda and the Taliban and received sanctuary from the Taliban in Afghanistan for its activity in Pakistan.

Location/area of operation

Afghanistan and Pakistan.

External aid

Unknown.

Liberation Tigers of Tamil Eelam (LTTE)

Other known front organizations

World Tamil Association (WTA)
World Tamil Movement (WTM)
Federation of Associations of Canadian Tamils (FACT)
The Ellalan Force
The Sangillan Force

Description

Founded in 1976, the LTTE is the most powerful Tamil group in Sri Lanka and uses overt and illegal methods to raise funds, acquire weapons, and publicize its cause of establishing an independent Tamil state. The LTTE began its armed conflict with the Sri Lankan government in 1983 and relies on a guerrilla strategy that includes the use of terrorist tactics.

Activities

The Tigers integrated a battlefield insurgent strategy with a terrorist program that targets not only key personnel in the countryside but also senior Sri Lankan political and military leaders in Colombo and other urban centers. The Tigers are notorious for their cadre of suicide bombers, the Black Tigers. Political assassinations and bombings are commonplace. The LTTE refrained from targeting foreign diplomatic and commercial establishments.

Strength

The group's exact strength is unknown, but the LTTE is estimated to have 8,000 to 10,000 armed combatants in Sri Lanka, with a core of trained fighters of approximately 3,000 to 6,000. The LTTE also has a significant overseas support structure for fundraising, weapons procurement, and propaganda activities.

Location/area of operation

The Tigers control most of the northern and eastern coastal areas of Sri Lanka but have conducted operations throughout the island. Headquartered in northern Sri Lanka, LTTE leader Velupillai Prabhakaran established an extensive network of checkpoints and informants to keep track of any outsiders who enter the group's area of control.

External aid

The LTTE's overt organizations support Tamil separatism by lobbying foreign governments and the United Nations. The LTTE also uses its international contacts to procure weapons, communications, and any other equipment and supplies it needs. The LTTE exploits large Tamil communities in North America, Europe, and Asia to obtain funds and supplies for its fighters in Sri Lanka, often through false claims or extortion.

Mujahedin-e Khalq Organization (MEK or MKO)

Other names

> National Liberation Army of Iran (NLA, the militant wing of the MEK)
> People's Mujahedin of Iran (PMOI)
> National Council of Resistance (NCR)
> Muslim Iranian Student's Society (front organization used to garner financial support)

Description

The MEK philosophy mixes Marxism and Islam. Formed in the 1960s, the organization was expelled from Iran after the Islamic Revolution in 1979, and its primary support used to come from the Iraqi regime of Saddam Hussein. Its history is studded with anti-Western attacks as well as terrorist attacks on the interests of the clerical regime in Iran and abroad. The MEK now advocates a secular Iranian regime.

Activities

The MEK worldwide campaign against the Iranian government stresses propaganda and occasionally uses terrorist violence. During the 1970s, the MEK killed several U.S. military personnel and U.S. civilians working on defense projects in Tehran. It supported the takeover in 1979 of the U.S. Embassy in Tehran. In 1981, the MEK planted bombs in the head office of the Islamic Republic Party and the Premier's office, killing some 70 high-ranking Iranian officials, including chief justice Ayatollah Mohammad Beheshti, President Mohammad-Ali Rajaei, and Premier Mohammad-Javad Bahonar. In 1991, it assisted the government of Iraq in suppressing the Shia and Kurdish uprisings in northern and southern Iraq. Since then, the MEK has continued to perform internal security services for the government of Iraq. In April 1992, it conducted attacks on Iranian embassies in 13 different countries, demonstrating the group's ability to mount large-scale operations overseas. In recent years, the MEK targeted key military officers and assassinated the deputy chief of the Armed Forces General Staff in April 1999. In April 2000, the MEK attempted to assassinate the commander of the Nasr Headquarters — the interagency board responsible for coordinating policies on Iraq. The normal pace of anti-Iranian operations increased during the "Operation Great Bahman" in February 2000, when the group launched a dozen attacks against Iran. In 2000 and 2001, the MEK was involved regularly in mortar attacks and hit-and-run raids on Iranian military and law enforcement units and government buildings near the Iran-Iraq border. Since the end of the Iran-Iraq War, tactics along the border garnered few military gains and have become commonplace. MEK insurgent activities in Tehran constitute the biggest security concern for the Iranian leadership. In February 2000, for example, the MEK attacked the leadership complex in Tehran that houses the offices of the Supreme Leader and President.

Strength

The MEK has several thousand fighters, located on bases scattered throughout Iraq, and armed with tanks, infantry fighting vehicles, and artillery. The MEK also has an overseas support structure. Most of the fighters are organized in the MEK's National Liberation Army (NLA).

Location/area of operation

In the 1980s the MEK's leaders were forced by Iranian security forces to flee to France. When they resettled in Iraq in 1987, the group conducted internal security operations in support of the government of Iraq. In the mid 1980s, the group did not mount terrorist operations in Iran at a level similar to its activities in the 1970s, but by the 1990s, the MEK claimed credit for an increasing number of operations in Iran.

External aid

Beyond past support from Iraq, the MEK uses front organizations to solicit contributions from expatriate Iranian communities.

National Liberation Army (ELN) — Colombia

Description

The ELN is a Marxist insurgent group formed in 1965 by urban intellectuals inspired by Fidel Castro and Che Guevara. The group began a dialogue with Colombian officials in 1999 following a campaign of mass kidnappings — each involving at least one U.S. citizen — to demonstrate its strength and continuing viability and force the Pastrana administration to negotiate. Peace talks between Bogotá and the ELN, started in 1999, continued sporadically through 2001 until Bogota broke them off in August. Talks resumed in Havana, Cuba, by year's end.

Activities

ELN activities include kidnapping, hijacking, bombing, extortion, and guerrilla war. The group has modest conventional military capability. It annually conducts hundreds of kidnappings for ransom, often targeting foreign employees of large corporations, especially in the petroleum industry. It frequently assaults the energy infrastructure, and has inflicted major damage on pipelines and the electric distribution network.

Strength

The ELN has approximately 3,000 to 5,000 armed combatants and an unknown number of active supporters.

Location/area of operation

ELN members can mostly be found in rural and mountainous areas of north, northeast, and southwest Colombia and Venezuela border regions.

External aid

Cuba provides some medical care and political consultation.

Palestine Islamic Jihad (PIJ)

Description

The PIJ originated among militant Palestinians in the Gaza Strip during the 1970s. The PIJ-Shiqaqi faction, currently led by Ramadan Shallah in Damascus, is most active. The group is committed to the creation of an Islamic Palestinian state and the destruction of Israel through holy war. It also opposes moderate Arab governments that it believes were tainted by Western secularism.

Activities

PIJ activists conducted many attacks, including large-scale suicide bombings against Israeli civilian and military targets. The group increased its operational activity in 2001 during the Intifadah, claiming numerous attacks against Israeli interests. The group has not targeted U.S. interests and continues to confine its attacks to Israelis inside Israel and the territories.

Strength

Unknown.

Location/area of operation

The group is located and operates primarily in Israel, the West Bank and Gaza Strip, and other parts of the Middle East including Lebanon and Syria, where the leadership is based.

External aid

The PIJ receives financial assistance from Iran and limited logistic assistance from Syria.

Palestine Liberation Front (PLF)

Description

The PLF broke away from the PFLP-GC in the mid-1970s. It later split again into pro-PLO, pro-Syrian, and pro-Libyan factions. The pro-PLO faction is led by Muhammad Abbas (Abu Abbas), who became a member of the PLO Executive Committee in 1984 but left it in 1991.

Activities

The Abu Abbas-led faction is known for aerial attacks against Israel. Abbas's group also was responsible for the attack in 1985 on the cruise ship *Achille Lauro* and the murder of U.S. citizen Leon Klinghoffer. A warrant for Abu Abbas's arrest is outstanding in Italy.

Strength

Unknown.

Location/area of operation

The PLO faction was based in Tunisia until the *Achille Lauro* attack. Now it is based in Iraq.

External aid

The group receives support from a variety of middle Eastern factions. In the past, it received support from Libya and Iraq.

Popular Front for the Liberation of Palestine (PFLP)

Description

The PFLP is a Marxist-Leninist group founded in 1967 by George Habash as a member of the PLO. He joined the Alliance of Palestinian Forces (APF) to oppose the Declaration of Principles signed in 1993 and suspended participation in the PLO. He then broke away from the APF, along with the DFLP, in 1996 over ideological differences. Then he took part in meetings with Arafat's Fatah party and PLO representatives in 1999 to discuss national unity and the reinvigoration of the PLO but continues to oppose current negotiations with Israel.

Activities

The PFLP committed numerous international terrorist attacks during the 1970s. Since 1978, the group has conducted attacks against Israeli or moderate Arab targets, including killing a settler and her son in December 1996. The PFLP stepped up operational activity in 2001, highlighted by the shooting death of the Israeli tourism minister in October to retaliate for Israel's killing of the PFLP leader in August.

Strength

The group has approximately 800 members.

Location/area of operation

Syria, Lebanon, Israel, West Bank, and Gaza Strip.

External aid

The PFLP receives safe haven and some logistic assistance from Syria.

Popular Front for the Liberation of Palestine-General Command (PFLP-GC)

Description

The PFLP-GC split from the PFLP in 1968, claiming it wanted to focus more on fighting and less on politics. The group is violently opposed to Arafat's PLO. Led by Ahmad Jabril, a former captain in the Syrian Army, the PFLP-GC is closely tied to Syria and Iran.

Activities

The group carried out dozens of attacks in Europe and the Middle East during 1970 to 1980. The PFLP-GC is known for cross-border terrorist attacks into Israel using unusual means, such as hot-air balloons and motorized hang gliders. The primary focus now is on guerrilla operations in southern Lebanon, small-scale attacks in Israel, West Bank, and Gaza Strip.

Strength

Several hundred.

Location/area of operation

The PFLP-GC is headquartered in Damascus with bases in Lebanon.

External aid

The group receives support from Syria and financial support from Iran.

al-Qaeda

Description

Al-Qaeda was established by Osama Bin Ladin in the late 1980s to bring together Arabs who fought in Afghanistan against the Soviet Union. The group helped finance, recruit, transport, and train Sunni Islamic extremists for the Afghan resistance. The group's current goal is to establish a pan-Islamic Caliphate throughout the world by working with allied Islamic extremist groups to overthrow regimes it deems "non-Islamic" and expel Westerners and non-Muslims from Muslim countries. Al-Qaeda issued a statement under the banner of "The World Islamic Front for Jihad Against the Jews and Crusaders" in February 1998, saying it was the duty of all Muslims to kill U.S. citizens — civilian or military — and their allies everywhere. The group merged with Egyptian Islamic Jihad (Al-Jihad) in June 2001.

Activities

On September 11, 2001, 19 al-Qaeda suicide attackers hijacked and crashed four U.S. commercial jets, two into the World Trade Center in New York City, one into the Pentagon near Washington, D.C., and a fourth into a field in Shanksville, Pennsylvania, leaving about 3,000 individuals dead or missing. The October 12, 2000 attack on the USS *Cole* in the port of Aden, Yemen, killing 17 U.S. Navy members and injuring another 39 was conducted by al-Qaeda. The group also conducted the bombings in August 1998 of the U.S. embassies in Nairobi, Kenya, and Dar es Salaam, Tanzania, that killed at least 301 individuals and injured more than 5,000 others. The group claims to have shot down U.S. helicopters and killed U.S. servicemen in Somalia in 1993 and to have conducted three bombings that targeted U.S. troops in Aden, Yemen, in December 1992.

Al-Qaeda is linked to the following plans that were not carried out: to assassinate Pope John Paul II during his visit to Manila in late 1994, to kill President Clinton during a visit to the Philippines in early 1995, to conduct the midair bombing of a dozen U.S. trans-Pacific flights in 1995, and to set off a bomb at Los Angeles International Airport in 1999. Al-Qaeda also plotted to carry out terrorist operations against U.S. and Israeli tourists visiting Jordan for millennial celebrations in late 1999. (Jordanian authorities thwarted the planned attacks and put 28 suspects on trial.) In December, 2001, suspected al-Qaeda associate Richard Colvin Reid attempted to ignite a shoe bomb on a transatlantic flight from Paris to Miami.

Strength

Al-Qaeda may have several thousand members and associates. The group also serves as a focal point or umbrella organization for a worldwide network that includes many Sunni Islamic extremist groups, some members of al-Gama'a al-Islamiyya, the Islamic Movement of Uzbekistan, and the Harakat µl-Mujahidin.

Location/area of operation

Al-Qaeda has cells worldwide and is reinforced by its ties to Sunni extremist networks. Coalition attacks on Afghanistan since October 2001 dismantled the Taliban — al-Qaeda's protectors — and led to the capture, death, or dispersal of al-Qaeda operatives. Some al-Qaeda members at large probably will attempt to carry out future attacks against U.S. interests.

External aid

Osama Bin Ladin, member of a billionaire family that owns the Bin Ladin Group construction empire, is said to have inherited tens of millions of dollars that he uses to help finance the group. Al-Qaeda also maintains money-making front businesses, solicits donations from like-minded supporters, and illicitly siphons funds from donations to Muslim charitable organizations. U.S. efforts to block al-Qaeda funding have hampered al-Qaeda's ability to obtain money.

Real IRA (RIRA)

Other names

> True IRA

Description

Formed in early 1998 as a clandestine armed wing of the 32-County Sovereignty Movement, the RIRA is a "political pressure group" dedicated to removing British forces from Northern Ireland and unifying Ireland. The 32-County Sovereignty Movement opposed Sinn Fein's adoption in September 1997 of the Mitchell principles of democracy and nonviolence and opposed the amendment in December 1999 of Articles 2 and 3 of the Irish Constitution, which laid claim to Northern Ireland. Michael "Mickey" McKevitt, who left the IRA to protest its cease-fire, leads the group; Bernadette Sands-McKevitt, his wife, is a founder-member of the 32-County Sovereignity Movement, the political wing of the RIRA.

Activities

The RIRA conducts bombings, assassinations, and robberies. Many Real IRA members are former IRA members who left that organization following the IRA cease-fire, and they bring to RIRA a wealth of experience in terrorist tactics and bomb making. Targets include British military and police in Northern Ireland and Northern Ireland Protestant communities. RIRA is linked to and understood to be responsible for the car bomb attack in Omagh, Northern Ireland on August 15, 1998, that killed 29 and injured 220 persons. The group began to observe a cease-fire following Omagh, but in 2000 and 2001 resumed attacks in Northern Ireland and on the UK mainland against targets such as MI6 headquarters and the BBC.

Strength

The group has 100 to 200 activists plus possible limited support from IRA hardliners dissatisfied with the IRA cease-fire and other republican sympathizers. British and Irish authorities arrested at least 40 members in the spring and summer of 2001 including leader McKevitt, who at the time of this writing is in prison in the Irish Republic awaiting trial for being a member of a terrorist organization and directing terrorist attacks.

Location/area of operation

Northern Ireland, Irish Republic, and Great Britain.

External aid

RIRA is suspected of receiving funds from sympathizers in the United States and of attempting to buy weapons from U.S. gun dealers. RIRA also is reported to have purchased sophisticated weapons from the Balkans. Three Irish nationals associated with RIRA were extradited from Slovenia to the United Kingdom and are awaiting trial on weapons procurement charges.

Revolutionary Armed Forces of Colombia (FARC)

Description

Established in 1964 as the military wing of the Colombian Communist Party, the FARC is Colombia's oldest, largest, most capable, and best-equipped Marxist insurgency. The FARC is governed by a secretariat, led by septuagenarian Manuel Marulanda, aka "Tirofijo," and six others, including senior

military commander Jorge Briceno, aka "Mono Jojoy." The group was organized along military lines and includes several urban fronts. In 2001, the
group continued a slow-moving peace negotiation process with the Pastrana
administration that gained the group several concessions, including a
demilitarized zone used as a venue for negotiations.

Activities

The FARC is responsible for bombings, murders, kidnapping, extortion,
and hijacking, as well as guerrilla and conventional military action against
Colombian political, military, and economic targets. In March 1999 the
FARC executed three U.S. Indian rights activists on Venezuelan territory
after it kidnapped them in Colombia. Foreign citizens are often targets of
FARC kidnapping for ransom. FARC has well-documented ties to narcotics
traffickers, principally through the provision of armed protection.

Strength

FARC has approximately 9,000 to 12,000 armed combatants and an unknown
number of supporters, mostly in rural areas.

Location/area of operation

FARC operates in Colombia with some activities — extortion, kidnapping,
logistics, and R&R — and in Venezuela, Panama, and Ecuador.

External aid

Cuba provides some medical care and political consultation.

Revolutionary Nuclei (formerly ELA)

Other names

Revolutionary Cells

Description

Revolutionary Nuclei (RN) emerged from a broad range of antiestablishment
and anti-U.S./NATO/EU leftist groups active in Greece between 1995 and
1998. The group is believed to be the successor to or offshoot of Greece's
most prolific terrorist group, Revolutionary People's Struggle (ELA), which
has not claimed an attack since January 1995. Indeed, RN appeared to fill
the void left by ELA, particularly as lesser groups faded from the scene.
RN's few communiqués show strong similarities in rhetoric, tone, and theme
to ELA proclamations. RN has not claimed an attack since November 2000.

Activities

Beginning operations in January 1995, the group claimed responsibility for some two dozen arson attacks and explosive low-level bombings targeting a range of U.S., Greek, and other European targets in Greece. In its most infamous and lethal attack to date, the group claimed responsibility for a bomb it detonated at the Intercontinental Hotel in April 1999 that resulted in killing a Greek woman and injuring a Greek man. Its modus operandi includes warning calls of impending attacks, use of rudimentary timing devices, and strikes during the late evening-early morning hours. RN last attacked U.S. interests in Greece in November 2000 with two separate bombings against the Athens offices of Citigroup and the studio of a Greek-American sculptor. The group also detonated an explosive device outside the Athens offices of Texaco in December 1999. Greek targets included court and other government office buildings, private vehicles, and the offices of Greek firms involved in NATO-related defense contracts in Greece. Similarly, the group attacked European interests in Athens, including Barclays Bank in December 1998 and November 2000.

Strength

Group membership is believed to be small, probably drawing from the Greek militant leftist or anarchist milieu.

Location/area of operation

The primary area of operation is in the Athens metropolitan area.

External aid

Unknown, but believed to be self-sustaining.

Revolutionary Organization 17 November (17 November)

Description

This is a radical leftist group established in 1975 and named for the student uprising in Greece in November 1973 that protested the military regime. It is anti-Greek, anti-United States, anti-Turkey, and anti-NATO, and is committed to the ousting of U.S. bases, removal of Turkish military presence from Cyprus, and severing of Greece's ties to NATO and the European Union (EU).

Activities

Initial attacks were assassinations of senior U.S. officials and Greek public figures. The group added bombings in the 1980s. Since 1990, the group expanded targets to include EU facilities and foreign firms investing in Greece and added improvised rocket attacks to its methods. The most recent attack claimed was the murder in June 2000 of British Defense Attache Stephen Saunders.

Strength

Unknown, but presumed to be small.

Location/area of operation

Athens, Greece.

External aid

Unknown.

Revolutionary Peoples' Liberation Party/Front (DHKP/C)

Other Names

> Devrimci Sol (Revolutionary Left)
> Dev Sol

Description

The group was originally formed in 1978 as Devrimci Sol, or Dev Sol, a splinter faction of the Turkish People's Liberation Party/Front. Renamed in 1994 after factional infighting, it espouses a Marxist ideology and is virulently anti-United States and anti-NATO. The group finances its activities chiefly through armed robberies and extortion.

Activities

Since the late 1980s the group has concentrated attacks against current and retired Turkish security and military officials. The group began a new campaign against foreign interests in 1990. Members assassinated two U.S. military contractors and wounded a U.S. Air Force officer to protest the Gulf War. It launched rockets at the U.S. Consulate in Istanbul in 1992. It assassinated a prominent Turkish businessman and two others in early 1996, its first significant terrorist act as DHKP/C. Turkish authorities thwarted a DHKP/C attempt in June 1999 to fire-light an antitank weapon at the U.S. Consulate in Istanbul. The DHKP/C conducted its first suicide bombings, targeting Turkish police, in January and September 2001. A series of safe-house raids and arrests by Turkish police since 2000 has weakened the group significantly.

Strength

Unknown.

Location/area of operation

The DHKP/C conducts attacks in Turkey, primarily in Istanbul. It raises funds in Western Europe.

External aid

Unknown.

Salafist Group for Call and Combat (GSPC)

Description

The Salafist Group for Call and Combat (GSPC) splinter faction that began in 1996 eclipsed the GIA since approximately 1998, and currently is assessed to be the most effective remaining armed group inside Algeria. In contrast to the GIA, the GSPC gained popular support through its pledge to avoid civilian attacks inside Algeria (although, in fact, civilians have been attacked). Its adherents abroad appear to have largely co-opted the external networks of the GIA, active particularly throughout Europe, Africa, and the Middle East.

Activities

The GSPC continues to conduct operations aimed at government and military targets, primarily in rural areas. Such operations include false roadblocks and attacks against convoys transporting military, police, or other government personnel. According to press reporting, some GSPC members in Europe maintain contacts with other North African extremists sympathetic to al-Qaeda, a number of whom were implicated in terrorist plots during 2001.

Strength

Strength is generally unknown; there are probably several hundred to several thousand inside Algeria.

Location/area of operation

Algeria.

External Aid

Algerian expatriates and GSPC members abroad, many residing in Western Europe, provide financial and logistics support. In addition, the Algerian government accused Iran and Sudan of supporting Algerian extremists in previous years.

Sendero Luminoso (SL)

Other names

Shining Path

Description

Former university professor Abimael Guzman formed Sendero Luminoso in the late 1960s, and his teachings created the foundation of SL's militant Maoist doctrine. In the 1980s SL became one of the most ruthless terrorist groups in the western hemisphere — approximately 30,000 persons have died since Shining Path took up arms in 1980. Its stated goal is to destroy existing Peruvian institutions and replace them with a communist peasant revolutionary regime. It also opposes any influence by foreign governments as well as by other Latin American guerrilla groups, especially the Tupac Amaru Revolutionary Movement (MRTA).

In 2001, the Peruvian National Police thwarted an SL attack against "an American objective," possibly the U.S. Embassy, when they arrested two Lima SL cell members. Additionally, government authorities continued to arrest and prosecute active SL members, including Ruller Mazombite, aka "Camarada Cayo," chief of the protection team of SL leader Macario Ala, aka "Artemio," and Evorcio Ascencios, aka "Camarada Canale," logistics chief of the Huallaga Regional Committee. Counterterrorist operations targeted pockets of terrorist activity in the Upper Huallaga River Valley and the Apurimac/Ene River Valley, where SL columns continued to conduct periodic attacks.

Activities

The SL has conducted indiscriminate bombing campaigns and selective assassinations. The group detonated explosives at diplomatic missions of several countries in Peru in 1990 and included an attempt to car bomb the U.S. Embassy in December. Peruvian authorities continued operations against the SL in 2001 in the countryside, where the SL conducted periodic raids on villages.

Strength

Membership is unknown but estimated to be 100 to 200 armed militants. SL's strength was vastly diminished by arrests and desertions.

Location/area of operation

Peru, with most activity in rural areas.

External aid

None.

United Self-Defense Forces of Colombia (AUC)

Description

The AUC — commonly referred to as the paramilitaries — is an umbrella organization formed in April 1997 to consolidate most local and regional paramilitary groups, each with the mission to protect economic interests and combat insurgents locally. The AUC — supported by economic elites, drug traffickers, and local communities lacking effective government security — claims its primary objective is to protect its sponsors from insurgents. The AUC now asserts itself as a regional and national counterinsurgent force. It is adequately equipped and armed and reportedly pays its members a monthly salary. AUC political leader Carlos Castaño claimed that 70 percent of the AUC's operational costs are financed with drug-related earnings, the rest from "donations" from its sponsors.

Activities

AUC operations vary from assassinating suspected insurgent supporters to engaging guerrilla combat units. Colombian National Combat operations generally consist of raids and ambushes directed against suspected insurgents. The AUC generally avoids engagements with government security forces and actions against U.S. personnel or interests.

Strength

Strength of the AUC is estimated to be 6,000 to 8,150, including former military and insurgent personnel.

Location/area of operation

AUC forces are strongest in the northwest in Antioquia, Córdoba, Sucre, and Bolívar departments. Since 1999, the group demonstrated a growing presence in other northern and southwestern departments. Clashes between the AUC and the FARC insurgents in Putumayo in 2000 demonstrated the range of the AUC to contest insurgents throughout Colombia.

External aid

None.

appendix e

Explosive materials

From Department of the Treasury, Bureau of Alcohol, Tobacco, and Firearms. The information listed in this appendix was updated on April 26, 2002, and is still valid based on the ATF Web site at http://www.atf.treas.gov/pub/fire-explo_pub/listofexp.htm.*

COMMERCE IN EXPLOSIVES

Pursuant to the provisions of section 841(d) of title 18, United States Code (U.S.C.), and 27 CFR 55.23, the Director, Bureau of Alcohol, Tobacco and Firearms, must publish and revise at least annually in the Federal Register a list of explosives determined to be within the coverage of 18 U.S.C. chapter 40, Importation, Manufacture, Distribution, and Storage of Explosive Materials. This chapter covers not only explosives, but also blasting agents and detonators, all of which are defined as explosive materials in section 841(C) of title 18, U.S.C. Accordingly, the following is the 2002 List of Explosive Materials subject to regulation under 18 U.S.C. Chapter 40. It includes both the list of explosives (including detonators) required to be published in the Federal Register, and blasting agents.

The list is intended to include any and all mixtures containing any of the materials on the list. Materials constituting blasting agents are marked by an asterisk. While the list is comprehensive, it is not all inclusive. The fact that an explosive material may not be on the list does not mean that it is not within the coverage of

* For further information, contact Arson and Explosives Programs Division, Bureau of Alcohol, Tobacco and Firearms, 650 Massachusetts Avenue, NW, Washington, DC 20226 (Phone: 202-927-7930).

the law if it otherwise meets the statutory definitions in section 841 of title 18, U.S.C. Explosive materials are listed alphabetically by their common names followed, where applicable, by chemical names and synonyms in brackets.

In the 2002 List of Explosive Materials, ATF has added five terms to the list of explosives, has further defined two explosive materials, and has made amendments to two explosive materials to more accurately reference these materials. The five additions to the list are as follows:

1. Azide explosives
2. HMTD [hexamethylenetriperoxidediamine]
3. Nitrate explosive mixtures
4. Picrate explosives
5. TATP [triacetonetriperoxide]

The ATF staff has added these explosive materials to the list because their primary or common purpose is to function by explosion. ATF has encountered the criminal use of some of these materials in improvised devices. "Nitrate explosive mixtures" is intended to be an all-encompassing term, including all forms of sodium, potassium, barium, calcium, and strontium nitrate explosive mixtures.

The two explosive materials that we have further defined by including their chemical names are listed as follows:

1. DIPAM [dipicramide; diaminohexanitrobiphenyl]
2. EDNA [ethylenedinitramine]

The two amendments to previously listed explosive materials are as follows:

1. "Nitrates of soda explosive mixtures" has been deleted and replaced with "Sodium nitrate explosive mixtures" to reflect current terminology.
2. PBX was previously defined as "RDX and plasticizer." We are changing the definition to reflect that PBX is an acronym for "plastic bonded explosive."

This revised list supersedes the List of Explosive Materials dated September 14, 1999 (Notice No. 880, 64 FR 49840; correction notice of September 28, 1999, 64 FR 52378) and became effective on April 26, 2002.

List of explosive materials

A

Acetylides of heavy metals
Aluminum containing polymeric propellant
Aluminum ophorite explosive
Amatex
Amatol
Ammonal
Ammonium nitrate explosive mixtures (cap sensitive)
*Ammonium nitrate explosive mixtures (non-cap sensitive)
Ammonium perchlorate composite propellant
Ammonium perchlorate explosive mixtures
Ammonium picrate [picrate of ammonia, Explosive D]
Ammonium salt lattice with isomorphously substituted inorganic salts
*ANFO [ammonium nitrate-fuel oil]
Aromatic nitro-compound explosive mixtures
Azide explosives

B

Baranol
Baratol
BEAF [1,2-bis (2,2-difluoro-2-nitroacetoxyethane)]
Black powder
Black powder based explosive mixtures
*Blasting agents, nitro-carbo-nitrates, including non-cap sensitive slurry
    and water gel explosives
Blasting caps
Blasting gelatin
Blasting powder
BTNEC [bis (trinitroethyl) carbonate]
BTNEN [bis (trinitroethyl) nitramine]
BTTN [1,2,4 butanetriol trinitrate]
Bulk salutes
Butyl tetryl

C

Calcium nitrate explosive mixture
Cellulose hexanitrate explosive mixture
Chlorate explosive mixtures
Composition A and variations
Composition B and variations
Composition C and variations
Copper acetylide
Cyanuric triazide

Cyclonite [RDX]
Cyclotetramethylenetetranitramine [HMX]
Cyclotol
Cyclotrimethylenetrinitramine [RDX]

D

DATB [diaminotrinitrobenzene]
DDNP [diazodinitrophenol]
DEGDN [diethyleneglycol dinitrate]
Detonating cord
Detonators
Dimethylol dimethyl methane dinitrate composition
Dinitroethyleneurea
Dinitroglycerine [glycerol dinitrate]
Dinitrophenol
Dinitrophenolates
Dinitrophenyl hydrazine
Dinitroresorcinol
Dinitrotoluene-sodium nitrate explosive mixtures
DIPAM [dipicramide; diaminohexanitrobiphenyl]
Dipicryl sulfone
Dipicrylamine
Display fireworks
DNPA [2,2-dinitropropyl acrylate]
DNPD [dinitropentano nitrile]
Dynamite

E

EDDN [ethylene diamine dinitrate]
EDNA [ethylenedinitramine]
Ednatol
EDNP [ethyl 4,4-dinitropentanoate]
EGDN [ethylene glycol dinitrate]
Erythritol tetranitrate explosives
Esters of nitro-substituted alcohols
Ethyl-tetryl
Explosive conitrates
Explosive gelatins
Explosive liquids
Explosive mixtures containing oxygen-releasing inorganic salts and
    hydrocarbons
Explosive mixtures containing oxygen-releasing inorganic salts and
    nitro bodies
Explosive mixtures containing oxygen-releasing inorganic salts and
    water-insoluble fuels

Explosive mixtures containing oxygen-releasing inorganic salts and
  water-soluble fuels
Explosive mixtures containing sensitized nitromethane
Explosive mixtures containing tetranitromethane (nitroform)
Explosive nitro compounds of aromatic hydrocarbons
Explosive organic nitrate mixtures
Explosive powders

F

Flash powder
Fulminate of mercury
Fulminate of silver
Fulminating gold
Fulminating mercury
Fulminating platinum
Fulminating silver

G

Gelatinized nitrocellulose
Gem-dinitro aliphatic explosive mixtures
Guanyl nitrosamino guanyl tetrazene
Guanyl nitrosamino guanylidene hydrazine
Guncotton

H

Heavy metal azides
Hexanite
Hexanitrodiphenylamine
Hexanitrostilbene
Hexogen [RDX]
Hexogene or octogene and a nitrated N-methylaniline
Hexolites
HMTD [hexamethylenetriperoxidediamine]
HMX [cyclo-1,3,5,7-tetramethylene 2,4,6,8-tetranitramine; Octogen]
Hydrazinium nitrate/hydrazine/aluminum explosive system
Hydrazoic acid

I

Igniter cord
Igniters
Initiating tube systems

K

KDNBF [potassium dinitrobenzo-furoxane]

L

Lead azide
Lead mannite
Lead mononitroresorcinate
Lead picrate
Lead salts, explosive
Lead styphnate [styphnate of lead, lead trinitroresorcinate]
Liquid nitrated polyol and trimethylolethane
Liquid oxygen explosives

M

Magnesium ophorite explosives
Mannitol hexanitrate
MDNP [methyl 4,4-dinitropentanoate]
MEAN [monoethanolamine nitrate]
Mercuric fulminate
Mercury oxalate
Mercury tartrate
Metriol trinitrate
Minol-2 [40% TNT, 40% ammonium nitrate, 20% aluminum]
MMAN [monomethylamine nitrate]; methylamine nitrate
Mononitrotoluene-nitroglycerin mixture
Monopropellants

N

NIBTN [nitroisobutametriol trinitrate]
Nitrate explosive mixtures
Nitrate sensitized with gelled nitroparaffin
Nitrated carbohydrate explosive
Nitrated glucoside explosive
Nitrated polyhydric alcohol explosives
Nitric acid and a nitro aromatic compound explosive
Nitric acid and carboxylic fuel explosive
Nitric acid explosive mixtures
Nitro aromatic explosive mixtures
Nitro compounds of furane explosive mixtures
Nitrocellulose explosive
Nitroderivative of urea explosive mixture
Nitrogelatin explosive
Nitrogen trichloride
Nitrogen tri-iodide
Nitroglycerine [NG, RNG, nitro, glyceryl trinitrate, trinitroglycerine]
Nitroglycide
Nitroglycol [ethylene glycol dinitrate, EGDN]
Nitroguanidine explosives

Nitronium perchlorate propellant mixtures
Nitroparaffins Explosive Grade and ammonium nitrate mixtures
Nitrostarch
Nitro-substituted carboxylic acids
Nitrourea

O

Octogen [HMX]
Octol [75% HMX, 25% TNT]
Organic amine nitrates
Organic nitramines

P

PBX [plastic bonded explosives]
Pellet powder
Penthrinite composition
Pentolite
Perchlorate explosive mixtures
Peroxide based explosive mixtures
PETN [nitropentaerythrite, pentaerythrite tetranitrate, pentaerythritol
   tetranitrate]
Picramic acid and its salts
Picramide
Picrate explosives
Picrate of potassium explosive mixtures
Picratol
Picric acid (manufactured as an explosive)
Picryl chloride
Picryl fluoride
PLX [95% nitromethane, 5% ethylenediamine]
Polynitro aliphatic compounds
Polyolpolynitrate-nitrocellulose explosive gels
Potassium chlorate and lead sulfocyanate explosive
Potassium nitrate explosive mixtures
Potassium nitroaminotetrazole
Pyrotechnic compositions
PYX [2,6-bis(picrylamino)]-3,5-dinitropyridine

R

RDX [cyclonite, hexogen, T4,
   cyclo-1,3,5,-trimethylene-2,4,6,-trinitramine;
   hexahydro-1,3,5-trinitro-S-triazine]

S

Safety fuse

Salts of organic amino sulfonic acid explosive mixture
Salutes (bulk)
Silver acetylide
Silver azide
Silver fulminate
Silver oxalate explosive mixtures
Silver styphnate
Silver tartrate explosive mixtures
Silver tetrazene
Slurried explosive mixtures of water, inorganic oxidizing salt, gelling
    agent, fuel, and sensitizer (cap sensitive)
Smokeless powder
Sodatol
Sodium amatol
Sodium azide explosive mixture
Sodium dinitro-ortho-cresolate
Sodium nitrate explosive mixtures
Sodium nitrate-potassium nitrate explosive mixture
Sodium picramate
Special fireworks
Squibs
Styphnic acid explosives

T

Tacot [tetranitro-2,3,5,6-dibenzo-1,3a,4,6a tetrazapentalene]
TATB [triaminotrinitrobenzene]
TATP [triacetonetriperoxide]
TEGDN [triethylene glycol dinitrate]
Tetranitrocarbazole
Tetrazene [tetracene, tetrazine, 1(5-tetrazolyl)-4-guanyl tetrazene
    hydrate]
Tetryl [2,4,6 tetranitro-N-methylaniline]
Tetrytol
Thickened inorganic oxidizer salt slurried explosive mixture
TMETN [trimethylolethane trinitrate]
TNEF [trinitroethyl formal]
TNEOC [trinitroethylorthocarbonate]
TNEOF [trinitroethylorthoformate]
TNT [trinitrotoluene, trotyl, trilite, triton]
Torpex
Tridite
Trimethylol ethyl methane trinitrate composition
Trimethylolthane trinitrate-nitrocellulose
Trimonite
Trinitroanisole

Trinitrobenzene
Trinitrobenzoic acid
Trinitrocresol
Trinitro-meta-cresol
Trinitronaphthalene
Trinitrophenetol
Trinitrophloroglucinol
Trinitroresorcinol
Tritonal

U

Urea nitrate

W

Water-bearing explosives having salts of oxidizing acids and nitrogen
   bases, sulfates, or sulfamates (cap sensitive)
Water-in-oil emulsion explosive compositions

X

Xanthamonas hydrophilic colloid explosive mixture

appendix f

Homeland security state contact list

Contact information, telephone numbers, and Internet Web site details are primarily from the official White House Web site. It should be noted that many states have consolidated intelligence or fusion centers for the purposes of homeland security as well as Joint Terrorism Task Forces (JTTF). The contact information outlined below may not be an investigative point-of-contact.

State homeland security contacts

Alabama
James M. Walker, Jr., Homeland Security Director
Alabama Department of Homeland Security
PO Box 304115
Montgomery, AL 36130-4115
334-956-7250
Main Fax: 334-223-1120
http://www.dhs.alabama.gov

Alaska
BG Craig Campbell
PO Box 5800
Ft. Richardson, AK 99505-0800
907-428-6003
http://www.ak-prepared.com/homelandsecurity

Arizona
Frank Navarette, Homeland Security Director
1700 West Washington Street, 3rd Floor
Phoenix, AZ 85007
602-542-7030

Arkansas
John Brackin, Director
PO Box 758
Conway, AR 72033
501-730-9781
http://www.adem.state.ar.us

California
Matt Bettenhausen, Director
Office of Homeland Security
State Capitol, 1st Floor
Sacramento, CA 95814
916-324-8908

Colorado
Joe Morales, Executive Director
Colorado Office of Public Safety, Preparedness and Security
700 Kipling Street
Denver, CO 80215
303-239-4398

Connecticut
James M. Thomas, Commissioner
Department of Emergency Management and Homeland Security
25 Sigourney Street – 6th Floor
Hartford, CT 06106-5042
860-256-0800 or 800-397-8876
http://www.ct.gov/demhs/

Delaware
David Mitchell
Acting Homeland Security Advisor
Department of Safety and Homeland Security
303 Transportation Circle
PO Box 1321
Dover, DE 19903
302-744-2680

District of Columbia
Robert Bobb
Deputy Mayor for Public Safety
1350 Pennsylvania Ave, NW #327
Washington, DC 20004
202-727-4036
http://www.dcema.dc.gov/dcema/site/default.asp

Florida
    Kenneth "Ken" S. Tucker
    Deputy Commissioner, Florida Dept. of Law Enforcement
    PO Box 1489
    Tallahassee, FL 32302-1489
    850-410-8300
    http://www.fdle.state.fl.us/osi/DomesticSecurity/

Georgia
    Mike Sherberger
    Acting Director of Homeland Security
    PO Box 1456
    Atlanta, GA 30371
    404-624-7030
    http://www.gahomelandsecurity.com/

Hawaii
    BG Robert Lee
    Adjutant General
    3949 Diamond Head Road
    Honolulu, HI 96816-4495
    808-733-4246
    http://www.scd.state.hi.us

Idaho
    MG Lawrence "Larry" Lafrenz
    Adjutant General
    4040 West Guard Street
    Boise, ID 83705-5004
    208-422-5242
    http://www.state.id.us/government/executive.html

Illinois
    COL Jill Morgenthaler
    Deputy Chief of Staff of Public Safety
    Homeland Security Advisor
    207 State House
    Springfield, IL 62706
    217-524-1486

Indiana
    Eric Dietz, Executive Director
    Indiana Department of Homeland Security
    Indianapolis, IN 46204
    317-232-3986
    http://www.in.gov/sema/

Iowa
  MG Ron Dardis
  Homeland Security Advisor
  Adjutant General of Iowa
  Hoover State Office Bldg
  1305 E. Walnut
  Des Moines, IA 50319
  515-252-4211
  http://www.iowahomelandsecurity.org

Kansas
  MG Tod Bunting
  Homeland Security Advisor
  2800 SW Topeka
  Topeka, KS 66611-1287
  785-274-1011

Kentucky
  Alecia Webb-Edgington
  Director of Homeland Security
  200 Metro Street
  Frankfort, KY 40622
  502-564-2081
  http://homelandsecurity.ky.gov/

Louisiana
  MG Bennett C. Landreneau
  Adjutant General and Director
  Louisiana Office of Emergency Preparedness
  7667 Independence Blvd.
  Baton Rouge, LA 70806
  504-278-2812
  http://www.loep.state.la.us

Maine
  BG John Libby
  Adjutant General
  Homeland Security
  1 State House Station
  Augusta, ME 04333-0001
  207-626-4205

Maryland
  Dennis Schrader
  Homeland Security Director
  State House, 100 State Circle

Annapolis, MD 21401
410-974-2389
http://www.mema.state.md.us

Massachusetts
Edward A. Flynn
Homeland Security Policy Advisor
Executive Office of Public Safety
1 Ashburton Place, Rm. 2133
Boston, MA 02108
616-727-7775

Michigan
COL Tadarial Sturdivant
Director of State Police
Capt. Kriste Etue
713 South Harrison Road
E. Lansing, MI 48823
517-333-5042
http://www.msp.state.mi.us

Minnesota
Michael Campion
Acting Commissioner of Public Safety
Director, Homeland Security
DPS, North Central Life Tower
445 Minnesota St., Ste. 1000
St. Paul, MN 55101
651-215-1527
http://dps.state.mn.us/homelandsecurity/index.htm

Mississippi
Edwin L. Worthington
Director, Office of Homeland Security
PO Box 4501
Jackson, MS 39296-4501
601-346-1499
http://www.homelandsecurity.ms.gov

Missouri
Mark James, Director
Missouri Office of Homeland Security
PO Box 749
Jefferson City, MO 65102
573-522-3007
http://www.homelandsecurity.mo.gov

Montana
  Dan McGowan
  Acting Homeland Security Advisor
  Department of Military Affairs – HAFRC
  Montana Disaster and Emergency Services
  1900 Williams Street
  PO Box 4789
  Helena, MT 59604-4789
  406-841-3911
  http://www.discoveringmontana.com/css/default.asp

Nebraska
  Rick Sheehy
  PO Box 94848
  Lincoln, NE 68509-4848
  402-471-2256
  rick.sheehy@email.state.ne.us

Nevada
  Giles Vanderhoof
  Homeland Security Advisor
  2525 S. Carson Street
  Carson City, NV 89710
  775-684-4556

New Hampshire
  Bruce Cheney
  State Homeland Security Advisor
  Director, Office of Emergency Management
  10 Hazen Drive
  Concord, NH 03305
  603-271-6911

New Jersey
  Jim McElwain, Director
  N.J. Office of Counter-Terrorism
  PO Box 091
  Trenton, NJ 08625
  609-341-5050
  http://www.njcounterterrorism.org

New Mexico
  Tim Manning
  Homeland Security Director
  PO Box 1628
  Santa Fe, NM 87507-1628
  505-476-0267

New York
James McMahon, Director
Office of Public Security
Executive Chamber
633 3rd Ave, 38th Floor
New York, NY 10017
212-867-7060
info@security.state.ny.us

North Carolina
Bryan Beatty, Secretary
Dept. of Crime Control and Public Safety
4701 Mail Service Center
Raleigh, NC 27699
919-733-2126
http://www.ncgov.com/asp/subpages/safety_security.asp

North Dakota
Greg Wilz
Homeland Security Coordinator/Emergency Management Director
Fraine Barracks Lane, Bldg 35
Fraine Barracks
Bismark, ND 58504
701-328-8100
http://www.state.nd.us/dem/homesec.html

Ohio
Kenneth L. Morckel
Director of Public Safety
1970 W. Broad Street
Columbus, OH 43223-1102
614-466-3383
http://www.homelandsecurity.ohio.gov

Oklahoma
Kerry Pettingill, Director
Oklahoma Office of Homeland Security
PO Box 11415
Oklahoma City, OK 73136-0415
405-425-7296
okohs@dps.state.ok.us
http://www.youroklahoma.com/homelandsecurity

Oregon
Beverlee Stilwell, Director
Office of Homeland Security

400 Public Service Bldg.
Salem, OR 97310
503-378-3056

Pennsylvania
Roland R. Mertz, Director
Pennsylvania Office of Homeland Security
2605 Interstate Drive
Harrisburg, PA 17110
717-651-2715
www.homelandsecurity.state.pa.us

Rhode Island
BG John Enright
Adjutant General
222 State House
Providence, RI 02903
401-275-4333

South Carolina
Robert M. Stewart, Chief
S.C. Law Enforcement Division (SLED)
PO Box 21398
Columbia, SC 29221-1398
803-737-9000

South Dakota
John A. Berheim, Director
Division of Emergency Management
500 East Capitol Avenue
Pierre, SD 57501
605-773-3450

Tennessee
Dave Mitchell, Interim Director
Office of Homeland Security
312 8th Avenue, North
Wm. R. Snodgrass TN Tower, 25th Floor
Nashville, TN 37243
615-532-7825
dave.mitchell@state.tn.us

Texas
Steve McCraw, Director
Office of Homeland Security
512-936-1882

Utah
> Verdi White, Director
> Division of Emergency Services
> 210 State Capitol
> Salt Lake City, UT 84114
> 801-538-3400
> http://www.cem.utah.gov

Vermont
> Chris Reinfurt, Captain
> Director of Vermont's Homeland Security
> 103 South Main Street
> Waterbury, VT 05671-2101
> 802-241-5357
> http://www.dps.state.vt.us/homeland/home_main.html

Virginia
> Robert P. Crouch, Jr.
> Assistant to the Governor for Commonwealth Preparedness
> Patrick Henry Building
> 1111 East Broad Street
> Richmond, VA 23219
>
> For regular U.S. mail, please use the following address:
> PO Box 1475
> Richmond, VA 23218
>
> Phone Numbers:
> 804-692-2595
> Fax Line: 804-225-3882
> http://www.commonwealthpreparedness.state.va.us
>
> Virginia State Police BCI – Fusion Center
> Criminal Intelligence Division
> PO Box 27472
> Richmond, VA 23261-7472
> 1-866-217-6717
> VFC@vsp.virginia.gov

Washington
> MG Timothy J. Lowenberg
> Adjutant General and Director
> State Military Department
> Washington Military Dept., Bldg. 1
> Camp Murray, WA 98430-5000
> 253-512-8201

West Virginia
  James Spears, Secretary
  Dept. of Military Affairs and Public Safety
  State Capitol Complex, Bldg. 6, Rm. B-122
  Charleston, WV 25305
  304-558-3795

Wisconsin
  MG Al Wilkening
  Homeland Security Advisor
  PO Box 7865
  Madison, WI 53707-7865
  608-242-3000
  http://www.homelandsecurity.wi.gov

Wyoming
  Joe Moore, Director
  Wyoming Office of Homeland Security
  Herschler Bldg., 1st Floor East
  122 W. 25th Street
  Cheyenne, WY 82002-0001
  307-777-4663
  http://www.wyohomelandsecurity.state.wy.us

American Samoa
  Leiataua Birdsall V. Ala'ilima
  Special Assistant to the Governor
  Office of Territory Emergency Mgmt.
  American Somoa Government
  Pago Pago, AS 96799
  011-684-633-4116

Guam
  Frank Blas
  Homeland Security Advisor
  PO Box 2950
  Hagatna, GU 96932
  671-475-9600/9602

Northern Mariana Islands
  Patrick J. Tenorio
  Special Advisor for Homeland Security
  Caller Box 10007
  Saipan, MP 96950
  670-664-2280

Puerto Rico
  Julio Gonzalez
  Homeland Security Advisor
  La Fortaleza
  PO Box 9020082
  San Juan, PR 00902-0082
  787-977-7730/7731

U.S. Virgin Islands
  BG Eddy L. Charles
  Adjutant General
  21-22 Kongens Gade
  St. Thomas, VI 00802
  340-712-7711

appendix g

Publication references

107th Congress, HR 3162
  Uniting and Strengthening America by Providing Appropriate Tools Required to Intercept and Obstruct Terrorism Act of 2001 (also known as The PATRIOT ACT of 2001)

Presidential Decision Directive-39
  This directive provides an unclassified synopsis of the U.S. national policy on terrorism and counterterrorism as laid out in Presidential Decision Directive-39 (PDD-39)

Presidential Decision Directive-62
  "Protection Against Unconventional Threats to the Homeland and Americans Overseas," dated May 22, 1998

The National Strategy for Homeland Security: Office of Homeland Security (PDF)
Office of Homeland Security, July 2002
  This document is the first national strategy for addressing homeland security issues in the United States. Topical material includes threat and vulnerability, organizing for a secure homeland, critical mission areas such as intelligence and warning, border and transportation security, domestic counterterrorism, protecting critical infrastructures and key assets, defending against catastrophic threats, and emergency preparedness and response.

The Country Report on Terrorism (formerly Patterns of Global Terrorism)
United States Department of State, published each year since 1993
  This document provides a chronological breakdown and dates of significant terrorist incidents as well as providing excerpts of the terrorist activity that took place and the locations.

The National Strategy for the Physical Protection of Critical Infrastruc-
    tures and Key Assets (PDF)
    White House, published February 2003
    This document identifies the road ahead for a core mission area iden-
        tified in the President's National Strategy for Homeland Security.
        It covers cross-sector priorities, securing critical infrastructures, and
        protecting key assets.

National Strategy for Combating Terrorism (PDF)
    White House, published February 2003
    This publication looks at the nature of the terrorist threat today and
        the availability of weapons of mass destruction. Reviewed are
        the goals and objectives of defeating, denying, and diminishing
        terrorist activities.

Project Megiddo — FBI
    "Project Megiddo" is the culmination of an FBI research initiative
        that analyzed the potential for extremist criminal activity in the
        United States by individuals or domestic groups who attach
        special significance to the year 2000.

The Directory of Homeland Security
    This directory provides contact information for over 500 state and
        federal agencies. The following is provided: over 150 pages of
        contacts; key local and federal personnel for each office; informa-
        tion on national organizations working on homeland security;
        agency-specific procurement information and contacts; helpful
        resources on selling products to the federal government; and a
        listing of select companies, including names of homeland security
        directors, number of employees, homeland security products/
        services, and key personnel.

The documents listed below are readily available on various Web sites,
but the majority can be found on the government's counterterrorism
training Web site www.counterterrorismtraining.gov, which was based
on a workgroup convened by the Department of Justice's Bureau of
Justice Assistance.

Assessing the Threats (PDF)
    Center for Defense Information, 2002
    Examined in this document are threats to security and stability as
        perceived from four perspectives: American, West European,
        Russian, and Northeast Asian. Chapters include information
        focusing on current security problems, weapons of mass destruc-
        tion, and various terrorist activities.

Assessing Threats of Targeted Group Violence: Contributions from Social Psychology (PDF)
National Threat Assessment Center, 1999
Recent increases in domestic and international acts of extremist violence perpetrated against American citizens prompted an increased need for information. To help understand and evaluate the threat posed to U.S. targets by extremist groups and their individual members, this article summarizes research on group behavior and the effects of group membership on individual behavior, proposes specific questions to consider in evaluating the risk for violence by groups and by individuals influenced by groups, and suggests further research needs.

Bioterrorism in the United States: Threat, Preparedness, and Response (PDF)
Chemical and Biological Arms Control Institute, 2000
Reviewed in this report are current programs that address the health and medical dimensions of national response to bioterrorism in the United States.

Combating Terrorism: Assessing the Threat of Biological Terrorism (PDF)
RAND, October 2001
Presented in this report is testimony before the House Subcommittee on National Security, Veterans Affairs, and International Relations on biological terrorism, the feasibility and likelihood of terrorist groups using biological or chemical weapons, and what the government can and should do to deal with biological or chemical threats.

Combating Terrorism: Assessing Threats, Risk Management, and Establishing Priorities
Center for Nonproliferation Studies, July 2000
Presented in this report is testimony before the House Subcommittee on National Security, Veterans Affairs, and International Relations on terrorism threat assessments and risk management strategies.

Cyber Protests: The Threat to the U.S. Information Infrastructure (PDF)
National Infrastructure Protection Center, 2001
Discussed in this report is the growing threat of cyber protests. Examples of recent events are provided.

Defending America: Asymmetric and Terrorist Attacks with Biological Weapons (PDF)
Center for Strategic and International Studies, February 2001
Explored in this report are various aspects of bioterrorism, including possible avenues of attack, potential threats, and possible solutions and preventative measures.

Defending America: Redefining the Conceptual Borders of Homeland
    Defense: The Risks and Effects of Indirect, Covert, Terrorist, and
    Extremist Attacks with Weapons of Mass Destruction (Final Draft) (PDF)
    Center for Strategic and International Studies, February 2001
    Examined in this report is the threat of terrorist attacks as well as
        more conventional means of attack (including how the two might
        overlap), the impact of technological change on homeland defense,
        and challenges for response planning.

Domestic Terrorism: Resources for Local Governments (PDF)
    National League of Cities, 2000
    This guidebook helps local decision makers develop and implement
        domestic terrorism preparedness plans. It surveys national strategy
        and describes the resources available to state and local govern-
        ments for planning, training and exercises, equipment, intelligence,
        and medical services.

Homeland Security: Key Elements of a Risk Management Approach (PDF)
    U.S. General Accounting Office, October 2001
    Described in this report are key elements of a good risk manage-
        ment approach, including assessment of threat, vulnerability,
        and criticality.

International Crime Threat Assessment
    President's International Crime Control Strategy, 1998
    This global assessment examines the threat posed by international
        crime to Americans and their communities, U.S. business and
        financial institutions, and global security and stability. It was
        prepared by a U.S. federal interagency working group in support
        of the President's International Crime Control Strategy.

Protective Intelligence and Threat Assessment Investigations: A Guide
    for State and Local Law Enforcement Officials (ASCII or PDF)
    National Institute of Justice, January 2000
    Described in this report are protective intelligence and threat assess-
        ment investigations, focusing on protocols and procedures for law
        enforcement and security agencies responsible for protecting public
        persons and others who are vulnerable to targeted violence.

The Sociology and Psychology of Terrorism: Who Becomes a Terrorist
    and Why?
    Federal Research Division, Library of Congress, September 1999
    In an effort to help improve U.S. counterterrorism methods and
        policies, this study examines the types of individuals and groups
        that are prone to terrorism. The relevant literature with which to
        assess the current knowledge of the subject is examined, and

psychological and sociological profiles of foreign terrorist individuals and selected groups are developed to use as case studies in assessing trends, motivations, and likely behavior, as well as in revealing vulnerabilities that would aid in combating terrorist groups and individuals.

The World Factbook
Central Intelligence Agency
The first classified factbook was published in August 1962, and the first unclassified version was published in June 1971. The 1975 Factbook was the first to be made available to the public with sales through the U.S. Government Printing Office (GPO). This publication provides statistical information on all the countries in the world, including data on populations, militaries, geography, governments, and transnational issues.

Patterns of Global Terrorism
U.S. Department of State
Examined in this report is the danger that terrorism poses to the world and efforts of the United States and international partners to defeat it. Aspects of the war on terrorism include diplomatic actions to form a global coalition against terror, cooperation among intelligence agencies, enhanced and cooperative law enforcement efforts, economic actions to deny financial support to terrorism, and military operations and assistance. The report is issued annually per congressional mandate. See the archive for reports from 1995 through 1993.

Political Violence Against Americans, 1998 (PDF)
U.S. Department of State, 1998
An overview of the political violence that American citizens and interests encountered abroad in 1998 is provided in this report. Incidents included were selected based on their seriousness, the use of unusual tactics or weapons, or the specific targeting of representatives of the United States.

Significant Incidents of Political Violence against Americans, 1997 (PDF)
U.S. Department of State, 1997
Provided in this report is an overview of the political violence that American citizens and interests encountered abroad in 1997.

The Sociology and Psychology of Terrorism: Who Becomes a Terrorist and Why?
Library of Congress, Federal Research Division, 1999
This report was prepared under an interagency agreement, and it provides approaches to terrorism analysis, general hypotheses of

terrorism, psychology of the terrorist, and terrorist profiling, based on research.

Terrorism in the United States, 1999 (PDF)
  Federal Bureau of Investigation, 1999
  This annual publication reviews the year's terrorist incidents, suspected terrorist incidents, arrests that prevented terrorist attacks, and other significant events. The report also describes 30-year feuds in domestic and international terrorism and the FBI's response.

1997 Bombing Incidents (PDF)
  Federal Bureau of Investigation (FBI) Bomb Data Center
  This bulletin provides statistics on criminal bombing incidents that occurred in the United States in 1997. Bombing data are presented by state, region, target, time of occurrence, and time of year.

Office for Domestic Preparedness (ODP) Information Clearinghouse
  The ODP Information Clearinghouse is a searchable virtual library of publications and other resources on domestic preparedness, counterterrorism, and weapons of mass destruction. The clearinghouse also offers an electronic newsletter that provides e-updates on domestic preparedness news, such as conference or training events, new ODP programs, and new publications.

Homeland Security Act of 2002 (H.R. 5005)
  Signed into law on November 25, 2002, this act restructures and strengthens the executive branch of the federal government to better meet the threat posed by terrorism. In establishing a new Department of Homeland Security, the act, for the first time, created a federal department with a primary mission that is to help prevent, protect against, and respond to acts of terrorism.

Protecting Democracy: States Respond to Terrorism
  The National Conference of State Legislatures created Web pages for counterterrorism legal issues of interest on the state level. Its state legislation database is updated monthly and is searchable by state, category, date/range, status, bill number/type, and keyword.

In addition to publications produced by governmental entities or those funded through the government, many leading authorities have authored a variety of crime/intelligence based books. Below is a listing of analytical and intelligence publications that can be found through a variety of sources. This list is by no means complete but will enable one's ability to grasp a firmer understanding of many of the tools and techniques available to analysts.

Crime/intelligence analysis publications

The Enemy Within: Intelligence Gathering, Law Enforcement, and Civil Liberties in the Wake of September 11, Stephen Schulhofer, Twentieth Century Fund, 2002, ISBN 0-87078-482-X.

Defending The Homeland: Domestic Intelligence, Law Enforcement, and Security, Dr. Jonathan White, Thomson/Wadsworth, 2004, ISBN 0-534-62169-4.

Psychology of Intelligence Analysis, Richards Heuer, Center for the Study of Intelligence (CIA), 1999, ISBN 1-929667-00-0.

Applications in Criminal Analysis, Marilyn Peterson, Praeger, 1998, ISBN 0-275-96468-X.

Criminal Intelligence Analysis, Paul Andrews and Marilyn Peterson, Palmer Enterprises, 1990, ISBN 0-912479-08-8.

Crime Analysis: From First Report to Final Arrest, Steven Gottlieb, Sheldon Arenberg, and Raj Singh, Alpha Publishing, 1998, ISBN 0-9634773-0-7.

Introduction to Crime Analysis: Basic Resources for Criminal Justice Practice, Deborah Osborne and Susan Wernicke, The Haworth Press, 2003, ISBN 0-7890-1867-3.

Using Microsoft Office to Improve Law Enforcement Operations: Crime Analysis, Community Policing, and Investigations, Mark Stallo, Analysis Consulting & Training Now, Inc., 2003, ISBN 1-59109-886-6.

Mapping Crime: Principle and Practice, Keith Harries, Ph.D, National Institute of Justice, December 1999, NCJ 178919.

Applied Crime Analysis, Karim Vellani and Joel Nahoun, Butterworth-Heinemann, 2001, ISBN: 0750672951.

Intelligence Analysis: A Target-Centric Approach, Robert Clark, CQ Press, 2004, ISBN 1-56802-830-X.

Law Enforcement Counterintelligence, Lawrence Sulc, Varro Press, 1996, ISBN 1-888644-74-5.

Geographical Profiling, D. Kim Rossmo, CRC Press, 1999, ISBN 0849381290.

Advanced Crime Mapping Topics, National Law Enforcement and Corrections Technology Center (NLECTC), www.nlect.org/cmap/cmap_adv_topics_symposium.pdf.

The following books can be obtained through the Police Executive Research Forum:

Crime Mapping Case Studies: Success in the Field (Volume 1) Nancy LaVigne and Julie Wartell, eds., 1998, ISBN 1-878734-61-X, 150 pp.

Problem-Oriented Policing: Crime-Specific Problems, Critical Issues and Making POP Work (Volume 1), Anne Grant and Tara O'Conner Shelley, eds., 1998, ISBN 0-878734-60-1, 430 pp.

Problem-Oriented Policing: Crime-Specific Problems, Critical Issues and Making POP Work (Volume 2), Corina Solé Brito and Tracy Allan, eds., 1999, ISBN 0-878734-70-9, 412 pp.

Mapping Across Boundaries: Regional Crime Analysis, Nancy LaVigne and
   Julie Wartell, 2001, ISBN 1-878734-74-1, 130 pp.
Crime Mapping Case Studies: Success in the Field (Volume 2), Nancy LaVigne
   and Julie Wartell, eds., 2000, ISBN 1-878734-71-1, 140 pp.
Police Crime Analysis Unit Handbook, LEAA, National Institute of Law
   Enforcement and Criminal Justice 1973, 100 pages.
Intelligence 2000: Revising the Basic Elements, Marilyn B. Peterson, Bob
   Morehouse, and Richard Wright, eds. (LEIU), 2000, ISBN 0-970-6887-0-9,
   245 pages.
Information Management and Crime Analysis: Practitioner's Recipes for Success,
   Melissa Miller Reuland, ed., 1997, ISBN 1-878734-48-2, 152 pp.
Crime Analysis Through Computer Mapping, Carolyn Rebecca Block,
   Margaret Dabdoub, and Suzanne Fregly, eds., 1995, ISBN 1-878734-34-2,
   297 pp.
*Solving Crime and Disorder Problems: Current Issues, Police Strategies and
   Organizational Tactics,* Melissa Reuland, Corina Solé Brito and Lisa
   Carroll, eds., 2001, ISBN 1-878734-75-x, 208 pp.

The following are free government publications available online in .pdf format:

Crime Analysis in America – 1/28/200 (http://www.cops.usdoj.gov/
   mime/open.pdf?Item=790)
   This is the final report of a COPS-funded study conducted by the
   University of South Alabama concerning the nation's law enforcement crime analysis units. Researchers conducted national telephone interviews, mail surveys, and site visits in order to develop
   a comprehensive understanding of the state of crime analysis in
   the United States. The researchers also provide recommendations
   on ways that local law enforcement agencies can enhance and
   develop their own crime analysis capabilities.

Crime Analysis in America: Findings and Recommendations – 4/1/2003
   (http://www.cops.usdoj.gov/mime/open.pdf?Item=855)
   While crime analysts have traditionally emphasized tactical analysis
   activities like identifying offenders, community policing encourages more focus on strategic and problem analysis functions. This
   includes identifying the underlying conditions that give rise to
   community problems, developing responses to them that are
   linked to these analyses, assessing the effectiveness of responses,
   and developing long-term organizational operational plans. This
   guide is a product of the findings of a study conducted by the
   University of South Alabama documenting the state of crime
   analysis in the nation's law enforcement agencies. These findings
   and recommendations are intended to inform police managers of
   the structural issues to address when considering a crime analysis
   function within a community policing context. They are also

intended to expose the current limitations of crime analysis and the policies that those findings imply.

Problem Analysis in Policing – 4/21/2003 (http://www.cops.usdoj.gov/mime/open.pdf?Item=847)

This report introduces and defines problem analysis and provides guidance on how problem analysis can be integrated and institutionalized into modern policing practices. The 64-page report is not a "how-to" guide on conducting problem analysis, but is a summary of what problem analysis is, what skills and knowledge are necessary to conduct it, and how it can be advanced by the law enforcement community, academia, the federal government, and other institutions. The ideas and recommendations in this report come primarily from a two-day forum conducted in February 2002 by the Police Foundation and the COPS Office that brought a group of academics, practitioners, and policy makers together to discuss problem analysis and make recommendations for its progress. This report is a culmination of the concepts and ideas discussed in the forum and includes specific, relevant statements made by participants.

Problem-Solving Tips: A Guide to Reducing Crime and Disorder through Problem-Solving Partnerships – 7/29/2002 (http://www.cops.usdoj.gov/mime/open.pdf?Item=441)

This guide is intended to serve as a reference for those in all stages of implementing the problem-solving approach. It contains insights into every stage of the process, most of which are drawn from the experience of law enforcement officers in the field, and relies on the SARA model: scanning, analyzing, response, and assessment of problems.

Tackling Crime and Other Public-Safety Problems: Case Studies in Problem-Solving (http://www.cops.usdoj.gov/default.asp?Item=583)

This compilation provides detailed descriptions of nearly 50 problem-oriented policing efforts dealing with a wide variety of specific crime and social disorder problems. Editor's notes are included after each section detailing the noteworthy aspects of each effort.

The Law Enforcement Tech Guide: How to Plan, Purchase and Manage Technology (Successfully!) – 9/1/2002 (http://www.cops.usdoj.gov/default.asp?Item=512)

The Law Enforcement Tech Guide presents best practices in strategic IT planning and procurement, reveals pitfalls to avoid, consolidates and expands upon various sources of relevant information currently available, and reviews best practices to help create a user-friendly product that will provide law enforcement with the tools they need to successfully achieve their IT goals. Contact the U.S. Department of Justice Response Center at 800-421-6770 to obtain hard copies.

Using Analysis for Problem-Solving: A Guide Book for Law Enforcement – 9/14/2001 (http://www.cops.usdoj.gov/mime/open.pdf?Item=342)

This guide provides law enforcement practitioners with a resource for conducting problem analysis. It summarizes many challenges of the analysis phase of the problem-solving process, identifies tools for analysis, and proposes tips for effectively using each tool. This book builds on the foundation presented in Problem-Solving Tips: A Guide to Reducing Crime and Disorder Through Problem-Solving Partnerships, and complements the Problem-Oriented Guides for Police Series.

appendix h

Government legislative references

The origins of the listed documents are from the http://www.counterterrorism-training.gov Web site (unless otherwise noted). The counterterrorism training Web site documents are based on recommendations made by the Counter-Terrorism Training Coordination Working Group convened by the U.S. Department of Justice's (DOJ's) Office of Justice Programs to examine the counterterrorism tools available to law enforcement and first responder communities.

Working group participants included the Bureau of Justice Assistance, the Executive Office for U.S. Attorneys, the Federal Bureau of Investigation, the Federal Emergency Management Agency, the Federal Law Enforcement Training Center, the National Institute of Justice, the Office for Domestic Preparedness, the Office of Community Oriented Policing Services, the Office of Homeland Security, the Office of Justice Programs, the Office of the Police Corps and Law Enforcement Education, the U.S. Customs Service, and the U.S. Department of Labor. Working group membership will expand to include other federal agencies as well as nongovernmental organizations that represent affected constituencies.

National Security Institute: Counter-Terrorism Legislation
http://nsi.org/terrorism.html
This is a one-stop shop for links to counterterrorism legislation, executive orders, terrorism facts, terrorism precautions, and related sites.

Code of Federal Regulation-28 CFR Part 23
http://www.iir.com/28cfr/guideline.htm and www.iir.com/28cfr
This provides complete text and guidelines from the Institute for Intergovernmental Research.

United States Code Title 18 — Crimes and Criminal Procedure
   http://www.access.gpo.gov/uscode/title18/title18.html and http://
   uscode.house.gov/usc.htm
   A complete detailed listing of guidelines and procedures for a wide
   array of crimes in five parts: covering crimes, criminal procedures,
   prisons and prisoners, correction of youthful offenders, and immunity of witness. Chapters cover a wide range of material, including
   biological and chemical weapons, terrorism, and sabotage.

Cyber Security Research and Development Act (H.R. 3394, Public Law
   107–305)
   Signed into law on November 27, 2002, this legislation will establish
   computer security research centers and fellowship programs
   through the National Science Foundation and the National Institute
   of Standards and Technology.

Effective Counterterrorism Act of 1996 (H.R. 3071)
   Signed into law on April 24, 1996 (as S.735, Public Law No. 104–132),
   this bill sets penalties for providing terrorist organizations with
   material support, expands federal jurisdiction over bomb threats,
   adds terrorism offenses to the money laundering statute, and
   establishes or increases other penalties related to acts of terrorism.
   It also authorizes funding for specialized training or equipment
   to enhance the capability of metropolitan fire and emergency
   service departments to respond to terrorist attacks.

Foreign Intelligence Surveillance Act of 1978 (FISA) (U.S. Code Title 50,
   Chapter 36)
   Under a November 18, 2002, FISA ruling by an appeals panel of the
   U.S. Foreign Intelligence Surveillance Court of Review, police
   were given broader power in the use of surveillance against terror
   and espionage suspects. This action affirms the implementation
   of new U.S. Department of Justice procedures that allow easier
   information access between federal domestic police agencies and
   intelligence agencies.

Homeland Security Act of 2002 (H.R. 5005)
   Signed into law on November 25, 2002, this act restructures and
   strengthens the executive branch of the federal government to
   better meet the threat posed by terrorism. In establishing a new
   Department of Homeland Security, the act, for the first time,
   creates a federal department with a primary mission that will be
   to help prevent, protect against, and respond to acts of terrorism.

Illegal Immigration Reform and Immigrant Responsibility Act of 1996, Program to Collect Information Relating to Nonimmigrant Foreign Students and Other Exchange Program Participants (Public Law No. 104–208, Section 641)

A final rule promulgated under this law established the Student and Exchange Visitor Information System (SEVIS), an Internet reporting and tracking system that will track "F," "M," and "J" visa participants from the time they receive their documentation until they graduate/leave school or conclude/leave their programs. Schools have until January 30, 2003, to enter data on new, nonimmigrant students and until August 1, 2003, to complete entries on current students. This information will be available to law enforcement, school officials, and certain U.S. State Department and Immigration and Naturalization Service personnel.

Immigration and Nationality Act of 1952 (U.S. Code Title 8)

The U.S. Immigration and Naturalization Service (INS) asked state and local police to voluntarily arrest aliens who violated criminal provisions of the U.S. Immigration and Nationality Act or civil provisions that render an alien deportable, and who are wanted as recorded by the National Crime Information Center. The National Security Entry-Exit Registration System Fact Sheet details the purpose and procedures called for by the INS National Security Entry-Exit Registration System. On December 6, 2002, the INS issued a statement emphasizing the registration requirements for visiting foreign nationals from the 18 countries affected. On December 18, 2002, the INS updated special registration requirements to include certain nonimmigrants from Pakistan and Saudi Arabia.

Maritime Transportation Security Act of 2002 (Public Law 107–295) (PDF)

Signed into law on November 25, 2002, this bill amends the Merchant Marine Act of 1936 to establish a program to ensure greater security for U.S. seaports. The act directs the Secretary of Transportation to assess port vulnerability and to prepare a National Maritime Transportation Antiterrorism Plan for deterring catastrophic emergencies.

Preparedness against Terrorism Act of 2000 (H.R. 4210)

Referred to the Senate committee on July 26, 2000, this bill requires the president to ensure that federal emergency preparedness plans and programs are adequate and carried out in the event of an act of terrorism or other catastrophic event.

Safe Explosives Act (Homeland Security Act of 2002, Public Law No.
    107–296, Section 1121)
    Included as part of the Homeland Security Act of 2002 and signed
        by President George W. Bush on November 25, 2002, the Safe
        Explosives Act empowers the Bureau of Alcohol, Tobacco and
        Firearms (ATF) to apply stricter controls on the purchase of
        explosives. Effective May 24, 2002, any person who wants to
        transport, ship, cause to be transported, or receive explosive
        materials must first obtain a federal permit. ATF prepared a
        special online reference page to keep the public informed of
        resulting regulations.

Terrorist Bombings Convention Implementation Act of 2002 (Title I) and
    Suppression of the Financing of Terrorism Convention Implementation
    Act of 2002 (Title II) (H.R. 3275, Public Law No. 107–197)
    This bill was enacted as Public Law Number 107–197 on June 25, 2002.
        Title I implements the International Convention for the Suppres-
        sion of Terrorist Bombings, which was signed by the United States
        on January 12, 1998. This convention imposes legal obligations
        on state parties to submit for prosecution or to extradite any
        person within their jurisdiction who unlawfully and intentionally
        delivers, places, discharges, or detonates an explosive or other
        lethal device in, into, or against a place of public use, a state or
        government facility, a public transportation system, or an infra-
        structure facility. Title II implements the International Convention
        for the Suppression of the Financing of Terrorism, which was
        signed by the United States on January 10, 2000. This convention
        imposes legal obligations on state parties to submit for prose-
        cution or to extradite any person within their jurisdiction who
        unlawfully and willfully provides or collects funds with the
        intention that they should be used to carry out various terrorist
        activities. State parties are subject to the obligations of these
        conventions without regard to the place where the alleged acts
        included in these conventions take place.

The below-listed legislative hate crime references can be located on the
Department of Justice's National Criminal Justice Reference Service Web site
at http://www.ncjrs.org/hate_crimes/legislation.html.

Hate Crimes Prevention Act of 1999 Bill (H.R. 1082)
    This act amends 18 U.S.C. 245 that prohibits persons from interfering
        with an individual's federal rights (e.g., voting or employment)
        by violence or threat of violence due to his or her race, color,
        religion, or national origin. This act allows for more authority for
        the federal government to investigate and prosecute hate crime
        offenders who committed their crime because of perceived sexual

orientation, gender, or disability of the victim. It also permits the federal government to prosecute without having to prove that the victim was attacked because he or she was performing a federally protected activity.

Church Arson Prevention Act of 1996 (18 U.S.C. 247)
This act created the National Church Arson Task Force (NCATF) in June 1996 to oversee the investigation and prosecution of arson at houses of worship around the country. The NCATF brought together the FBI, the ATF, and Department of Justice prosecutors in partnership with state and local law enforcement officers and prosecutors. In addition to the NCATF's creation, the law allowed for a broader federal criminal jurisdiction to aid criminal prosecutions, and established a loan guarantee recovery fund for rebuilding.

Hate Crimes Sentencing Enhancement Act (Section 280003 of the Violent Crime Control and Law Enforcement Act of 1994)
As a part of the 1994 Crime Act, the Hate Crimes Sentencing Enhancement Act provides for longer sentences when the offense is determined to be a hate crime. A longer sentence may be imposed if it is proven that a crime against person or property was motivated by "race, color, religion, national origin, ethnicity, gender, disability, or sexual orientation."

Hate Crime Statistics Act of 1990 (28 U.S.C. 534)
This act requires the Department of Justice to collect data on hate crimes. Hate crimes are defined as "manifest prejudice based on race, religion, sexual orientation, or ethnicity." The FBI, using the Uniform Crime Reporting system, compiles these statistics. The Crime Act of 1994 also required the FBI to collect data on hate crimes involving disability.

Glossary of terminology

Cyber terminology

Back door A hole in the security of a computer system deliberately left in place by designers or programmers or established maliciously by manipulating a computer system.

Code master An individual who epitomizes the art of computer usage, programming, and in the case of cyber terror, malicious activity.

Denial of service (DOS) A malicious activity that renders a server, or a service, useless. This is often done through transmission of a virus or a repetitive electronic attack.

Domain name service (DNS) A distributed Internet directory service. DNS is used mostly to translate between domain names and IP addresses, and to control e-mail delivery. Most Internet services rely on DNS to work.

Hacker An individual who gains unauthorized access to a computer system.

Pharming The misdirecting of users to fraudulent sites or proxy servers, typically through DNS hijacking or poisoning.

Phishing Use of "spoofed" e-mails to lead consumers to counterfeit websites designed to trick recipients into divulging financial data such as credit card numbers, account usernames, passwords, and social security numbers.

Phreak A technologically savvy individual who understands the inner workings of communication and phone systems and uses that knowledge to exploit illicit cyber activity. (phreaking, verb).

Ping A networking computer program that verifies Internet protocol (IP).

Script kiddie Individuals who break security on computer systems without truly understanding the exploit they are using.

Trojan horse A hidden script attached to a program that appears legitimate but contains code allowing unauthorized collection, exploitation, falsification, or destruction of data on a host computer.

Worm A type of virus that acts as an independent program that replicates itself from machine to machine across network connections in an effort to cause a denial of service.

General terrorist-related terminology

Berserker Term considered and posed by Jonathan White in 2000 to better explain actions of a single-event terrorist. These individuals are crazed true believers who went too far and possibly crazy for their cause.

Hard target A well-fortified and secure location that is extremely difficult to penetrate, e.g., military installation, government facility, and nuclear site.

Lone wolf Considered a one-hit wonder and an extremist. This type of terrorist is often leaderless, acts on his own, and once he commits the violent act, will vanish.

Militia Any number of American paramilitary right-wing groups that focus their beliefs and issues on taxes, white supremacy, gun control, abortion, and antigovernment.

Soft target A less-fortified and often more attractive target for a terrorist due to its relative ease of accessibility, e.g., hotel, market, and arena.

Wolf packs American right-wing extremist term for small groups of activists operating below a militia.

Islamic terminology

It is important to note that depending on the source or translation there may be variations of some terms. Also, this listing is not all-inclusive but merely represents some of the more common terms seen in publications or writings.

Cell leadership structure terms

Al Awlani - The leader

Al Hakeem - Medic/doctor

Al Jare - Courrier; infantryman

Al Kannas - Sniper/killer with one shot

Al Mukabir - Communications/Intelligence

General Islamic terms

Adhan The Islamic way of calling Muslims to the five obligatory prayers

Allah The Muslim name for the one and only God — there are no others

Allahu akbar Statement said by Muslims numerous times — means Allah is the greatest

Amin Custodian or guardian — one who is loyal or faithful

Asr The late-afternoon prayer

Ayatullah Title of major Shi'a cleric; translation means "Sign of God"

Barakat Blessings

Barakate Reference to Osama bin Laden used at Guantanamo Bay, Cuba

Barzakh Translation means "The Partition;" the time between death and resurrection

Bayaat Allegiance to

Dajjal The anti-Christ

Eid Festivity, a celebration, a recurring happiness, and a feast. In Islam, there are two major 'Eids, namely the feast of Ramadan ('Eid Al-Fitr) and the Feast of Sacrifice ('Eid Al-Adhha).

'Eid ul adha Islamic holiday at the end of the Hajj

'Eid ul Fitr Islamic holiday at the end of the Ramadan fast

Esa Islamic name for Jesus

Fajr The dawn prayer

Fatwa Legal ruling or opinion issued by an Islamic scholar

Hadith Sayings and practices of the Prophet Mohammed that were collected after his death

Hajj Annual pilgrimage to Mecca that takes place in the 12th month of the Islamic calendar

Hajji Translation means "Pilgrim;" title given to person who completes Islamic pilgrimage

Halaqa Study circle

Hijab Head scarf worn over the hair

Imam Sunni Islamic leader; person who leads congregational prayers

Iman Faith and trust in Allah

Isha The night prayer

Jihad Arabic term for the "struggle"

Khalifa Supreme leader of the Muslim community; translation means the "caretaker"

Maghrib The sunset prayer

Masjid Proper name for a Muslim house of worship; also referred to as a mosque

Mecca Southwestern Arabian city founded by Abraham's wife Hagar and
their son; birthplace of Muhammad

Medina First capital city of Islam in 622 when Muhammad fled Mecca

Muslim Follower of the religion of Islam

Nabi A prophet from God

Nika Islamic marriage ceremony

Qiblah Direction of Mecca toward which all Muslims face when they pray

Qur'an Islamic Holy Book

Ramadan Ninth month of the Islamic lunar calendar

Sadaqa Islamic term for charity

Sayyid A leader or chief

Shahadah The Creed of Islam

Shaheed (Shahid) Islamic term for martyr

Shari'ah The term for Islamic Law

Shi'a Second largest sect of Islam

Surah The Qur'an is composed of 114 chapters, each of which is called a Surah

Sunni Largest sect of Islam

Ummah Muslim community or motherland

Wudu Islamic practice of washing the face, hands, and feet with water

Yahudi Arabic term for a Jew

Zuhr The afternoon prayer

Klanspeak terminology

The culture and makeup of many domestic groups has led to them developing
their own terminology and lingo. In his book *Blood in the Face*, James Ridgeway
provides an example of what is referred to as "Klanspeak." The following
terms and definitions are shown as represented in his work and are provided
as an example of just one group's use of distinct terms.

Dominion Five or more counties of a Realm

Empire The national Ku Klux Klan organization

Exalted Cyclops Head of a Klanton

Giant Head of a Province

Grand Dragon Head of a Realm

Great Titan Head of a Dominion

Imperial Wizard Head of national Ku Klux Klan

Kladd Assistant to Exalted Cyclops

Klaliff Vice president to Exalted Cyclops

Klanton or Den Local chapter

Klavern Local meeting place

Kleagle An organizer

Klokard National lecturer

Kludd Chaplain

Realm The Klan in a particular state

index

n

o

p

q

r